EMBEDDED REAL-TIME SYSTEMS

WILEY SERIES IN
SOFTWARE ENGINEERING PRACTICE

Series Editors:

Patrick A.V. Hall, *The Open University, UK*
Martyn A. Ould, *Praxis Systems plc, UK*
William E. Riddle, *Software Design & Analysis, Inc., USA*

Fletcher J. Buckley • Implementing Software Engineering Practices

John J. Marciniak and Donald J. Reifer • Software Acquisition
Management

John S. Hares • SSADM for the Advanced Practitioner

Martyn A. Ould • Strategies for Software Engineering
The Management of Risk and Quality

David P. Youll • Making Software Development Visible
Effective Project Control

Charles P. Hollocker • Software Review and Audits Handbook

Robert L. Baber • Error-free Software
Know-how and Know-why of Program Correctness

Charles R. Symons • Software Sizing and Estimating
Mk II FPA (Function Point Analysis)

Robert Berlack • Software Configuration Management

David Whitgift • Methods and Tools for Software Configuration Management

John S. Hares • Information Engineering for the Advanced Practitioner

Lowell Jay Arthur • Rapid Evolutionary Development
Requirements, Prototyping and Software Creation

K. C. Shumate and M. M. Keller • Software Specification and Design
A Disciplined Approach for Real-Time Systems

Michael Dyer • The Cleanroom Approach to Quality Software Development

Jean Paul Calvez • Embedded Real-time Systems
A Specification and Design Methodology

EMBEDDED REAL-TIME SYSTEMS

Jean Paul Calvez
IRESTE Nantes, France

Translators

Alan Wyche and Charles Edmundson
ECS Langues & Communications S.A., Nantes, France

JOHN WILEY & SONS
Chichester · New York · Brisbane · Toronto · Singapore

Embedded Real-time Systems: A Specification and Design Methodology,
by Jean Paul Calvez, is a translation from the French book
Spécification et conception des systèmes: une méthodologie © Masson,
Editeur, Paris, 1990.

Other Wiley Editorial Offices

John Wiley & Sons, Inc., 605 Third Avenue,
New York, NY 10158-0012, USA

Jacaranda Wiley Ltd, G.P.O. Box 859, Brisbane,
Queensland 4001, Australia

John Wiley & Sons (Canada) Ltd, 22 Worcester Road,
Rexdale, Ontario M9W 1L1, Canada

John Wiley & Sons (SEA) Pte Ltd, 37 Jalan Pemimpin #05-04,
Block B, Union Industrial Building, Singapore 2057

Library of Congress Cataloging-in-Publication Data
Calvez, Jean Paul.
    [Spécification et conception des systèmes. English]
    Embedded real-time systems : a specification and design
methodology / Jean Paul Calvez ; translators, Alan Wyche and Charles
Edmundson.
        p.   cm. —(Wiley series in software engineering practice)
    Translation of: Spécification et conception des systèmes.
    Includes bibliographical references and index.
    ISBN 0 471 93563 8
    1. Electronic digital computers—Programming.   2. Real-time data
processing.   3. Embedded computer systems—Programming.   I. Title.
II Series.
QA76.6.C338313   1993
004'.33—dc20   92-36522
                                                             CIP

British Library Cataloguing in Publication Data

A catalogue record for this book is available from the British Library

ISBN 0 471 93563 8

Produced from camera-ready copy supplied by the author
Printed and bound in Great Britain by Biddles Ltd, Guildford and King's Lynn

*To my wife Catherine
and my children*
       Sébastien,
       Estelle,
       Anne-Laure.

CONTENTS

Part 6 : IMPLEMENTATION

Part 7 : PROJECT MANAGEMENT

PREFACE

The formalization of a methodology is a long-term effort. I could never have completed this work alone and without a testing ground.

I would sincerely like to thank my colleagues who have been a great deal of help to me since the start of this work by accepting responsibility for projects in industry and experiments using the methodology. In particular, Pascal Clodic, Gérard Duchene, Jocelyn Frappier, Eric Friot and Gérard Thibaut.

I would also like to thank the students and audiences who have attended methodology training courses at various times.

First, I would like to mention the students of the DESS "Design and Use of Electronic Systems". They used the methodology on industrial projects over a period of four years as part of their training, and provided me with an experimental base. The fruitful contacts that I still maintain with some of them who use this Methodology in their work as engineers, and are able to impose it within their companies, bear witness to the pedagogical achievements made during their training.

Second, system design forms an integral part of the IRESTE (Institut de Recherche et d'Enseignement aux Techniques de l'Electronique) Engineer Training Program on Electronic Systems and Industrial Data Processing. During their first year, students have to carry out a six month industrial project in industry, and become aware of the real extent of this training and its essential advantages for the competitiveness of our companies. This provides them with a major asset which satisfies manufacturers' current and long-term concerns.

I would also like to thank the companies that showed confidence in our team and engineers, and have consequently realized that the Methodology injects a new vitality into system development.

Finally, I would like to mention the considerable amount of work involved in typing and formatting this book. I would like to thank Marie-Thérèse Saloux who did the typing work very efficiently, Olivier Debon and Franck Bertaud who produced the figures and prepared the page layout.

Jean Paul CALVEZ

July 1992

METHODOLOGY OVERVIEW

Part 1 introduces the Electronic Systems Design Methodology (MCSE in French) by describing the application class concerned, the intended objectives and the main principles.

Chapter 1 defines the overall objective of the book. The described methodology is intended for system designers and industrial computing specialists, and is a work tool for improving productivity and quality of project developments.

Chapter 2 outlines the field of applications concerned by MCSE. For these applications, so called real-time systems, are defined by their characteristics. It also mentions techniques used and the skills needed.

Chapter 3 describes the life cycle for the development of any product. The life cycle model is useful for introducing the various phases, and shows the iterative nature of the development process and the field covered by MCSE.

Chapter 4 describes the basis for most methodologies. In particular, it justifies the breakdown into steps and the need for description models.

Chapter 5 gives the reader an overall view of the MCSE methodology, including models and the procedure.

Chapter 6 introduces the procedure using a fairly simple, but sufficiently realistic example, to give the reader a fairly accurate idea about the methodology by giving him a synthetic view of the various steps.

1

INTRODUCTION

This book describes the MCSE methodology (Méthodologie de Conception des Systèmes Electroniques) for the specification, design and implementation of industrial computing systems. These systems integrate Electronic and Computer techniques and deal with applications in a wide range of fields and with very variable complexities. Examples include a centrifuge control system, a large building centralized management technique, automatic management of a warehouse including wire-guided trolleys, and the monitoring of oil platform anchor chains. These types of examples are found in the industrial field.

These are real-time systems for dedicated applications; this means that every application is the subject of a special development that must directly produce an operational industrial product satisfying customer requirements, costs and deadlines.

A methodology can be seen as a tool box containing a variety of tools - models, methods, solutions - to help the designer to do his work. All activities involved in bringing a product, system or application from its requirements definition to its finalized implementation specification are concerned by the MCSE methodology. These activities are broken down into three steps: writing specifications, preparing the functional design and then defining the implementation specification.

In order to illustrate the usefulness of this book, we will mention the objectives of a development and the related difficulties. A methodology is one answer to this problem.

1.1   OBJECTIVES FOR A DEVELOPMENT

We will consider the normal case of a system development for a customer. Another situation would be to develop a product for our own needs. This is a special and more simple case since the designer is also the customer.

What do we expect of designers? Several essential skills, in addition to the technical ability to handle the problem:

- **to satisfy the customer's requirements**: this is a fundamental point. The customer contractually finances the development. A product that the designer feels satisfactory will not necessarily satisfy the customer's expectations.

- **to respect deadlines and costs.** Normally, a development is the subject of a negotiated contract based on proposals including deadlines and costs. On this basis, the customer defines a company strategy, for example sale or integration into a product series. Non respect of deadlines or costs leads to extra expenditure or a loss of part of the market, together with a loss of credibility for the development team.

- **to satisfy quality criteria.** Apart from the obviously essential need to work properly, the main criteria are: product robustness (reliability, tolerance to errors), understandability of documents and the product itself, maintainability to facilitate correction of remaining bugs and expansion of system capabilities. Thus, quality in systems has repercussions on the global cost of all operations involved in the product life cycle.

1.2   DIFFICULTIES OF THE DESIGNER'S WORK

The designer is normally faced with the question : How should he proceed to develop a specific system in working order and satisfying all the above-mentioned requested characteristics.

It is easy to note the complexity of system designers' work. There are three sources of complexity: first, the diversity of techniques and resources to be used, second the gap between the nature of the problem and the nature of the technique used, and third the range of application complexities and sizes.

Firstly, the implementation constituents must be mastered; but the range of techniques is very wide - analog electronic, digital electronic and VLSI components, programming and computer science, industrialization problems, etc. Since techniques evolve and diversify very quickly, a major effort is continuously necessary, if only to keep informed about techniques. Implementation of systems also requires a good understanding of hardware and software development methods. The stated problem may require expertise in other fields - signal processing, telecommunications, algorithms, physics, etc.

Second, the designer is not the customer. Therefore, he must get involved in the customer's field. A dialog is essential. The objective of a system is to satisfy the requirements of the customer, who is probably neither an electronics nor computer expert. Consequently, the designer is required to interpret the request as best as he can, such that the system gives satisfaction.

Third, with the increased application complexity, systems can no longer be developed by a single person. Project management, human resources, work organization in teams, and overall consistency problems etc, are required. Note also that electronic systems are in a competitive market. The only survivors will be good products and competitive companies. With the fast evolution of techniques and concepts, an industrial product must be manufactured as quickly as possible. Costs and quality criteria have become essential.

Between 20 to 30% of the development effort should be dedicated to analysis, specification and preliminary design. Any error during these phases involves very expensive corrections. This has been known for many years. However, specifications are often badly produced, resulting in exorbitant product redesign and modification costs. Why? Is it the engineers' "fault" because they do not spend enough time or do not carry out the analysis work correctly? There are other reasons. First, few designers are trained and encouraged to analyze complex systems. Second, designers cannot learn one or more methods by themselves, since few books have been written on the subject. Finally, reading a book is not sufficient; experienced engineers must be guided through projects if they are to acquire appropriate experience.

How does each person become competent? By acquiring know-how which gradually expands during new developments. Each problem dealt with helps to enrich the designer's experience. It is not surprising to note that industrial system development know-how is normally specific to relatively small groups and, consequently, methods developed from collective work remain very restricted. There is also a considerable difference in the work habits in different companies, and even in different groups within the same company.

The most frequently observed procedure consists of three phases: requirements definition, design and implementation. Designers use the document produced by the customer directly, with no particular method. A solution is produced after carrying out an analysis. The solution may be described in many different forms: flow chart, block diagrams, use of high-level languages or any other description form. Very often, hardware solutions have already been chosen explicitly or implicitly for a given project. However, the dependence of implementation on design which should exist is not as obvious as it might be. It is no exaggeration to note that selected implementation solutions very often have an effect on the design, rather than the inverse way.

During the development, the separation of the hardware and software implementation activities is not obvious either, since there is a large degree of coupling between the two parts. If there is no prior precise definition of what is to be carried out by each part, the integration work consisting of combining the two parts requires a considerable amount of time for a project carried out in this way. The situation becomes worse later since a great deal of time must be spent on maintenance, improvements and modifications to such completed systems. Maintenance includes improvements, modifications and corrections, as well as system troubleshooting. This situation, which is the result of correcting design and specification or even product definition errors, is not viable.

1.3 ADVANTAGES OF A METHODOLOGY

The designer has many techniques and tools available to help him solve his problem, but he still needs to know how to put these tools into use.

Although an incremental procedure may have appeared to be adequate for several years, the increase in the number of problem types, the variety of techniques and the complexity of tools make it necessary to have global methods for efficiently moving on from the problem to an appropriate solution. This type of procedure forms a methodology.

All developments involve a large number of decisions. Knowledge about the problem, techniques and tools form essential information which help decision making, whereas a procedure leads to decision chronology.

Consequently, when faced with a problem, the three main aspects - methods, techniques, tools - must be well understood as shown in Figure 1.1.

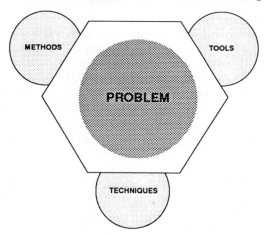

Figure 1.1   The three main aspects of solving a problem.

The technique is the support for the implementation. Tools are used to implement the technique. Methods help to progress from the problem to an implementation.

What can be expected of a methodology? It must:

- **guarantee obtaining a result**. It must be sufficiently global to cover a variety of problems and techniques, but must also be precise, efficient and simple.

- **facilitate early evaluation of the application feasibility**, the development cost and time.

- **increase designer's productivity and the quality of the result**, by encouraging maximum automatic production of solutions which by inference will then be error free.

- **increase thought at design level**; this should be as independent as possible of the technology to lead to a better understanding of the problem and produce more easily reusable specifications and general solutions.

- **allow project organization and management**, in order to manage complex developments which require the participation of teams and various specialists.

1.4 GENESIS OF THE MCSE METHODOLOGY

Why do we need a methodology for industrial data processing systems? Various reasons have led to this necessity. First, during the last 20 years, there have been considerable developments in available techniques for electronics and data processing, and this trend will continue. Using these techniques, more and more complex applications of all types are becoming possible. To satisfy this type of demand, specific abilities must be available or quickly acquired, and the organization of development teams has become an essential concern.

Second, unlike general systems or mass produced products which are the result of gradual developments, real-time systems for dedicated applications have to go into production immediately in their final version with guaranteed results. Consequently, activities to be carried out before implementation, writing specifications and the design, are essential to satisfy constraints such as deadlines, costs and quality.

In addition to necessities related to the previous points, we have seen during the last decade that a methodology is comparable to any other essential long-term investment for companies. The return on investment is not easily estimated beforehand, and can be expressed in various forms: reduction of costs and development times, improved customer's satisfaction, longer developed product life, significant reduction of maintenance costs.

A methodology is the result of a long-term determination to make a complete, efficient and coherent procedure available to developers. At the present time, any methodology requires almost ten years to reach maturity. This time period can easily be explained. For authors, a methodology is the result of an incremental bottom-up process, since this is the only possible way of analyzing difficulties, searching for solutions, preparing conceptual designs in the form of models and methods, experimenting to verify and validate each proposal, and then structuring the whole to make a directly usable complete global top-down process available.

No methodology can become generally accepted without being a subject for experimentation. Developers' problems cannot be satisfied without understanding their problems: scope of activities, nature of difficulties, etc. Participation in industrial projects is essential. Experimentation requires that all or part of the methodology be applied for these industrial developments. Observation of problems, difficulties and results is also necessary since it may be the source of corrections. Finally, experimentation concerns developers and users of the methodology, and not its author. Designers therefore have to be trained in the methodological approach in order to be able to observe design results and any remaining difficulties in acquiring concepts, together with problems during use.

Since there are so many aspects, progress is very slow. We have worked with and for manufacturing companies since 1978: prototype development, training in techniques and methods, transfer of know-how and methodology, creation of products followed by their transfer to manufacturing companies for production and marketing.

Since 1980, the MCSE methodology has been taught to engineers and technicians, although not in its current version. It started by training people in the use of the system description model: functional and executive models, and we quickly observed designers' difficulties in finding a solution complying with the model. The accent was then put on the methods aspect - how to determine a solution complying with the model from a specification? At the same time, we observed that it was impossible to disassociate the design step from the other phases: the earlier specification phase and the later implementation phase. The methodology was then gradually extended to the entire development cycle.

Towards 1985, after realizing that designers did not necessarily produce quality solutions when using the method, we searched for a tool other than the methods aspect which would have the ability to induce solution ideas (obviously quality solutions). An analysis of developments was then undertaken and demonstrated a relative similarity of solutions in the same problem class. This contributed to the introduction of template solution models.

The work carried out during the last ten years will not end with this book since we are far from the end of the road. We need to increase the number and quality of trained designers, and to pursue the development of concepts and methods to increase automatic solution production possibilities and to encourage the creation of computer-aided tools as supports and guides in the use of the methodology.

1.5   OBJECTIVE OF THIS BOOK

Few methods are taught at the present time, and even fewer methodologies. The reasons are fairly simple: there are few books available on the subject and few specialist instructors have complete knowledge of a methodology, since this also necessitates a wide knowledge of usable techniques and considerable experience in industrial project development.

We will mention the main existing methodologies for real-time systems. Part 2 contains bibliographic references and a brief description of each.

- **SADT** (Structured Analysis and Design Technique) for the specification phase [ROSS-85].

- **SA/SD** (Structured Analysis, Structured Design) by DeMarco, Yourdon and Constantine for specification using data-flow diagrams and structured design [DEMARCO-79, JENSEN-79].

- **JSD** (Jackson System Development) by Jackson, covering all development phases [JACKSON-83].

- **OOD** (Object Oriented Design) by Booch [BOOCH-83], and the GOOD, HOOD, MOOD, OOSD variants.

- **OOA** (Object-Oriented Analysis) by P. Coad and Yourdon [COAD-90] and the **OMT** (Object-Modeling Technique) [RUMBAUGH-91].

- **RTSA** (Real-Time Structured Analysis) which is an extension to SA/SD by Ward and Mellor, and by Hatley and Pirbhai for dedicated real-time systems [WARD-85, HATLEY-87].

- **DARTS** (Design Approach for Real-Time Systems) for the specification and design of real-time applications and DARTS/DA for distributed applications [GOMAA-84, 89]. Use of this method with ADA implementation [NIELSEN-88].

- **SDWA** (System Design With ADA) [BUHR-84] and currently SDWMC (System Design With Machine Charts) [BUHR-89] for the design of intensive behavior systems.

These methodologies differ in their application field, development phases, models and methods. Which should be used? one of those mentioned above, MCSE, or should a new one be developed based on other concepts?

The purpose of this book is to improve methodological knowledge. Therefore, it is concerned with the acquisition of concepts and methods rather than with technical knowledge. To make the best use of it, the reader should have prior knowledge of analog electronics, digital electronics, microprocessor systems, process control and instrumentation systems, computer tools and high-level languages.

The aim of this book is to propose a complete methodology for system development. Consequently, it concerns companies and particularly the engineers responsible for product or system design, and also technicians and engineering students oriented towards this type of activity.

At least four categories of engineers and technicians are concerned by all or part of this book:

- **project managers,** who are responsible for project estimating, planning and management;

- **specifiers or analysts and designers,** who are responsible for carrying out all development work prior to implementation;

- **implementers,** who must use and therefore must understand the results of the design;

- **instructors,** who are responsible for developing a methods awareness in their listeners for specification writing, design and system implementation.

The book is broken down into three interest levels in order to satisfy these four user categories:

- The **overview level,** which gives an idea of what a methodology is. After delimiting the scope of application, Part 1 briefly describes the concepts and steps involved in the MSCE methodology. It is illustrated by a case study. In conclusion, Part 8 considers three aspects - methods, tools and designers as users of methodologies - to describe the long-term effort and therefore the motivation necessary for the use of a methodology, together with foreseeable development prospects for computer-aided tools as support.

- The **methodologies and project management level,** which gives a fairly wide vision for the organization of developments. Part 2 gives an insight into known methodologies in the real-time system field. Part 7 presents the main project management problems and principles.

- The **reference manual level,** which explains concepts, principles and processes in detail for each MCSE step. This level forms the body of the book and is the designer's working tool. It includes Part 3 describing the role and procedure for the first specification writing step, Part 4 which deals with the functional design step, Part 5 describing the implementation specification step, and Part 6 describing problems and techniques for hardware and software implementations. There is a summary of the main points dealt with at the end of each chapter.

After reading the overview level, the reader is advised to refer either to the methodologies and project management level, or the Reference Manual level, depending on whether he would first like to have an overall view of the methodologies subject and projects, or would like to get into the details of the MCSE methodology in order to make use of it.

The user should realize that if he wants to become competent in design, he will have to make a long-term investment of his own time. Reading a book alone is not sufficient; if he wants to apply the concepts, he will also need to develop projects and take the time to make a critical analysis of good and bad results in order to gradually increase his experience.

2

SYSTEMS CHARACTERISTICS

This book concerns systems for which implementation is the result of combining hardware and software. The term system designates the part to be developed which is actually only one part of the application. The design and development process for this type of system depends on the nature of its environment and the characteristics required for the application.

Before starting to describe the principles used, it seems useful first to characterize the systems for which the MCSE methodology was developed. This chapter then describes the evolution of electronics techniques and tools and discusses the industrial data processing field, and finally describes the problem classes concerned and implementation tools for dedicated systems, the characteristics of real-time systems and quality criteria for a system.

2.1 EVOLUTION OF IMPLEMENTATION TECHNIQUES AND METHODS

Starting from the transistor and then integrated circuits, considerable technological evolution has led to diversification of available techniques for implementation of electronic systems. Some landmarks are the change from analog to digital techniques, and then the change from wired logic to programmed or programmable logic used in programmable devices (PLD) and microprocessors. The advantages are obvious: a given hardware structure can solve a whole family of problems and is not restricted to the problem concerned. Note the present widening gap between the technological and technical characteristics of the hardware part and the features available for applications created with these components. Thus, a single support can be used for many applications, and conversely a variety of technologies are available for a single application. The system operation specification for a precise application is defined more and more by programming.

Reuse of hardware becomes possible, and possibilities of product modification and improvement become greater due to software. Thus, starting from a purely hardware solution, implementations have gradually evolved towards a hardware/software distribution with an increasing software part. On average, for all system types combined, the software part is currently estimated at over 70%. Consequently, electronics and data processing are frequently interrelated within applications.

More recently, due to communication techniques and tools, the increased complexity of components and the diversity of available functions have made it possible to replace centralized solutions by implementations in which the structure is very close to the geographical distribution of the application. Part of the complexity is then handled by an interfunction communication system. Naturally, previously independent systems are currently more and more interconnected.

All these techniques are relatively well known and mastered. As complexity increases, available objects become closer and closer to the required functions and implementation becomes simpler. A microprocessor is becoming easier to put into operation than a 2-transistor amplification stage.

Tools available for the implementation of systems have also followed the technical progress. An electronic engineer's main working tools used to be his measuring instruments and a soldering iron, but he is now much closer to being a computer scientist. The computer as a working tool is now used by everyone.

Computer-aided design tools help designers to define, check and then manufacture components and electronic systems. In addition to the use of standard components, the electronics engineer can even develop his own special components (ASICs).

For the software, the developer has a variety of available support tools such as microcomputers and computer systems, and development tools such as cross-compilers, logic and performance analyzers, and various software packages.

2.2 THE INDUSTRIAL DATA PROCESSING FIELD

Electronic Systems (in the widest sense) are used in a large number of applications. There is no point here in listing the diversity of fields influenced or concerned by electronics. As a manufacturing technique, it is used as support for many activities, thus contributing to improving functions, performance, safety, operating flexibility, etc.

Analog, Digital and Programming techniques are used. Today it is more realistic to consider global synergy rather than trying to define the boundary between electronics and data processing, when considering them from the implementation technique aspect. Electronic systems include more and more data processing tools, while computers, sensors, actuators, peripherals and interfaces are necessary as supports for application implementations for data processing systems. Consequently, the Industrial Data Processing field has appeared as an intermediate discipline during the last decade.

For a designer, a system is composed of two parts:

- The **hardware part** (the visible part) which consists of an analog part in which only voltages and currents are important, and a digital part in which Boolean or digital states are sufficient at the user level. The boundary between the two depends only on the observation level.

- A **software part**, not directly visible since it is defined by Boolean states 1 and 0 in the computer memories or in the mass storage memories. Specific equipment (computer and software) is used to produce and manipulate this type of data.

The analog part is more or less significant depending on the application. It always exists to a certain extent since every system is coupled to its environment through interfaces which transport voltages and currents. There are also some other functions which cannot be carried out by digital techniques: high frequency transmission/reception, signal transformation and generation, etc.

The digital part consists of an assembly of LSI and VLSI components, each carrying out a complex function. These components are becoming more and more programmable, thus justifying an architecture built around one or several microprocessors.

The proportion of the software part can vary considerably. Functionality is more and more frequently obtained by software, whereas the hardware is only the implementation support. In extreme cases, computer systems are considered as complete functional supports used to develop an application without the need to consider the hardware part.

The global functionalities result from a good match between all parts: correct assembly of all components, programming suitable for the use of components and satisfying specific features of the application.

Therefore, designing and building this type of system requires technical ability in three fields: analog electronics, digital electronics or industrial data processing, and computer engineering. Other complementary abilities could be added: integrated components when they have to be designed, power electronic components when the environment uses high currents, communication networks when coupling is necessary between systems or assemblies, etc. But we must also consider the suitability for catering to the needs of customers in all disciplines who require the implementation of a system, and a good understanding of the development process. It is easy to imagine the difficulties involved in this subject, and the responsibility of the industrial data processing expert as system development coordinator.

2.3 EMBEDDED SYSTEMS

For the applications discussed in the previous section, the customer may ask for the implementation of a so-called "dedicated" system. This means that the system is developed to satisfy a well-defined need at a given moment. Its operating limit is defined: several years or even several decades. Therefore, long life is important. The system should be perfected as far as possible, in its final version using current technology. Its possibilities for future development are limited to a few improvements for the same application. Therefore, this is not a general system, such as a computer or microcomputer, nor is it a prototype which operates well at a given moment.

A dedicated system is installed once and for all. Therefore, the development procedure must lead to a correct operational system since the solution is not the result of an incremental development or of successive experiments.

The technique to be implemented must be correct, suitable and sufficient for the problem in order to reduce development costs and time, and reproduction costs.

Many techniques are available for implementing this type of system:

- the use of complete systems: microcomputer, programmable controller, regulation system, image processing system, terminals, computers, etc;
- use of boards, sub-assemblies and program packages: microprocessor boards, power supplies, interface boards, mass storage memories, databases, report generators, multi window systems, etc.

Reuse reduces development times. It is absolutely essential for hardware since the user cannot manufacture his own components and each reproduction implies a cost. Although less restrictive for software, the designer may (wrongly) want to completely develop his application software, arguing that the developed program will be more appropriate than one which results from the reuse of an existing program, a software library or a more general program package, etc.

2.4 REAL-TIME SYSTEMS

Let us consider the functional characteristics of a system from the application point of view. The functionality is then explained using the vocabulary of the application rather than the vocabulary of the technique used. The term "environment" is used to represent the application part excluding the system.

The environment of a dedicated electronic system consists of various natures of objects (in the general sense): some are physical and others are human. Objects are dynamic - their actions generate events, information, data. Similarly, they are sensitive to external actions. Consequently, the systems to be developed are said to be of the functionally reactive type since they react in response to stimuli from the environment. The frequency of these actions is then an important parameter.

To satisfy the objective assigned to it, the system is coupled to these objects by interfaces for observation and control. These systems thus have multiple inputs and outputs. There are two classes of interfaces: man-machine interfaces and physical interfaces. Exchange procedures between the system and its environment must take account of the nature of these interfaces.

Since the physical environment is often composed of several simultaneous and sometimes physically remote activities, the application requires the use of a system which can simultaneously:

- observe information to monitor evolution of the environment;
- take account of random events;
- evaluate decisions based on events and observations;
- generate actions in the environment to make the entire application operational.

Due to the large number of inputs and outputs to be monitored globally, an electronic system must carry out concurrent processing. The degree of parallelism is a function of the implementation technique. It is complete when a hardware part is assigned to each process. It is pseudo-simultaneous when a processor shares its activity to carry out several tasks. The operation of this type of processor is then called multitasking.

Coupled to its environment, an electronic system is also concerned with the reaction time of objects surrounding it. Control of an elevator, a wire-guided trolley, or an aircraft is related to the speed at which these objects move.

Although information exchanges for man-machine type interfaces are of the order of a second or 1/10th of a second, the reaction time of a system to physical processes is of the order of a millisecond. The response times required by electronic systems are thus significantly closer to the reaction time of the technology used (100 µsec to 1 ms for microprocessors). This type of system is called real-time.

By definition, a system is said to be a real-time system when it carries out all its activities respecting timing constraints. The important interaction with the environment brings out several types of timing constraints, some of which are severe, and have to be respected:

- high frequency for actions incoming from the environment - event frequency, data transfer rate, etc;
- high frequency for actions to be undertaken on the environment, for example high frequency for the control of a fast response time process;
- a maximum limit for reaction times between the moment at which an event appears and the moment at which the resulting action is completed (deadline).

If one of these constraints is not respected, the application may malfunction, which could lead to very serious consequences, endangering human life in extreme cases.

Real-time systems are thus different from so-called interactive systems which are preferably qualified as "online" systems. Coupled to operators, they require short response times which do not lead to serious consequences if they are not respected. For example, in a bank management system, the response time for transactions must remain low for user comfort. A delay is acceptable provided it is only occasional.

2.5 SYSTEM QUALITIES

A system can also be observed according to its qualities, each contributing to satisfying a specific objective. In particular, a system may be:

- **adequate**: its behavior with respect to the environment satisfies the customer's wishes;

- **efficient**: all timing constraints are satisfied and system response times are acceptable;

- **robust**: the system remains operational, either completely or in degraded mode, even in the presence of unforeseen faults or events coming from the environment;

- **progressive**: the system allows evolution of its characteristics and functions. This is necessary to satisfy unforeseen developments in the specification list;

- **maintainable**: after implementation, the system will have to be kept in operation throughout the life of the application. Corrections and improvements also form part of the tasks carried out by maintenance;

- at **optimum cost**: the system can be developed and produced at a reasonable cost acceptable to the customer.

These qualities are objectives for any development. A methodology for the development of real-time systems for dedicated applications must encourage the development of solutions satisfying these kinds of criteria.

2.6 SYSTEM CATEGORIES

To conclude this chapter, we will attempt to classify systems based on the main technique used. For the classification, which can only be approximate, we will consider disciplines closely related to industrial data processing, namely electronics, automation, signal processing (words and pictures), communications, data processing. Each discipline is represented by a circle on Figure 2.1. The disciplines partially overlap.

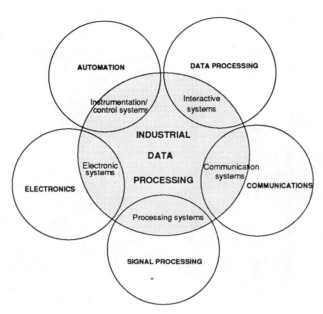

Figure 2.1   System categories.

This book considers systems which require the use of different techniques in greater or lesser degrees. These systems are represented in the industrial data processing circle. Very specific systems in a field are excluded since they require a specific methodology directly related to the concepts and techniques to be used specific to the discipline.

The following kinds of systems are thus concerned by the MCSE methodology:

- **typically electronic systems**: mainly implying the development of hardware such as function and component design, assembly of components;
- **instrumentation and process control systems**, dominated by monitoring and control problems for applications including all types of physical processes to be controlled;
- **interactive systems** concerned by the use of high-level interfaces for man-machine dialogs;
- **communication systems**: dominated by data transfer. These systems receive, transform and transmit message flows;
- **data processing systems**: mainly concerned by processing all forms of information: signals, pictures, voice, etc.

3

SYSTEM DEVELOPMENT LIFE CYCLE

After characterizing systems by their application fields, techniques used and specific real-time features, we will characterize the application development process.

We will not go into all the reasons - poor organization, unsuitable tools, lack of methods, lack of test and integration plans and procedures, lack of specifications, no customer investment in the project - why even good projects do not necessarily lead to a success. The most essential objective is to express what procedure should be followed to efficiently develop a system satisfying the customer's requirements.

To characterize the development activity, it must first be placed in the company context. A development is part of the activities of a project, and each project is integrated into a company objective. Obtaining results implies the need for a procedure to plan, organize and control project developments. Project management necessitates modeling the development process itself. The general term "application or product life cycle" is used to describe this type of model. Introduced around 1975, this kind of model is used as a support to describe the details of the procedure to be followed, and then to control it.

This chapter shows that a system development requires a more complex organization than simply sequencing specification, design and implementation steps. Moreover, a development model can also be used as a basis for a methodology. The model proposed for electronic systems at the end of the chapter defines the range in which the MCSE methodology is useful.

3.1 DEVELOPMENT CONTEXT

The term "development" is used here to characterize all technical activities involved in progressing from user requirements to the industrial product satisfying the need.

For the company or organization responsible for the development, these activities form an integral part of a project. A project is characterized first by objectives and second by its progress. It has a start and an end which corresponds to objectives satisfied. A project also interacts with other activities (or projects) in that it necessarily shares resources.

Characterizing the context of a development consists of positioning it within the context of the company as shown in Figure 3.1.

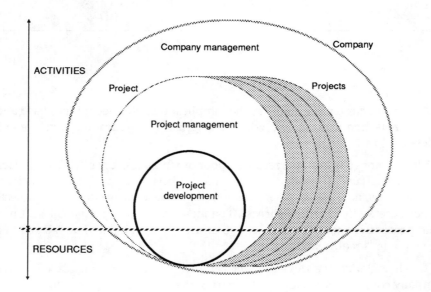

Figure 3.1   Global development context.

Company activity in the wider sense concerns a set of projects. The development of an application and a system is only part of a project. In order to carry out its activities, the company has physical and human resources that it distributes between the various activities.

The development activity can be better characterized by defining what the project is and its management.

A project can be characterized by its life cycle. This cycle starts by a requirements expression phase and is completed by a finalization phase.

Three intermediate phases are shown in Figure 3.2 : project definition, planning and organization and development [RUSKIN-82].

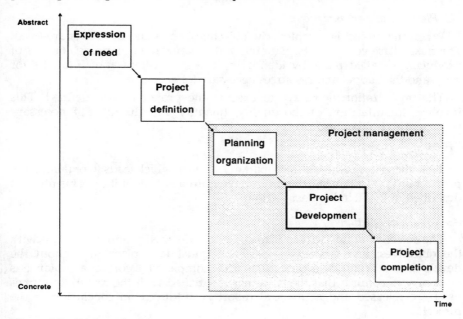

Figure 3.2   Project phases.

-A- *Expression of need*

A project starts by the need or wish to satisfy an objective. The objective may vary a great deal in nature and form. For example, it may be required to develop a system for the control of large buildings, but the objective may also be expressed as the wish to provide an aid to building control.

Therefore, the first phase concerns the expression of a need to satisfy objectives, which leads to expressing a concept and identifying essential constraints. This phase gives no indication about the manner of achieving these objectives. Different techniques can be used, particularly creativity and value analysis techniques (value engineering).

-B - *Project definition*

This phase involves a preliminary project study. First, the project is characterized by a feasibility study based on assumptions about the different ways of achieving objectives, decision criteria, constraints, potential obstacles, resources, budgets and deadlines.

Second, the global approach to be followed to satisfy these objectives is then selected. The project definition step results in a description in sufficient detail to allow the development of a clear proposal.

All aspects of the development must be considered in the project definition phase, but it does not require project implementation.

- C- Planning and organization

When the project is accepted, the objectives, costs and deadlines are fixed. The next phase concerns its planning and organization. Planning consists of producing detailed plans by identifying tasks, deadlines and durations for each, and the budget and resources necessary for each task.

The organization necessary to execute the project is also defined. This involves identification of the quality, quantity and duration of necessary physical and human resources.

-D- Project development

This phase forms the technical part of the work which leads to obtaining the product or application starting from the requirements definition. This phase is described in detail in the next section.

-E- Project completion

The objective of this activity is to check that the final product conforms with the objectives, and whenever possible it must take place throughout the development. When the product has been completed, a formal acceptance is necessary to confirm that the customer is satisfied with the result. Resources used are released and a financial report is produced on conclusion of the project.

As shown in the previous figure about the development work, project management concerns planning and organization activities, and the management and control of the development.

The MCSE methodology is not concerned with the management part of a project. Some guidelines are described in Part 7, to illustrate the complementary nature of development and project management activities, since management is based on a model of the system development process, also called the development cycle or product life cycle.

3.2 DEVELOPMENT PHASES

The life cycle of an application or a product is a purely descriptive representation. It breaks down the development process into a series of interrelated activities, based on the initial need to produce an operational product. The term "cycle" is related to the fact that any product developed normally generates new needs.

Several models have been produced. Before getting involved in the differences between them, we will note that all have the essential phases of every development in common. With a few variations depending on the author, we distinguish at least five phases:

- definition or specification;
- design;
- implementation;
- production;
- operation.

The normal meaning of each of these phases is described below.

-A- Definition and specification

A project is generally the result of a request formulated in the form of a document describing user requirements. This document is called the requirements definition. This is a starting point for the design team, to express a proposal which must contain all specifications.

Although descriptions in the requirements definition may appear clear to the customer, this type of document normally contains few details, and it is consequently inadequate for characterizing the complete project. Consequently, during the definition phase, objectives are listed which must be satisfied by the final system. The purpose is to produce a detailed description of the external behavior of the system. This description describes functions to be fulfilled, constraints to be respected, interfaces to be used, and all complementary information specifying the system size, the execution speed, performance and other characteristics to be satisfied, etc. The resulting document is called a requirements specification.

-B- Design

The design work consists of going on from the requirements specification to an implementation definition, in other words the documents necessary to undertake the implementation. Initially, the designer directly uses specifications to produce a decomposition in terms of internal functions. As decisions are taken, refinement continues by expressing how each function considered as a black box contributes to achieving the objectives.

This is a simplified view, since design involves several intermediate stages. In each stage, every requirement is transformed into a corresponding implementation by a sequence of decisions.

Although this outline is now conventional, particularly for software projects, useful intermediate stages depend on the class of problems being processed. For the category of real-time systems considered in this book, the design must produce a simultaneous definition of hardware and software to be used (hardware/software co-design). Therefore, the process is more complicated.

-C- Implementation

The implementation phase concerns hardware and software development, followed by the integration of the software into the hardware infrastructure. This implementation leads to a running system which can be industrially reproduced and which satisfies all requirements.

-D- Production

This stage concerns experimentation on a prototype to evaluate its characteristics. Production is started after this evaluation. Complementary industrialization criteria are introduced at this stage.

-E- Operation

When the product has been mass produced and marketed, it goes into operation. The exploitation phase starts, which implies maintenance.

Various types of maintenance are possible: corrective to eliminate residual errors, adaptive to take account of new requirements, preventive to increase system reliability.

The last two phases do not necessarily form part of the project. However, regardless of the organization, the company is always responsible. For example, other groups or departments can be responsible for production and maintenance of developed products.

3.3 LIFE CYCLE MODELS

In addition to the advantage of a work breakdown structure, decomposition of the project into steps facilitates control of the development by defining plannable and measurable objectives to be achieved for each phase. A model prepared for development can therefore be used as a basis for project management.

Several models have been suggested to represent the development process. In the following sections, we will describe the most common models presented for software development.

3.3.1 The "Waterfall" model

This first model describes the life cycle as a series of steps in which all description levels between the problem and the implementation are found, starting from the definition and ending with operation and maintenance [BOEHM-76].

Each step is linked to the next step to represent chaining, and to the previous step to represent corrections by feedback. Each step is associated with a verification phase, the purpose of which is to check that the selected solution conforms to the step input specifications. Any lack of conformity will mean that the step or the results of the previous step has to be revised as shown in Figure 3.3.

This first model shows that the development cannot take place using a top-down progress only. As suggested by the closed loop control theory, uncertainties or errors and omissions are corrected by loopbacks as soon as variations are observed. Obviously, this is only possible if the result at the end of each phase is observable and can be compared with an objective.

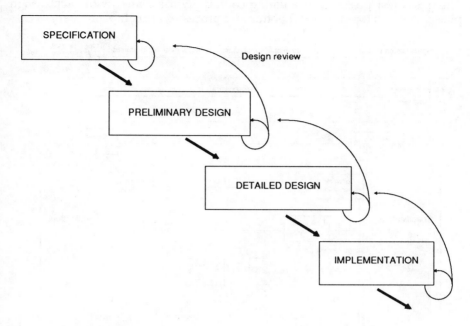

Figure 3.3   The Waterfall model.

A large amount of validation work during the early phases facilitates fast correction of early errors, since their correction later can be very expensive.

This model is somewhat limited, and only partially takes account of the real iterative nature of the development.

3.3.2 The V cycle

This model also considers the project verification and evaluation phases for each stage of its implementation. It clearly demonstrates that the specification and design procedure is globally top-down and the implementation and test phase is globally bottom-up, since the various constituents are assembled to obtain functionalities. Figure 3.4 shows a typical example of a development plan.

The horizontal axis represents the project phases and the duration of each. The vertical axis represents the abstraction level for the application. The specification and design phases lead to more and more detailed description levels. Coding is the most detailed form for a software application. The conformity of the implementation at each level of the design can be evaluated during the integration, test and verification phases, starting with the most elementary parts and gradually progressing towards the complete product. There is a test phase for evaluating conformity associated with each design phase. The two top-down and bottom-up processes are complementary.

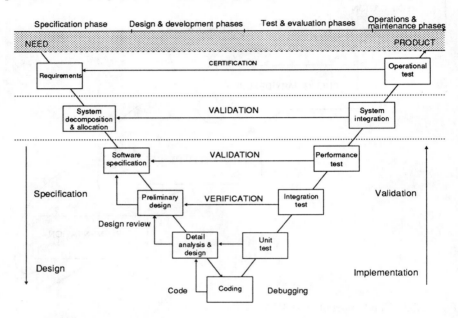

Figure 3.4   Example of V life cycle.

This model facilitates the planning of dates for production and for reading documents at the completion of each phase, and for verification validation procedure deadlines. However, it is particularly applicable to software development.

3.3.3 The "Spiral" model

The previous models are applicable to the creation of a single product. They are not very suitable for the description of a set of products and activities related to these products: feasibility, prototyping, etc.

The Spiral model [BOEHM-88, WILLIAMS-88] describes development as an iterative four phase process, for combining the various approaches: expression of needs, feasibility, prototyping and development of the final product as shown in Figure 3.5.

There are four phases, one in each quadrant, concerning:

- planning subsequent phases;
- definition of objectives, alternatives and constraints;
- solution evaluation, risk analysis;
- product development and verification.

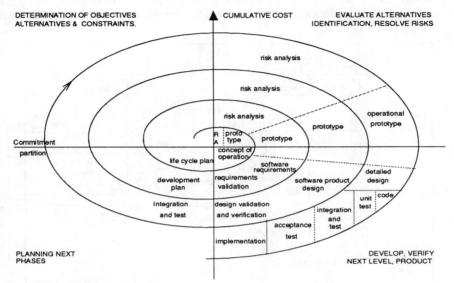

Figure 3.5   The Spiral model.

The distance of any point on the curve from the center represents the accumulated cost leading up to this stage of the development.

3.3.4 The "Contractual" model

Any development requires an interaction between the customer and designers. This model (Figure 3.6) shows this point of view. Each development phase is considered to be the subject of a contract between two parties - the customer and the supplier (designers) [COHEN-86].

A development phase involves moving on from a description to the next description. The customer validates the result. Completion of each phase is signalled by customer agreement meaning that the supply satisfies the terms of the contract.

This model shows the designer ways to satisfy the customer. The first phase is particularly difficult since it consists of formalizing the customer's wishes which are not clearly and fully expressed.

3.4   A FEW OBSERVATIONS

3.4.1 Phase overlapping

The previous models tend to give the idea that phases are clearly identified and separate. The reality is more complex. At the beginning of each phase, decisions taken in previous phases are modified or added to by loopbacks.

Therefore, phase overlaps are necessary as shown in Figure 3.7 [HATLEY-87]. Therefore, for example, design can start before the specification is completed.

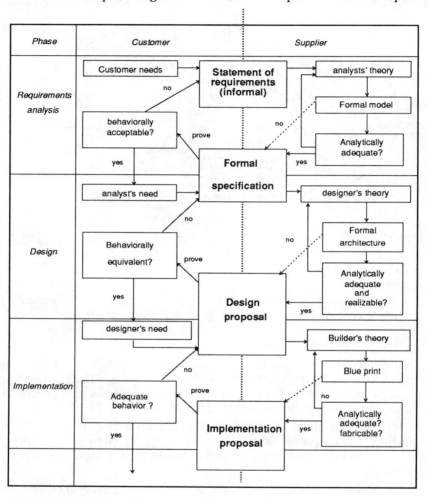

Figure 3.6   The Contractual model.

Figure 3.7 shows that all phases start almost simultaneously but the amount of effort varies with progress. Note that, with the other phases, the test phase starts very early. Even during the first phases, the objective is to prepare test and validation criteria and procedures. This can result in taking specific design decisions early, hence the necessity of developing a test system. Similarly, specifications are normally only rarely completed since new revisions are received from the customer.

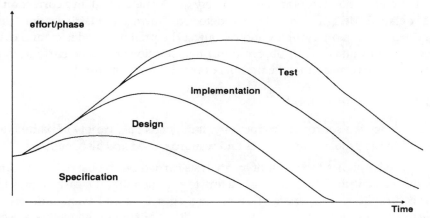

Figure 3.7   Desirable phase overlap.

3.4.2 Cost of error correction

Costs and times are reduced by reducing errors. It is fairly obvious that errors detected very late in the life cycle, and particularly during production and operation, are difficult to delimit and correct. They are also more expensive when they concern the first essential decisions: specifications, performance, need. Figure 3.8 shows the exponential cost of error correction.

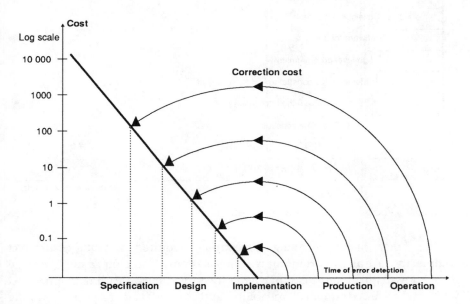

Figure 3.8   Error correction cost curve.

Implementation errors are detected very quickly and result in a correction at the detailed design level. Errors detected during industrialization and production are more complex and can affect the preliminary design and even some specifications. Errors observed during operation are particularly serious, since these may mean that the product does not satisfy the need.

3.4.3 Productivity factors

Efficiency is a source of productivity. It depends on a variety of parameters related to the problem, techniques and resources used and also methods.

Figure 3.9 shows the result of an analysis carried out by Barry Boehm, and shows the contribution of a set of factors to productivity. It clearly shows the low contribution of experience factors: languages, tools and even applications. The essential factor is team ability. This ability is related to the methods used, and hence the long-term advantage of investing in methods expertise.

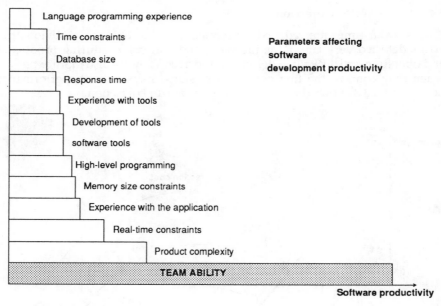

Figure 3.9   Factors affecting software costs.

The other factors - timing constraints, required reliability, product complexity - are all important for real-time systems. Therefore, a methodology must allow managing the complexity at the same time as leading to a product with the required quality, reliability and safety, and respecting timing constraints.

3.4.4 Effort distribution

In order to achieve his objective, the designer must spend a minimum amount of time on analysis, synthesis, verification and experimentation. Variations from this minimum time depend largely on the method used.

Without a method, an intuitive approach could be used to start the implementation fairly quickly. The solution would then be a result of trials, errors and corrections. Error detection and correction inevitably lead to additional time and money.

Assuming that a method is used, decomposition into steps is not sufficient. The amount of effort must be considered for each phase. Obviously, the distribution depends on the nature of the problem, but it is also a function of the required development strategy.

Although some strategies may be known through structured approach principles and the use of high-level languages, this is not the case for all phases in the life cycle, and particularly for the early stages. Specification and design activities are not very visible, and may be judged to be unproductive. A natural tendency is to think that engineers and technicians are more efficient and more productive when they are busy with electronic boards or programs than when they are producing preliminary specification and design documents.

To minimize the cost of errors and to obtain an efficient implementation, effort must be transferred to the early phases, namely specification and design. Figure 3.10 shows two opposed strategies. The effort at any moment expresses the human resources assigned to the development. The integral of this effort gives an investment chart for the project.

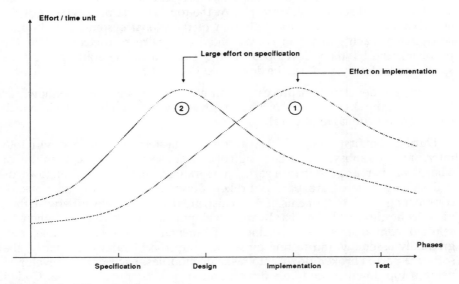

Figure 3.10   Effort distribution.

Curve 1 shows a traditional process in which a large amount of effort is invested during the implementation phase. The result of this is that a large part of the analysis work is carried out during this stage. Curve 2 shows the necessity for a large amount of effort during the specification and then in design. The higher investment of resources in the early phases in curve 2 is then largely compensated by a cost reduction during the implementation, test, production and maintenance phases.

The conclusion of the above analysis is that it is vital that the development process be controlled as well as possible. In addition, planning, organization, guidance and management of the development are essential if the project is to be a success.

3.5 DEVELOPMENT OF AN ELECTRONIC SYSTEM

After analyzing a few life cycle models for a product development and a few essential points which affect its progress, we will consider the details of the process for the development of electronic systems for real-time applications, in order to characterize the development process model selected for MCSE.

It must be remembered that electronic systems are composed of two main parts - the hardware and the software - and that these two parts must be coherent for dedicated systems. In order to manage the complexity, a system is then described following a set of hierarchical levels: definition, external description, brief description, detailed description.

If it is to take account of these aspects, a project development must be seen as a hierarchical set of developments. At the top, the first phases concern the specification and preliminary definition of the global system. This implies subsystems. Each subsystem corresponds to a more restricted part of the problem, and is then developed in the same manner, starting with its specification. Subsystems can be developed in parallel.

Thus, the development process for an electronic system can be shown as follows. Figure 3.11 shows that the design follows hierarchical levels which vary from functional to physical.

During the first design stage, a complex system is broken down into interconnected subsystems. The design of each subset includes the definition of a hardware part and a software part. Still working from a specification towards a design, the hardware part is broken down into a set of functions or components. The components, if they exist, are directly usable, otherwise they have to be designed. The hardware development hierarchy stops when all selected components are available. Implementation is then possible, and gradually assembly and testing by working up the hierarchy. Similarly, the software part is broken down into tasks or modules. Each part is developed using a top-down procedure - design and structured programming. Coded modules are tested and then assembled.

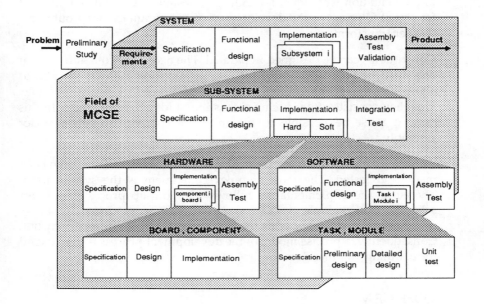

Figure 3.11   Hierarchical model for a system development process.

A few comments can be made on this presentation.

- Observing the hierarchy, it is seen that every implementation is a component developed as an independent item but which can be integrated into a more complex assembly.

- Each component is developed iteratively: analysis, synthesis, verification and correction by loopbacks when necessary.

- The specification, design, implementation definition, assembly and test phases are repeated for each constituent. Therefore, the terminology - specification, design, implementation - is not related to a specific description level. There is a great deal of confusion about the definition of these terms, particularly between specification and design. For the moment, we will consider that a specification concerns an external view of the object considered, whereas subsequent phases concern the inside, and therefore the solution.

- Although the approach may be global (system approach) at the top of the hierarchy, when going down into the hierarchy the designer of a constituent must be more and more a specialist in a specific field or implementation technique: for example, design of an ASIC component for signal filtering, or the development of a program carrying out a fast Fourier transform, etc.

- Constituents can be designed in parallel. The necessary constraint is that one must be able to produce the specification for each component to allow subsequent integration. A bottom-up procedure is also possible. This then consists of producing a constituent for subsequent use. In this case, it must be possible to integrate the component into a wider assembly.

- A system only becomes operational when all its constituents have been made and tested. The most complex constituent is the system itself. Therefore, the implementation follows a bottom-up process. A project schedule (for example, a PERT diagram) can be produced to satisfy deadline objectives only after the decomposition has been carried out. Consequently, a precise model of the development process is very useful for planning and therefore for project management.

3.6 SCOPE OF MCSE

The previous figure can also be used to specify the scope and levels of development covered by MCSE. This is a global methodology since its starting point is a need expressed by a requirement. It covers the specification, design and implementation phases at the system level as well as for hardware and software parts.

However, as mentioned at the beginning of the chapter, it does not cover the initial phase or the project definition phase which concerns the feasibility evaluation, a value analysis and negotiation. The starting point is the need of a product to be developed defined by objectives, costs and deadlines. However, a good understanding of the proposed methodology can considerably facilitate the preliminary study.

Nor does it cover the last design stages which concern the implementation of specific functions. For hardware, it may involve components or sub-assemblies which require specific competence in a given field: power electronics, analog electronics, etc. For software, this involves the development of individually written programs (programming-in-the-small as opposed to programming-in-the-large [NIELSEN-88]).

MCSE does not concern levels relatively close to the implementation; this is not a disadvantage since automatic production tools already exist: electronic CAD for boards and silicon compilers for components, cross-compilers for programs. Note that the methodology produces the documents necessary as input to these tools; this is the essential point.

Nor is it a methodology for project management. Project management tasks - planning, organization, personnel assignment, guidance and control - are not explicit in MCSE, but obviously the hierarchical model proposed for the development is very useful as a basis for the creation of a project guidance strategy.

The field in which MCSE is useful is therefore essentially system development and particularly specification and design for systems or global applications, and for the hardware and software parts. It seems a complete and efficient answer to the hardware/software co-design issue.

4

METHODOLOGY BASIS

A methodology goes beyond simply breaking down work into steps. To lead to a complete and thorough understanding of MCSE and before considering its characteristics, it will be useful to bear in mind what the term 'methodology' means and implies.

Several aspects are discussed in this chapter. First, design is a human activity, with all its associated advantages and disadvantages. Second, a method does not describe a solution, but how to reach a solution. Therefore every method is dependent on the nature of the solution to be found, thus leading to the necessity for a description model useful for every solution.

This chapter shows how models, methods, techniques and design tools are complementary. When organized, the whole forms a methodology.

4.1 TERMINOLOGY

First, we will define the terms used in this book which could otherwise lead to confusion.

4.1.1 Problem: definition, solution

The term "Problem" is always related to a subject or a situation. There are two classes of activities around this term - problem definition (what do we want?, what do we need?, the WHAT), and the problem solution (HOW to do it?).

A problem may be well or badly defined. When it is well defined, the solution activity alone is needed; this is the designer's work. However, both activities are necessary for a badly defined problem. The problem has first to be defined before it can be solved.

Solving a problem consists in analyzing the situation in which the problem exists, determining possible solutions about what must or must not be done, and then deciding upon a solution.

4.1.2 Model and modeling

Modeling is an activity that we all carry out, either consciously or unconsciously. It precedes any decision or expression of an opinion. It is not an end in itself. It must be able to answer the initial question for which a model was developed.

A MODEL is an explicit interpretation by its user of the understanding of a situation, or more simply of the idea that he has about the situation. It can be expressed mathematically, by symbols or words, but essentially it is a description of entities and relations between them. Modeling therefore comes down to the creation of a more or less abstract partial view of the actual situation [WILSON-86].

4.1.3 Method and methodology

A method to solve a problem or a technique is characterized by a set of well-defined rules which lead to a correct solution to the problem.

A methodology has a wider scope than a method. It is a structured and coherent set of methods, guides and tools for determining the way in which a problem can be solved. A methodology leading to the use of techniques can be used to determine whether or not a specific technique is appropriate. It is therefore a combination of methods and techniques from various fields.

A design methodology is expressed in particular by the progress through successive steps and the tools for efficiently developing a solution to the stated problem and respecting quality criteria.

4.2   DESIGN WORK CHARACTERIZATION

4.2.1 Design: a human activity

The design activity is a decision-making process. Carried out by man, it is an individual creative activity based on the use of acquired knowledge and not on intuition [JENSEN-79]. All normal procedures consist of:

- formulating the problem;

- analyzing the problem to bring out sufficient detail;

- searching for potential solutions;

- determining the most appropriate solution by evaluating and comparing solutions;
- describing a detailed description of the selected solution.

Acquired knowledge deals with two information categories:
- knowledge in one or more than one field. Knowledge is acquired gradually and deals with the description, behavior and properties of what exists;
- methods and techniques. These are also acquired and assimilated very gradually by solving problems.

These two categories which are apparently very different are actually complementary and essential to the development activity: knowledge provides information necessary for decision-making, whereas methods and techniques structure the decision sequence.

As shown in Figure 4.1, the design activity is comparable to a transformation procedure, expressed by a set of related actions, necessary to move on from the problem to a solution.

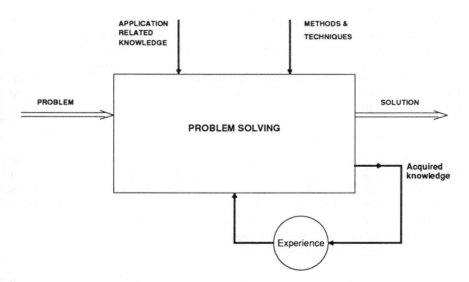

Figure 4.1   Problem-solving procedure.

Solving problems improves acquired skills by enhancing experience. Experience has the special property of being reusable. Knowledge, methods and techniques are not sufficient, and what is important for a designer is to know how to make the best use of all components to suit each individual problem. Experience is this ability and since it is personal, each designer only acquires it by individual work.

To solve these problems, the designer must have the following minimum qualities:

- reasoning ability - important for analysis and decision taking;
- the ability to acquire knowledge - curiosity, a synthetic mind;
- communication skills, since he has to solve the customer's problem.

Since design activity is individual, the problem must be broken down to a stage accessible by each, such that communication becomes possible. It must be possible to integrate all contributions for any one project; this is the purpose of a methodology, a process or procedures.

In addition, since it is a human activity, it is a source of errors. Therefore checks are necessary to reduce design errors.

Another different but complementary way of viewing the design activity is to consider whether it can be broken down into two coupled subsets [WILSON-86]:

- a system of activities, representative of the methods, techniques or a methodology;
- a social system, representative of participants in the design activity.

This point of view is useful, since it suggests that results may be bad even when using a satisfactory system of activities. Conversely, results can be obtained without a methodology, but undoubtedly with less guarantee. A satisfactory result is only possible if the company system and therefore individual designers use the methods or techniques correctly. When a methodology is felt to be necessary, the organization responsible for the team has an additional responsibility. Chances of success are reduced without strong internal commitment.

4.2.2 The design process

In order to characterize a methodology, the design process has to be modeled [DASGUPTA-89]. Conventionally, this is carried out in the form of a sequence of steps [KOOMEN-85]. A form of the solution description is used as the interface between two successive steps. There are two natures of description interfaces intermediate between each step:

- formal data (m): specifications, diagrams, schemes, components, etc;
- less formal data (c): text, description, constraints, etc.

At the beginning of a project, all available data is informal by nature. During design, they are gradually transformed into formal data, but some remain informal. These are called constraints since they will have an effect later on the final result.

Thus, designing consists of gradually increasing the level of detail in the formal description, gradually building in constraints described by the informal part, until all constraints disappear. In this way, the final solution can be observed as a set of hierarchical levels equivalent to the sequence of descriptions.

Each transition between two description levels forms a step, as shown in Figure 4.2.

Mi composed of *mi* and *ci* is the solution description for level i. A specification (*S*) is considered as a formal description of the need with the system properties and constraints, whereas an implementation (*I*) (or solution) is a formal description of a structure of constituents which satisfy these specifications. The transformation *S* --> *I* necessitates that the designer makes use of knowledge *Ki* and methods *Di*. The verification of the conformity of *I* relative to *S* is an essential condition for reducing errors.

Chaining steps requires that an implementation at the completion of one step can be used as a specification for the next step.

According to this model, the nature of design work is creative. In some special cases it can also be of a transformation type; it can then be formalized and the transformation can be carried out automatically.

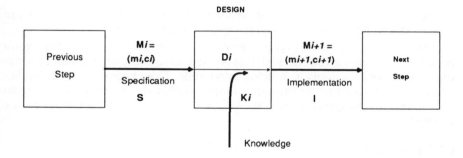

Figure 4.2   A design step.

4.2.3 Refinement and abstraction

The procedure for going from one description level to another is possible in two directions, one towards more detail (refinement) and the other towards less detail (abstraction). For each direction, solution derivation rules can be expressed which can serve as a basis for a method:

for refinement:

- mirror: a model of the environment is placed in the system;
- enhancement: descriptions are added to the current state;
- decomposition: functions are described by more elementary subsets;
- association: this is a composition operation subsequent to a decomposition and/or enhancement operation.

Refining a solution thus consists in increasing the level of detail by adding additional information which will subsequently be used as constraints for the implementation.

for abstraction:
- - simplification: (as opposed to enhancement), descriptions are eliminated to reduce complexity;
- - composition: (as opposed to decomposition), several description sets are combined into one;
- - reduction: descriptions are replaced by an equivalent less detailed description.

The abstraction process describes an element by a purely external view to make it usable within a set at a higher description level.

The refinement technique encourages a top-down approach to the problem towards the detailed solution, whereas the abstraction technique is justified more as a bottom-up procedure.

4.3 MAIN FEATURES OF A METHODOLOGY

Therefore, a methodology is the expression of a progress by steps, which can efficiently reach the objective respecting quality criteria.

The development process is broken down into steps. The observable result between two steps can be checked; this is essential to eliminate inevitable errors due to the human activity as quickly as possible. This chapter showed that the design process consists in finding a more detailed description starting from input data used as specifications. We will go on to define the main features of a methodology.

4.3.1 Description model

Observing that chaining steps is only possible if the output result of one step can be used as a specification for the next step and that a description level resulting from one step is a refinement of the previous level, a global methodology leading from a problem to its solution is necessarily based on a hierarchical description model.

The model for each description level then acts as a constraint for the solution description issuing from the step which produces it.

In Figure 4.3., *Si* and *Ci* form specifications for step *i*. The description of the selected solution *Ii* must satisfy the description model *MDi*. *Si+1* corresponds to all or part of *Ii*. Note that any solution respecting the model will have the characteristics and properties of the model

For a system, the first and most abstract description is a purely external view called the specification and the most detailed description is the complete implementation description.

When the description model for a system has been defined, the methodology scheme as an expression of a sequence of steps is also defined by a description model which is then the development process model. The latter is a result of the former, not the converse.

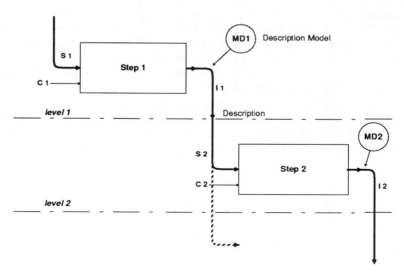

Figure 4.3   Chaining steps and description levels.

4.3.2 Method and technique for each step

Specifying and designing is determining a description from a previous abstract description and by using complementary information as constraints. The output results must fulfill the description model for the level. To satisfy this, the deduction process has to use rules, a guide and recommendations which specify the constraints to be taken into account at each stage to introduce them into the solution. Decision criteria are then necessary to satisfy the various choices.

One or more than one method isthen related to each step, whereas a steps sequence defines the global outline of the methodology.

4.3.3 Solution models

The design process is a human activity. Although the solution is sometimes the result of pure transformations, there is nevertheless a large amount of creative work. How can we ensure that most designers produce correct and, if possible, quality solutions? We must be capable of encouraging solution concepts adapted to the problem.

It is therefore useful to have solution models available, also referred to in this book as template models, since they can help find a variety of solutions, each specific to the problem to be solved and deduced from the objective to be satisfied.

Although the previous aspects - description model, methods - are conventional, the advantage of template models has recently become apparent as a result of pedagogical experiments. The result is very promising. Moreover, looking forward to the future, in the same way that increased productivity is a result of automatic production of products and even of earlier solution descriptions, automation of a step inevitably requires that a production tool be based on one or more solution models.

The MCSE methodology introduced in the next chapter is based on these concepts: a three-dimensional system description model, a four-step development process model, a method associated with each step, solution and template models to help the designer.

5

MCSE OVERVIEW

This chapter describes the MCSE methodology distinguishing features and the process. First, it introduces the model used to describe any system. Second, the various methodology steps are subsequently described based on this model. Finally, there is a summary of the main points of MCSE at the end of this chapter. However, before beginning, we will summarize the gradual bottom-up process followed during the last ten years to bring this methodology to maturity by pointing out the characteristic thought stages.

5.1 DEVELOPMENT OF THE METHODOLOGY

At the present time, the methodology described covers the specification, functional design (preliminary design), implementation specification (detailed design), and implementation phases.

This development was started around 1977/78, and dealt mainly with the design step. Defining a design procedure required prior development of a description model for all applications and real-time systems. This model was defined in 1980, and has three dimensions: functional, temporal, executive. It has demonstrated its usefulness as a basis for application developments by successive refinements of requirements resulting in an implementation solution including hardware and software and satisfying various criteria.

With hindsight, it is interesting to note that the selected model is an invariant. Its suitability has been gradually confirmed during projects development for various companies and for many types of problems.

We then consider the refinement of methods to be followed to find a solution with technical and economic qualities. The design step must not be isolated from prior or subsequent steps. Prior to the design step, one needs to develop a

47

method for producing a specification document which efficiently be used for design. The Specification method is based upon an initial approach by modeling the system environment. This type of approach greatly facilitates the subsequent design process.

After the design, we considered the various implementation techniques for defining the procedure for selection based on a functional design for the most appropriate implementation technique (technology, hardware/software distribution, respect of timing constraints, etc.).

A great deal of methodology experimentation has shown the importance of the description model, and also the importance of rules and advice to help designers produce quality solutions. In recent years we have gone past this stage and we have noted that quality solutions can be expressed in the form of generic models. Therefore, knowledge of this kind of generic solution model or template model for various problem classes facilitates the designer's task and encourages the production of quality solutions leading to improved readability, maintainability, efficiency and therefore reducing total cost.

The MCSE methodology has been developed particularly for real-time process control applications. It has been applied to many industrial problems, and has thus been validated. The resulting model is very suitable for the problems dealt with and has a definite advantage in the detailed design phase, proposing a systematic procedure for selecting the hardware/software solution (co-design).

Although this methodology is particularly concerned with the real-time systems field, the procedure followed for the initial development phases (specification, functional design) are implementation-independent since a system approach is used. Interesting experiments have been carried out on its use for various applications: process control systems, networks and protocols, multiprocessor and distributed systems, interactive tools, design of application-specific integrated circuits (ASICs).

It is systematically used for the specification and design of systems on request by companies and research laboratories.

Some studies are mentioned below:

- Design of an electronic system for programming and control of high performance centrifuges;

- Feasibility study of an entirely digital solution for the control of DC/DC converters;

- Implementation of an automatic 6-battery test system. Another version for 64 batteries was subsequently developed;

- Data acquisition system for the monitoring of anchor chains for oil platforms;

- Design of a centralized management and heat regulation system for a large building with the development of a local area network at 2 Mbits/s.

The size and complexity of these problems is highly varied. The centralized large building management system dealt with the simultaneous management of 600 inputs/outputs.

5.2 THE DESCRIPTION MODEL

MCSE is based on the simple idea that any system (its internal view, in other words the HOW) can be observed in three views:

- a **functional view**, which characterizes the system's internal functions;

- a **temporal view**, describing the behavior of internal functions thus expressing the contribution of each;

- a **hardware view**, specifying the physical part of the system.

To illustrate this idea, consider the case of a control system for heating a building. The functional view will show dialog and building supervision functions, regulation functions for each area, etc. These functions are inter-related to satisfy the objective - message exchanges for the heating schedule, access to the main characteristics such as outside temperature, water temperature, etc.

The behavioral view explains the contribution of each function. For example, regulation of each zone calculates valve control values every minute using the formula:

$$cv = k1*(Tc-Ti) - k2*To - k3* (To-To\_prev)$$

where Tc = control temperature, Ti = inside temperature, To = outside temperature, To_prev: previous outside temperature measurement.

The hardware view is a set of microprocessor systems interconnected by a 2-wire pair cable used as a common bus.

No single view is sufficient for complete understanding of the system. Each explains a specific aspect and thus adds an additional information dimension to describe the "how" of the system. These three views prove to be necessary and complementary.

Therefore, the selected conceptual model has three dimensions [CALVEZ-82]:

- the **structural dimension**, described by the functional model (or functional structure);

- the **behavioral dimension**, which uses temporal models to describe the behavior of functional components;

- the **executive dimension**, described by an executive structure which expresses hardware components and interconnections necessary to operate the system.

The first two dimensions describe the structure and behavior of a system, disregarding implementation techniques and methods. The resulting description, called the "functional description", should be independent of implementation techniques to be selected or imposed.

The third dimension describes computer and electronic resources used to generate the evolution described by the functional description, satisfying all temporal, technical and technological constraints of the application.

Figure 5.1 shows this three-dimensional model.

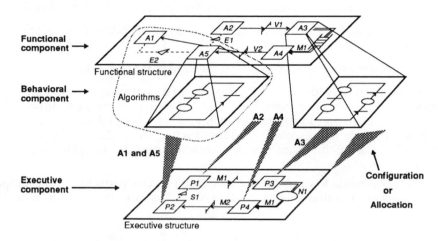

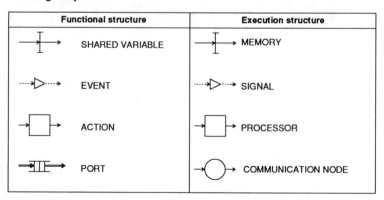

Meaning of symbols

Functional structure		Execution structure	
┼	SHARED VARIABLE	┼	MEMORY
▷	EVENT	▷	SIGNAL
□	ACTION	□	PROCESSOR
Ⅱ	PORT	○	COMMUNICATION NODE

Figure 5.1   The three-dimensional model.

This figure shows that the function behavior and functional structure combination is integrated into the execution support structure using an integration or allocation correspondence, also called configuration.

We will briefly describe each of the model dimensions.

5.2.1 The functional model

The functional model is a structure built using functions and relations between them.

A function usually designates the entity carrying out a specific system activity. Decomposition into functions corresponds to a "topological" rather than a temporal point of view of application activities.

Relations between functions are particularly suitable for real-time systems. Three types are used:

- The **synchronization relation**, expressed by an event. It is used to define the complete or partial order in which the various functions participate in the overall activity of the system. Interventions take place on the appearance of events which generally express system state changes. This type of relation is particularly suitable for event-driven applications.

- The **shared variable relation** (state variable). In this type of relation, several functions can know an item of information by reading it, or can instantaneously modify its value. This is an important relation for real-time applications, particularly for coupling physical processes with a control system. Some functions must have an immediate influence on their environment, or a precise and instantaneous knowledge of the state of this environment.

- The **information transfer relation**, by message exchange. This relation is used to pass information from one function to another. This type of relation suggests that the ownership of the information changes. This is a producer --> consumer type relation. A function is only activated when the information necessary is available and is transmitted to it in the form of a message. We can therefore say that function-related activity is synchronous to a particular event type signalling the availability of some information. This type of exchange generates a totally time-ordered relation for the activity of resulting functions.

Functions considered in this model may be elementary or complex. By successive refinements, a complex function can be decomposed into the form of a structure. Functions and relations are those necessary to satisfy the objective and are in no way concerned with technological aspects. A good functional description must be independent of the technology.

Figure 5.2 illustrates this model for the heating control system example. Its graphical nature makes it particularly useful for fast overall understanding of the model. The solution consists of a supervision function related to the operator, and as many regulation functions as there are heating zones to be controlled.

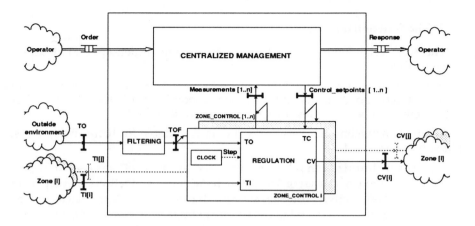

Figure 5.2   Functional structure example for heating control.

By its hierarchical nature, this model allows the designer to proceed by abstraction and refinement of the structure. This structural dimension can also be used to represent the complementary nature of two organizational dimensions, namely the vertical dimension to express a structure in service levels, and the horizontal dimension expressing the data-flow and time dependencies of the level.

The advantage of the three relation types rather than, for example, a version unified by messages, is its ability to simultaneously describe event-driven and data-driven type behavior and direct variable exchanges between processes (state space).

5.2.2 The behavioral model

This model describes the contribution of the function to its environment. This is therefore its specification. A function should be understood as an input and output transformation operator. Described by a behavioral model which has to be simple, its evolution is necessarily sequential and cyclic. All sequential behavior model types can be used - finite state diagram, Grafcet, algorithm, etc.

Each function carries out one transformation at any one time. Two behavior types are considered:

- a **permanent evolution**: the function continuously carries out its transformation role, without any activating event or message input. It is therefore a permanent function.

- a **temporary evolution**: the function carries out its role whenever a message or event type input appears. It is therefore a temporary function.

The following example in Figure 5.3 shows the algorithmic description given for temperature regulation in each zone. The regulation function is driven by a clock controlling the sampling rate.

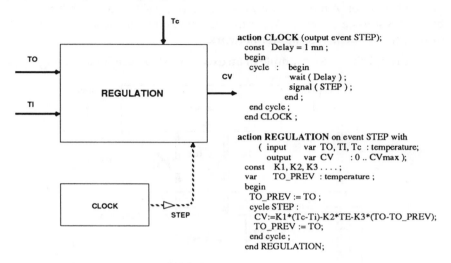

Figure 5.3   Regulation function behavior.

Permanent evolution is expressed by the statement CYCLE: <Statement> end cycle; and temporary evolution by the statement CYCLE <ev>: <Statement> end cycle;

This type of description is formal and therefore checkable, and can be used for a very fast implementation, particularly for a software development.

5.2.3 The executive model

This model specifies the hardware part. It is based on the fact that every electronic system consists of:

- **processors**, a wide word expressing active objects for information transformation and decision making;
- **memories**, for storing data;
- **communication nodes**, as intermediate elements for information transit points.

These three interrelated types of technological elements produce a hardware solution description using a structure called an "executive" structure. Exchanges between processors take place:

- by interprocessor signalling for direct coupling;
- by memory sharing for indirect coupling;
- through a network of communication nodes for message transfers.

The terms "processor", "memory" and "communications node" should be taken in their most general sense. A processor is programmable, for example like a microprocessor, or specific such as an operational amplifier or a digital to analog converter. A memory may be restricted to a single register, but may also be a mass storage memory. A communication node may be a single RS232 line or may be a node in a computer network.

Figure 5.4 shows an example of an executive structure for a heating control.

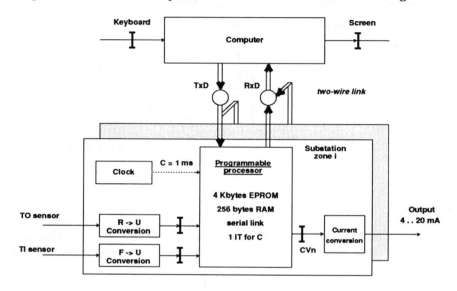

Figure 5.4   Executive structure for a heating control system.

The executive dimension model is similar to that proposed for the functional dimension but with a different meaning of functions and relations. The existence of this third dimension facilitates the searching for or expression of the most appropriate hardware support for each application. The similarity of the two models makes it possible to proceed by deduction defining the executive structure as a reduction of the functional structure.

5.2.4 Advantage of this model

This three-dimensional model allows a description facilitating gradual understanding of a system by first considering relations between internal functions necessary to satisfy objectives, then the behavior of each of them, and finally the resources which actually make the system work. It can be used to structure the presentation of a system based on a four-level hierarchy:

- the **external description**, as level 1. This level describes the complete application specifications before considering any type of internal solution;

- the **functional description**, as level 2. Based on the functional model and the expression of the behavior of internal functions, it explains the internal solution as an application-oriented point of view;

- the **executive description**, as level 3. This is the result of associating the description of the previous level with a chosen or imposed executive structure for the hardware support;

- the **final description** (level 4), as the last level containing the detailed application hardware and software descriptions.

The functional description is an application-oriented description and does not take into account technological characteristics. Thus, this type of solution facilitates new implementations when technological changes occur.

The executive description is the association of the three dimensions linked together by allocation or configuration which describes the implementation of the functional description on the executive support. The principle is that a subset of the functional description is located in each processor. For programmable processors such as microprocessors, the functional structure subset allocated on this processor is described by a software implementation diagram.

The four-level description model increases understandability and consequently maintainability. Moreover, it is usable as a basis for decomposing the development process into steps. The model is also useful for the description of complex systems since it is invariant with scale: ASIC component or multiprocessor application, simple microprocessor implementation or a complex computer information system.

5.3 THE DEVELOPMENT PROCESS

A methodology is a guide for project developments. The proposed MCSE process is globally top-down. It recommends starting from the customer's problem to search for an appropriate implementation by successive approaches. Decomposition into steps is based on the possibility of describing any system at several levels.

The design process is based on the use of the above model. It expresses the thought process that the designer must follow to end with a description that conforms to the model and satisfies quality criteria: robustness, modularity, understandability, maintainability. Each description level is intermediate between two successive steps.

The development process is carried out in four steps:

- the **specification step**, to express a purely external view of the system (WHAT), starting from the needand requirements;

- the **functional design step**, the objective of which is to find the functional description composed of the first two model dimensions (application-oriented HOW);

- the **implementation specification step** (also called detailed design), the purpose being to find an executive structure and a software implementation scheme on the selected hardware with respect to all technological constraints: geographic distribution constraints, time constraints, electrical constraints, etc;

- the **implementation step** leading to an operational system.

Figure 5.5 describes the sequence of these four steps.

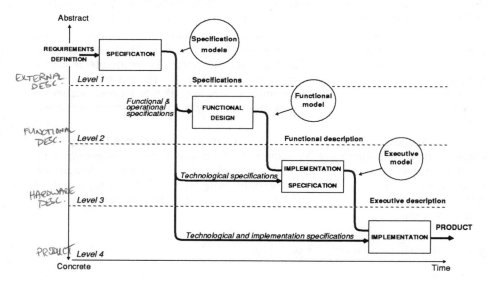

Figure 5.5   Steps for MCSE.

In each step, the designer must use as inputs the intermediate level description resulting from the previous step, and the additional information defined by constraints imposed in the specifications. The step produces a description for the next level. A conformity verification is possible after each step.

Without entering into detail, we will review the various methodological steps in the next sections, and will describe the principles involved.

5.3.1 The specification step

Specifications must be available before design can start. The word specification means a complete but purely external description of a system to be designed. It is easier to find a solution when these specifications are more detailed and expressed with formal models. However the specification must be verifiable, particularly by the customer. To satisfy these objectives, a specification must comply with a specification model which has all expected properties and qualities.

The first important question to ask is therefore: how can we model any system without describing its internal solution since this is the unknown to be defined subsequently during the design?

The starting point is the requirements definition describing the customer's need. To describe what a system must do, the system is considered to observe and act upon objects in its environment. Therefore, the first essential step is to know this environment. Knowing it initially involves modeling objects without the system, and second, describing existing relations between them in the form of a functional description.

After that, the role of the system must be described, and so expressing its specifications consists of stating and characterizing the requested functions. This is generally done by describing the required behavior of objects in the environment under the control of the system together with all imposed constraints.

Using this approach, the methodology brings out a similarity of reasoning between the specification process and the design process. The environment analysis leads to a synthesis of reality in the form of a model. Introducing objectives to be achieved enhances the previous model, also taking the system contribution into account.

Three types of specification are produced in this step:

- **functional specifications**: these include a list of system functions for the application (external functions) and a description of the behavior of the environment under the control of the system for these functions;

- **operational specifications** which concern the behavior, performance, information details, and methods to be used in the system;

- the **technological specifications** which include timing and geographic distribution constraints, interface characteristics and various implementation constraints.

The functional and operational specifications are used in the functional design step, whereas the technological specifications are only used in the implementation specification and implementation steps. Some specifications are specific to the implementation step.

5.3.2 The functional design step

The solution for this step is deduced from an analysis of the functional specifications. The functional structure is sought first starting from the system delimitation by characterizing its inputs and outputs. A first functional decomposition is then carried out. This approach is important since it leads to quality or non-quality for the rest of the development.

The design process then consists of successive refinements for each function to be designed in order to search for the necessary, and if possible sufficient, characteristic internal variables and events. Functions which use and update these variables are then deduced, together with the behavior of each function. Refinement is continued until elementary functions are obtained which can be expressed by a purely sequential description.

Experience has shown that this data-based approach leads to functional structures which are simple (reduction of coupling expressing order relations) and more structured than the function-based approach which expresses the structure as describing a sequence of transformations.

5.3.3 The implementation specification step

The third step consists in searching firstly for the executive support, and second for the means of implementing software functions.

First, the functional description must be refined, detailed and enhanced to take account of the technological constraints: geographic distribution (if necessary), physical interfaces, user interfaces.

Timing constraints are then analyzed to determine the hardware/software distribution. The hardware part is specified by an executive structure. Integration, which includes allocation, completely describes the implementation of the functional description into the executive structure.

Each functional subset to be implemented by software is described by a software implementation diagram which expresses the priority of each task and the spatial (based on data) and temporal dependence relations between tasks. This layout is the result of using rules for carrying out transformations on the functional structure. This is done by taking account of the hardware support and aiming to minimize the software organizational part in order to reduce the development time.

5.3.4 The implementation step

The two parts - the hardware support and the software implementation - facilitate the work involved in making a prototype, integration and testing.

At this stage, it is necessary to be aware of the variety of implementation strategies which depend on at least three factors: technological specifications, techniques to be used, tools and methods available for development.

Implementation is a bottom-up process since it consists of assembling. The solution has to be developed in individual parts, bringing out more and more abstract functionalities to approach the objective. Each level of the implementation is validated by checking compliance with specifications for the corresponding level in the top-down process. Hardware and software implementations can be developed simultaneously involving specialists in both fields, thus reducing the total implementation time.

The objective of integration and testing at the end of the implementation is to combine all parts of the development in order to provide an operational system which satisfies the customer's wishes.

5.4 MCSE CHARACTERISTICS

The proposed methodology is a complete process for progressing from a problem to a product. We will repeat here the main points presented as objectives in previous chapters to show why and how MCSE satisfies all these points.

-A- A basic description model

Every methodology is necessarily based on one or more description models, allowing decomposition into levels and steps. MCSE is based on an internal three-dimensional description model. It facilitates the description of any system in a hierarchy of description levels. Each level is intermediate between two steps. Models are mostly graphical, thus facilitating overall and rapid understanding.

-B- A globally top-down design process

Each step of the methodology is used to move from one description level to the next more detailed description level, by enhancing the solution with added information.

Therefore, the progression is globally top-down since it starts from the stated problem and ends in an operational implementation.

-C- An iterative progression

No development can take place without errors or omissions. Corrections are always necessary. Based on corrections by feedback, a verification phase at the end of each step allows error detection and induces iterative work with loopbacks within the step or to previous steps.

-D- A specific method for each step

The solution description model to be respected at the end of each step (the WHAT) is not sufficient. The designer must have a precise guide for each step explaining HOW to pass from the input specification to a solution having the required qualities.

This guide is the method to be followed: analysis technique, decision sequence, selection criteria synthesis. Unlike an intuitive search, the use of a method guarantees that a solution, probably a quality solution, will be obtained more quickly.

Beyond the method aspect, there is an unquestionable advantage in the concept of template solution models. These model types are used to induce multiple functional decomposition solutions since they have intrinsic qualities: understandability, maintainability, simplicity, suitability for the global MCSE model. We have observed that 80% to 90% of designers can achieve satisfactory developments if they are familiar with these models in addition to the methods.

-E- A globally bottom-up implementation process

Assembly is not possible before components are available. Therefore, implementation starts by making the smallest subsets, and then gradually assembling and integrating them into more general functions. The implementation work is represented by a triangle adjacent to the design triangle as shown in Figure 5.6. The width of the triangle for each stage indicates the quantity of information to be handled.

Each implementation level can be checked, proving its conformity with the corresponding design level. The two processes - top-down and bottom-up - are therefore complementary.

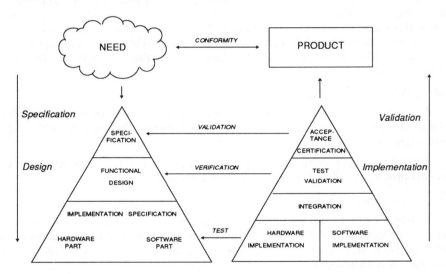

Figure 5.6   Double triangle form for the development process.

-F- A hierarchical development cycle model

For a relatively complex system, the above double triangle model is not accurate enough.

The hardware and software parts are defined during the implementation definition phase. Each part has therefore to be developed using a three-phase process: specification, design and implementation, until the necessary components are available (hardware or software components).

The development cycle is thus a series of interrelated developments. Figure 5.7 shows MCSE as a hierarchical development process model.

At the first level, the design is general and concerns the overall application. As the solution is refined, developments concern more specific problems related to the implementation: development of a component, a specific function, a software module, etc. A specification serves as an objective for an implementation. The component or subset is the usable result.

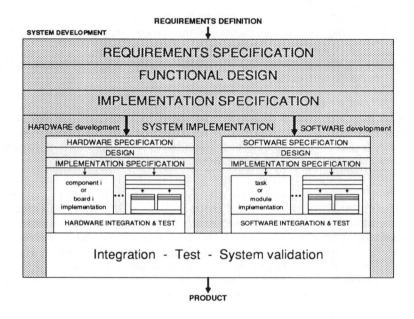

Figure 5.7   Hierarchical model for the development cycle.

-G- A documentation guide

The description model directly leads to the structure of documents to be produced during the development. Each document is the result of a step and provides information for the next step.

Respecting the process of using successive steps, the documentation is thus generated during the development, and not after it has been finished. Its form and content are then of high quality since they describe, in addition to the solution, the procedure followed and the argument justifying major decisions.

Produced in this manner, the documentation can be used throughout the development cycle for checking phases in an author-reader cycle, for observation of progession, and also in later steps and particularly for manufacturing and maintenance.

-H- A project management guide

The development cycle model is used for the implementation of a management procedure for a set of projects. This activity concerns the following procedure for each project:

- management: project planning, organization, direction, control;
- obtaining conformity: scheduling tests, nature of technical tests to be used, results, conformity and certification;
- documentation management: document specification, review scheduling, management methods, updates, etc;
- maintenance management: maintenance scope and procedures, solutions and tools, scheduling;
- quality management: quality assurance, method for obtaining quality, inspection procedures.

-I- An open and complementary methodology

MCSE is not restricted to a very specific field and does not use just one particular method. On the contrary, several methods can be used for each step and the designer chooses one of these methods depending on a given criterion, whichever is most useful to him in solving the problem.

Initially developed for real-time microprocessor process control systems, experience has shown that it is suitable for a wide range of applications and techniques, and particularly for applications using electronics and computers. MCSE is not to be opposed to other methodologies; on the contrary, it is intended to be complementary. Most models proposed by various authors can be used. For example, SADT, Ward and Mellor's and Hatley's, OOA and OMT specification methods facilitate the problem analysis task. In some aspects, the Jackson methodology is fairly close to MCSE. Gomaa's DARTS and Buhr's SDWMC methodologies have some points in common.

-J- A support for tools

Today, it is difficult to conceive of a methodology without thinking about computer-aided design tools as a development and project management aid.

Based on a formal model, MCSE has all the characteristics which facilitate the development of such tools. It should be understood that a tool does not imply a methodology, but rather the inverse. A tool is only used to assist with the application of a methodology. A tool as a support can only be developed after the formalization of a methodology.

This brief description is not sufficient to give a complete idea about the methodology. The following chapter illustrates its use on a rather simple example in order to give a more complete view of the process.

6

AN ILLUSTRATIVE EXAMPLE

In order to illustrate the principles of the MCSE methodology, this chapter describes an example of a relatively simple problem, but sufficiently complex to justify the use of a method. It helps to understand the main points of the recommended process, and the role of each step. It facilitates understanding the three views of the conceptual model and the solution description levels.

The reader is not expected to understand all the details of the example. It is recommended rather, that he reads this chapter quickly, simply to get an overall idea of the methodology. Later, after having read parts 3 to 6 which explain each step of the method in detail, he should return to this example for complete understanding.

The example is a system for controlling a vehicle cruising speed.

This example is taken from the book *Strategies for Real-Time System Specification* by Hatley and Pirbhai [HATLEY-87] in which a solution is described. The same example is given in the book *Structured Development for Real-Time Systems* Volume 2 and Volume 3 by Ward and Mellor [WARD-85].

Additions and modifications have been made to the requirements, particularly to the technological specifications in order to propose a complete and realistic solution satisfying the need.

6.1 REQUIREMENTS DEFINITION

This control system is to be considered as a possible option on some vehicle models. The essential functions of the system deal with routine operations and maintenance tasks, namely:

- monitoring the cruising speed;
- monitoring the average speed;
- monitoring fuel consumption;
- vehicle maintenance.

These functions are described in more detail below, such that a preliminary study can be carried out together with a solution evaluation, development cost and time estimate, and a reproduction cost estimate.

6.1.1 Cruising speed control

When the driver selects this mode, this function keeps the vehicle at a constant speed. It is only active when the engine is running. The function is obviously inactive at the moment the engine is started.

The driver can act on the system by means of several commands:

- regulator activation;
- stop;
- acceleration;
- return to the previous speed (cruising speed regulation).

When the driver activates the regulation mode, the vehicle speed at that instant is maintained if it is greater than 50 kph. The STOP command allows the driver to take control again.

The vehicle speed is deduced from the wheel rotation speed and the engine speed is controlled by means of a valve controlling fuel injection. The valve can only be forced in the open direction (acceleration). It is automatically returned by a spring. Obviously, the acceleration pedal always acts mechanically on the valve; the most important displacement action defines the vehicle speed.

When the regulator is active, the driver can use the START ACCELERATION command to request a gradual increase in speed. This action is maintained until the END ACCELERATION command is given: use of the same acceleration key acting as a bistable. The vehicle then maintains this speed as a cruising speed.

The driver can increase the vehicle speed at any time by pressing the accelerator pedal, or reduce speed by pressing the brake pedal. The vehicle returns to the cruising speed when the accelerator pedal is released. The system is de-activated when the brake pedal is pressed or when the gear shift is withdrawn from its engaged position. When the brake is released with the speed lever in position, the "return to cruising speed" command will return the vehicle to the previously selected speed.

If a STOP command is given in the mean time, the RETURN command is inoperative.

The system must have its own speed indicator. Since the speed, and therefore the distance travelled, is a function of the size of the tyres, it must be possible to calibrate the system on installation. Two additional commands are available on the rear face: START KM MEASUREMENT and STOP KM MEASUREMENT.

After pressing START, the driver travels 1 km and then presses STOP. In calibration mode the system must record the number of wheel revolutions which will then be used as a reference for speed and distance calculations.

6.1.2 Monitoring average speed

The system must inform the driver about his average speed. The driver uses the START RUN command to inform the system that he is starting a run, and whenever he requests the average speed by pressing REQUEST AS, the system will display the average speed after pressing START RUN.

6.1.3 Monitoring fuel consumption

When filling the tank, the driver informs the system about the amount of fuel that has just been added. The system then calculates and displays the consumption between two fillings.

6.1.4 Maintenance

The system must monitor the kilometers run by the vehicle and inform the driver when maintenance is due, to satisfy the following constraints:

- oil and filter change: 7,500 km;
- air filter change: 15,000 km;
- major service: 30,000 km.

250 km before these limits are reached, an appropriate slowly flashing message should be displayed. The message should become continuous at 50 km beforehand and should stay on until the driver clears it by pressing the MAINTENANCE COMPLETED command.

6.1.5 Complementary characteristics

The specification phase obviously requires discussions with the customer to clarify some points. The decisions to be made are described below.

- The accelerator pedal is in parallel on the electrical valve control. The action requiring the highest speed takes priority. The electrical control is proportional between complete valve closure at 0 volt and complete opening at 8 volts.

- The system measures the speed by counting pulses received by a sensor placed on a wheel.

- When the system detects that the speed is more than 3 kph above the selected speed, the valve must be completely closed (going down a steep hill). For any other speed, the control should be proportional to the speed variation, except when the valve is completely open. This should only arise for a variation of 3 kph. The control should only be updated every second to avoid stability problems.

- To prevent too sudden acceleration, the valve actuator must not operate faster than 10 seconds for the entire opening variation range. On the other hand, it can be closed at any speed. Mechanical engineers estimate that using these constraints, the vehicle can maintain its speed within + or - 2 kph on normal slopes.

- When the system is in the acceleration phase, acceleration should be maintained at 2 kph/s. The valve should be fully closed if the acceleration reaches 3 kph/s and fully open if it is equal to 1 kph/s. Between these two values the degree of opening is proportional to the acceleration variation.

- The user dialog system must have a set of function keys and an LCD type screen.

- The user interface must be "intelligent" - all magnitude inputs must be validated (fuel quantity, etc.).

6.2 SPECIFICATIONS

The specification process consists firstly of considering the system environment by creating an application model containing entities external to the system and excluding the system itself. The system functionalities then have to be specified by describing the behavior of the entities with the system.

This first step produces an external description of the system to be designed.

6.2.1 Modeling the environment

-A- The entities

The following entities are concerned by the system:
- the vehicle driver (the installer for calibration);
- the vehicle with its engine for displacing it via its wheels.

-B- Events, conditions, observations

A list is then made of related events in the specification, produced by entities and which require a reaction by the system.
- Start and stop vehicle (driver);
- Regulator activation and stop (driver);
- Start acceleration, end acceleration (driver);
- Return to previous speed (driver);
- Acceleration by pedal, brake (driver);
- Start km measurement, and Stop km measurement (installer);
- Start Run, request AS (driver);
- Maintenance completed (driver);
- Add fuel (driver).

Similarly, conditions to be taken into account can be listed:
- S > 50 kph (vehicle);
- S = SR: cruising speed for regulation (vehicle);
- Gear engaged (vehicle);
- Fuel quantity (driver);
- Maximum valve variation: 10 sec for the entire range on opening.

Some entity observations are:
- Distance covered (D);
- Vehicle speed (S);
- Average speed over a distance (AS);
- Average consumption (avC);
- Flashing for 250 km limit;
- Permanent display for 50 km limit.

-C- Entity behavior

The driver may request a particular behavioral item relative to his vehicle at any time. He is the generator of events concerning the vehicle, and is also observer of his vehicle's reactions and information.

The vehicle can be modeled, very simply, by assuming that when the engine is rotating and a gear is engaged, the displacement speed is roughly proportional to the position of the valve. Obviously, factors such as the slope of the road and the load are also essential parameters affecting the speed.

$$S = F \text{ (max (Paccelerator, Ctl\_valve), slope, load...)}$$

Paccelerator is the position of the accelerator pedal and Ctl_valve is the electric valve control.

The largest difference between the accelerator pedal position and the electric valve control position takes priority.

The influence of the slope, load, etc. terms makes a closed loop command necessary to obtain the regulation effect.

-D- System context delimitation

The delimitation shown in Figure 6.1 specifies coupling between the system and its environment.
- For commands received from the driver, all events mentioned in B are shown; similarly for observations. The fuel quantity has to be added.
- The only control acting on the car is the valve position.
- Observations include vehicle speed, distance travelled and gear engaged.

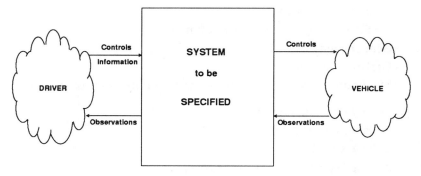

Figure 6.1   System context delimitation.

6.2.2 Functional specifications

These are the functions that must be carried out by the system on its environment, and the characteristics of these functions must be described as accurately as possible.

Since the functions cannot be described directly (if it were possible, the design would already be complete), an attempt is made to produce an indirect description of them by detailing the behavior of entities under the influence of the system.

-A- List of system functions

The system must:

- regulate the vehicle speed at cruising speed when necessary;
- provide driving information;
- provide maintenance assistance.

Each of these functions is described below.

-B- Speed regulation

Before the driver can make use of this function, he will need to coordinate (sequence relation) the events that he generates. The vehicle will then behave as the driver has wished. This specification is shown in Figure 6.2.

Therefore, the specification must model the required states for the vehicle under the control of the driver.

S is the current speed of the vehicle and SR represents its cruising speed, and acts as a control value for regulation. Acceleration is a Boolean condition specifying whether or not the driver is accelerating.

To complete the specification, actions to be undertaken for the active regulator phases must be defined. The acceleration pedal is active for other phases. Therefore, Ctl_valve = 0.

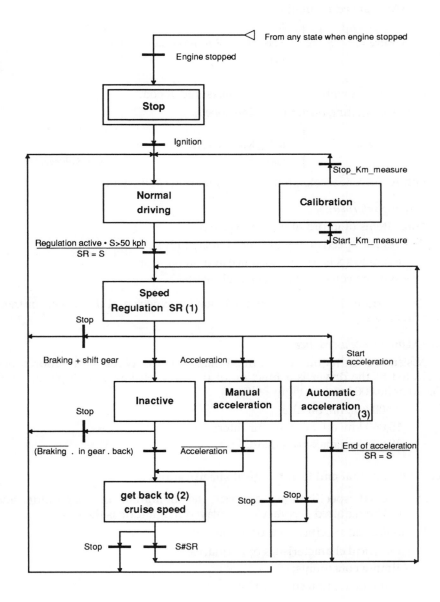

Figure 6.2   Vehicle behavior for regulation.

- PHASE: speed regulation -

$$Ctl\_valve = \begin{cases} 0 & \text{for } S - SR > 3 \text{ Kph} \\ Max * (SR - S)/6 + Max/2; & \text{for } |SR - S| < 3 \text{ Kph} \\ max; & \text{for } SR - S > 3 \text{ Kph} \end{cases}$$

with max = 8 volts,   S: measured speed.

- PHASE: getting back to cruising speed,

$$Ctl\_Valve = \begin{cases} 0 & \text{for } A > 3 \text{ Kph/sec} \\ K * (2Kph/sec - A) & \text{else} \\ max; & \text{for } A < 1 \text{ Kph/sec} \end{cases}$$

with A: current acceleration,   K : regulation coefficient.

-C- *Driving information*

Three items of information are required:

- vehicle speed at any instant (display only);
- average speed over a distance and on request;
- average consumption when filling up.

The diagrams Figure 6.3 show the behavior expected of the driver for these two functions.

-D - *Maintenance assistance*

Assistance is required for three maintenance types. The information indicated to the driver is a function of the value in km: a multiple of 7,500, 15,000 or 30,000 km (see Figure 6.4).

- 7,500 km: oil, oil filter;
- 15,000 km: oil, oil filter, air filter;
- 30,000 km: major overhaul.

6.2.3 Operational and technological specifications

Operational specifications concern the definition of magnitude and accuracy. The required accuracy of displayed magnitude is the unit.

Technological specifications describe:

- electrical characteristics of interfaces;
- timing constraints;
- implementation constraints.

-A- *Interfaces*

Two interface types have to be considered:

- coupling between vehicle and the system;
- coupling with the user.

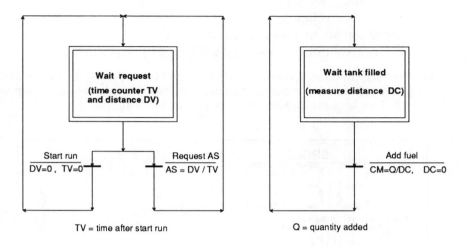

Figure 6.3   Behavior imposed on the driver for driving assistance.

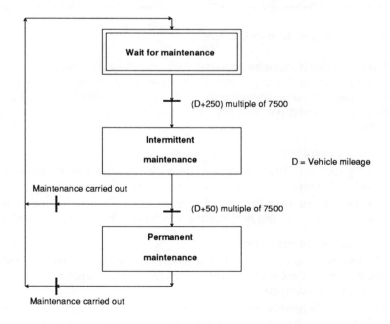

Figure 6.4   Driver's behavior related to maintenance.

For vehicle-system interfaces:

- incremental encoder for speed and distance measurements, 10 pulses per wheel revolution;
- closed contact, for gear engaged and braking;
- electrical control between 0 and 8 V for the valve position.

For the user interface, it was decided to use an LCD type display device and a set of keys to select the required mode. A draft of this interface is shown in Figure 6.5. Two keys are located on the back panel for calibration.

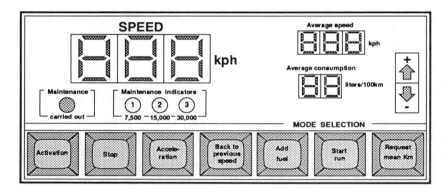

Figure 6.5   Draft of the user interface.

Fuel quantity is input by pressing the + and - keys instead of using a numeric keyboard. During this input, which starts as soon as the + key is pressed, the average consumption display unit lights up. The average quantity per 100 km is given by pressing the "add fuel" key. The behavior of this function is shown Figure 6.6.

-B- Timing constraints

For regulation stability purposes, the valve position control must not exceed a period of one second (not a severe constraint).

The system reaction time for driver requests must be of the order of one second maximum, except for braking which must be as fast as possible.

-C- Implementation constraints

The assembly must be developed based on microprocessor technology. The reproduction cost must be as low as possible since a large number of systems may have to be produced.

The system is battery powered. The system must store the main magnitudes even when the battery is disconnected: kilometers run by the vehicle, calibration parameters, etc.

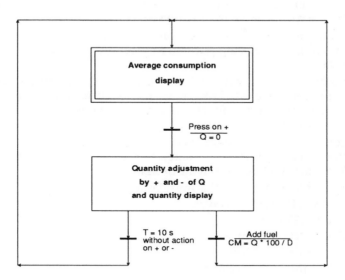

Figure 6.6   Behavior for the average consumption dialog.

Environmental constraints deal with temperature, relative humidity and vibrations.

6.3 FUNCTIONAL DESIGN

The functional design starts with the development of an initial functional approach. This is created starting from a delimitation of functional system inputs/outputs, searching for the main functions necessary to satisfy the specifications.

The solution search must be purely functional, identifying the characteristic internal variables. Normally, if the functional specifications have been well written, they will contain these main magnitudes. Interfaces necessary for observing or controlling entities should be excluded such that only the true application variables are considered. This comment is essential for a good functional delimitation of inputs/outputs. The recommended method thus develops a solution independent of the technology.

This second step produces an initial internal solution level.

6.3.1 System delimitation

The driver is the source of many events: pressing the buttons, inputting fuel quantity.

In order to be independent of the user interface, all commands are considered as messages. For display, all outputs will also be messages, each containing the nature of the information concerned.

The information to be observed on the vehicle are the speed, the total distance travelled since being put into service, and the braking state and gear engaged state.

Delimitation of the system with its functional inputs/outputs is therefore obtained by replacing all links with the environment expressed in the specification by appropriate functional model relations - synchronization, state variable, message transfer. Figure 6.7 represents this delimitation.

It is considered, at this stage, that the system will be powered by the car battery through the ignition key. Therefore, there is no point in considering the engine "ON" and "OFF" events in the design.

All input and output variables must be specified:
- BRAKE, IN_GEAR: Boolean;
- V: 0 to 199 kph;
- D: 0 to 100,000 km;
- Ctl_Valve: 0 to Max;
- CTL = [Maintenance done |
          Regulator activation |
          Stop regulator |
          Start acceleration |
          End acceleration |
          Return to previous speed |
          Start km measurement |
          Stop km measurement |
          Start run |
          Request AS |
          Fuel quantity: 0 to 99 1];
- DISPLAY = [Speed: 0 to 199 kph |
          Average speed: 0 to 199 kph |
          Consumption: 0 to 99 1 |
          Maintenance + case];

where case indicates one of the three maintenance cases.

Flashing is obtained by successive display of the "Maintenance" and "Null" messages.

6.3.2 Initial functional structure

This initial structure is deduced by an efficient analysis of the functional specifications, searching particularly for the internal variables strictly necessary to solve the problem.

The phases involved are analysis, decomposition, construction, verification.

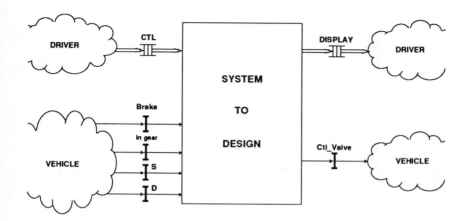

Figure 6.7   System delimitation.

-A- Analysis

According to the specifications, the three system FSM specified in Section 6.2.2. are independent since there are no common variables.

Internal variables appear in the specification (conditions or actions):

- SR: for the cruising speed to be maintained,
- DV and TV: distance travelled and time since the start of the run,
- DC: distance travelled since the last time the tank was filled.

-B- Solution construction

Let us consider the following functional structure (Figure 6.8). It is based on the previous analysis by considering the variable VR as essential. In relation to the two entities - the driver and the vehicle - the functional structure represents a supervision/control type decomposition: supervision as a driver-related function, and speed control as a vehicle control function.

The SPEED_CONTROL function is activated by a periodic event acting as a sampling step for regulation.

The MODE variable defines the three operating cases for this function:

MODE: (STOP, REGUL, ACCEL.). The REGUL mode corresponds to the 2 states (1) and (2) in the vehicle specification on Figure 6.2, the ACCEL mode corresponds to state (3) for an automatic speed increase, and the STOP mode applies to other states.

In order to produce a uniform solution for the supervision activation, it was decided to integrate the BRAKE or NOT IN_GEAR and BRAKE and IN_GEAR events as messages in CTL. SUPERVISION is thus a temporary action which sequentially processes the message stream. This is equivalent to considering all external transitions used in the specification diagrams as messages.

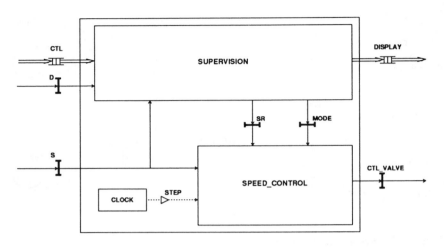

Figure 6.8   First functional draft.

-C- Verification

Before continuing refinement, we must make sure that the proposed solution can satisfy the specifications.

The FSM given in the specification will correspond to SUPERVISION behavior.

The speed regulation phase (1) and the get back to cruising speed phase (2) are combined and included in SPEED_CONTROL. This is specified by MODE when it is in the REGUL state. The transition between phase 2 and phase 1(S # SR) is produced internally within SPEED_CONTROL.

Another comment: S must be displayed regularly in order to give a correct speed reading; this is impossible with the proposed solution since SUPERVISION is a temporary function synchronous with CTL. In addition, a variable T is necessary to measure the time from the start of the run. Finally, SUPERVISION must have a permanent nature in order to be able to monitor the kilometers run by the vehicle, D, for maintenance purposes. The maintenance message must also flash.

The corrected solution also shows the MAINTENANCE function activated every second, and the TIME_GENERATION function (Figure 6.9).

Display of S requires a link between the SPEED_CONTROL function and the output to the DISPLAY port.

This type of check is also carried out naturally by continuing with the complete refinement, and a final coherence check validates the initial approach. Loopbacks are often necessary. However, a simple initial structure at the beginning leads to a better decomposition.

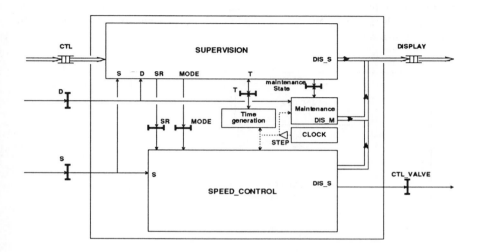

Figure 6.9   First functional structure.

6.3.3 Refinement

To continue with the design, each function has to be reconsidered to express a solution, which may be another functional structure, or a behavioral description. In each case, the first question that has to be asked is: "Is it possible to write a behavioral specification". It is possible, if the function has a sequential behavior.

This is the case for SPEED_CONTROL which is activated by the STEP event. SUPERVISION is activated by each CTL message. Therefore this function has a sequential behavior. However, several FSM have to be included in its behavioral description.

Functional refinement is not recommended at this stage, since it introduces a complexity which is not helpful for software implementation. The sequential behavior of each function will be described in detail in the next sections.

6.3.4 Speed control function

On the changeover to REGUL mode, this temporary action synchronous with STEP (1 second) must first reach the cruising speed by constant acceleration and then by speed regulation. The system must be inactive in STOP mode.

The behavior deduced from the specifications is therefore as shown in Figure 6.10.

The behavior during the acceleration and regulation phases was specified in the functional specifications. The acceleration variable is deduced by taking the difference between two consecutive speed measurements (1 second apart). The "manual acceleration by the driver" state (priority) in Figure 6.2 is carried out by the regulation state.

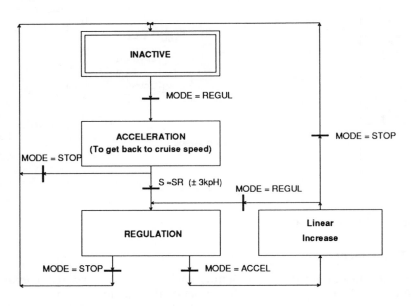

Figure 6.10   SPEED_CONTROL specification.

The algorithmic description is deduced directly from this analysis by simply transcribing the above specification. Variable types are defined as follows:

```
T_SPEED = 0..199;
T_DIS = Record
        NATURE:("Speed", "average speed",
                        "consumption", "null", "maintenance");
        SPEED:T_SPEED;
        CONSUMPTION:T_QUANTITY;
        end;

action SPEED_CONTROL on STEP event with
                        (inputs var S, SR: T_SPEED;
                                var MODE: (STOP, REGUL, ACCEL);
                         outputs var CTL_VALVE: 0..max;
                                message DIS_S: T_DIS);
    const Max, K, INC:...;
    var STATE: (inactive, acceleration, regulation, increase);
        R: 0...Max;
        A, SPREV: T_SPEED; A_MESS: T_DIS;
    begin
        STATE:=inactive;
        CTL_VALVE:= 0; SPREV:=S;
```

```
                CYCLE STEP:
                        begin
                        case STATE of
                        inactive:
                                if MODE = REGUL then STATE = acceleration;
                        acceleration:
                                if MODE = STOP then
                                        begin
                                        STATE:=inactive
                                        CTL_VALVE:= 0;
                                        end
                                    else
                                        if (S>SR-3) and (S<SR+3) then
                                                        STATE:=Regulation
                                        else
                                        begin
                                        A:=S-SPREV;
                                        if A>3 then CTL_VALVE:=0
                                        else
                                        if A<1 then CTL_VALVE:=Max
                                        else
                                        CTL_VALVE:=K*(2-A);
                                        end;
                        Regulation:
                                if MODE = STOP then STATE:=inactive
                                        else
                                        if MODE = ACCEL then STATE:=increase
                                    else
                                        begin
                                        if S-SR>3 then CTL_VALVE:=0
                                        else
                                        if S-SR<-3 then CTL_VALVE:=Max
                                        else
                                        CTL_VALVE:= (Max*(SR-S)/3+Max)/2;
                                    end;
                        increase:
                                if MODE = STOP then STATE:=inactive
                                        else
                                        if MODE = REGUL then STATE:=regulation
                                    else
                                        SR:=SR+INC;
                        end case;
                SPREV:=S;
                A_MESS.NATURE = "speed";
                A_MESS.SPEED:= S;
                send(A_MESS,DIS_S);
                end;
        end cycle;
    end SPEED_CONTROL;
```

6.3.5 Supervision function

For each message taken from CTL, this action performs the necessary actions and state transitions.

According to the specifications, this function includes three FSM and controls the maintenance function. For regulation, the behavior is simplified since two states are carried out by the SPEED_CONTROL function. The T_CTL specification is as follows:

```
T_CTL = Record
        NATURE:(Maintenance_done, fuel_quantity,
                start_run, request_AS, activation,
                stop,start_acceleration, end_acceleration,
                brake, end_brake, start_km_measurement,
                stop_km_measurement,Return_to_cruising_speed);
        QUANTITY: 0..100;
        end;

action SUPERVISION on message E_CTL:T_CTL with
                                (input var D: T_DISTANCE;
                                input/output var T: integer;
                                Output var SR:T_Speed;
                                  var MODE: (STOP, REGUL, ACCEL);
                                  var MAINTENANCE_STATE: (wait...);
                                  message DIS_S: T_DIS);

Var STATE: (normal, regulation, manual, inactive, calibration);
    DC,DT,DM: T_Distance;
    A_MESS:T_DIS;
    BRAKE_STATE:(true,false);
begin
DC:= 0; DM:= 0; DT:=0;
MODE:= STOP;
MAINTENANCE_STATE:=wait;
STATE:=normal;
cycle E_CTL:
        case E_CTL.NATURE of
          Maintenance_done:
                        MAINTENANCE_STATE:=Wait;
          Fuel_quantity:
                        begin
                        A_MESS.NATURE:="consumption";
                        A_MESS.consumption:=E_CMD.quantity/(D-DC);
                        send(A_MESS,DIS_S);
                        DC:=D;
                        end;
          Start_run:
                        begin
                        DT:=D; T:=0;
                        end
          Request_AS:
                        begin
                        A_MESS.NATURE:="Average_speed";
                        A_MESS.speed := (D-DT)/T;
                        Send (A_MESS,DIS_S);
                        end;
          activation:
                        if (STATE = normal) and (S>50) then
                                begin
                                VR:=V; MODE:=REGUL;
                                STATE:=Regulation;
                                end;
          Stop_regulation:
                        begin
                        STATE:=normal; MODE:=STOP;
                        end;
          Start_acceleration:
                        if STATE=regulation then
                                begin
                                STATE:=inactive;
                                MODE:=ACCEL;
                                end;
```

```
            end_acceleration:
                    if STATE=inactive then
                            begin
                            SR:=S;
                            STATE:=Regulation;
                            MODE:=REGUL;
                            end;
        brake:
                    if STATE=Regulation then
                            begin
                            STATE:=inactive;
                            MODE:=STOP;
                            BRAKE_STATE:=true;
                            end;
        end_brake:    BRAKE_STATE:=false;
        Return_to_cruising_speed:
                    if STATE=inactive and BRAKE_STATE=false then
                            begin
                            STATE:=regulation;
                            MODE:=REGUL;
                            end;
        Start_Km_Measurement:
                    if STATE=normal then STATE:=calibration;
        Stop_Km_Measurement:
                    if STATE=calibration then
                            begin
                            Constant calibration calculation;
                            STATE:=normal;
                            end;
        end case;
      end cycle;
  end SUPERVISION;
```

It will be observed that writing the algorithm is relatively simple since the action checks whether the system is in a correct state (receptivity) for each received message. If so, it carries out the corresponding actions. If not, the event is simply eliminated. The algorithm is derived from the specification by simple translation.

6.3.6 Maintenance function

This temporary function is synchronous with STEP to monitor the increase of the distance D, and in particular to produce the flashing display between 250 km and 50 km before maintenance.

The behavior is given in the specifications in the form of a 3-state automata. Initialization in the "wait" state is carried out by SUPERVISION on reception of the "Maintenance done" event.

```
Type T_Maintenance=(wait, intermittent, permanent);
Action MAINTENANCE on event STEP with
                    (input/output Var MAINTENANCE_STATE:T_Maintenance;
                    output message DIS_M:T_DIS);
Var   STATE: (off, on);
      A_MESS:T_DIS;
begin
STATE:=off;
```

```
cycle STEP:
     case MAINTENANCE_STATE of
          wait:
                    begin
                    A_MESS.NATURE:="null";
                    Send(A_MESS, DIS_M);
                    if (D+250) DIV 7500 = 0 then
                    MAINTENANCE_STATE:=intermittent;
                    end;
          intermittent:
                    if (D+50)DIV 7500 = 0 then
                              MAINTENANCE_STATE:=permanent
                              else
                              case STATE of
                               on:begin
                                 STATE:=OFF;
                                 A_MESS.NATURE:="null";
                                 Send(A_MESS,DIS_M);
                                 end;
                               off:begin
                                 STATE:=ON;
                                 A_MESS.NATURE:=
                                 "maintenance";
                                 Send(A_MESS, DIS_M);
                                 end;
                              end case;
          permanent:
                    begin
                    A_MESS.NATURE:="maintenance";
                    Send(A_MESS,DIS_M);
                    end;
     end case;
   end cycle;
end MAINTENANCE;
```

6.3.7 Time_generation function

This function simply updates T by adding the value STEP_DURATION on each STEP event.

```
action TIME_GENERATION on event STEP with(input/output T:integer);
  const STEP_DURATION= 1s;
  begin
   cycle STEP: T:= T + STEP_DURATION;
       end cycle;
  end TIME_GENERATION;
```

6.4 IMPLEMENTATION SPECIFICATION

The functional model was obtained deliberately disregarding all technological aspects, such as the nature of sensors for D and S, the characteristics of the user interface, thus leading to a solution independent of the technology. Obviously, the solution to be deduced during this step must take account of all these technological constraints and timing constraints.

The following must be defined during this third step, which will result in obtaining level 2 of the internal description, or the executive description:

- hardware specification;
- software specification.

In particular, this involves making use of the technological specifications. Proceed as follows:

- introduce physical distribution if necessary (not the case in our problem);

- introduce interfaces with the environment;

- analyze real-time constraints;

- hardware/software distribution;

- software specification;

- executive structure specification.

6.4.1 Interfaces introduction

The links with both environment entities -the vehicle and the driver - must be added around the functional solution.

We will use the template model proposed by Hatley (Template Architecture) which proposes a decomposition of the implementation solution into four subsets as shown in Figure 6.11 [HATLEY-87].

The functional model described above is the hard core of the application, independent of the technology used.

The deliberate separation of the user interface from other inputs/outputs makes it possible to take special care with this interface in order to obtain a particularly user-friendly product.

The "Maintenance, self-test, etc" subset influences other components to improve the application reliability and safety. This subset is not dealt with in this example.

-A- Input interfaces

We are concerned here with all information to be observed on the vehicle.

According to the technological specifications, the speed S cannot be directly observed. A pulse encoder on a wheel is used for this purpose. The same applies to D. D is deduced by observing the number of wheel revolutions and therefore the number of encoder pulses during a determined time interval (which could be one second). This is the principle of the frequencemeter.

$$S = K * NB\_IMP$$

K is a constant which depends on the size of the tyres. Therefore, this constant K is the result of the calibration phase, already developed in the functional model. K must correspond to the displacement for 1/10 of a wheel revolution, since the encoder outputs 10 pulses per revolution.

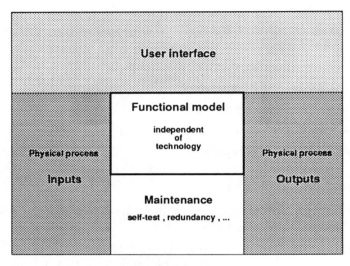

Figure 6.11   Template implementation model.

D is the integral of S. It is also obtained by taking the total number of wheel revolutions multiplied by the distance travelled per revolution. Therefore, D := D + K; for each encoder pulse. The functional solution for the two observations D and S is as shown in Figure 6.12.

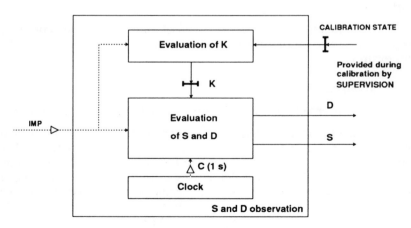

Figure 6.12   Functional structure for S and D observations.

Note that the evaluation of K, which only takes place during the calibration state, requires the observation of the number of pulses during 1 km, which can be used to deduce the length of a wheel revolution. The interface with the functional model is also modified to determine the "CALIBRATION STATE" variable from SUPERVISION which indicates whether or not the system is in the calibration phase.

The specification is completed with the behavioral descriptions of the actions.

```
action EVALUATION_S_AND_D on events IMP and C with
                                (input var K: T_K;
                                input/output var D:T_DISTANCE;
                                output var S: T_SPEED);
    Var NB_IMP: integer;
    begin
    S:=0; NB_IMP:=0;
    cycle
            C:          begin
                        S:=K * NB_IMP;
                        NB_IMP:=0;
                        end;
            IMP:        begin
                        NB_IMP:=NB_IMP + 1;
                        D:=D + K;
                        end;
            end cycle;
    end EVALUATION_S_AND_D;

action EVALUATION_K on event IMP with
                (input var CALIBRATION_STATE: (calibration, other);
                output var K: T_K);
    Var    STATE: (OFF, ON);
           N: integer;
    begin
    STATE:=off;
    cycle
            IMP:        case STATE of
                        off:
                                if CALIBRATION_STATE=calibration then
                                        begin
                                        STATE:=on;
                                        N:=0;
                                        end;
                        on:
                                if CALIBRATION_STATE<>calibration then
                                        begin
                                        STATE:=off;
                                        K:=1000/N;
                                        end else N:=N+1;
                        end case;
            end cycle;
    end EVALUATION_K;
```

-B- *Output interface*

The only output toward the vehicle is the valve control. This is an electronic signal between 0 and 8 V. Therefore, CTL_VALVE must be transformed into an analog signal.

Technologically, the digital to analog conversion may be done simply with a PWM type (pulse width modulation) control. The advantages over a conventional digital-analog convertor are:

  - purely digital operation;
  - logic power control;
  - opto-electronic isolation possibility.

The functional solution is given in Figure 6.13 without going into the details of the behavior of the elementary actions. The principle of the function is to use a counter-down P initialized every N*T to the value CTL_VALVE and decremented every T. CA is active so long as P is strictly positive.

-C- User interface

To be technology independent, all events incoming from or outgoing to the driver have been specified as messages. For example, the solution for the method used in the technological specifications for inputting the fuel quantity was not developed in the functional model since it is independent of the user interface.

This interface was outlined in Figure 6.5. It can be seen that there are ten keys which the driver can press, plus another two at the rear face. There are four display areas, giving a total of eight decimal digits and three binary states.

Management of the interface is based on periodic scanning of all keys, excluding simultaneous key presses. Display is obtained by decoding messages and transmission towards the destination display unit.

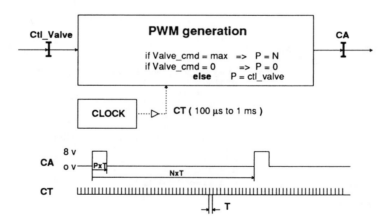

Figure 6.13   Valve control output interface.

A special case arises for selecting the fuel quantity: the display must follow the variation resulting from pressing the + and - keys. Consequently, the interface directly produces the display messages.

Figure 6.14 shows the functional solution selected to satisfy these specifications.

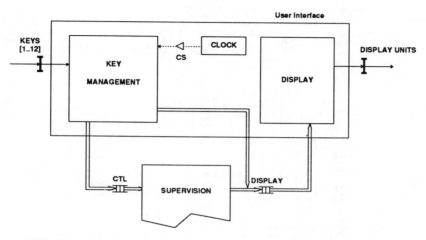

Figure 6.14   User interface.

The behavior for these two functions is not described in detail below. The user interface always takes up a large number of programming lines and therefore development time. The functional approach given below can be used to program the user interface following a general model, leading to greater efficiency.

6.4.2 Timing constraints analysis

This analysis considers:

- activation frequencies of all actions (event frequency);
- response times for output events.

It must eventually make it possible to decide upon the hardware/software distribution, based on the principle of including a maximum number of functions in the software part.

Before deciding upon the distribution, the number of generated clock-type events must be minimized. Therefore, we start with a generator for the maximum frequency. Other events are then obtained by frequency division.

Figure 6.15 summarizes the complete functional structure considered for the timing constraint analysis, and then the choice of hardware/software distribution.

The following events are shown on the global functional structure:

- CTL: negligible period defined by the user's reaction;
- IMP: 500 Hz approximately for 200 kph and 1 m tyres;
- C: 10 kHz (for CT);
- CP: 10 to 100 Hz (for CS, STEP and C1s).

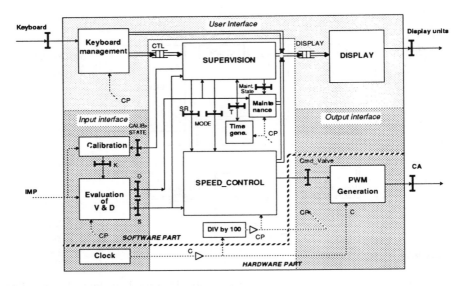

Figure 6.15   Complete functional solution.

There is only one response time constraint in the technological specifications: the one second reaction time which is not a severe constraint for an electronic solution. However, braking must be immediate. A sampling step of 0.1 sec will be taken for braking. Therefore, CP = 10 Hz.

6.4.3 Hardware/software distribution

The analysis consists firstly of classifying functions into two categories:
- functions which are necessarily carried out by hardware, for example clocks, fast functions with a period less than 50 to 100 µs;
- those which can be implemented by software or hardware.

For this second category, and in order to decide whether or not a function can be implemented by software, the activation frequency must be considered and the probable execution time evaluated for the function using the selected or imposed technological assumption.

The two functions which may cause a problem are:
- PWM generation;
- divide by 1,000.

We will use a hardware solution here for the PWM generation function for technological reasons, and the divider by 1,000 can easily be done by software. The clock function must also be added. All other functions can be located on a single microprocessor, considering the activation frequencies and execution times which remain low. The microprocessor load rate confirms this choice.

6.4.4 Software specification

Nine functions which can run in parallel are to be implemented by software, obviously on a microprocessor which is "just a sequential machine".

Specifying the software implementation effectively involves specifying the sequencing of these functions on a microprocessor, in other words their progress with time. For this purpose, the priority of each function has to be defined, including those which are invoked by an interrupt input and software synchronizations between time-dependent functions.

Some simple principles help to define the solution. Functions activated by a hardware function are implemented under an interrupt. The execution priority for these functions is proportional to the activation frequency. All functions activated by a single event are treated in sequence. Permanent software functions are implemented in the background task (main task).

Software synchronization by events or messages are implemented by a procedural call if the destination function may have a higher priority at the time of execution.

There is a difficulty due to the fact that the D and V evaluation action is activated by two events. The solution is to split this action into two parts, each of which is activated by one event. The variable NB_IMP, common to the two parts, is then a shared variable requiring mutual exclusion.

A software implementation specification is given in Figure 6.16 in the form of a diagram which expresses:

- horizontally: inputs from hardware at the left, software functions at the center, and outputs to hardware at the right;

- vertically: the distribution of tasks in an increasing priority and the software relations between them.

The lowest priority task is the background task. The double vertical line represents a procedural call which can only be used in the increasing priority direction.

The proposed implementation leads to any function in the background task. Therefore, it could be used for self-test inputs, for example.

The implementation coherence verification consists of making sure that all temporal constraints are satisfied in the worst cases and that the processor remains operational: activity ratio < 1 for actions other than those included in the background task.

Using the above diagram, verification is simple by making sure that for all actions:

- Tresponse max < T execution max,

- Tocc max = Σ (Texecution max/minimum activation period) < 1.

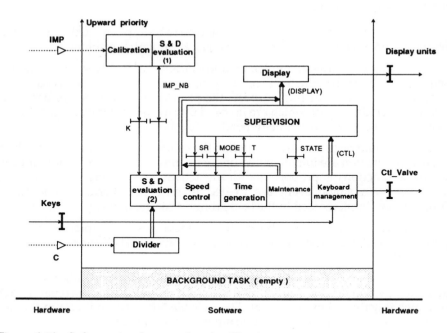

Figure 6.16   Software implementation specification.

Additional points such as the format of internal variables to satisfy accuracies and calculation techniques, will need to be studied to completely specify the implementation. In particular, the format of K, S, D, CTL_VALVE and the multiplication and division calculations have to be clarified. Obviously, the formats will be integer or fractional and operations will be carried out using integers.

6.4.5 Hardware implementation specification

This last phase defines the hardware support through an executive structure. It is defined by abstraction from the complete functional structure replacing all actions implemented in software with a programmable processor which will carry out execution.

The processor specification can be made more general by including the clock and even the PWM generator as shown in Figure 6.17.

The technician responsible for the implementation will be a specialist in commercially available VLSI components, and will take account of imposed implementation constraints and make use of these specifications to produce a detailed hardware solution in the form of an electronic drawing. For this application, in 1989, the choice might have been made from the following single chips:

- Intel 8051 and derivative family;
- Nec 78 XX family;
- Motorola 687XX family.

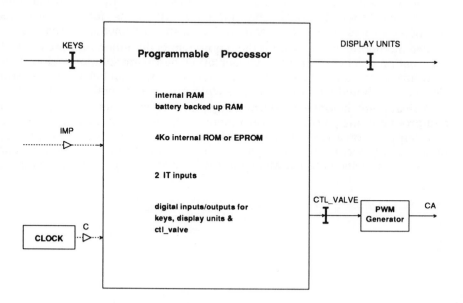

Figure 6.17   Hardware implementation specification.

6.5 CONCLUSIONS: SOME REMARKS

Now that we have completed the overview of the design process using an example , we will quickly summarize the benefits of the MCSE methodology.

First, after having become familiar with the requirements definition only and therefore before having seen the proposed solution, the reader should be able to answer the three main questions which interest the customer:

- development time (contract duration),
- development cost (obtaining an industrial type prototype),
- system manufacturing cost.

A fairly good idea of the solution is necessary to answer this: hardware for the cost estimate, software complexity for the time estimate. The odds are that few readers feel comfortable reading these requirements, unless they have considerable experience in the microprocessor system development field.

One may think that everyone would have a clear understanding of the method and of the solution after reading this conceptual design document: about the operation of the system, about the principles used to produce the solution, about solutions to conventional problems found in a variety of applications. If so, the reader has already assimilated the main elements of the methodology and has enhanced his abilities in the real-time application field, simply by reading a solution document.

The ease with which a solution is understood is a result of the description models used, which are mainly graphical: diagrams for specifications, functional structure, executive structure, software implementation diagram.

The methodology starts from the requirements definition and provides all information necessary for the implementation: hardware solution architecture, software organization, algorithmic description of function behavior in Pascal. Verification should guarantee that this will result in an operational product.

A final point: before even starting any practical implementation (prototype and programming), a complete document exists: as a guide to understanding, as a support for a critical analysis of the solution, and later as a product maintenance document. Subsequently, it will simply be necessary to add hardware implementation drawings and a software listing with comments.

References Part 1

BOOKS

[BOOCH-83]
Software Engineering with ADA
G. Booch
Benjamin/Cummings, Menlo Park, CA. 1983

[BUHR-84]
System Design with ADA
R.J.A. Buhr
Prentice-Hall, Englewood Cliffs NJ 1984

[BUHR-89]
System Design with Machine Charts: A CAD approach with ADA examples
R.J.A. Buhr
Prentice-Hall 1990

[CALVEZ-82]
Une Méthodologie de Conception des Systèmes Multi-microordinateurs pour les Applications de Commande en Temps-réel
J.P. Calvez
Thèse de Doctorat d'Etat, Université de Nantes, Novembre 1982

[COAD-90]
Object-Oriented Analysis
P. Coad, E. Yourdon
Yourdon Press, Computing Series 1990

[COHEN-86]
The Specification of Complex Systems
B. Cohen, W.T. Harwood, M.I. Jackson
Addison-Wesley Publishing Company 1986

[DASGUPTA-89]
The Structure of Design Processes
S. Dasgupta
Advances in Computers, Academic Press, Vol 26, 1989, p 1-67

[DEMARCO-79]
Structured Analysis and System Specification
T. DeMarco
Yourdon Computing Series, Yourdon Press, Prentice-Hall 1979

[FATHI-85]
Microprocessor Software Project Management
E.T. Fathi, C.V.W. Armstrong
Marcel Dekker, Inc NY 1985

[HATLEY-87]
Strategies for Real-time System Specification
D.J. Hatley, I.A. Pirbhai
Dorset House Publishing New York 1987

[JACKSON-83]
System Development
M. Jackson
C.A.R Hoare series, Prentice-Hall 1983

[JENSEN-79]
Software Engineering
R.W. Jensen, C.C. Tonies
Prentice-Hall International, Inc 1979

[NIELSEN-88]
Designing Large Real-time Systems with ADA
K. Nielsen, K. Shumate
MacGraw Hill Book Company NY 1988

[RUSKIN-82]
What every Engineer should know about Project Management
A.M. Ruskin, W.E. Estes
Marcel Dekker, Inc NY 1982

[WARD-85]
Structured Development for Real-time Systems
P.T. Ward, S.J. Mellor.
Vol.1: Introduction and Tools
Vol.2: Essential modeling Techniques
Yourdon Computing Series, Yourdon Press, Prentice-Hall 1985

[WILSON-86]
Systems: Concepts, Methodologies and Applications
B. Wilson
John Wiley and Sons NY 1986

PAPERS

[BOASSON-87]
Modeling in real-time systems
M. Boasson
Computer Standards and Interfaces 6-1987, p 107-114

[BOEHM-76]
Software engineering
B.W. Boehm
IEEE Transactions on Computers Vol 25 No 12, Dec 1976, p 1226-41

[BOEHM-88]
A spiral model of software development and enhancement
B.W. Boehm
IEEE Computer Vol 21 No 5, May 1988, p 61-72

[CALVEZ-84]
*Méthodologie de conception pour les systèmes complexes de commande
en temps-réel*
J.P. Calvez, Y. Thomas
RAIRO Automatique Vol 18 No 2 1984, p 251-266

[CALVEZ-86]
*Some microsystems design methodology and its application to industrial
problems*
J.P. Calvez, E.Friot, Y.Thomas
*Proceedings of IECON'86, Twelfth annual IEEE Industrial Electronics
Society Conference* Milwaukee USA 29 Sept-3 Oct 1988, p 675-680

[GOMAA-84]
A software design method for the real-time systems
H. Gomaa
Communications of the ACM Vol 27 No9 Sept. 1984

[GOMAA-89]
A software design method for distributed real-time applications
H. Gomaa
Journal of Systems and Software No9 1989, p 81-94

[KOOMEN-85]
The Entropy of design: A study on the meaning of creativity
C.J. Koomen
IEEE Transactions on Systems, Man, and Cybernetics Vol 15 No 1 Jan 1985
p 16-30

[NADLER-85]
Systems methodology and design
G. Nadler
IEEE Transactions on Systems, Man, and Cybernetics Vol 15 No 6
Nov.1985, p 685-697

[ROSS-85]
Applications and extensions of SADT
D.T. Ross
Computer April 1985, p 25-34

[WILLIAMS-88]
Software process modeling: A behavioral approach
L.G. Williams
Proceedings of 10th International Conference on Software Engineering
Singapore 1-15 April 1988, p 174-186

PART $\mathcal{2}$

MODELS AND METHODOLOGIES

Before describing the MCSE methodology in detail, it will be useful to consider the various methodologies and models on which these are based. This knowledge is justified since one methodology should not be put in competition against others. On the contrary, some approaches and some points of view and models are useful and usable for the class of problems which concern us. The designer thus discovers everything that he may or could find in his "tool box".

The three development phases which interest us, particularly for the analysis of methodologies, are: specification, functional design or preliminary or architectural design, implementation specification or detailed design.

When a methodology is specific to a phase, it is preferable to talk about a method. A method is based on the use of a model. Therefore, it is essential to be familiar with these models.

A global methodology is a result of the concatenation of several methods, each of which is particularly well suited to a phase. This is explained by the fact that it is necessary to use different concepts and points of view and therefore different models for each solution abstraction level.

Chapter 7 describes the best known methods and methodologies in the real-time applications field in more or less chronological order. The models used are indicated for each.

Chapter 8 is a synthesis of the most frequently used model categories. Model types for specification and design are described in detail, and preferential uses are described. A methodology is described by a trajectory in a set of modeling spaces.

If he wishes, the reader can browse quickly through Chapter 7; however it is recommended that he reads Chapter 8 carefully since this will help him to become familiar with the models used in MCSE and to understand the proposed design process.

PART 2

MODELS AND METHODOLOGIES

7

METHODOLOGIES SURVEY

> *Some Methodologies concentrate on the management framework rather than on its technical substance. The danger is that the development team gets locked into a framework that is totally inappropriate for their project. That is why many developers do not like methodologies and think them a waste of time.*

> **J.R. Cameron**

This chapter briefly describes existing methodologies in the real-time system field. In order to be able to interpret the characteristics and special features of each and the differences between them, we will briefly recall the basis for any methodology introduced in Part 1, and will then give a classification and history of methodologies.

A methodology is used to express a solution using a model. It is therefore mandatorily based on the use of description models for input and output of each phase; these models follow on from a set of concepts. The method itself is specified by a thought model expressing how to proceed to specify or design. Tools as working supports are necessary for the analysis, description and validation of solutions, and to produce an implementation. They are only meaningful as an assistance in the application of a method. Thus, a methodology can be analyzed by considering three points : models, methods and tools, successively. We will deliberately restrict ourselves to the two essential points, models and methods, in this chapter.

Concerning the system description model, it cannot be based on the assumption that descriptions at different abstraction levels differ only by the scale - the ZOOM principle. Various components participate in a system: external view, functional view, structural view, hardware view etc., which depend on the point of view used for the observation: user, hardware, software, manager.

To understand methodologies, it is therefore useful to bear in mind that several concepts are necessary for the description using several abstraction levels. Each corresponds to a point of view:

- external point of view;

- organizational or structural point of view;

- temporal point of view;

- tools and resources point of view.

A methodology is thus a combination of a set of models and methods.

Although a methodology may be analyzed based on three components: - model(s), method(s) and tool(s) - another aspect concerns the style of the thought procedure to be followed which may vary from an "authoritarian" style to a "liberal" style. According to C.J. Tully, the style must differ depending on the objects concerned [TEICHROEW-83].

In order for a methodology to be clear and unambiguous, it must be authoritarian for concepts and models, since these induce description precision, and subsequently efficiency in the development process and tools. Consequently, a clear model with explicit semantics is a necessity for a good model - and even more so for an efficient tool.

On the other hand, the method must not constrain the designer in selecting solutions, in order to make the best use of the individual creativity. A method must thus be an expression of a set of recommendations, and the model expresses the rules.

The efficiency of recommendations is another important method comparison criterion. The objective of a methodology is to allow the highest possible percentage of designers to produce quality developments.

7.1 METHODOLOGY CLASSIFICATION AND HISTORY

The classification proposed in the following table deals with real-time system-oriented methodologies. It gives a rough idea of the life cycle phase or phases concerned by each methodology, and the essential concept as a model.

PHASE	METHOD	CONCEPT
Specification	SADT (Ross)	Activities
	SA (DeMarco)	Data-flow diagrams
	RTSA (Ward, Hatley)	Control flow extension
	JSD (Jackson)	Jackson diagram
	SREM (Alford)	Stimuli-response charts
	OOA (Coad)	Object model
Design	SD (Yourdon)	Data-flow diagrams and structured charts
	JSD (Jackson)	Data structures and process network
	SYSREM (Alford)	R-NETS and F-NETS diagrams
	DARTS (Gomaa)	Data-flow diagrams and functional decomposition.
	OOD (Booch)	Object encapsulation
	OMT (Rumbaugh), HOOD	Object model
	SDWMC (Buhr)	Machine charts
Implementation	Structured programming	Algorithms
	Object programming	Object model

Figure 7.1 summarizes the birth of methodologies and shows a few temporal dependencies related to the models used.

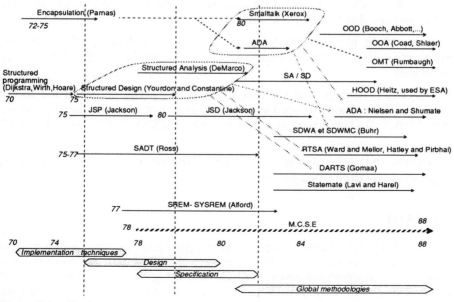

Figure 7.1   Evolution in the methodologies field.

Interest in methodologies started in the 1970s at the level closest to the final products, in other words the implementation level. For the hardware, system complexity has led designers to develop more and more complex components, but which are simpler to use due to the reuse of already designed "hardware objects" and making use of integration possibilities.

For software, the complexity of programs and the variety of processors has made it necessary to have high-level languages and a methodology to help to write these programs. This is how structured programming appeared. This method brought a number of benefits, but it only partially solved the complexity problem. The method is the result of the necessity for structuring into modules. It is the start of an architectural approach corresponding to the design phase. It is also the very beginning of the object approach with the encapsulation concept.

The need for specifications for design purposes became evident by two convergent approaches almost simultaneously:

- approach from the problem which must be defined correctly in order to be able to search for a solution;

- bottom-up approach starting from the design which justifies a description level of the objective to be satisfied.

Specification methods differ depending on the point of view adopted: activity diagrams (SADT), data-flow diagrams for processing systems (DFD), entity-relation diagrams for information systems (E-R), finite state and stimuli-response type diagrams for real-time control systems.

In the 1980s, global methodologies were gradually developed covering the entire life cycle by combining already proven methods (SA/SD, JSD, SREM-SYSREM).

The object concept and the emergence of the ADA language led to the creation of new object-oriented approaches, first as implementation techniques (Smalltalk, ADA), and then as a design method (OOD, GOOD, HOOD, OMT, etc).

The rest of this chapter describes the best known system-oriented methods, approximately in chronological order.

7.2 SADT

The SADT (Structured Analysis and Design Technique) methodology was developed between 1972 and 1977 by Softech [ROSS-85, IGL-82]. Essentially, it covers the requirements analysis phase, the design phase and specification document phase, in order to facilitate communication between analysts, designers and users.

7.2.1 The model

The method is based on the use of the SADT model. It makes use of a set of a linked "boxes" to describe activity partitioning (Actigrams) and data transformation (Datagrams). Each "box" in the diagram has four types of link with its environment as shown in the notation below.

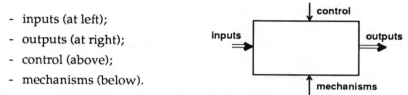

- inputs (at left);
- outputs (at right);
- control (above);
- mechanisms (below).

For example, for the function Y = (A * X + B), X is the input data, Y is the output result, A and B are control parameters and the mechanisms are the calculation operators.

Each box can be refined using an SADT model. This is therefore a hierarchical model, but the relations expressed are of the horizontal type and the diagram can be drawn completely "flat" as shown in Figure 7.2.

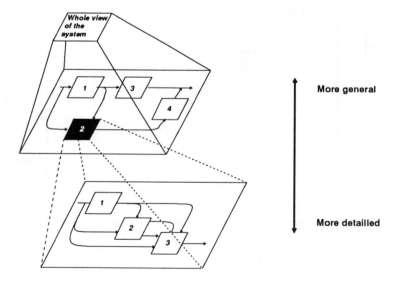

Figure 7.2   SADT hierarchical description example.

This model is intermediate between a structural description and a behavioral description since it only partially expresses order relations. It is close to data-flow diagrams, without the concept of storing information (data files).

Two model types can be used in SADT:

- The Actigram model, which expresses transformation functions (rectangles) acting on data (the links). Each rectangle corresponds to verbs and links correspond to nouns.

- The Datagram model, which gives an opposite representation. Rectangles represent data (nouns), and the links represent transformations on these data.

These models are dual and redundant, such that the completeness of an analysis can be checked. One expresses the decomposition of activities by showing manipulated objects, and the other expresses the decomposition of data by showing the activities which create or use them.

An example of an actigram is given in Figure 7.3 to illustrate this model. This model is a general tool for expressing, understanding, manipulating and validating problems. It is therefore, typically, a specification assistance tool.

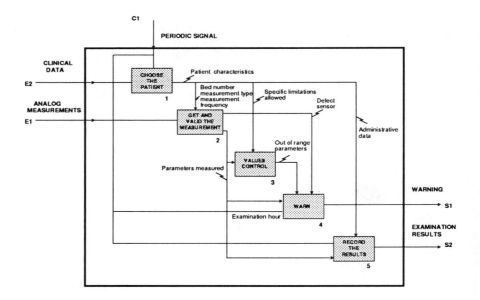

Figure 7.3   Example of SADT diagram.

7.2.2 The method

The Structured Analysis (SA) method is used. First, this is a discipline of thought. The method is based on a data-flow oriented analysis work which shows all the activities. The process recommends gradual refinement of each activity, leading to hierarchical diagrams. The analysis work leads to the construction of a functional SADT model by passing through the following phases:

- produce system actigrams and datagrams;
- define cross-references between diagrams;
- correct, complete the system analysis;
- introduce possible activity sequencing;
- identify mechanisms which can help to implement functions.

Two principles are stated as being essential:
- context delimitation. Each action must be seen as forming part of a wider system which forms its context;

- limitation of information quantity. This limits the decomposition of a diagram to a maximum of six boxes.

The first phase is the most critical. Diagrams are obtained as a result of prior interviews with experts in the field, in order to collect the necessary information.

The work can be carried out in a group, several authors produce the subset specifications simultaneously and independently. Documents thus produced are then assembled and distributed to readers (or at least the other authors). Each author takes account of the comments and corrects and improves his analysis and then re-submits it for approval. This working formula based on checking and validation by others thus ensures continuous evaluation of the quality of produced documents.

This methodology is considered to be general and applicable to any situation and any problem. It is also usable either by an individual or by teams in large projects. Although useful for a problem analysis, the SADT methodology is restricted to the specification phase.

7.3 STRUCTURED ANALYSIS

This method was developed by DeMarco to produce specifications for a system or an application [DEMARCO-79]. It can describe all problem activities and data. This method is typically a very useful analysis aid, currently used by several methodologies in the specification phase.

7.3.1 The model

This method is based on the data-flow diagram. It includes the diagram itself which expresses relations between activities, activity specification in natural structured language, and the data specification (Jackson diagram and entity-relation model).

This diagram (Data-Flow Diagram - DFD) is suitable for the analysis of transformations undergone by the data. It specifies the data-flow through functions or activities starting from the input data and producing the output data. Four kinds of elements are used in this type of diagram:

- the activity or process: these are actions carried out on the input data;

  - the memory variable or the file - it is used as a data storage;
  - the source and the sink: a source is an external entity as a source for input data, and a sink is a destination for output data;
  - the link, oriented and labeled by data in transit between activities.

The activities diagram thus described (Figure 7.4) expresses ordering relations between activities by means of links between the output data from one activity and the input data to subsequent activities. The file is an information store for subsequent use.

The characteristics of a correct diagram are:
  - all identified inputs are at the left;
  - all outputs are at the right;
  - data must be named for identification and definition of the contents;
  - transformation functions or activities must be named to allow understanding of what is done on the data;
  - there are no loops in this type of diagram.

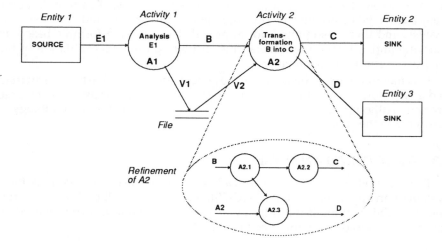

Figure 7.4   Data-flow diagram example.

The model is hierarchical. It thus facilitates a top-down approach by refinement, since each activity can be described by a data-flow diagram. For a bottom-up approach, it also allows coordination of approach made by several analysts on subsets. It is very useful as a communication tool between designer and customer during the specification phase.

One limitation is that it does not express temporal behavior or control of actions. However, since each transformation is procedural, performance constraints can be added along information paths.

7.3.2 The method

Before producing an application specification, the existing situation has to be analyzed so that the required functionalities can be characterized. Two description levels are thus possible: the physical level, and the logical or conceptual level.

The procedure to be followed, proposed by DeMarco, is shown in the data-flow diagram in Figure 7.5.

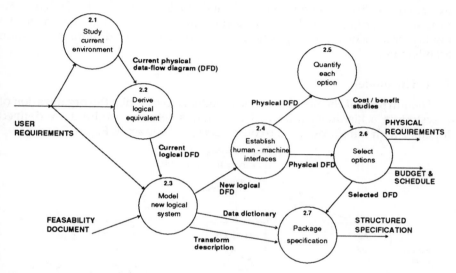

Figure 7.5   SA analysis process. (Tom DeMarco, *Structured Analysis and System Specification,* © 1979, p 6. Adapted by permission of Prentice-Hall, Inc., Englewood Cliffs, New Jersey.)

The analysis of the current environment at the physical level leads to the logical level by abstraction. The functionalities introduced at the logical level are then transformed to the physical level.

The successive phases are therefore:

- description of the current physical environment by analysis of this environment;

- transformation into an equivalent logical description to obtain WHAT is done and not the HOW;

- creation of the logical description of the required system: DFD, data and activity specifications;

- production of the final document which involves transforming the logical description into a physical description: man-machine interfaces, operational characteristics and performances.

This method is efficient for a global approach to applications, thus explaining its current use in several methodologies for the specification phase. It seems to be less efficient when an approach is made starting from system environment entities.

7.4 STRUCTURED DESIGN

This method was developed by Yourdon and Constantine and then extended by Meyers between 1975 and 1980 [JENSEN-79]. Suitable for preliminary design, it is based on a transformation technique based on the quality criteria of a decomposition. It is very useful for designing program architecture.

7.4.1 The model

The purpose of the Structure Chart model is to describe the organization of a system in a hierarchical form. The relations between modules are defined together with interfaces and the control access as shown in Figure 7.6.

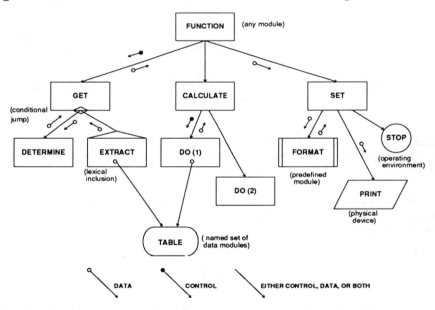

Figure 7.6   Structure Chart example. ("Software Design", in *Software Engineering*, Jensen/ Tonies eds.,© 1979, Figure 3.20 p170. Reprinted by permission of Prentice-Hall, Inc., Englewood Cliffs, New Jersey.)

The rectangles represent modules. Rounded shapes represent data accessible in the form of tables. The chart partially expresses temporal progress by using the basic control structures: sequence, call, iteration, alternative. Data or control information exchanged are marked on the hierarchical links corresponding to procedural calls. The result follows on from a structured analysis.

It is used as a model for the preliminary design of a sequential program and is used before structured programming [JENSEN-79, MARTIN-88].

7.4.2 The method

The input to this methodology is the analysis result of DeMarco data-flow diagrams, and the solution is expressed as structure charts and module structures.

The approach is based on transforming data-flow diagrams for a problem into a module structure, using a specification analysis technique and decomposition criteria.

Jensen and Tonies [JENSEN-79] describe the design process dynamics as a combination of two forces (Figure 7.7):

- the first generates the transformation: data-flow into module structure;

- the second generates the transition from a high-level description to a detailed description through successive refinement levels.

The transformation technique for producing a structure consists of identifying, on the specification, the three element classes for activities - inputs, actions and outputs. If two groups are chosen, the third can be deduced. At the highest level, inputs and outputs interface with the environment. A three branch structure can then be produced: inputs/transformation/outputs.

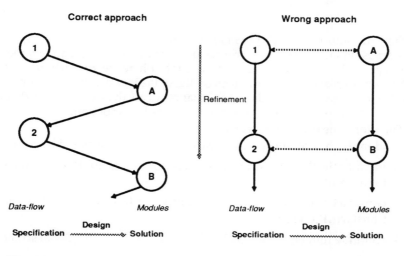

Figure 7.7   Module structure search processes.

This is equivalent to dividing the data-flow diagram into three parts as shown in Figure 7.8.

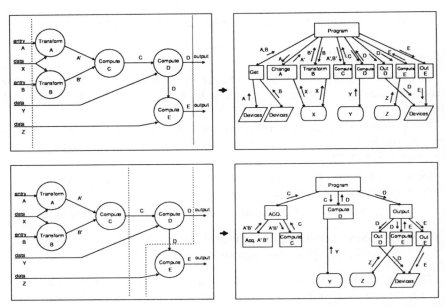

Figure 7.8   Influence of partitioning on the structure. ("Software Design", in *Software Engineering*, Jensen/Tonies eds.,© 1979, Figure 3.28 and 3.29 p186, Figure 3.34 and 3.35 p191. Reprinted by permission of Prentice-Hall, Inc., Englewood Cliffs, New Jersey.)

Several solutions are possible for the structure depending on the decomposition used. Decision criteria are used on the DFD, mainly a reduction in coupling between parts and functional coherence of each part. This is equivalent to placing partition lines on the data-flow diagram to minimize the number of crossings. The data-flow diagram can thus be used to determine module structures and functional relationships by induction.

Therefore, the procedure is as follows:

- identify the data-flow and construct the corresponding diagram;

- identify the three transformation sets: for inputs, for the central part and for outputs;

- construct a decomposition into modules or functions based on the three transformation sets;

- continue refinement for each subset and optimize the global structure.

7.4.3 Comments

This methodology is also called SA/SD, and the only point in common with SADT is the data-flow type approach for the analysis. It is also restricted to the design of sequential programs.

The system architecture is a direct result of the first modular decomposition. If this is not appropriate, which is only detected during advanced design stages, the work must be restarted. This is the result of the fact that the method leads to a monolithic solution using vertical hierarchical relations only.

7.5 JACKSON'S METHODOLOGY (JSD)

This methodology was initially developed about 1975 for program design: JSP (Jackson Structured Programming), was then extended between 1975 and 1980 to system design: JSD (Jackson System Development). At the present time, it covers three phases: specification, preliminary design, and detailed design or implementation. It is suitable for the design of information systems and real-time systems [JACKSON-83, CAMERON-86].

This methodology is based on data modeling, unlike SA which is based on modeling activities by data-flow.

The essential concept of this method is that the structure of the system to be designed, can be determined from the structure and evolution of data that it must manage. The system is designed as an element for transforming input data into output data. It is particularly efficient when event scheduling in time is significant.

7.5.1 The models

Jackson's methodology uses several models, each adapted to the level required for the description:

- Jackson's diagram for the data structure and the behavior of entities, when preparing the specification;
- process network for the functional design;
- JSP language for the implementation.

- A - JACKSON'S DIAGRAM FOR ENTITIES

Jackson's diagram is used to describe the evolution of an object or an entity by expressing the sequencing of actions and events for the object. It is a tree-type structure. The leaves are the elementary actions, and the nodes are sequencing operators. Therefore, this diagram can be used for dynamic modeling of data, in other words its behavior.

The diagram is constructed and based on three symbols corresponding to three control structures:

- sequence
- iteration
- selection

It thus describes the sequence of events concerning the entity, without expressing the duration between each. The example shown on Figure 7.9 describes the state evolution of a book.

This type of diagram can be directly translated into a pseudocode type syntactical description (Jackson Programming Language).

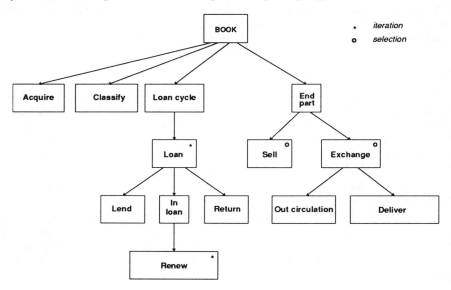

Figure 7.9   Example of Jackson diagram for an entity behavior.

B - Jackson process network

This model is composed of entities considered as "processes". Each process has its data inputs and outputs and carries out some processing.

Sequential processes are represented by rectangles. Circles and diamonds are used for relations describing two communication mechanisms:

- the circle representing the data stream, consists of messages produced by one process and used by another. The circle represents an unlimited size FIFO file;

- the diamond represents the status vector of the connected process, which is a form of global variable. Any process can only read the state of another process (one writer only, several readers).

For a process network (see Figure 7.10), a rectangle represents only the process type and not the instances. However, communications are between instances. The double lines (on the producer side) indicate the communication multiplicity, and therefore the multiplicity of the producer processes, in other words all instances of the type of this process. The concatenation of input links indicates concatenation of messages before reading to form one message only, thus expressing a synchronization.

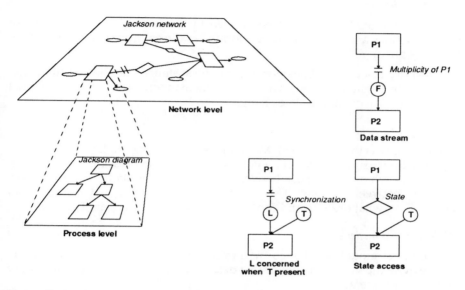

Figure 7.10   Jackson network example and notation.

For this model, each process is described by an internal structure based on sequences, selections and iterations. This can be represented by any behavioral model, particularly by Jackson diagrams, and then by a structured description such as JSP.

7.5.2 The process

The methodology recommends decomposing the work into three phases:
- modeling the environment by search and description for real-world entities;
- specification of the necessary functions to obtain outputs;
- timing constraints description and implementation definition.

The development procedure consists of six steps:
- the entity action step;
- the entity structure step;
- the initial model step;
- the function step;
- the system timing step;
- implementation step.

Each step is described in detail below to give an overall view of the proposed methodology.

- A- The entity action step

Firstly, the SUBJECT has to be defined by describing reality in terms of entities, actions and events. These are located in the environment of the system to be designed.

An entity has its own behavior outside the system. It can be identified and described by events and actions in an ordering manner. An action is considered to be atomic. An event is a state change.

- B- The entity structure step

Each entity is then described. Modeling is made using the Jackson diagram, which expresses its temporal evolution, i.e. an expression of temporal constraints which may exist between actions, but without specifying the duration between actions. This modeling is essentially dynamic (What happens?, in what order?), and concerns each instance of the entity type.

- C- The initial model step

The initial model is obtained by introducing into the system a simulation process with the same behavior as that described by the diagram for each entity in the environment.

To allow it to monitor the state of the real entity, the state of the internal process is updated by system connections with the real world so as to keep informed about actions and events in the environment. The model prepared in -B- can thus be used to deduce the necessary observations. The figure below describes the initial model for a book showing wait points for events incoming from the environment.

Processes remain throughout the entity life. They remain permanently waiting for external events. The state only changes when an event appears.

The process state is internal to the process and gives no additional information than the corresponding real entity. But this state can be used to define data to be stored for each entity: actions define what happens and data defines what is to be stored on what happens.

Information or events incoming from the environment may not be conform with the model, for example: two consecutive loans for the same book. This observation of non-conformity can then result in the production of error procedures, leading to the introduction of an input subsystem for error detection and correction, see Figure 7.11.

For the subsequent implementation, all identical processes will be implemented in the form of a single procedure working with data specific to each entity. All data is then stored in a table or database. Actions then correspond to database updates.

It is important to note that this process results in modeling the environment in the system by a data model, and not by an event model. According to Jackson, modeling by data deduced from events is much more stable than modeling from events directly, which may quickly change when specifications are modified.

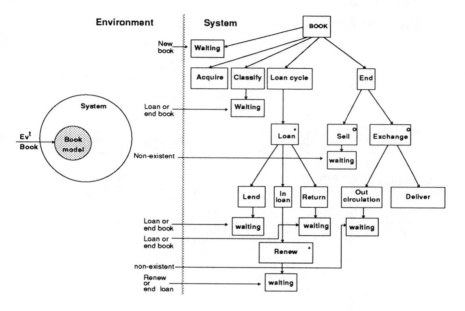

Figure 7.11   Example of initial book model.

- D- The function step

The designer then specifies system functions in terms of the model. This is carried out by adding processes to satisfy the customer's requirements and, if necessary, by modifying existing processes. Processes may need to be added for several reasons:

- production of results data determined from data representing entities;

- processing environment to model non-conformity errors;

- the necessity for interactivity with users: production of outputs as reactions to input requests.

Therefore, the development takes place incrementally. Processes are interconnected in accordance with the process network model, and relation types are message transfer and state consultation. Message transfers are used to specify to another function that actions are to be carried out according to an order relation. A state vector is used for data coupling between temporarily independent functions.

Figure 7.12 shows four types of processes:
- entity model process;

- error processing function;

- output function;

- interactive function.

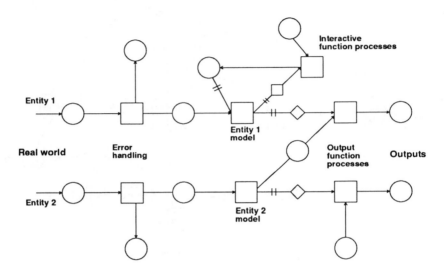

Figure 7.12   Process network example.

The complete specification of the solution contains two description levels:
- the network of communicating sequential processes;

- the behavior of each process expressed by a structured diagram or by a description in a structured language.

The functions introduced in the network are generally mutually independent. They can thus be developed separately. This facilitates team work and the addition of new functions.

- E- The system timing step

Up to this step, the design takes place without any time considerations. However, the real world generates events satisfying temporal specifications. Delays may take place due to the solution selected for implementation. Potential delays must therefore be expressed and acceptable delays determined with the user: data validity, delay in processing an event, conformity of the model with reality, etc. These decisions act as constraints for the implementation phase.

- F- The implementation step

Two problems have to be solved:

- execution of all processes on a hardware structure with less processors;

- storage of application data.

The first point deals with sharing the processor or processors. This requires deciding upon a sequencing strategy. This is carried out by transforming processes into procedures, passing the current context as an argument. This transformation makes it possible to separate data from executable code. There must be a copy of specific data or the context for each process.

Moreover, the combination of processes may simplify the implementation. For example, a network of processes is transformed into a main program and a hierarchy of subprograms. Jackson recommends the inversion technique to reduce the complexity. The following figure shows the result of this transformation technique. For the example in Figure 7.13, R is only active when F and G exist.

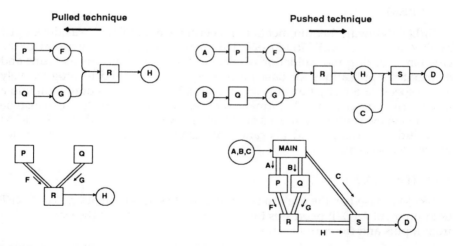

Figure 7.13   Transformation examples for implementation.

In the pulled technique, R uses a procedural call to request information F from P, and then G from Q. In the pushed technique, functions are always invoked by calling procedures, but in the data stream direction.

7.5.3 Comments

The JSD method leads to a hierarchical solution. Although this is not a result of a completely top-down process; the specification and design are more of an incremental approach.

The environment model acts as a context for functional specifications: all possible functions for the system are induced by the model. Entity models are more stable than functions. If the view of reality, and therefore the specification changes, functions must also change, but not necessarily the models (difference between structure and behavior). The recommended procedure is to first describe the reality. The functions specification is then used to describe something new. However, it is not always easy to define a model of reality without also having some idea of the purpose of the model.

Steps A to E are user-oriented, whereas step F is purely technical. Steps C and D produce a design solution in the form of an internal structure before writing specifications. The method mixes specification and functional design by iteration. Therefore, the resulting solution cannot be optimized and this work is carried out during implementation.

This methodology appears complete and appropriate for the design of information systems. This process is fairly similar in principle to some concepts used in MCSE, but MCSE is more applicable specifically to real-time systems.

7.6 SREM

SREM (Software Requirements Engineering Methodology) was developed by TRW after 1975 [ALFORD-82,-85]. This methodology is mainly useful for the creation, checking and validation of specifications, and concerns real-time and distributed applications for data processing. It can be used to progressively create specifications by transforming the initial requirements definition into a more formal description. Performances expected from the system can also be included in the specification. This methodology was then extended by SYSREM to include the design and allocation of resources, and then by DCDS for distributed systems.

7.6.1 The model

SREM is based on the use of a structured finite state automata called R-NET (Requirement-Net). It expresses the evolution of outputs and the state starting from inputs and the current state.

This model is produced from the finite state diagram with extensions giving it a high-level structured nature. It is used to specify processing on a set of inputs to produce a set of outputs. This is a stimulus/response type diagram. Inputs are structured into sets of messages, each supplied by an interface connected to the environment. Outputs are structured similarly. The state S of the network is the Cartesian product of information known by the system.

Each R-Net diagram describes the transformation of an input message and the current state into a number of output messages and a new state. Figure 7.14 shows an example of a graph. The model uses the following symbols:

- the START symbol;

- the input interface, which accepts a message from the outside;

- the output interface, which transmits a message to the outside;
- the ALPHA functions which specify transformations;
- a sub-net defining a processing graph with an input point and an output point;
- an OR node to introduce state conditions;
- an OR-REJOIN node to express an OR convergence;
- an AND node to introduce parallel processing;
- a AND-REJOIN node to express an AND convergence;
- the SELECT node for selection of an input message, taking account of the current state;
- the FOR-EACH node specifies that all elements in a list must be processed.

This model is hierarchical since it allows progressive refinement of sub-network type nodes using R-NET diagrams.

It is appropriate for expressing stimulus ==> responses relations, and it can also be used to describe performances to be satisfied and timing constraints. Constraints are expressed by minimum and maximum times attached to paths through the R-NET diagram. Characteristic network points for these performance checks are called validation points.

Diagrams are then translated into RSL (Requirements Statement Language) based on the elements, attributes, relations and structures.

7.6.2 The SREM method for specification

The SREM methodology for the production of specifications stipulates work breakdown into the following phases:

- identification of the interface between the system and the environment, and data description and processing;
- produce an initial description using R-Nets;
- specify data and behavior of ALPHA functions in RSL;
- add management information: deadlines, analysis points, tools;
- validate the specification by a functional simulation using validation points;
- identify performance specifications and timing constraints;
- carry out a feasibility study to guarantee a solution to the system.

7.6.3 The SYSREM method for design

The problem of the transition from specifications to a design solution then arises. This is the objective of SYSREM.

A global view of the method is given in Figure 7.15.

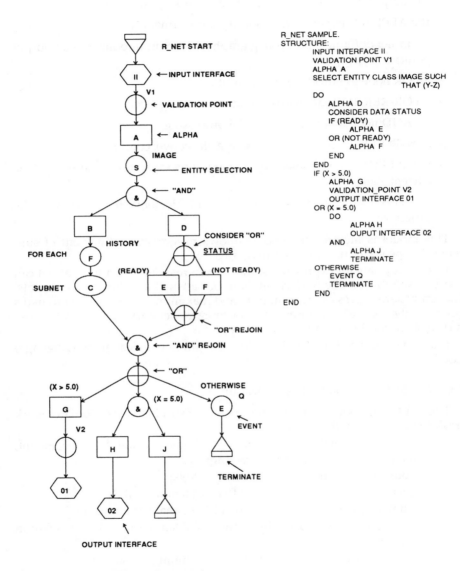

Figure 7.14   R-NET graph example.

R-Net subsets are translated into the form of tasks. ALPHA functions induce a modular decomposition into procedures for tasks. Tasks are allocated on a hardware architecture.

A solution is developed using the following phases:

- system definition, in accordance with SREM;
- identification of components and subsystems involved in the system;
- system decomposition, based on the principles stated below. Function sequencing and parallelism are expressed in this way;
- allocation of functions on subsystems or components, by association. Several solutions are possible;
- feasibility and cost estimate. Each subsystem has to be evaluated, taking account of the allocation. All interfaces are defined to ensure functional coupling between subsystems;
- evaluation of critical parts and resources;
- introduction of fault tolerance by addition of functions;
- integration and test plan;
- design optimization.

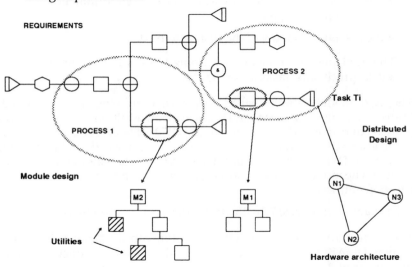

Figure 7.15   An overall view of the SYSREM method.

7.6.4 Comments

The SREM method is useful for specification making use of the stimulus-response model which can produce an efficient approach starting from the environment and expressing performance constraints. Coherence verifications are also possible.

One limitation is that specifications must be described in a great deal of detail, since they are not based on a hierarchical model. So, the step from specification to preliminary design is not obvious.

Unusable for specifying the design of a distributed solution, the SYSREM method was extended by DCDS (Distributed Computing Design System).

7.7 WARD AND MELLOR'S METHODOLOGY (SDRTS OR RTSA)

This methodology (Structured Development for Real-Time Systems), also called RTSA (Real-Time Structured Analysis), was developed for the specification and design of real-time applications [WARD-85]. It provides the necessary additions to SA/SD to improve the limitations of data-flow diagrams and structured design for real-time systems.

7.7.1 The model

The methodology is based on the use of two models:

- The essential model is composed of two parts:

  - the environment model which describes the environment within which the system will operate;

  - the behavioral model of the system to be designed.

- The implementation model describing the solution in three hierarchical levels: processors, tasks and modules.

The two models above, called transformation schemas, are based on DeMarco's data-flow diagram (DFD) to which an additional diagram is added to express control over the evolution of the DFD. This part is called the Control Flow Diagram (CFD) and is shown as a dashed line. An activity in this diagram which acts on DFD activities is specified by a finite state model (FSM, decision table, etc.). The model also uses entity-relation diagrams for specifying data and application entities.

The example in Figure 7.16 illustrates this specification model.

There are three types of activity evolution control actions: ENABLE for activation, DISABLE to stop the activity, TRIGGER for a single activation. There are two types of data lines: event driven or continuous (double arrow).

As for the data-flow diagram, this model allows a progressive approach to the specification by refining activities as shown in Figure 7.17.

The implementation model is structured into three levels:

- The processor level, which always describes the application processors, relations and interfaces between them by a data-flow type diagram. Each processor will be responsible for an essential part of the model.

- The task level, which expresses tasks and relations between them for each processor. This level models the software architecture.

- The module level, specifying each task decomposition. The recommended model is the Structure Chart.

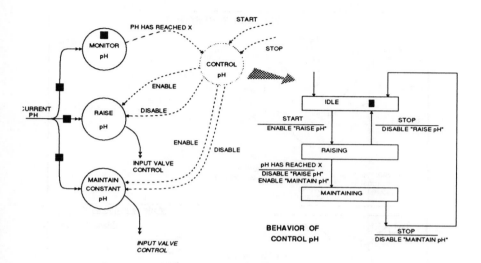

Figure 7.16   The Ward and Mellor specification model. (Paul T. Ward/Stephen J. Mellor, *Structured Development for Real-Time Systems*, © 1985, Vol I Figure 3.20 p102. Reprinted by permission of Prentice-Hall, Inc., Englewood Cliffs, New Jersey.)

7.7.2 The procedure

An application development consists of finding two models. First, the search for the essential model phase consists of [WARD-85,vol.2]:

- An environment model which necessitates:

    • describing the context diagram (system delimitation);

    • finding the set of events that the system must satisfy.

- System modeling, which expresses its behavior in response to events in the environment. For this, the transformation schema (DFD + CFD), then the data schema, and activity and data specifications have to be expressed by successive refinements.

The implementation model search phase then consists of making sure of the correspondence between portions of the essential model and each unit of implementation technology. It requires the following steps [WARD-85, Vol.3]:

- Identification of necessary processors as support for the essential model. This is obtained by reorganizing the essential model.

- Reorganization of the transformation diagram for each processor, in order to show the tasks, interfaces, data management and data scheduling.

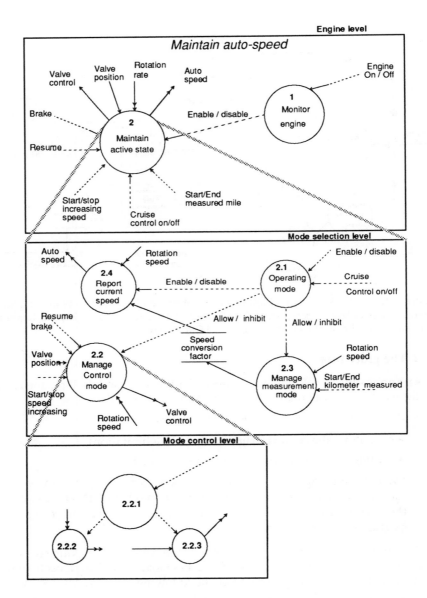

Figure 7.17   Refinement example for the essential model.

- Definition of the implementation schema for each task in the form of a
  hierarchy of modules (use of Yourdon and Constantine's method
  [JENSEN-79]).

Figure 7.18 illustrates these three description levels and shows that each subset of a level is a refinement of a higher level activity. Figure 7.19 shows this type of result.

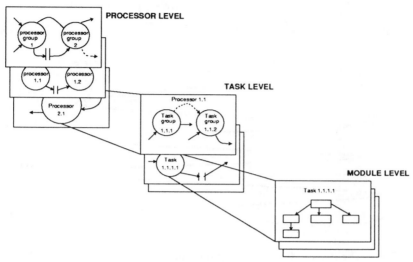

Figure 7.18   The 3 implementation model levels.

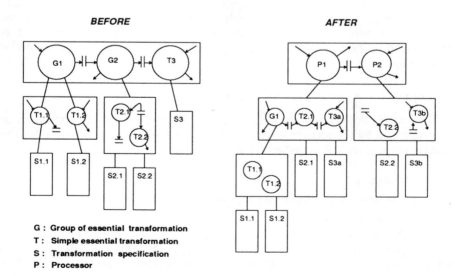

Figure 7.19   Result of a reorganization. (Paul T. Ward/Stephen J. Mellor, *Structured Development for Real-Time Systems*, Vol III © 1986 , Figure 5.3 p 67, Figure 1.4 p 7, Figure 3.1 p 19. Reprinted by permission of Prentice-Hall, Inc., Englewood Cliffs, New Jersey.)

According to the authors, several development processes are possible based on both models. Extreme cases are:
- complete essential model, then implementation model;
- iteration by levels between the two models (spiral model).

Figure 7.20 shows the iteration process.

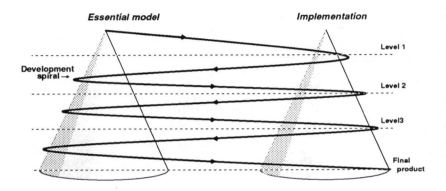

Figure 7.20   The two models and the spiral process.

In conclusion, if the data-flow diagram approach proves to be efficient, this method appears complete and suitable for multi-task real-time applications. However, it only concerns the software part, since the hardware part is assumed to be defined and nothing in the methodology shows how it can be deduced.

7.8 HATLEY AND PIRBHAI'S METHODOLOGY

This methodology is very similar to Ward and Mellor's methodology, in principle and by the recommended models. It is therefore also suitable for the specification of real-time systems [HATLEY-87].

7.8.1 The model

A system definition consists of two parts:
- the system specification;
- the system architecture.

The specification model is the data flow diagram (DFD or process model) to which a control specification (CFD or control model) is added. Figure 7.21 shows an example. This model is very similar to WARD's model, except that it has a different notation for control activities and a different meaning for specifying transformation activity active and inactive states. It is more structuring for the control part.

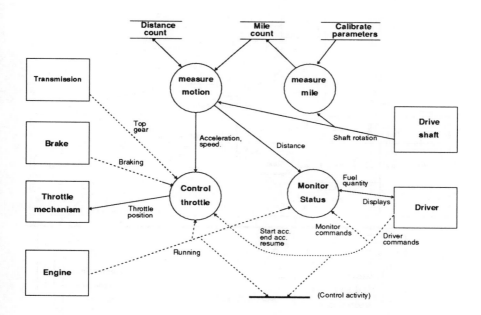

Figure 7.21   Example of (DFD + CFD) specification.

The architecture model specifies partitioning the system into its physical subsets. The architecture flow diagram (AFD) defines the modules and functional relations between them. The architecture interconnect diagram (AID) defines the means of making exchanges between modules. This model is shown in Figure 7.22.

The transformation from specification - supposedly technology independent - to architecture requires the addition of the interface parts: input, output, and man-machine interface which are related to the technology. The recommended structuring or decomposition model is shown on Figure 7.23.

Four subsets - input interface, output interface, user interface and test and safety maintenance functions - to be determined are added around the "hard core" described by the technology independent system specification.

7.8.2 The process

The process consists of finding the two parts of the system specification. The method consists first, of searching for all technology independent specifications. The model is then enhanced by interfaces: inputs, outputs, user and maintenance and safety aspects. Finally, the system architecture is deduced with the two parts, the hardware and software. This process is illustrated in Figure 7.24.

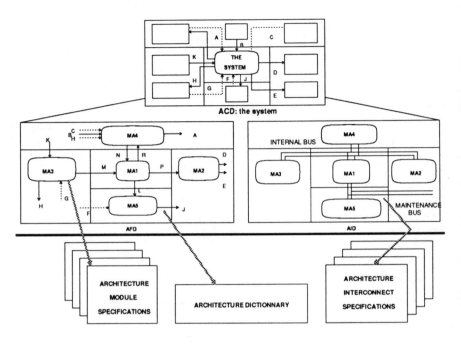

Figure 7.22   A system architecture model.

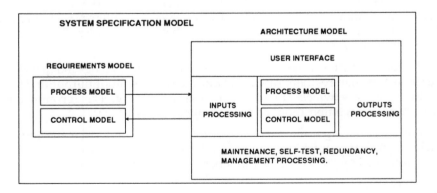

Figure 7.23   Requirements-to-architecture iterative loop for the Hatley methodology. (Figures 11.6 p133, 2.14 p24, 2.16 p26, 25.1 p287, 25.2 p288 reprinted with permission from Dorset House Publishing. Copyright © 1988, 1987 Dorset House Publishing, 353 W. 12 Street, New York, NY USA. Reprinted from *Strategies for Real-Time System Specification* by Derek J. Hatley and Imtiaz A. Pirbhai.)

The development can take place by separating the two parts, but also and especially, using an iterative procedure (spiral model) between the specifications and the architecture for the three parts - the system, hardware and software (same as Ward).

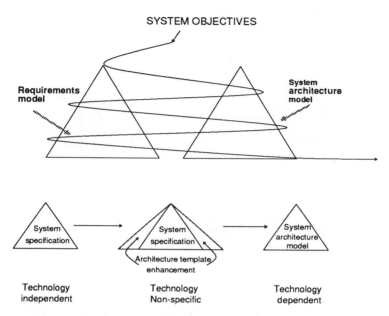

Figure 7.24   A system specification procedure.

7.9 LAVI AND HAREL'S METHODOLOGY (STATEMATE AS A TOOL)

This methodology is based on the association of three views for system modeling: activities, control and implementation. Harel's statechart control model is used. Statemate was developed as a computer-aided design tool [HAREL-88, LAVI-88].

7.9.1 The ECS (Embedded Computer Systems) model

This model describes a single or multi-computer system and the associated software subsets and modules according to a multi-level decomposition. It is based on the principle of decomposing a system into subsystems each carrying out a functionality, and a controller responsible for coordination between subsets. Figure 7.25 illustrates this model.

This conceptual model represents data and control links between the environment and the system, and internal links between subsystems. Each subsystem carries out a specific function defined by its behavior. It can also be decomposed according to the ECS model. The behavior is defined by a data-flow type diagram.

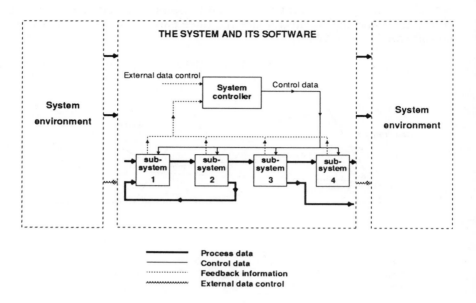

Figure 7.25   The ECS model.

The controller defines the behavior of the set of subsystems dependent on it: modes, transitions, activations. Its activity is normally described by a finite state machine, or more specifically by an extension called statechart.

Statechart [HAREL-87] was developed as an extension of the finite state diagram in order to reduce its limitations. Essentially, it is used to represent a hierarchical and structured description of simultaneous activities or actions, and of complex transition conditions.

Restricting ourselves to the main characteristics of this model, it allows:

- refinement by detailing a state by one, or more than one, diagram. When several diagrams are used, they evolve in parallel (equivalence with AND convergence and AND divergence of the Grafcet);

- the explicit or default specification of an initial state for a set of diagrams, and multiple synchronizations;

- the association of timing constraints with states, such as timeouts.

Figure 7.26 shows the advantage and simplicity of this model in an example.

The complete model thus allows a three view description of the system being developed as shown in Ffigure 7.27:

- the architecture specification (module-charts) which describe the logical and physical modules, and the environment;

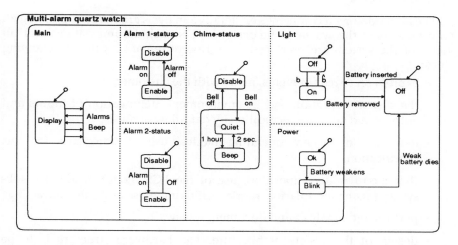

Figure 7.26   Watch operation specification.

- the activity specification (activity-charts) including a data-flow part and a control part (description similar to Ward's description);
- the control specification (statecharts).

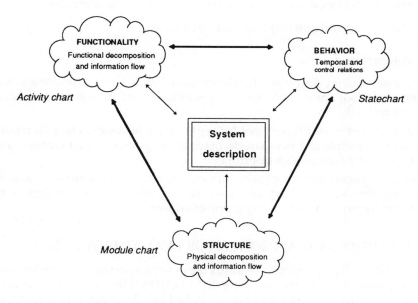

Figure 7.27   The three views for a system description.

7.9.2 The process

The methodology recommends an iterative analysis gradually expressing all requirements of the system to be designed. For each decomposition level, all views of the system are produced. The procedure consists of the following steps:

- expression of requirements, made with the customer;

- the system definition and its environment: delimitation of inputs and outputs and system specification by data-flow analysis;

- definition of system operating modes: use of statecharts for this specification;

- first modular decomposition: use of the ECS model to identify sub-systems using modularity criteria facilitating reuse and sub-contracting;

- performance analysis and document review;

- design of the system architecture. The hardware structure is to be defined: multi-computer system, communication system, etc;

- identification of activities and data-flows: specification of the activities of each subsystem, modules and links between them;

- dynamic analysis and design of the controller. The detailed analysis of the global system behavior using operational modes (statecharts), and the role of modules is used to deduce the solution for the controller;

- check coherence, prototyping and simulation.

7.9.3 Comments

This methodology developed for the needs of Israel Aircraft Industries, and the Statemate tool are suitable for the specification and design of embedded real-time systems.

The statechart is an efficient tool for expressing a behavior. The ECS model is similar in principle to a two-part decomposition: operative part (subsystems or modules), and control part (controller).

The tool appears to be complete. Structured around a database, it allows interactive simulation, report and document generation, testing and code production. Inputs are made using graphics editors.

7.10 DARTS (DESIGN APPROACH FOR REAL-TIME SYSTEMS)

This methodology is oriented towards the development of software for real-time applications. A recent extended DARTS/DA version concerns applications distributed on a set of nodes linked by a local network [GOMAA-84, 89].

Models used by DARTS include the data-flow diagram for the specification, an internal structure description model of the solution called the "process structure chart" deduced from the Activity Channel-Pool (ACP) diagram of the MASCOT (Modular Approach to Software Construction Operation and Test) methodology [COOLING-91]. DARTS includes a set of rules explaining how to create the process diagram from a data-flow diagram.

7.10.1 The DARTS model

The graphic model for the design describes the system structure as a set of data type and process type objects, each associated with activities operating on data. The interprocess relations thus described represent communication and synchronization mechanisms.

A simple synchronization between processes is represented by an event, whereas interprocess communications are possible by:

- a shared variable (pool);

- a channel allowing the transfer of one or several messages using a weak coupling (asynchronous tasks) or a tight coupling (send with acknowledgement for synchronous tasks).

Figure 7.28 shows an example of this type of model.

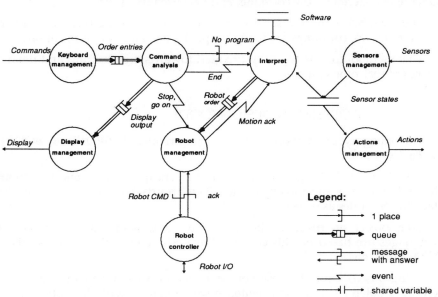

Figure 7.28   Example of process structure chart.

7.10.2 The process

The methodology recommends the following steps:

- Create the specification using data-flow diagrams. Use the RTSA method.

- Determine parallel evolution tasks starting from DFDs and based on a set of rules: input/output dependency, periodic execution, functional coherence, etc.

- Define interfaces or tasks by determining coupling relations starting from the DFDs: communication, data sharing or synchronization. This leads to the PSC (Process Structure Chart).

- Design for each task.

The Structured Design Technique is used to describe the internal structure of processing or transaction-oriented tasks. An approach using finite state machines or statechart is preferable for control tasks.

The DARTS/DA extension includes two steps after the specification production step.

Firstly, the system has to be decomposed into subsystems. Each subsystem will be located on a network node. The structure decomposition is based on functional coherence, low coupling, and performance criteria.

The interface between subsystems then has to be defined. Located on different nodes, couplings are made simply by message communications.

This methodology is typically oriented towards architectural and detailed design of real-time systems.

7.11 OBJECT-ORIENTED DESIGN (OOD)

This category of methodologies is data-oriented [ABBOTT-86, BOOCH-83, 86, COX-86].

Object-oriented design is based on the encapsulation concept initially defined by Parnas and then by Guttag. This approach considers all resources, data and modules as objects.

Each object encapsulates its data and data manipulation procedures. Languages are based on this concept: Smalltalk, C++, objective C, SIMULA, ADA, Eiffel, etc.

Using this concept, the designer can create his own abstractions necessary for the problem. The object-oriented development is typically bottom-up. A software component trade would thus be possible, facilitating reuse as indicated by Cox.

7.11.1 The object model

An object is an abstraction of an entity of the problem under consideration. It is a dynamic entity with an internal state. A boundary called the interface separates its "inside" from its "outside", the only part visible for its use [BOOCH-83, 86].

From a user point of view, the object is described by a specification, in other words, services or actions that it can carry out for its environment. Requests are made by inputs (generally procedures). Internally, the object has its own structure. It responds to external requests and changes its internal state.

So, an object corresponds to a high functional cohesion logical entity. Coupling between objects is weak and each is protected by encapsulation. Therefore, in this technique, the "object" is the logical decomposition unit, and not the action or procedure as in structured programming.

Different authors use different terminologies for the term object:

- module or package for the ADA language, according to Booch [BOOCH-83, 86];

- interpreter for Abbott [ABBOTT-86];

- software component for Freeman [FREEMAN-86] and Cox [COX-86];

and associate it with different characteristics:

- abstract data type (data encapsulation);

- autonomous evolution (task type object);

- inheritance (Smalltalk object). An object inherits characteristics from upper objects.

In the following, the objects considered do not have the inheritance property. The ADA language is a typical example of a description type tool suitable for an object-oriented implementation of real-time applications. Each ADA package consists of a specification and a body. Compilation of the specification alone is sufficient before use.

Several object types exist depending on the role [BOOCH-83]:

- the PROCEDURE object, as encapsulation of a set of sequential actions;

- the PACKAGE object as encapsulation of resources: data, programs;

- the TASK object as an independent entity;

- the GENERIC object as a software component model.

According to Booch, these object types are shown graphically in Figure 7.29.

Figure 7.30 shows an example of a solution representation using these objects. Each object is defined for its environment by its input points and its visible part.

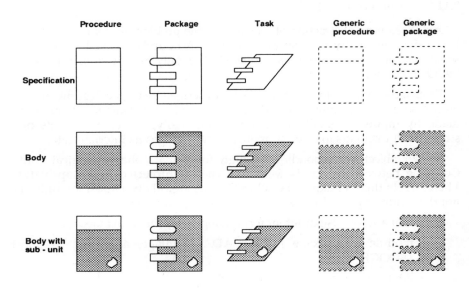

Figure 7.29   Symbols for representing object types according to Booch.

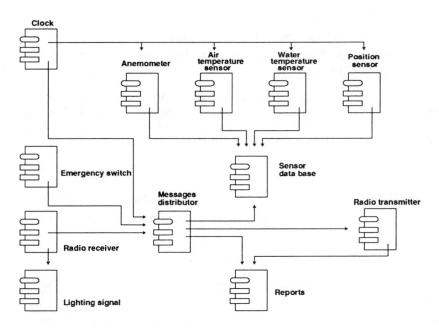

Figure 7.30   Example of representation showing objects and links between them.

7.11.2 Design process

The design process proposed by Booch can be summarized by the following steps:

- problem definition;
- solution definition at design level;
- strategy formalization.

The strategy formalization step includes the following phases [BOOCH-86]:

- Object identification: this involves identifying the objects in the problem to be solved, together with their characteristic properties. This phase is obviously particularly difficult and is highly dependent on the amount of analysis work carried out previously using other methods.

- Operation identification: the objective is to identify actions undergone and done by the object. Specification verbs provide indications about operations.

- Define the object visibility: relations with other objects are to be established, starting from characteristics and operations. This is equivalent to integrating each object into the solution structure.

- Establish the interface: this is equivalent to defining specifications for an object by characterizing its interface with the environment.

- Implementing objects: the internal behavior of the object is written during this final phase.

Another author, Abbott, also recommends the object-0riented design as a technique for implementing application constituents [ABBOTT-86]. His methodology is based on the use of four software component categories:

- data objects: data types, data structures, storage units. These objects are purely passive;

- operations objects: these are the basic functions;

- transducer objects: these components transform input data into output data;

- driver objects: these components control the other components.

To define the application architecture based on such interconnected components, the author previously adopts a data-flow oriented design as a guide. He suggests organizing the system so that the data-flow determines components or objects and their intervention order. Object identification is then deduced in this case from a data-flow analysis (SA method).

The implementation of each object must comply with its specification. This conformity is simpler to obtain when the implementation is the result of a very systematic translation. Therefore, the nature of the specification is very important. For this purpose, Abbott recommends the specification of each object using a finite state diagram that he calls a Roadmap. This specification is particularly well suited to the interpreter concept, and is fairly equivalent to a program structure as shown in the example in Figure 7.31.

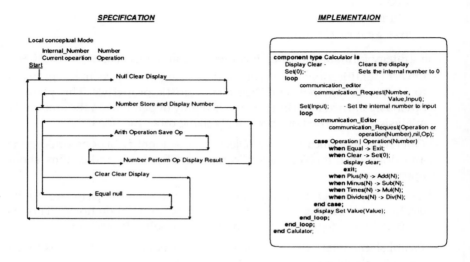

Figure 7.31   Object example using the Abbott method.

This example shows the two external and internal aspects of an object:

- The behavior to be respected by the user, in the form of a syntactical diagram which thus specifies the accepted language. Other sequences are invalid.

- The internal behavior followed by the object under the influence of external requests to impose the required behavior on the user.

The object approach is fairly recent and has a number of advantages for implementation:

- object protection by well-defined interfaces;

- reuse of objects, thus reducing development costs (software components);

- object independence: an internal change does not induce external changes.

The object concept is thus very useful, but a lot of work on methodology remains to be done for it to have an efficiency, similar to that provided by structured programming, for writing programs.

The difficulty with the object method lies in the object identification phase. What analysis should be done to deduce objects? Does an analysis based on modeling the real problem entities lead to a rational solution? The answer will not be simple.

Still referring to Booch in [BOOCH-86], the method described above concerns software design and implementation phases only, and therefore covers only part of the life cycle. The author stipulates that this type of method must be associated with prior analysis and specification methods such as Jackson's JSD, and DeMarco's or Sarson's data-flow oriented techniques, in order to create a model of the problem.

Several other object-oriented methodologies have been formalized, for example:

- GOOD (General Object-Oriented Software Development) created by Seidewitz and Stark for the specification and design phases for an ADA oriented software development. The data-flow diagram leads to entity identification [SEIDEWITZ-88].

- HOOD (Hierarchical Object-Oriented Design) derived from an approach by abstract machines and selected by the European Space Agency [HEITZ-87]. The integration of object concept, structure by hierarchy and control expression, facilitates the development of large applications.

- MOOD (Multiple-View Object-Oriented Design Methodology) using Ward and Mellor's RTSA analysis method for identification of objects and tasks [KERTH-88].

- OOSD (Object-Oriented Structured Design) defined for system architectural design. The graphic model for the architecture representation allows a transition between the Structured Design and the Object-Oriented Design methods [WASSERMAN-89].

- OOA (Object-Oriented Analysis) developed by Coad and Yourdon [COAD-90], is a methodology to define a complete specification model.

- OMT (Object-Modeling Technique) [RUMBAUGH-91], is a four steps methodology. The specification is elaborated based on a three-dimensional model: object model, dynamic model (statechart), functional model (DFD). The others steps are: architecture design, object design, object implementation.

- PAMELA (Process Abstraction Method for Embedded Large Applications) developed by Cherry and oriented towards embedded real-time systems. This methodology is oriented towards sequential communicating processes, with a direct transcription using an ADA task structure [KELLY-87].

To overcome the difficulty of identifying objects during design, thoughts have been undertaken to induce objects from the specification phase. This leads to the development of object-oriented specification methods [BAILIN-89, KURTZ-89, WARD-89, COAD-90, RUMBAUGH-91].

7.12 SYSTEM DESIGN WITH MACHINE CHARTS

This methodology (SDWMC) is recommended by Buhr as an evolution of SDWA (System Design With ADA) which was specified for an ADA implementation [BUHR-84, -89].

Suitable for behavior-intensive applications, it is based partly on the central idea that a system architecture is the association of a structure and a behavior, and secondly on the fact that diagrams are the best way to represent both aspects so as to allow the use of CASE tools or CAD tools. The structure is represented by Machine Charts, and the JRBS (Joint Refinement of Behavior and Structure) method is recommended.

7.12.1 The model

The model recommended for representing a system architecture is a description using Machine Charts. The icon syntax is relatively simple, each has precise semantics expressing the intercomponent behavior. A graphical representation is a natural method of thinking for engineers, and also simplifies communication between participants. The notation is derived from Buhr diagrams [BUHR-84].

The objective of using machine charts is to express:

- the abstract architecture of a system;

- the behavior, for example by expressing temporal diagrams based on event scenarios;

- abstract or formal operational specifications as a basis for the analysis, animation and implementation: use of finite state machines or pseudo-code.

Machine Charts are based on a set of symbols represented very summarily on Figure 7.32. The objects are boxes corresponding to an autonomous structure modularity (packages, modules, units), "robots" which are the objects representing the behavior modularity (actors, processes, tasks), and the "engines" which are the active components.

Relations are represented by "buttons" and "fingers", and the terminology directly expresses the semantics of the required interaction. Two types of push and push-pull relations are used to represent asynchronous interactions (immediate activation) and synchronous rendez-vous type interactions (conditional activation).

Figure 7.33 shows the semantics of these two link types.

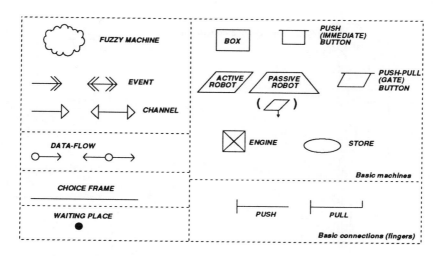

Figure 7.32   Machine Chart basic icons.

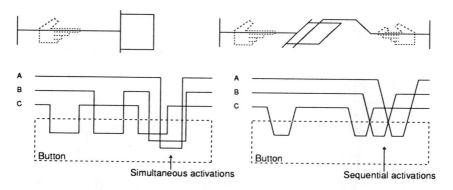

Figure 7.33   Notation and behavior for interactions.

The Buhr notation given here is very abbreviated. Figure 7.34 gives an idea of the recommended graphical representation, and Figure 7.35 shows a diagram of the behavior induced by the structure.

7.12.2 The method

According to Buhr, the Machine Chart notation uses tools to allow the "compilation" of a design or program skeleton for the implementation in a fairly automatic manner. Therefore, the objective of a methodology is to allow designers to progress from specifications to design. This is the objective of SDWMC.

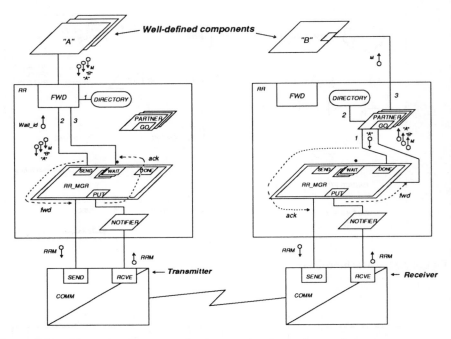

Figure 7.34   Example of structure for a remote exchange by rendez-vous.

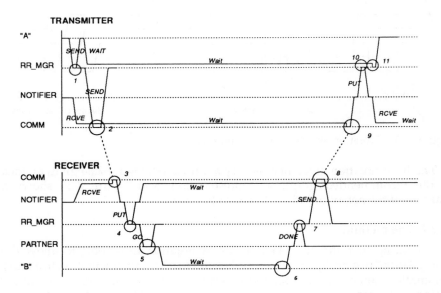

Figure 7.35   Representation of the behavior for the previous example.

The JRBS method consists of expressing the solution while simultaneously searching for the two views: structure and behavior. Behavior concerns the global solution and therefore interactions between objects in the structure, but not the objects themselves. This latter behavior is a result of a so-called functional refinement which is deduced later.

The design process is as follows:

- Specification by Event Flow Diagrams (EFD). The application is decomposed into subsets. Events represent interactions between these subsets for coordination and data exchanges. This is a structural diagram whereas DFD is a functional one.

- Search for architecture components. The designer is free to proceed sequentially, or by mixing structural and behavioral approaches. The structural approach involves defining components. Event relations are then transformed into explicit connections between components. The behavioral approach is simpler, starting from behavioral specifications. Data flow links are transformed into connections thus inducing a structure.

- Express the functionality of each component. This is distinct from the interaction between components; the objective is to describe the internal data and processing on these data.

Figure 7.36 summarizes this methodology, indicating the three types of views and possible iterations between the views.

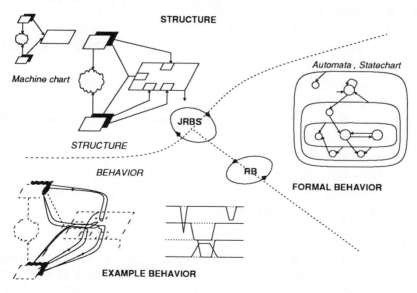

Figure 7.36   Overview of the method SDWMC.

7.12.3 Comments

This methodology is specific to the preliminary design phase. The solution is sought and expressed at the architectural level. The graphical notation facilitates understanding, checking and automatically producing the application skeleton. It is simple to add the functionality of each component in an algorithmic form. This is therefore a useful step towards the use of CAD tools.

The graphical notation is nevertheless complex and is fairly close to implementation problems: synchronous or asynchronous exchange, resource sharing, and relatively closely related to ADA concepts and mechanisms.

The design method does not clearly describe how to progress from specifications to an architecture, since specification models are not defined.

7.13 NIELSEN AND SHUMATE'S METHODOLOGY

This methodology is recommended by its authors for the design of complex real-time applications using ADA (ADA Design Methodology) [NIELSEN-88]. It is the result of associating the DARTS method for the real-time aspect, and structured design and object-oriented design approaches. This methodology is based on two concepts: Virtual Machines (LVM) and Object-Oriented Design (OOD).

7.13.1 The models

The system modeling is based on the use of one model per level, from specification down to implementation:
- the data-flow diagram for specifications;
- a Process Structure Chart (PSC) to describe the functional solution (see the DARTS method);
- a Concurrent Process Graph (CPG) which describes the implementation of the previous diagram;
- an ADA Package Graph (APG) which specifies objects with their contents and interfaces;
- a Structure Graph (SG) of ADA objects and their specifications using BUHR diagrams;
- the Structure Chart to describe the decomposition of each task into procedures (see structured design).

7.13.2 The design process

The process to be followed is easily deduced from the previous model. We will restrict ourselves here to stating the various steps together with a brief illustration to show the nature of models at each level and the gradual level by level process alternating between specification and design, see Figure 7.37.

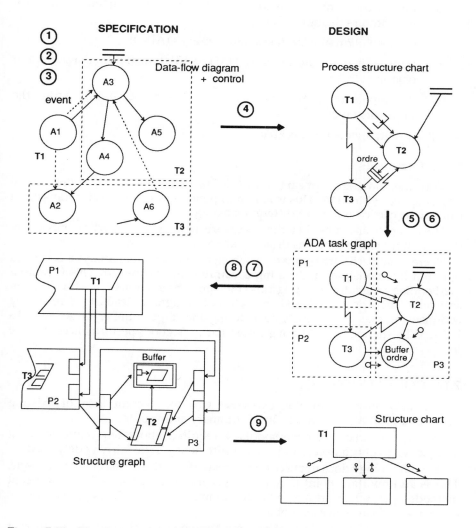

Figure 7.37   Illustration of the design process by its models.

1.   delimitation of interfaces;

2.   association of a process for each peripheral, or input, or output;

3.   specification of the central part of the system by a data-flow diagram;

4.   concurrence determination and therefore processes (PSC);

5.   determination of interfaces between processes;

6. introduction of intermediate tasks for the implementation of interprocess relations (CPG);

7. encapsulation of ADA tasks into packages (APG);

8. translation of the design into ADA: specification of Buhr diagrams and objects;

9. decomposition of complex tasks (SD and OOD) and write the implementation;

10. design review for checking.

7.13.3 Comments

This methodology appears complete for real-time applications to be implemented with ADA. This is not an imperative constraint since translation can also be carried out into a different language.

However, it assumes that the hardware part as a support is previously defined. It therefore concerns the software part exclusively.

There is no preliminary phase in which an environment analysis is carried out, and functionalities and timing constraints are expressed. This is more a methodology intended for design and then implementation of real-time system software. The approach based on data-flow diagrams leads to a relatively complex internal architecture, considering the large number of ADA tasks induced by the method. Although modularity is good, performances may be low.

7.14 CONCLUSION

The only purpose of this overview was to give an idea of existing methodologies. We will make a brief summary at this point.

Firstly, note that each methodology required about ten years before it became relatively complete and known sufficiently to be fairly widely used.

A methodology does not necessarily cover the entire development life cycle. This is an important point to note. However, the purpose of the most recent methodologies which are a result of combining proven methods, is to cover the entire life cycle as well as possible.

We have to note the lack of any methodology which leads to a coherent deduction of solutions both for the hardware and software parts (co-design). Most methodologies assume that the hardware part is known, and are thus more oriented towards software engineering.

Obviously, tools are developing as support for these various methodologies. This is a necessary condition industrially, to facilitate management and monitor large development projects. Allowing for the turbulence in this field of Computer-Aided Software Engineering (CASE) tools, we have deliberately not mentioned existing methodology computer-aided tools. We leave the task of searching for information about the products, which may be useful to each individual, for when they need it. To help in this task, we have included a guide in Part 8 in the form of a requirements definition for a CAD tool. However, the reader should remember that tools act as support for the application of a methodology, and not the inverse: a tool does not lead to a methodology. Therefore, a correct opinion of the benefit of a tool cannot be made without knowledge about methodologies. This is why this chapter is useful, since many tools are based on models and methods described in it.

This methodologies overview is obviously not exhaustive; it is not easy to know them all, and then to summarize them in a few lines. Some are derived from other methodologies. The number of them suggests that there is a real need.

It is thus important to remember that all methodologies are based on a system model. It is easier to compare methodologies by considering the models and analyzing problems, and the specification, design and implementation models.

Note the importance of the four model categories which are found in most methodologies:

- the data-flow diagram to specify activities;
- the finite state diagram with its variants for control;
- the structured diagram for program decomposition;
- the structure diagram to express the architecture.

A variety of models exists in each category. Which are the most appropriate models? How should the MCSE methodology be situated relative to those which have been described above? The next chapter presents a models survey for use as a guide in searching for and understanding methods. It also describes the MCSE point of view.

8

MODELS SURVEY

A model represents a description of a real system, or a system which will become reality after its design, at a given level of detail. As application views, models differ depending on the description to be expressed: external description for a specification, abstract internal description for a preliminary solution, detailed internal description for an implementation solution.

A model is also used to describe the characteristics of a system to be designed. It is then used as a basis for verifying its properties. The more detailed, and therefore formalized the model is, the more it facilitates the analysis work. Characteristics specified by a model depend on the nature of the model. Thus, to express a specific property, the class of models which induce this property should be selected.

Due to the quantity and the variety of models, this chapter first presents a classification of model types. Methodologies are essentially based on conceptual models.

Based on the methodologies described in the previous chapter, this chapter describes representation spaces commonly used to express the specification and the design. This overview makes it possible to define the essential models described by category.

As a synthesis facilitating our understanding and comparison of methodologies, it is shown that a methodology can be expressed as a trajectory in three representation spaces. The end of the chapter explains the MCSE development strategy.

8.1 BASIS FOR MODEL ANALYSIS

8.1.1 Model qualities

A model is an abstract representation of all or part of the real world. The term "abstract" should be taken in the simplest sense, in other words the elimination of non-useful details. In order to be usable, a model must have some general qualities:

- **Abstraction**: this quality is necessary in order to be useful for the description of complex systems. It satisfies the necessity to express the behavior of the whole without referring to the details of all its parts.

- **Refinement**: it must be possible to describe a subset of the model using another model: of the same type for a progressive description, or of a different type to complete the description or to express a different point of view.

- **Readability**: the model must be simple to interpret. Graphical representations are thus generally preferred to textual descriptions.

It is interesting to note immediately, the advantage of graphical models, which facilitate readability by global understanding, thus improving communication and validation. Most models using a graphical representation make use of a chart structure composed of nodes and links between these nodes, together with an interpretation to express the model semantics.

8.1.2 Model classification

The interpretation of a system, understanding of an object or a phenomenon, can lead to a wide variety of possible models. In order to describe models by major categories, we will use the classification given by Wilson [WILSON-86]. A distinction is made between four model forms:

- **icon models**, which are miniature reproductions of an object: for example, vehicle, aircraft, building model for wind tunnel studies;

- **analog models**, which use a physical appearance different to the phenomenon or object to be characterized: for example, electrical network for an analog simulation of a vehicle suspension;

- **analytic models**, which use mathematical or logical relations to represent physical behavioral laws;

- **conceptual models**, based on the use of symbols to represent qualitative aspects.

In sequence, the modeling approach uses conceptual models before using analytic models. Analytic models allow checks by direct simulation or by transformation into analog models. A designer most frequently uses these two categories.

8.1.3 Analytic models

Analytic models are very widespread and very varied. They are used as tools for predicting or estimating the behavior of some aspects of the object or the situation concerned. They are also used for validation purposes. Wilson describes a model classification into four categories as shown in Figure 8.1.

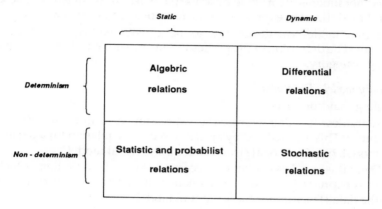

Figure 8.1   Analytic model categories.

The columns in the matrix show the difference between time-independent and time-dependent models. The rows separate certain and predictable behavior from uncertain behavior.

8.1.4 Conceptual models

This chapter deals particularly with the conceptual model category. They satisfy various objectives:

- to clarify a situation: for example, structure of a company and links between its services;

- to illustrate a concept: for example, closed loop diagram for process control;

- to define a structure, relations: cause and effect interaction between entities;

- to describe a method: for example, life cycle steps for the development.

In practice, the latter two cases are the most frequently used in design.

The two types of conceptual models differ depending on the nature of the information or situations to be represented. The classification can be made based on several criteria. Categories are complementary. Some criteria types will now be described.

- A - Structural model - Behavioral model

Some models represent an entity topology. This type of model is said to be structural. Entities are interrelated by dependency relations. Dependency may concern data, activities, events, resources, etc. This dependency is not temporal, it expresses a functional dependency only.

Many other models are used to describe the behavior of an entity. These are behavioral models, often expressed in the form of a temporal behavior.

These two model categories are to be considered as independent or "orthogonal". The definition of properties for one category adds no information to the other category.

- B - Activity model - Data model

Modeling may concern:

- Activities: in other words, the expression of actions specific to the entity. This is translated by an action sequence relation for a behavioral model, or a functional structure for a structural model.
- Data: this is a description of successive states of a data item which are thus expressed by a sequence relation for the behavioral model, or by the data structure for the structural model.

It is useful to keep in mind the duality that can exist between activities and data. A behavioral model for an activity induces the possibility of describing the evolution of the output data, and modeling for data induces, by duality, the behavior of the activity to ensure evolution of the data.

- C - Vertical model - Horizontal model

A structural description can be made along two axes:

- The vertical axis: a more detailed level results from refinement of each high-level entity. Relations exist only between consecutive levels. This is a hierarchical dependency.
- The horizontal axis: refinement can appear in horizontal relations only. Dependencies are of a functional nature.

- D - Continuous model - Discrete model

The continuous model describes the continuous evolution of a behavior, whereas the discrete model represents only specific states of the object at specific times.

- E - Synthesis of categories

Each conceptual model can be positioned using the table given in Figure 8.2. This figure can also be used to position methods by analyzing the nature of models used. As a reminder, analytic models fall into the category of behavioral models.

Considering the three phases - specification, design, implementation - we can say, in general, that:

- behavioral models are used particularly to express function specifications;
- structural models describe the architecture of the design solution.

	Structural		Behavioral	
Activities				
Data				
	Vertical	**Horizontal**	**Continous**	**Discrete**

Figure 8.2   Conceptual model categories.

Considering design in particular, in the same way as a problem solution simultaneously expresses structural and behavioral relations for activities and data, this classification shows that a methodology cannot be based on a single model. Completely describing a system (and therefore designing it) requires the ability to express different concepts at different abstraction levels. Each corresponds to a point of view: organizational, temporal, resources.

8.2   OBJECTIVES OF MODELS FOR SYSTEMS

One observation, based on the previous chapter dealing with the various methodologies, is that most categories of conceptual models are used. Therefore, after having making an initial classification of model types, we will consider in more detail those which are useful to describe systems to be designed. To grasp the essentials, we will first differentiate between two modeling objectives:

- **Specification**: the purpose is to express the characteristics of the "objects" to be developed, in as much detail as possible from an external point of view: behavior, properties, constraints.

- **Design**: an internal description of the solution is necessary in as much detail as possible: structure, behavior of constituents.

We will detail the modeling principles for each of these two problems.

8.2.1 Modeling for specification

To respect the term "specification", a model for specification must be a purely external view. It then exclusively expresses the observable behavior, described by a set of statements in a formal language: use of rules, relations, pre-conditions and post-conditions, predicates and axiomatic description. It is obvious that this modeling technique is little used in methodologies due to its complexity and lack of understandability, particularly by the customer.

Another modeling technique is to use so-called explicit models. The term "explicit" should be understood in the sense of using primarily internal data, or states. For example, a data-flow diagram shows internal data and activities, a finite state machine considers internal states of the specified object. Models for all methodologies mentioned in the previous chapter fall into this category. One essential reason justifies this choice: the objective is to design, starting from the specification, therefore the earlier that internal information is available, the more quickly the design can be carried out. However, the specification and the solution must not be confused.

The "explicit" model of a system depends on the application field and consequently the point of view adopted. For specifications at the present time, there is a consensus for modeling in three complementary views as shown in Figure 8.3. The three views correspond to three representation spaces:

- data space
- state space
- activity space

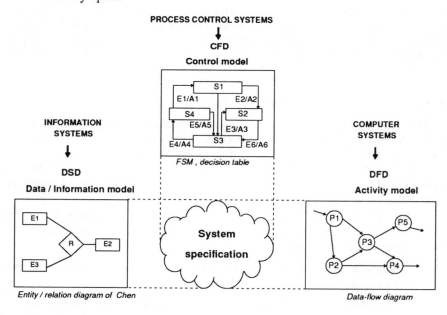

Figure 8.3   Modeling according to three complementary views.

Data modeling (Jackson's diagram, entity/relation diagram) is the main point of view for information systems. State models (finite state machine, decision table, statechart) is the point of view for control systems whereas the activities model (data-flow diagram) is the point of view for processing or computer systems. Since systems are becoming more and more complex and include multiple functions, the three views have become necessary and complementary. For industrial computing applications, the large number of routines has made it necessary to consider the data-flow approach. Similarly, the increased quantity of information managed makes it necessary to consider the organization of all these data. This explains why the specification proposed by Ward and Mellor in RTSA includes three components: activity diagram, addition of a part for activity control, data specification between activities [WARD-85].

8.2.2 Modeling in design

The internal description of a system requires the expression of two information types:

- the structure, to be understood as a set of more elementary constituents and relations between these constituents;

- the behavior to specify an evolution.

The structure may concern functions, data and resources. Resources here refer particularly to hardware constituents necessary for the application. For the object approach, functions and data form a whole.

The behavior description may concern each constituent (function, data item, resource) or interactions between constituents.

The description of a system can therefore be made from two views - the functional view and the resource view. Each view requires associating a structure with the behavior of constituents. This can be represented diagrammatically as shown in Figure 8.4.

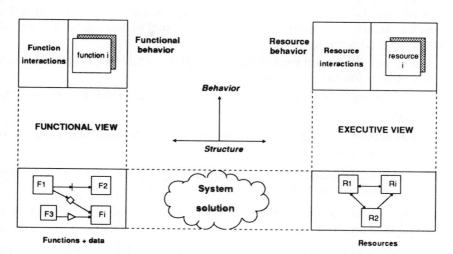

Figure 8.4   Modeling a system with two complementary views.

The resources view is considered here as being different from the functional view, and acts as a necessary support for it. It is not often used since most methodologies require the hardware to be available.

8.3 MODELS SURVEY

The previous analysis has shown that models useful for specification and design fall into two categories: structure models and behavior models. In the following, we will first review the main structure models, and then the behavior models that it needs to be familiar with, outlining the use of each.

8.3.1 Activities model

The data-flow diagram is an example of a model describing activities. It is a structural model but for the specification. The global behavior is only partially expressed by this model. The reader should refer to the SA model for representation rules (see Section 7.3). It is used as an initial specification for design in several methodologies. Its advantage is that it can be used for global modeling of an application without modeling each entity.

8.3.2 Data models

Two categories of structural models are used, depending on whether the data under consideration forms an indivisible whole or as a collection of interrelated data items.

- A- Jackson's diagram

Large sets of data, or data containing a variety of information must be described by their structure. High-level languages such as Pascal and ADA allow this description type in a textual form. "Typing" of data can be considered to be a logical description.

At a higher abstraction level (semantic level), the structure of a data item can be described using four symbols:

- the terminal element (rectangle), which is an indivisible and typed data item;

- the composition operator, which represents the Cartesian product of contained data;

- the set operator, which designates a group of identical elements (dynamic size, including the case of 0 elements);

- the alternative operator, which associates a special data item for each value of an attribute.

Oriented links between symbols represent access paths. Figure 8.5 shows an example, for illustration purposes.

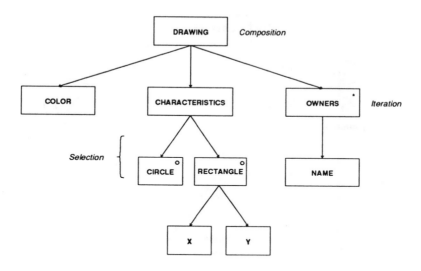

Figure 8.5   Jackson diagram for data structures.

These diagrams are very simple to understand. It is easy to deduce the logical structure starting from this representation, for example when using Pascal.

- B- Entity-relation model

This model is used to represent a "world" in terms of entities, their attributes and relations between these entities [MARTIN-88].

An entity is a "thing": object, person, information, etc. Each falls into a category (entity type). Entities are not necessarily physical objects. They can also be abstractions such as an aircraft flight. Each entity type has its own attributes (or properties) which make it possible to differentiate between entities. Attributes take on values, for example: measurements of an object such as height and weight.

When entities are interrelated, relations express facts for the "world" considered. The semantics of each element in a phrase used to express characteristics of data or information, induces its category:

- entities are subjects, objects, nouns;
- the relation is the verb;
- the attributes are modifiers.

Figure 8.6 shows an example of an entity-association diagram to express a model.

Numbers on the links show the cardinality of entities for each relation.

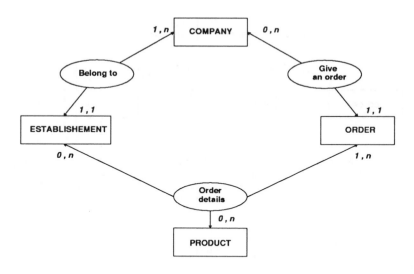

Figure 8.6   Representation of an entity-association model.

A single number is used in Chen's notation, and two numbers are used in the French notation: 0 means that not all entities are necessarily linked by relations, 1 means that each entity is used once only in the relation, and n means that it is used in several relations. For example, not all companies pass orders, but one may pass several orders.

This model does not describe temporal characteristics. It is a static description model. Databases, the heart of information systems, are based on this type of so-called relational model.

8.3.3 Function models

This model class is used to represent a set of interconnected functions by a structure. These models may be at the functional, executive or resource level.

- A- Hierarchical function diagram

This diagram type expresses the decomposition of a complex system into a collection of subsets linked by input/output relations. It allows refinement and abstraction. It is a vertical model and an example is given in Figure 8.7.

It does not indicate the temporal chronology for its constituents. For example, it does not express sequencing or conditions on information for inputs: X2 and Z1, X2 or Z1, X2 followed by Z1, nor is it a concurrent or sequential behavior. The expression of the hierarchy is therefore an essential structuring ingredient, but it is not sufficient in itself.

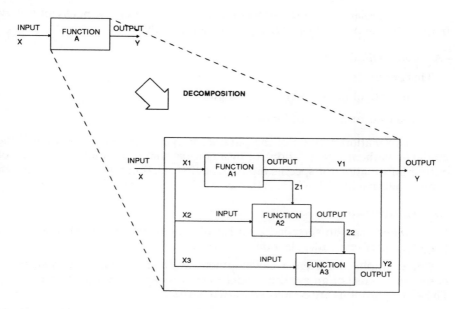

Figure 8.7   Function hierarchy example

- B- *The functional structure model*

The structural model proposed in MCSE also allows refinement and abstraction. There are three types of relations between functions: synchronization, variable sharing, message transfer. The model is associated with an interpretation expressing the behavior of interactions between functions (see Part 4). The existence of this interpretation reduces the designer's degrees of freedom, but on the other hand adds efficiency, since it is then sufficient to complete the description by the internal behavior of each function.

The executive structure model in MCSE is similar, but its objective is to express the structure of a hardware set.

The Process Structure Graph model used in DARTS which is derived from MASCOT, is relatively similar but has more relation types to express data transfers.

- C - *Object structure model*

Booch's, Buhr's, Wasserman's, and Bishop's diagrams fall into this category. This model represents each object by a diagram with input and output points. The form of the object and the characteristics of input points precisely define its type and therefore its role relative to its environment. Connections between objects are of the requester or transmitter type towards requested or receive objects.

8.3.4 Behavior models

There is a relatively wide variety of models in this category. Behavior is very frequently, but not exclusively, expressed temporally.

- A - Mathematical model

This describes:

- the field of input and output variables;

- the transformation of inputs to outputs.

Transformation may be of the parametric type: expression by an analytic model (a mathematical relation), or by a non-parametric relation: expression of output information for specific inputs. The first relation type normally uses an explicit internal model, whereas the second is a real external description.

- B - Formal models

A system may be specified by a set of statements expressed in a formal language (grammar rule, algebraic rules, etc.).

For example, the Vienna Development Method (VDM) (IBM Vienna) is based on the use of an explicit model to express specifications [COHEN-86]. These specifications are composed of two parts:

- the abstract definition of data and variables to represent the internal state of the system;

- the definition of operations and functions acting on the data and variables. This is carried out by expressing the operation name and the input and output parameters, a pre-condition on the value of input parameters and the initial state which defines the execution, and a post-condition which specifies values taken on by variables and the final state after completion of the operation.

- C- Pseudocode

Another general way of describing behavior consists of using a structured textual description. The language can be very close to spoken language or very close to computer languages: for example, Pascal or ADA.

- D- Finite state machine (FSM)

This model allows a simple behavioral description, by expressing the discrete states of an entity and state change conditions. It is essentially a computer science and industrial data processing model.

An FSM is characterized by states and links between states representing possible transitions. One of the states is the initial state. Two model types are well known, Mealy's model in which actions are associated with transitions, and Moore's model in which actions are associated with states, see Figure 8.8.

The latter is more imple but less practical for specifications. A combination of the two models is very useful to express a behavior fairly concisely. The bar on the transition link is used for reasons of clarity.

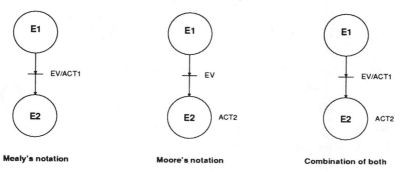

Mealy's notation   **Moore's notation**   **Combination of both**

Figure 8.8   Notation for the finite state machine.

The expression of concurrent evolutions necessitates the combination of several diagrams with coupling expressed by transition conditions which depend on the states of other diagrams or events produced by them. It is similar to Grafcet when it does not make use of parallelism. It is not suitable for representing the complexity, since it is a "flat" model and therefore limited for refinement.

This model is sometimes extended by the use of variables or counters such as the Extended Finite State Machine. Grafcet is also an extension of this model allowing the representation of parallelism.

- E- Statechart

Developed by Harel [HAREL-87], the statechart corrects the main limitations of the finite state machine (see Section 7.9.1). We advise readers to look at this model carefully, since it is extremely attractive for expressing simultaneous sequential behaviors for control systems.

- F- Petri net

The Petri net is a bipartite graph composed of places and transitions. The place token concept expresses temporal sequencing and concurrency [NUSSBAUMER-84].

Evolution rules are very simple: a transition can only be fired when all previous places have each at least one token. When it is fired (without considering when), one token is removed from all previous places and one token is added into all subsequent places. The basic structures are shown on Figure 8.9.

When the output of a place is linked to several transitions, there is a possibility of conflict (competition). In this case, the token is only used for firing a single transition.

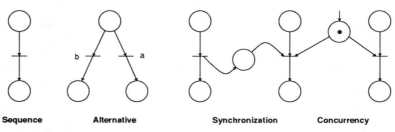

Figure 8.9   Petri net basic structures.

Various interpretations are given to places and transitions:
- place = activity, transition = end condition;
- place = state, transition = evolution condition and associated atomic action;
- place = resources, transition = activity.

For the third case, each activity can only take place when input resources are available (tokens in preceding places), thus producing output resources. Petri nets can thus be used, for example, to represent production processes. Figure 8.10 represents the inspection process in a medical analysis laboratory and the corresponding Petri net.

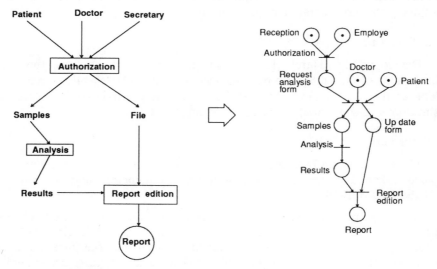

Figure 8.10   Petri net description example.

Petri nets can be used to check very useful properties for parallel systems: safe, clean and alive nets.

This model is useful for expressing and validating the specification for the behavior of a set of entities, and then for validating a design resulting from this specification.

Despite these advantages, the essential limitations are similar to those for finite state machines. It is a "flat" model, and the Petri net quickly becomes complex. However, the refinement technique can be used if a transition has only one input and one output link. Another consideration is that it limits the specification to a description of the control evolution, excluding the data. However, control often depends on the state of the data.

G- Communication nets

This model is derived from the Petri net for the special case of the state chart (one incoming link and one outgoing link for each transition). It is also called a Communication Finite State Machine (CFSM). The place represents a wait state. Each transition is associated with:

- a firing condition, generally reception of an event or a message;

- generation of an action when the transition is fired: for example, sending a message.

This message is particularly useful for specifying communication protocols [ORR-88]. It is of the stimulus/response type. According to its authors, it is expressed in several forms as shown in Figure 8.11.

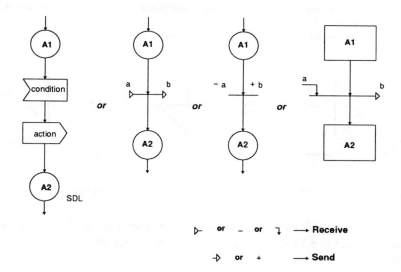

Figure 8.11   Communication machine representation examples.

The specification validation and property evaluation are normally carried out by considering the equivalent Petri net.

8.4 CONCLUSION: THE MCSE MODELS

We showed in Part 1 that a methodology is based on one or several models. In this chapter, we showed that modeling a system requires several views and therefore several model types. Consequently, a methodology can be defined by a trajectory within a modeling space. To illustrate this point of view, Figure 8.12 shows the case of the Nielsen and Shumate methodology by separating the three model types: specification, functional description, and executive or implementation description [NIELSEN-88].

The specification leads to data-flow diagrams by successive approaches.

Design starts by searching for functions (process) directly starting from activities. Data is then specified as interfaces and function behavior follows.

Since the hardware support is imposed, the software implementation is deduced by transformation of the process structure. The same applies to behavior.

All methodologies described in the previous chapter can be represented in the same manner, given that the models used differ depending on the method. Therefore, the comparison is not very easy.

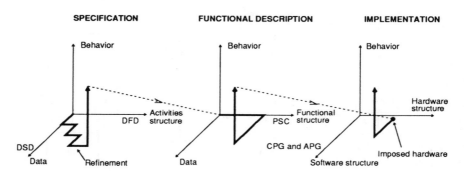

Figure 8.12   Trajectory for Nielsen and Shumate's methodology.

We now have all elements necessary to characterize the approach proposed in MCSE. Figure 8.13 shows the development trajectory for the three modeling levels.

This Figure explains the methodology described in subsequent parts of this book:

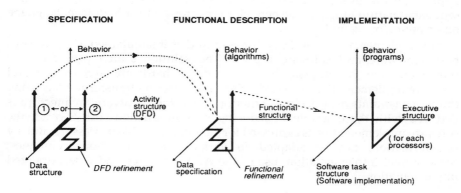

Figure 8.13   MCSE explained by a trajectory in three spaces.

- Part 3 shows that, depending on the complexity, the specification is obtained according to two possible trajectories: low complexity (1), since it is then possible to directly express the global behavior for each entity, and higher complexity (2) then requiring the characterization of application activities.

- Part 4 describes the design process for determining a functional description, which consists of starting with data and then functions, leading to a functional structure. Iteration by refinement is possible. The description is obtained when the internal behavior of the basic functions is defined.

- Part 5 specifies the order in which constituents are found: first, processors, then software tasks on programmable processors, ending with the behavior imposed on each processor by tasks.

For specifications, the three-dimensional modeling space is similar to most methodologies. Suitable for real-time systems, MCSE recommends using the behavioral dimension in preference to the activities dimension. This is justified since the problem analysis must start from environment entities. The behavior of these entities under the influence of the system can then be expressed. The process based on activities will be more efficient if it transpires that the preceding approach is not simple (many badly defined entities).

For design, the functional model is simple and independent of the implementation technique. The solution is the result of a data search and, therefore, prior relations between functions. This is an essential difference. Several methodologies deduce functions or processes by transformation, starting from specification activities. MCSE starts from the principle that the internal view is very different from the external view. Consequently, the designer must perform an analysis and synthesis work to develop a simple, appropriate and efficient functional architecture. When refinement results in a sequential nature function, the behavior is expressed by a high-level language description, for example Pascal.

For implementation, MCSE is different in that it simultaneously processes both hardware and software aspects. The solution search procedure for implementation is complete since it leads to hardware architecture and software implementation. The deduction takes place by transformations using timing constraints as a decision criterion. First, the hardware architecture is deduced with the objective of reducing its reproduction cost. Second, the software implementation is expressed for all programmable processors, and, by transformation, can be adapted to various implementation techniques: conventional implementation, use of the ADA language and object-oriented implementation.

References Part 2

BOOKS

[ABBOTT-86]
An Integrated Approach to Software Development
R.J. Abbott
WILEY, Interscience Publication, John Wiley&Sons 1986

[ALFORD-82]
Distributed Systems. Methods and Tools for Specification
M.W. Alford, J.P. Ansart, G. Hommel, L. Lamport, B. liskov,
G.P. Mullery, F.B. Schneider.
Lectures Notes in Computer Science Springer-Verlag 1982

[BOOCH-83]
Software Engineering with ADA
G. Booch
Benjamin/Cummings, Menlo Park, CA. 1983

[BUHR-84]
System Design with ADA
R.J.A. Buhr
Prentice-Hall, Englewood Cliffs NJ 1984

[BUHR-89]
System Design with Machine Charts: A CAD approach with ADA examples
R.J.A. Buhr
Prentice-Hall 1990

[CAPRO-86]
Systems Analysis and Design
H.L. Capro
The Benjamin/Cummings, Menlo Park, CA 1986

[COAD-90]
Object-Oriented Analysis
P. Coad, E. Yourdon
Yourdon Press, Computing Series 1990

[COHEN-86]
The Specification of Complex Systems
B. Cohen, W.T. Harwood, M.I. Jackson
Addison-Wesley Publishing Company 1986

[COOLING-91]
Software Design for Real-Time Systems
J. E. Cooling
Chapman and Hall 1991

[COX-86]
Object-Oriented Programming: an Evolutionnary Approach
B.S. Cox
Addison-Wesley Publishing Company 1986

[DAVIS-90]
Software Requirements. Analysis and Specification
A. M. Davis
Prentice-Hall 1990

[DEMARCO-79]
Structured Analysis and System Specification
T. DeMarco
Yourdon Computing Series, Yourdon Press, Prentice-Hall 1979

[HATLEY-87]
Strategies for Real-time System Specification
D.J. Hatley, I.A. Pirbhai
Dorset House Publishing New York 1987

[JACKSON-83]
System Development
M. Jackson
C.A.R Hoare series, Prentice-Hall 1983

[JENSEN-79]
Software Engineering
R.W. Jensen, C.C. Tonies
Prentice-Hall International Editions 1979

[MARTIN-88]
Structured Techniques-the Basis for CASE
J. Martin, C. Mc Clure
Prentice-Hall 1988

[NIELSEN-88]
Designing Large Real-time Systems with ADA
K. Nielsen , K. Shumate
Intertext Publications Inc. Mc Graw Hill, NY 1988

[NUSSBAUMER-84]
Informatique Industrielle II. Introduction à l'informatique du Temps Réel
H. Nussbaumer
Presses Polytechniques Romandes, Collection Informatique 1984

[RUMBAUGH-91]
Object-Oriented Modeling and Design
J. Rumbaugh, M. Blaha, W. Premerlani, F. Eddy, W. Lorensen
Prentice-Hall 1991

[TEICHROEW-83]
System Description Methodologies
Eds D. Teichroew, G. David
Proceedings of the IFIP TC2 Conference, Ungary North-Holland 1983

[WARD-85]
Structured Development for real-time systems
P.T. Ward, S.J. Mellor
Vol.1: Introduction and Tools
Vol.2: Essential Modeling Techniques
Vol.3: Implementation Modeling techniques
Yourdon Computing series, Yourdon Press, Prentice-Hall 1985

[WILSON-86]
Systems: Concepts, Methodologies and Applications
B. Wilson
John Wiley & Sons NY 1986

PAPERS

[ABBOTT-81]
Software requirements and specifications: A survey of needs and languages.
R.J. Abbott, D.K. Moorhead
The Journal of Systems and Software No 2 1981, p 297-316

[ALFORD-85]
SREM at the age of eight; The Distributed Computing Design System
M. Alford
Computer April 1985, p 36-46

[BAILIN-89]
An object-oriented requirements specification method
S.C. Bailin
Communications of the ACM Vol 32 No 5, 1989 p 608-623

[BOASSON-86]
Modeling in real-time systems
L. Boasson
Computer Standards & Interfaces North-Holland, Vol 1 1987, p 107-114

[BOOCH-86]
Object-oriented development
G. Booch
IEEE Transactions on Software Engineering Vol SE-12 No 2, Feb. 86, p 211-221

[BRACON-88]
La spécification du logiciel dans l'industrie
G. Bracon
Bigre No 58 Janvier 1988, p 12-19

[CAMERON-86]
An overview of JSD
J.R. Cameron
IEEE Transactions on Software Engineering Vol SE-12 No 2, Feb. 1986,
p 222-240

[DAVIS-86]
A practical Approach to Specification Technology Selection
M.J. Davis, D.R. Addleman
The Journal of Systems and Software No 6 1986, p 285-294

[DAVIS-88]
A comparison of techniques for the specification of external system behaviour
A.M. Davis
Communications of the ACM Vol 31 No 9, Sept. 1988, p 1098-1115

[FREEMAN-86]
Reusable software engineering concepts and research directions
P. Freeman
Software Reusability: tutorial, Computer Society Press of the IEEE No 750,
p 10-23

[GOMAA-84]
A software design method for the real-time systems
H. Gomaa
Communications of the ACM Vol 27 No 9, Sept. 1984

[GOMAA-89]
A software design method for distributed real-time applications
H. Gomaa
Journal of Systems and Software No 9 1989, p 81-94

[GOMAA-89]
Structuring criteria for real-time systems design
H. Gomaa
Proceedings of the 11th International Conference on Software Engineering 1989,
p 290-301

[HAGEMANN-88]
Requirements analysis for real-time automation projects
M. Hagemann
Proceedings of 10th International Conference on Software Engineering
Singapore 11-15 April 1988, p 122-129

[HAREL-87]
Statecharts: a visual formalism for complex systems
D. Harel
Science of Computer Programming North Holland, Vol 8, 1987, p 231-274

[HAREL-88]
Statemate: A working Environment for the development of complex reactive
systems.
D. Harel, H. Lachover, et al.
Proceedings of 10th International Conference on Software Engineering
Singapore 11-15 April 1988, p 122-129

[HEITZ-87]
HOOD, une méthode de conception hiérarchisée orientée objets pour
le développement des gros logiciels techniques et temps-réel.
M. Heitz
Bigre No57 Decembre 1987, Journées ADA France p 42-61

[IGL-82]
Introduction à SADT
Documentation IGL France 1982

[JOHNSON-88]
Deriving specifications from requirements
W.L. Johnson
Proceedings of 10th International Conference on Software Engineering,
Singapore, 11-15 April 1988, p 428-438

[KELLY-87]
A comparison of four design methods for real-time systems
J.C. Kelly
Proceedings of the 9th International Conference on Softward Engineering
Monterey, April 1987, p 238-252

[KERTH-88]
MOOD: A methodology for structured object-oriented design
N. Kerth
OOPSLA' 88, San Diego, CA 1988

[KURTZ-89]
An object-oriented methology for systems analysis and specification
B.D. Kurtz, D. Ho, T.A. Wall
Hewlett-Packard Journal April 1989, p 86-90

[LAVI-88]
Embedded computer systems: requirements analysis and specification:
An industrial course
J.Z. Lavi, M. Winokur
Proceedings of SEI Conference Virginia April 1988
Lecture Notes in Computer Science: Software Engineering Education
No 327 Ed. G.A. Ford Springer-Verlag p 81-105

[LUDEWIG-87]
Specification techniques for real-time systems
J. Ludewig, H. Matheis
Computer Standard and Interfaces No 6 1987, p 115-133

[ORR-88]
Systematic method for real-time system design
R.A. Orr, M.T.Orris, R. Tinker, C.D.V. Rouch
Microprocessors and Microsystems Vol 12 No 7, Sept. 1988, p 391-396

[RAMAMOORTHY-87]
Issues in the development of large, distributed, and reliable software
C.V. Ramamoorthy, A. Prakash, V. Garg, T. Yamaura, A. Bhide
Advances in Computers, Vol 26 -Purdue (LD-26), p 393-443

[ROSS-85]
Applications and extensions of SADT
D.T. Ross
Computer April 1985, p 25-34

[SANDEN-89]
An entity-life modeling approach to the design of concurrent software
B. Sanden
Communications of the ACM Vol 32 No 3, March 1989, p 330-343

[SEIDEWITZ-88]
General object-oriented software development: background and experience
E. Seidewitz
21st Hawaï International Conference and Systems Sciences 1988, p 262-270

[SHEMER-87]
Systems analysis: a systemic analysis of a conceptual model
I. Shemer
Communications of the ACM Vol 30 No 6, June 1987, p 506-512

[SOMMERVILLE-87]
Describing software design methodologies
I. Sommerville, R. Welland, S. Beer
The Computer Journal Vol 30, No 2 1987, p 128-133

[TSE-86]
  Integrating the structured analysis and design models: an initial algebra approach
  T.H. Tse
  The Australian Computer Journal, Vol 18 No 3, August 1986, p 121-127

[WASSERMAN-89]
  Concepts of Object-Oriented Structured Design
  A.I. Wasserman, P.A. Pircher, R.J. Muller
  Interactive Development Environments Inc, 1989

[WARD-89]
  How to integrate object-orientation with structured analysis and design
  P.T. Ward
  IEEE Software March 1989, p 74-82

[YAU-86]
  A survey of software design techniques
  S.S. Yau, J.J.P. Tsai
  IEEE Transactions on Software Engineering Vol SE 12 No 6, June 1986, p 713-721

PART **3**

SYSTEM SPECIFICATION

The first development work phase determines the required system specifications, so that it can subsequently be designed and implemented. Starting from the need expressed by the customer and users, a specification translates this need into a complete external description containing all information necessary for its development.

This is a difficult but essential step, since it is the first and also because it involves a long dialog between specifiers and the customer. Obtaining a complete description implies a transfer of expertise and information from the customer. A specification must also satisfy the request, and this needs verification which can only be done by the customer and users.

Part 3 describes the contents of the specification document and the procedure to be followed to produce it. The specification is defined so that it will be directly usable later in subsequent steps.

Chapter 9 deals with the requirements definition which describes the nature of the request as the expression of a need. Chapter 10 describes the objectives, nature and qualities of a specification. Chapter 11 describes modeling basis and tools available to help produce the specification.

Chapter 12 describes the structure and all components of the specification document, and the procedure to be followed to produce it. This procedure is illustrated by examples for which the solutions will be described in Parts 4 and 5.

9

System Requirements

The first contact between the customer and designers takes place when a need occurs. A customer may be a person, a company or an organization. A need is the apparent necessity for an electronic system-type device (to restrict ourselves to the field considered in this document) leading to improving a situation - quality, productivity, or features.

Designers (in the widest sense) are persons capable of analyzing the need and finding a solution. In the early phases, the work concerns analysts and specifiers, and in later phases it concerns designers and implementers.

Designers may belong to the same organization as the customer: for example they may belong to another department when the organization has the competence internally. However, designers are more usually external; in this case, the product design is subcontracted outside.

The general characteristics of this type of relation are as follows:

- the field concerned by the need has nothing, or little in common with electronic systems;
- the customer or other persons such as the users have an expertise in the product application field;
- designers, specialists in electronic systems, are not necessarily competent in the field of the need;
- typically, the need is neither clearly nor completely expressed to be directly usable by the designers.

The objective of this chapter is to clarify the role of the first contact phase beginning in a need. More specifically, the problem is to start from the initial situation described above and to analyze and synthesize the customer's instructions and requirements.

9.1   THE CUSTOMER: THE SOURCE OF THE NEED

The context in which a need appears can be very varied. Electronics systems as an implementation technology, can provide a solution to a tremendous variety of problems. It is therefore not surprising to realize that the customer does not have the necessary competence to develop the appropriate system. Neither does he have the technical vocabulary necessary to precisely express his need in terms directly usable by electronics designers.

Therefore, the problem to be solved is submitted outside with the objective to satisfy the need. It is then described in a language specific to the application field. The need must be confirmed internally before any external request is made. Is the need really a necessity? This is the first question to be asked. This task is the responsibility of the customer who must carry out a value analysis.

9.2   THE DESIGNER: EXPERT IN THE IMPLEMENTATION FIELD

The problem is explained to specialist designers of electronic and industrial data processing systems. Expressed in a terminology specific to the field of the need, the product definition is probably incomplete and not directly understandable by designers. The problem may not necessarily need the implementation of an electronic type system.

It is therefore unlikely that designers will be presented with a well-defined problem on which they can efficiently work to produce an implementation. It is certain that a large amount of work is necessary to understand the problem and to analyze the need. This work becomes more difficult as the difference between the fields of expertise of the two parties becomes larger.

9.3   THE REQUIREMENTS DEFINITION: EXPRESSION OF THE NEED

The requirements definition is the first document produced by the customer and describes the environment in which the system will exist, the objectives that it must satisfy and its properties and constraints. Its objective is to answer the first essential question which is the WHY of the system. It also acts as a first intermediate point between users who express their needs, and designers who find in it a description of this need [AMGHAR-89].

The description of the need is the result of a customer's discussion with his assistants who want the system, and put themselves in the place of the system to describe its role in the environment. The description then presents:

- a view of the system environment described in the customer's terminology;
- the problem to be solved and all necessary information to use the system;
- the characteristics and all constraints that the system must satisfy.

In general, the contents of the requirements definition are very variable depending on the customer and the problem concerned: very brief or very voluminous, very vague or very specific. As a guide, the customer can take inspiration from recommendation documents for the production of a functional requirements definition, for example such as AFNOR Standard X 50-151 in ISO 9000.

9.4 CUSTOMER'S WISHES

In expressing his problem, the customer expects a quick answer to several points:

- firstly, the feasibility of the problem;
- if feasible:
  - development time
  - development cost
  - reproduction cost if applicable
  - supply description

Based on this answer, the customer can decide whether or not to develop the system. Designers then provide services to the customer.

The customer may also wish to proceed on the basis of a predetermined objective ceiling cost. Determination of the price depends mainly on data external to the product (budget, contracts). In this case, the requirements definition is open and negotiable. Designers' motivation may be increased by a profit sharing principle.

9.5 REQUIREMENTS DEFINITION PURPOSE AND IMPLICATION

Every designer would like a requirements definition correctly defining the environment and system functions. Without questioning the good will of the customer and his ability to prepare this type of document, it is more realistic to assume that the requirements definition will generally be inadequate. Very probably, designers will have to start by producing this document themselves.

Therefore, an essential question arises: what information should be included in this requirements definition? We will return to the objectives to answer this.

The requirements definition clarifies and formalizes the relative responsibilities of the customer and designers. Its objective is thus to act as a contractual document between the customer as a person or organization, and the developers. The designers are then constrained by the contents of this document, since it defines the supply. This document will be used as a reference during the final system certification. This is particularly the case for calls for bids (for example, detailed technical specifications). The document must fully define what the product is to be, and nothing else.

Prior to writing the requirements, the customer or the designers must:

- collect pertinent information about the product under consideration;

- carry out a systematic and exhaustive analysis of the need;

- define appreciation criteria for the result.

However, the responsibility and consequently the freedom of choice of solutions must remain with the designers. The research field is then as wide as possible.

To achieve this objective, a dialog between all partners is essential. As a guide, the following questions define an initial framework for exchange with a customer:

- What are the reasons behind the system development? What are the customer's expectations: market, quality, brand image, etc.?

- Who are the users and how do they intend to use it? What do they expect of it? The nature of their expertise?

- What environmental characteristics does the system have to comply with? Existing or planned interfaces, etc.?

- What functions will the system perform, expressed in the customer's language? What information will it have to manage?

- What are all the constraints - hardware, temporal, economic - with which the system must comply?

- What will be the final form of the product: model, industrial prototype, mass production, product esthetics?

The designer needs to enter into a dialog with the customer, or to facilitate the analysis of an existing document if it is fairly complete. He must also bear in mind that too vague a description makes it difficult to estimate the development feasibility and cost and can therefore produce a high risk for the service company that will carry out the implementation. Similarly, a document which is too detailed, and in particular containing solution outlines, imposes constraints on the implementation. There may be an excess of information for two reasons:

- it may be easier to describe a system which solves a problem than the problem itself;

- the customer is tempted to believe that a document describing only the characteristics to be satisfied makes the designer's work more complicated.

What information should be included in the requirements specification? The following sections describe the structure of its contents.

9.6 REQUIREMENTS CONTENTS AND GUIDE

The procedure used to obtain the requirements is not important in itself. The important point is the quality of the document and the relevance of its contents. Together with a development plan and a cost estimate, it can be used to answer the request for a service. The logical procedure is as follows:

- formulate the need (made by the customer), including a market analysis, a system analysis and a value analysis;
- write a first version of the requirements definition;
- feasibility study and refinement of the need (customer - designers);
- development decision and write the final document.

An outline of the requirements definition is given below, as a guide for its structure:

1. Document introduction
- customer,
- document organization,
- conventions, terminology.

2. Product presentation
- general description of the problem,
- field,
- market,
- objective,
- users, organization,
- statement of need,
- put into operation,
- maintenance.

3. Description of environment
- entities: characteristics,
- information: attributes, relations,
- constraints.

4. Description of functions to be satisfied
- main functions,
- complementary functions,
- configurations, options, variants,
- characteristics and performances.

5. Constraints
- interface constraints,
- real-time constraints,
- usage constraints,
- implementation constraints,
- maintenance and extension,
- operational safety and reliability.

6. Documentation

- specification, design and implementation documents,
- user manuals, installation, maintenance and system management procedures.

7. Certification plan

- results evaluation criteria,
- test situations and scenarios,
- acceptance limits, flexibility.

8. Development plan

- development schedule,
- support for the development.

It is useful to consider the competence necessary to write this type of document. The customer is not always able to do it, and it is not logically the responsibility of the designers. The designers are probably more competent since they have experience in feasibility studies in project development and project management, and are thus aware of the importance of a good requirements definition.

9.7 ANSWER TO A REQUIREMENTS DEFINITION

The customer is responsible for product costs and designers propose a solution to achieve the objective. The requirements definition acts as a basis for consulting potential suppliers. Designers are requested to provide a proposal satisfying the need.

An example of an answer outline is given below which can be used to facilitate evaluation of proposals and, if necessary, make a comparison in the case of a public call for Bids.

1. Supplier description

- organization,
- competence in the field.

2. Description of proposal

- functions satisfied,
- proposed solution (outline, preliminary design),
- basic version, variants, etc.,
- quality, reliability, expandability.

3. Development plan

- schedule,
- support for the development,

4. Cost of service

- development cost (basic, variants),
- reproduction cost,
- installation cost, maintenance costs, etc.

Based on this kind of answer, the customer will have objective elements allowing him to decide on how to proceed with the product. He may decide to stop the project for various reasons - technical, economical, strategic, etc. Otherwise, he can decide to work with a supplier and then enter into the final contract negotiation and signature phase. The final specification will then become a contractual document.

9.8 PROBLEM EXAMPLES

The objectives of the two problems described in this section are first to show the nature of information supplied by the customer, and second to use the description of the two case studies to illustrate all steps of the methodology. Obviously, these are not complete requirements as described above. The examples are simple cases compared with complex problems raised by industrial companies, but are sufficient to help understand the recommended process.

Each designer can also consider various points: what do these problems suggest? Am I competent enough to solve these examples? Is all information available? Am I capable of evaluating the development cost and time? What solution should be adapted? What procedure followed, etc.

9.8.1 Centrifuge speed control system

The objective is to have a system for rotating a motor within a given speed template. A centrifuge is an application example.

However, this type of problem arises in a wide variety of applications - high speed displacement of a trolley (for example, an elevator), control of a furnace in accordance with a temperature template, etc.

More precisely, a motor is required to operate at a constant speed defined by the user before starting the operation. Rotation takes place for a given period, in this case fixed, since the speed increases and decreases at constant acceleration and deceleration. The speed variation chart is given in Figure 9.1.

The times TR, TC, TF are fixed but can be modified for each system.

The user has four push buttons for controlling the system:

- ON and OFF to start the cycle and interrupt it before the end if he wishes;
- MORE and LESS, to adjust the speed control setpoint. This adjustment is incremented each time a key is pressed, but when it is pressed for a long time, the progression becomes geometric: control value modified by single units, then by 10s, then by 100s.

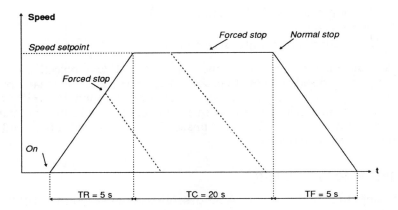

Figure 9.1   Description of a rotation cycle.

A four digit display of the current speed control value is given to assist the user in adjusting the speed. The control value is adjusted before the start of a cycle and it cannot be modified during rotation. The display unit then shows the control value. A red indicator also lights up when the motor is rotating.

The following constraints have to be satisfied:

- time precision: 0.1 %;

- speed precision: 10 rpm on the whole domain;

- PWM output to control the motor: 0.1 %;

- speed measurement with a shaft encoder: 100 pulses/rev;

- motor inertial time: 50 ms.

9.8.2 Automation with a wire-guided trolley

A wire-guided vehicle can be used to carry out handling operations in the workshop without human intervention. The problem is to transfer packets between two platforms.

The vehicle follows a closed trajectory defined by a wire installed in the floor. This wire emits a high frequency wave. The two platforms are on the trajectory.

There is a coupling between the platforms as issuers of commands, and the vehicle which executes them. Transmission takes place using an infrared technique which behaves as an RS232 link. The workshop implementation is shown in Figure 9.2.

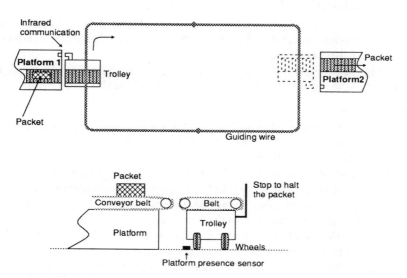

Figure 9.2   Workshop description.

-A- Trolley operation cycle

At rest, the trolley is at platform 1. It must be capable of automatically carrying out a complete cycle: load a packet on the trolley, transport the packet to platform 2, unload the packet, return to platform 1, and wait for the next command.

The following sequence is imposed for a cycle:

- First, platform 1 checks the presence of the trolley. To do this, it sends a presence interrogation message. The trolley immediately answers if it is present. A siren is sounded to inform the operator if platform 1 does not receive any response after time TI.

- If everything works correctly, platform 1 gives the load trolley command which rotates the belt on the trolley platform for a time TC (loading time).

- Platform 1 stops rotating its belt and issues a command to the trolley to go to platform 2.

- When it reaches platform 2, the platform detects the presence of the trolley. If platform 2 does not detect the arrival quickly, the trolley activates its siren.

- Platform 2 gives it the unload command: trolley and platform belt rotation for time TC.

- After TC and when commanded by the platform, the trolley leaves to return to platform 1.

- Its arrival is detected and the cycle can be restarted.

All platform ==> trolley dialog takes place through the infrared link. Detection of presence (and therefore arrival) at a platform is based on detecting the presence of a reflecting mark.

We are not concerned here with what happens when a siren is activated. The operator will take the necessary manual action to repair the installation.

-B- Trolley description

The vehicle has three wheels. The front wheel is free. Each rear wheel is directly controlled by a motor (M1, M2). If the velocities of the two wheels are different, the vehicle is rotated, see Figure 9.3.

The following information helps to understand the imposed operation:

- The nominal vehicle speed, VC, is fixed for each displacement.
- the speed of each wheel must be deduced from an incremental shaft encoder directly coupled to each motor.
- Two analog sensors, C1 and C2, are used to follow the wire. Each sensor translates the received high frequency wave into an analog signal (AC1 and AC2), which is inversely proportional to the distance. If the received wave is too weak, the sensor outputs a zero amplitude. The trolley position relative to the wire will be proportional to (AC1-AC2). The differential speed between the two wheels will thus be proportional to (AC1-AC2).
- The vehicle must stop and activate its siren when one of the two sensors does not detect a signal (trolley too far away) or when the radar on the front detects an obstacle.
- Starting and stopping must take place with linear speed variation in one second.

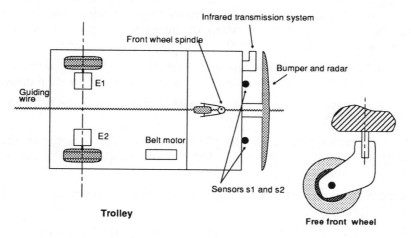

Figure 9.3   Wire-guided vehicle description.

C- Operational and technological characteristics

- The maximum speed VC is 5 km/hour, and the wheel diameter is 30 cm.
- The shaft encoders output 128 pulses/rev.
- For good trajectory following quality, commands must be sent to each motor at intervals such that the displacement does not exceed 2 cm.
- The accuracy of the speed must be 5%, and sensors C1 and C2 have a precision of 1%. The radar detector outputs a logical TTL level.
- Infrared link exchanges take place at 2400 bauds.
- An 8-bit microprocessor technology may be used.

9.9 SUMMARY

This chapter described the context and procedure for setting up a contractual relation between a customer and designers.

The essential points to be retained are as follows:

- A need is never clearly defined. A significant amount of collaboration between the various partners is necessary to produce an explicit document.

- The requirements definition document, if it is sufficiently explicit, can be used as a basis for inviting proposal from potential companies.

- The requirements definition and development proposals can help to decide the future of the product. If an implementation is required, a collaboration agreement will result in a development contract.

- Knowing how to write a requirements definition correctly is a result of experience, which is acquired gradually after developing and then managing projects.

10

SYSTEM SPECIFICATIONS

The requirements are expressed and written by the customer. They are used as a basis for initial discussions with the designers and are therefore a statement of the problem to be solved. This type of document describing the WHY is obviously very incomplete and does contain enough information to decide upon the implementation. However, before starting any collaboration, a financial estimate must be made initially that will lead to the signature of an agreement or a development contract. The estimating error at this stage may be very large.

Based on the requirements definition, customers and designers together have to carry out an initial brainstorming session to clearly express the objective to be achieved. The specifications are intermediate between the request and the design, and are useful to both partners:

- First to the customer, since he can be sure that his problem has been correctly interpreted by the designers, and that the implementation at the end of the development will comply with his wishes. The specification work may also bring out unexpressed needs, leading to better quality for the customer.

- Second to the designers, since in getting a precise idea of the problem raised, they can efficiently undertake the design and then the implementation work. A better estimate of the design cost is also possible, which may lead to an improvement in the service contract.

This chapter justifies the essential role played by a specification and describes its nature relative to the requirements. The qualities of a specification are then stated, together with an outline of the document contents and the basis for writing it.

10.1 SPECIFICATION ROLE

We will first analyze the situation of the various partners in a development to determine the precise role of a specification.

10.1.1 Distance between customer and designers

The customer, in the general sense as the requester of a development has expertise in the field of activity in which the system will be used. This field may have nothing in common with the designer's field of expertise, which in our case is that of electronic systems.

The wish expressed by the customer, transformed into an obligation in the form of a requirements definition, thus generally contains little information which can be directly understood and used by the designers. The designer may think he has understood the request, by visualizing a product useful to the customer, based on his own competence.

Due to the difference in fields of expertise between the two types of partners, the chances of success are low, unless a common effort is made to transfer knowledge between the customer and the designers. The designers may feel that the developed product is satisfactory, but it may be inappropriate and unusable by users.

10.1.2 Diversity of customer partners

To understand all the aspects of the problem, it is useful to know the various participants concerned, by the product at the customer's side. The term "customer" thus covers the following categories:

- The system purchaser, often a service negotiator and scheduler. He is the technical and/or financial manager for the operation. His objective is to satisfy the problem at minimum cost and within the stated deadlines, and to integrate this product into his organization's development plans.

- The users, very often different from the customer site development manager, will have to use the requested system. They are concerned by functionalities, performances and operating procedures. Users may be divided into categories, depending on the complexity of the system. The work method and the competence of this personnel category are indispensable elements to be considered if the product is to be a success.

- Installers, who will be concerned by the system on-site installation procedure. Some of the objectives to be satisfied are simplicity and low cost.

- The maintenance team, which must be concerned with qualities such as product maintainability, documentation, solution understandability, maintenance methods, etc.

- Manufacturers, when the system must be reproduced within the organization or by subcontracting for distribution of many copies. Methods managers are concerned with industrial reproduction qualities of the prototype.

Due to the diversity of people concerned with the product, each with his own objectives and constraints which are not necessarily compatible, the design of a system satisfactory to all of them becomes a difficult task.

10.1.3 Importance of verification

Allowing for the situation of each partner concerned by the result, it is obvious that the first essential task for designers is to get a good understanding of the problem. The work procedure, the dialog, thoroughness and objectivity in the analysis are essential points which help to produce successful results.

However, do the designers have a guarantee that they have correctly understood the problem? If there is no intermediate check, they proceed with the development and then the implementation. The resulting product can only be observed when it is finalized, and it will obviously then be checked by the customer. It is quite likely that some aspects will not be acceptable, for several reasons:

- The expression of the need in the requirements definition is not exhaustive, so that different interpretations are possible.

- Customer requirements can evolve during the development period. This point must be considered, since it is an inevitable situation.

- The designer's idea of the product may also evolve, but not in the same direction as the customer, due to the difference of competences and fields of activity.

- Without understandable information from the designers about what the system will be, the customer has a gradual tendency to doubt the results while waiting for the product.

These risks should be avoided. It is essential that the designer's understanding of the problem is checked. This check is obviously carried out by the customer, and results in:

- improving the resulting system definition;

- creating a climate of confidence between the customer and the designers, since as a result of analyzing the understanding, the customer has a precise vision of the final product, thus reducing his doubts;

- refining the definition and the limits of the contract, thus avoiding end of contract problems.

It is also essential that a description base is available for checking, despite the difference in fields of expertise between the two partners.

10.1.4 A specification as a formal verifiable document

To formalize understanding of the problem and the objective to be achieved, an intermediate document is necessary between the requirements expressing the WHY and the solution developed by the designers expressing the HOW. This intermediate description (the WHAT) must be verifiable by the customer for validation, and be directly usable by designers to search for and validate this solution.

This intermediate document is called the problem specification as shown in Figure 10.1.

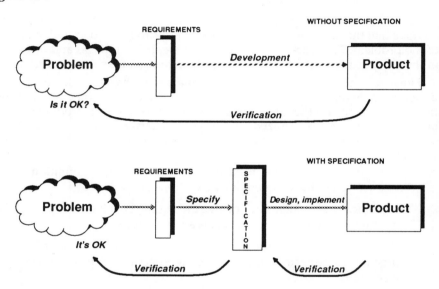

Figure 10.1   Advantage of a detailed specification.

The specification document is an essential interface between the customer and the designers, determined from the requirements by discussion with the customer and usable by designers to express a solution. It is used to correct the fact that what is not specified cannot be checked, and what is not checked may be wrong.

To better understand the meaning of the term "specification", we will consider an existing product such as an integrated VLSI component. For its use, the manufacturer produces a user document, which is in fact a detailed component specification. The available description is an external view of the component which describes its properties. In this case, a specification is of the same nature but has to be produced before the design.

As a definition, a specification describes the complete external characteristics of the system to be designed which operates in the environment specified in the requirements definition. It is therefore a description of a system as seen from outside, and which possesses properties and qualities expressed by the customer (WHAT), whereas the requirements describe the properties and constraints to be satisfied (WHY).

Consequently, an essential difference is made in MCSE between the requirements and the specifications, confirmed by many authors [ABBOTT-86, LUDEWIG-87, WARD-85, HATLEY-87, DAVIS-90].

Obviously, this intermediate step apparently increases the amount of work at the beginning of the project. Mentioned by Ludewig and Matheis in the software field, which can be extrapolated without major errors to electronic systems, almost two-thirds of the total cost of a project is related to activities which arise after debugging starts. This results in a high cost of corrective and evolutive maintenance. This cost goes down if the number of corrections and modifications are reduced, and by reducing the development complexity - complexity of circuits and boards for hardware and the number of program lines for the software. Similarly, Ramamoorthy [RAMAMOORTHY-87] indicates that 30% of errors found during testing and the start of running are due to a poor understanding of the problem, and very often lack of thoroughness of the user needs in the requirements definition.

A good specification helps to reduce these points. In order to reduce the global cost of a development, it is better to spend more time on the specification phase. Figure 10.2 [LUDEWIG-87] shows the advantage of this type of investment in a software project.

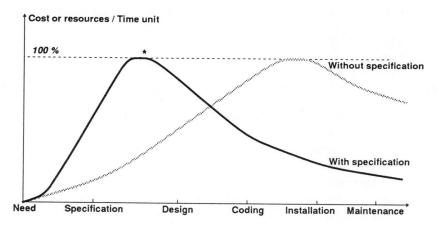

Figure 10.2   Effort per phase with and without specification.

The point marked * is critical for project control. It is the stage at which the specification is not yet completely coherent but at which the design has already been started based on the incomplete specifications. This is therefore the time at which the team may start to doubt the need for a good specification.

Parnas gives other advantages of a complete specification [PARNAS-86]:

- Duplications and inconsistencies must be avoided. Without a document, the same questions arise at different stages and different answers may be given.
- A complete document is also necessary to make a good estimate of the necessary work and resources.
- This is also a guarantee if personnel are transferred.
- It can be used to prepare a test plan.
- It can be used for a long time after the system has been put into operation.
- It serves as an interface between customer and designer, and exchanges are thus reduced.
- It can act as a negotiation and reference document for other similar jobs (reuse).

Ideally, this document would be written by users or their representatives. In fact, users are not often competent to carry out this task. Consequently, designers have to carry out this work and then have the result analyzed by the customer.

10.2 NATURE OF THE SPECIFICATION

Due to the essential role played by a specification, the first step of understanding and formalizing the problem is particularly difficult. The specifier's competence is essential for the success of the project. Before discussing the procedure to be followed, we will consider the nature of a specification.

The starting point for the discussion is that it is an intermediate step which can be verified by the customer and used by designers, despite the difference in expertise between the two parties. First, it is a paper document. There may also be a prototype for a subset of the project. This is the case for the specification by prototyping approach.

Subsequently and ideally [LUDEWIG-87, ABBOTT-86] the specification document should be:

- correct: it must reflect needs;
- complete: it must contain all characteristics and constraints;
- coherent: no ambiguities or contradictions;
- understandable: structured to facilitate reading, and easy to interpret both by the customer and designers;
- checkable: it must be possible to check the specification validity;
- usable by designers to efficiently deduce a solution;
- easy to write and modifiable: it must be possible to write the specification on paper and it must be easy to change it to incorporate missing items or required modifications.

To satisfy these objectives, a specification must respect the qualities described in the next section.

10.3 SPECIFICATION CHARACTERISTICS

The quality of a specification document can be evaluated by considering the following three points:

1. Understandability: a specification must be clear, unambiguous, and be written in a language accessible to the two groups of readers.

2. Testability: designers and the customer must be able to check conformity of the implementation with the specifications.

3. Maintainability: since needs generally tend to evolve during the design and implementation phases, specifications must be easily modifiable. If the document does not incorporate all accepted modifications made during design and implementation, it may be very difficult to check the results.

If it is to satisfy the objectives stated in the previous section, the specification document must satisfy at least the following characteristics.

-A- Communication support

A specification has been justified as an interface between the customer and designers to reduce distance and to create a basis for verification. Communication problems cannot easily be solved if there is no common language. As an intermediate step, the synthesis document can formalize the communication procedure. At the customer end, persons concerned first must answer questions raised by the specifier during the dialog, so that he can extract the essential elements and formalize them in the specification. Then as reader, the customer approves it or corrects errors and omissions. At the designer end, the document allows global transmission of information, thus avoiding repetition at different stages and inconsistent solutions.

-B- Structure

A specification is a reference: it is therefore necessary for it to follow, as for all documents of this type, a logical outline to facilitate its reading, occasional references and modifications.

A good document structure facilitates understanding, checking and use by designers. For the customer and therefore for users, the specification structure must be such that the system environment, well known by the reader, is described first, followed by a description of the functions of the system acting on this environment.

For designers, the document structure must facilitate the progressive search for a solution considering a functional approach to the subject, and later as an implementation support.

-C- *Simplicity and suitability*

Understanding is a function of the simplicity of the specification description. It is well known that graphical descriptions simplify understanding. However, symbols used must be clear enough to completely and unambiguously express a meaning. The choice of specification tools referred to in subsequent specification models is important to give the best compromise between simplicity, suitability and understandability.

-D- *Description accuracy*

The objective for a development is to reduce its cost. An attempt must be made to maximize automation in producing the solution and the corresponding implementation. Automatic production necessitates a formal specification of an object as an intermediate step between the need and the product. It is also necessary to be able to formalize the solution production procedure. To move in this direction, the use of formal specifications has to be increased, maintaining customer understandability for checking purposes.

-E- *Complexity management*

Specification models or tools must be able to describe all levels of system complexity. Due to limitations of the human brain to manage all the details of a complex system, specification tools must facilitate partitioning a system into subsystems. The specification must be based on hierarchical models for description by levels, and conceptual or abstract rather than physical models in order to eliminate details. A specification can thus be used to describe the system at different levels of detail and by parts.

10.4 SPECIFICATION CONTENT GUIDELINES

First, consider two quite different aspects:

- the specification document as a final result;
- the method used to obtain the document.

The essential point for the customer and designer is the final document. However, the cost of obtaining this document can be reduced by using a suitable method and by having specific analyst competence.

Like every document, the specification document must be structured. The plan and contents must answer the questions raised by its readers as clearly as possible. Before writing, each specification author must previously consider the following common sense questions:

- What questions should the document answer?
- Who are the readers?
- How will they use the document?
- What knowledge is necessary to understand it?

The document structure is a result of consideration of the above points. The following outline is given as a plan for writing specifications. Chapter 12 describes the contents of each part in detail.

1. Problem presentation: specification, brief analysis, terminology.

2. Characteristics and modeling of the environment for the product to be implemented.

3. System input and output specifications.

4. Functional specifications: system function description.

5. Operational specifications: operation sequence, accuracy.

6. Technological specifications: implementation constraints.

7. Additional information (technical explanations, documentation sources, etc.).

This plan shows that the specifier gradually builds up the document based on his meetings with all customer participants. He starts by acquiring expertise by analyzing the environment, and then gradually characterizes the system by successive refinements. The customer checks the document during its production.

10.5 SPECIFICATION WORK PROBLEMS

The specifier is in a difficult intermediate position between the customer and designers. The customer, as order issuer, is observer and judge of the results. Designers and implementers carry out a well-defined and interesting technical job, and relations between them are fairly simple since they work in the same field of expertise.

The situation is very different for the specifier. Relations with the customer (and therefore with all participants) and with designers require a constant negotiation effort. Occasionally, some participants are hostile to any dialog.

A specification is never finalized or entirely satisfactory. It is a result of compromises and the specifier, constrained by time, may feel frustrated. Moreover, the lack of methods and tools makes the task particularly difficult.

To specify correctly, he must be able to evaluate product feasibility and produce a cost estimate. For feasibility, the specifier must be able to determine possible solutions, justifying his design and implementation competence. The cost estimate is another difficulty since this type of expertise can only be acquired based on experience, and identical situations never arise.

A specification plays a defensive type of role. It is much more necessary to prevent errors than to guarantee success. Designers are naturally tempted to blame the intermediate specifications when difficulties arise, and the same applies for the customer who considers the specifier as responsible for the project.

Even if the specification results in a significant improvement on the project cost over the entire life cycle, nothing proves that this improvement is due to the specification phase. The additional cost of this task may even be individually identified.

Despite all these difficulties, industrial companies are more and more aware of the importance of a good specification, probably as a result of a defensive reaction resulting from multiple observations in difficulties in completing projects. The specifier's job is also essential, and even fascinating. At this point, we may quote DeMarco: *"So analysis is frustrating, full of complex interpersonal relations, indefinite and difficult. In a word, it is fascinating. Once you're hooked, the old easy pleasures of system building are never again enough to satisfy you!!"* [DEMARCO-79].

10.6 COMPETENCE FOR SPECIFYING

Specifications are deduced from information given by the customer. This task is not as simple as it appears. It is probably the most difficult task in the system development cycle.

At least three essential qualities are necessary if a good result is to be obtained: adaptable, communicative, and an analytic mind.

-A- Adaptable

Starting from a generalist competence, essential due to the variety of electronic system application fields, the specifier must be capable of acquiring the expertise necessary in the customer's field to be able to write the specification. Since the document must be usable by designers, he must also be an expert in electronic systems in order to be able to evaluate feasibility and to express specifications in terms which can be understood by the designers.

-B- Communicative

In order to acquire the expertise in the field under consideration, he must listen to all customer participants, who may not themselves be capable of judging the relevance of some aspects. It is thus up to the specifier to decide upon the essential points and to induce the dialog in order to efficiently obtain all necessary information.

He must also be able to clearly, synthetically and adequately express the system description to make it understandable by the two partners.

-C- Analytic mind

The specifier has an essential responsibility in the success of the project. The relevance of his analysis, guiding him in his interrogations and dialogs with the project partners, is an essential quality for success. On the other hand, he must eliminate all preconceived solutions from his mind. To isolate the important points will require a great deal of imagination. If the customer has no clearly defined ideas, the specifier's creative mind can help to improve quality.

10.7 SUMMARY

This chapter has shown the importance of the specification as an intermediate step between the requirements definition and the implementation. The main points discussed are as follows:

- The specification is a checkable document which can help to give a better understanding of the problem.

- To play its role correctly, the document must be understandable both by the customer and designers. It must therefore be easy to write, easy to read and easy to modify.

- The specifier has a particularly difficult job, which has an essential but immeasurable impact on the project. He must be competent in many fields.

11

MODELING CONCEPTS

The previous chapters showed the advantage and necessity for an intermediate description between the customer and designers. This description is called the specification and is essentially a document.

Two important points should then be considered: the contents of this document (information nature and structure), and the method used to produce this type of document. We will first consider the form and contents of the document and we will then describe the method.

The purpose of a specification is to characterize a system or a product to be designed without considering its internal structure: the WHAT and not the HOW. Describing a system from a purely external point of view is equivalent to producing a behavioral model of it. Any implementation with the properties of this model will comply with the specifications. The specification must be easy to write, easy to understand and easy to modify. To satisfy these objectives, a specification must comply with a specification model which has the properties and qualities expected of all specifications.

The first important question to ask in order to obtain a specification model is therefore: how can we model any system without describing its internal solution, since this is the unknown to be defined subsequently during the design?

The objective of this chapter is to answer this main question. First, note that the choice of a model is a real problem due to the large number of papers and books on the subject. However, the model type depends on the problem class considered. Therefore, in MCSE we have considered a combination of several description model types instead of a single model.

11.1   WHAT MUST BE CHARACTERIZED?

A specification is a purely external description of the object concerned. For any application requiring an electronic system, the system is never isolated from the rest of the world. Otherwise, without external links and therefore inputs and outputs, it would be of no use even if it were active; nothing could act on it nor observe the result of its activity.

Every system is therefore necessarily implied within an environment containing objects. Figure 11.1 shows the normal situation for a system. Objects may have various natures.

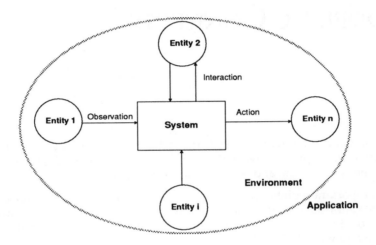

Figure 11.1   The system to be specified and its environment.

We will first define the terminology used.

An "application" in the physical sense of the term is considered here as the closed system (having no useful relation with the outside for the problem to be solved), formed by the system to be designed and objects related to it.

The "environment" is all application objects, excluding the system.

Objects in the environment are called "entities". An object has a dynamic behavior and has its own independence. It is necessarily a functional reality, but not necessarily physical.

An entity, like a system, has inputs and outputs and at least one internal state which characterizes its situation at any instant. It can be modeled by an external and internal description.

An entity strongly coupled to the system by inputs and outputs will be considered interacting with the system. This is naturally the case, for example, for the user entity.

As an illustration, consider the example of a control system for automatically loading a trolley. The objective of the application is to move material from P1 to P2 using a trolley. An electronic system is used to automatically carry out a complete cycle whenever an operator makes a cycle request: P2 ==> P1 ==> load ==> P2 ==> dump.

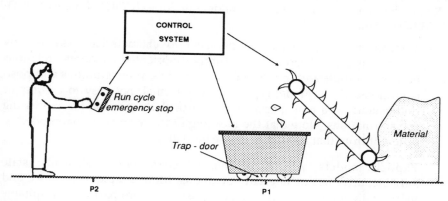

Figure 11.2   Application example.

This application includes four entities: the control system, the operator, the trolley, the belt-loader. Each entity has an internal state - position for the trolley, rotating or not rotating for the belt-loader - and an independent behavior influenced by its inputs.

The functionality of the application which is to automatically execute a cycle, is a result of the system entity providing coupling between the three other entities. The global behavior cannot be correct unless the system observes information such as the trolley position and user request in its environment, and acts on the trolley and the belt-loader.

Therefore, a system is mandatorily linked to the entities in its environment. To characterize the system, its inputs and outputs must be characterized too. System inputs are entity outputs defining their state, and system outputs are entity inputs and therefore action controls. The external description of the system behavior inevitably involves characterization of the entities.

Therefore, characterizing the system to deduce its specification concerns:

- its environment;

- its inputs/outputs;

- its behavior;

- its use.

11.2 CHARACTERIZATION NATURE: MODELING

The environment entities exist or will exist. Characterizing them is equivalent to describing the nature and behavior of each entity at a given level of detail. A real object therefore has to be modeled in the form of an abstraction. The concept of model, its types and qualities were described in Part 2 Chapter 8. Remember that there are two main model categories [COHEN-86, ALFORD-82, ABBOTT-86]:

- **External models**, which can be used to characterize a system by expressing its properties only (property-oriented): axioms, relations between outputs and inputs, algebraic models, pre-conditions and post-conditions. These model types are very formal, not easy to express or understand for a non-specialist and particularly suitable for expressing transformations. Note that the meaning of the term "external model" is different from that used in database modeling.

- **Explicit models**, which use internal characteristic elements: state variable, activities or internal operations. More simple to produce and more easily interpreted by non-specialists, they are particularly suitable for describing existing objects.

The model abstraction level is a function of the required behavioral details. For example, the trolley in the previous example can be modeled at least at two different levels:

- a macroscopic level, at which the trolley speed is represented by three values: 0 for stop, +VM for displacement to the right and -VM for displacement to the left;

- a more microscopic level, at which the trolley speed is a continuous function of the control input and the load which introduces an inertia effect.

On the other hand, a model can contain different views of the same object. This is then different projections of the object in its description space: for example static description, dynamic description, data description, activity description, etc.

11.3 ENTITY MODELING

Before discussing description models, we will first analyze what is an entity and what are the essential elements to describe it. Note that this analysis will also be used as a basis for the system specification since the system can be considered as an entity with the special property of not existing before its implementation.

11.3.1 Nature of an entity

An entity is a conceptual object for the application. It may have a physical or material existence, such as an operator or the trolley, but it may also be a functional or logical object for example, a department within a company, or a purely abstract object such as an aircraft flight which is a result of associating physical objects and data (aircraft, passengers, trajectory, etc.). An entity has its own identity defined by its name.

To facilitate modeling, entities are grouped into categories each of which has common characteristics. Each category is named thus defining an entity type - an entity name E is said to be of type T. E is also called an instance of T.

All entities of a single type are generally different. This is due to different values of the characteristic elements. We then say that elements of the entity type are its attributes. For example, a person as an entity type has weight and height as attributes.

11.3.2 Nature of characteristic elements

An entity type can be characterized by a set of elements and relations. This characterization is made using a model which expresses characteristic information of the object and relations between them.

In order to define appropriate model classes, we will consider categories of characteristic elements. For the kind of entities used in electronic systems, three element categories have to be considered:

- events
- data
- actions and activities

We will explain the nature of each category.

-A- Event

An event specifies the instant at which a significant state change takes place. This instant is therefore associated with a meaning. Two event types are useful for systems:

- A state change. The event name directly and completely defines the meaning. For example, event T50 means that the temperature has just exceeded 50°C.
- A data item occurrence. This event type is associated with a data item. The event defines the instant of occurrence and so the availability of the data item. The data item enhances the meaning of the event. For example, to the "temperature setpoint value has just been modified" event is associated the new setpoint value.

To avoid any ambiguity in the terminology when a distinction is necessary, the first type is called event and the second information. Thus, information has a limited existence in time and is characterized by its type which is that of the associated data item.

-B- Data item

A data item is a variable (or a set of variables), the existence of which is considered to be permanent. Its value only evolves with time. For example, the trolley is characterized by several variables which are its attributes: position, speed, quantity of transported material. We also say that a data item is a characteristic variable of the entity. A data item is defined by its type characterized by attributes with values domain.

A state variable is an important special case of a permanent variable acting to uniquely characterize the situation of the entity at the required abstraction level. An entity state is represented by the set of variables strictly necessary to characterize it at any instant. The nature of state variables depends on the required modeling type. For example for the trolley, modeling the behavior of the trolley requires that its speed V and position P are taken into account at all times. For a more macroscopic model, we may be satisfied with two discrete states P and V where:

- for position P: $P \leq P2$, $P2 < P < P1$, $P \geq P1$;
- for speed V: stop, left move, right move.

-C- Action and activity

An action is considered as an instantaneous operation acting at a given instant during the evolution of the entity. It is undecomposable. It is also said to be an atomic operation.

An activity represents a higher level view. It represents a sequence of actions. An activity thus covers a time period, also called a phase.

An activity can be characterized by a state, whereas an action is characterized by an event. For example, the action of starting the trolley by the system generates an event for the controlled entity, thus leading to the displacement activity and therefore the "displacement" state.

The boundary between action and activity is not very precise. Depending on the model level (for example, time scale), an action considered to be instantaneous for a microscopic level is an activity for a more detailed model. For example, the stop trolley action is not instantaneous if its inertia is taken into account.

11.3.3 Dependency between characteristic elements

Action and activity are the only types of generating (and therefore active) elements. The dependency relationship is indicated in Figure 11.3.

Since an action is atomic, its intervention time can only be determined by an event. Thus, an action is a response to an event. On the other hand, an activity may be in the active or inactive state. A state can only be changed by an event. If there is no input event the activity will always be effective, otherwise it would be useless.

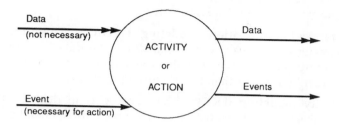

Figure 11.3   Dependency between element classes.

Activities and actions can produce events and information, modify data and states. For an action or activity input, and to distinguish between a data item or event, we will use a single arrow to denote events (and therefore also for information) and a double arrow for data, as proposed by Ward [WARD-85].

11.3.4 Nature of inputs and outputs

The dynamic nature of an entity is the result of internal actions and activities. The only coupling with its environment is through events/information, data and states.

As an input to the entity, data and states can be observed at any time (read). Events and information are fugitive: information no longer has any meaning after it has been taken into account. As output, data and states allow permanent external observations, whereas events and information generate external actions.

11.4   THREE VIEWS FOR AN ENTITY DESCRIPTION

Bearing the previous analysis in mind, how can an entity be modeled? The three essential elements are data, event, activity, so that:

- a state is a special case of data;
- an information is an event with a significant contents defined by its data type;
- an activity is a group of actions. An action can therefore also be understood as an atomic activity.

Dependency relations have to be added to these elements.

The structure of a data item has to be defined unless it is an elementary type. An activity only exists during periods in time. Characterizing an activity necessitates first, that it is detailed (for example by a specification), and second, that its external action in time is described, making it necessary to express temporal dependencies using events or information.

Due to the lack of a single model containing all these characteristics (see Section 8.2.1), a coherent description for an entity requires three complementary views shown in Figure 11.4.

- **Data and information modeling** (WHAT). This describes the characteristics of each data item. When the data is compound, the structure and definition domain type of each basic constituent have to be described. This is therefore exclusively a structural and static model.

- **Activity modeling** (HOW). The purpose is to describe the entity activities and relations with its environment by data and events. This is also a structural model.

- **Behavioral model** (WHEN). This involves describing the instants at which events and information appear, together with data state changes generated by activities. This is equivalent to modeling the behavior which may be that of activities or of data evolution.

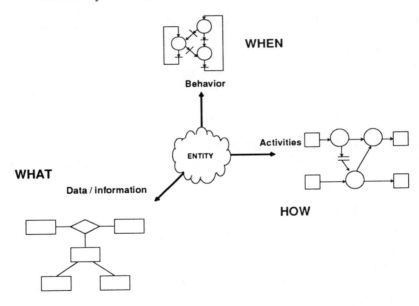

Figure 11.4   The three views for an entity modeling.

These three views are complementary and undissociable. To characterize an activity, the data used and produced have to be known. To characterize an entity, all activities and the reactions of each to input stimulus have to be known. Global coherence is a result of a correct specification for each view, thus providing a verification method because there is some redundancy between the evolution of data and of activities, since activities modify data.

The overriding effect of data on activities has to be recognized. The data for an entity (obviously as a type) is more stable than functions and their behavior. Hence the prime importance is attached to data in the model.

The result of this analysis is in agreement with modeling procedures recommended by other authors for real-time systems. Hatley recommends a two-view model: activities, behavior for control. In Appendix C of his book, he describes the third data view [HATLEY-87]. Ward and Mellor consider the three views of the model [WARD-85].

In the remainder of this chapter, we will describe the model recommended in MCSE for each of the three views. Some models have already been introduced in Part 2 and are repeated here so that this part can be read and used independently.

11.5 DATA/INFORMATION MODELING

Concerning data and information only, this modeling view is independent of the other two views. The objectives of the model are as follows:

- to allow a complete, concise and understandable definition of the nature and structure of the data: category, composition, type of each component;

- to be suitable for a large class of data: from Boolean to relations;

- be conceptual to exclusively describe the meaning and not an implementation.

11.5.1 Two-level models

The data modeling subject has been widely developed in the literature. Many authors have dealt with it [ABBOTT-86, DEMARCO-79, JACKSON-83, WARD-85, HATLEY-87, MARTIN-88]. The approach described here is similar to that for object-oriented models, and is therefore not limited to relational type models [DATE-86, GALACSI-86-89, BAILLY-87, VELEZ-89]. It is based on the idea that a data item (as a type) can be described from two element categories:

- the data entity (or the data object);

- the relation.

The data entity is considered here as a coherent set of attributes concerning a single subject. On the other hand, a relation expresses one fact among several subjects; it is therefore not a hierarchical dependency.

To avoid any ambiguity of interpretation, the subjects (or objects) are called entities within this book. For modeling by data, it is not necessary to know the entity behavior. It is sufficient simple to know the possible entity states. In this case, an entity can be modeled by a set of attributes defining and fully characterizing the data, hence the name data entity. For example, sufficient attributes for a car may be: purchase date, owner, registration number.

A relation concerns interrelated data to express a fact. For example, for the fact that "a person is the owner of a vehicle", the property relation links the two entities: the person and the vehicle.

An appropriate model exists for each of the two categories (see Section 8.3.2):

- The **hierarchical composition model** for data entities based on three operators: composition, alternative and set. This model is usual. Authors use fairly similar notations: graphic notation by Jackson, syntactical notation by DeMarco, Ward and Hatley. The dependency concept which is called the inheritance concept can also be added; an object (and therefore a data item in the special case) inherits all characteristics of the object on which it depends. This dependency limited to the data item leads to the type concept: a data item is defined by its type.

- The Chen **entity/relation model**, also with notation variants [MARTIN-88].

Figure 11.5 shows a graphical representation of the model for each category. The meaning of symbols is defined in the following sections.

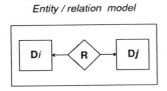

Entity / relation model

Hierarchical composition model

Figure 11.5   Data model.

Note that each model allows description of each Data item Di by refinement using one of the two models: decomposition into relations, decomposition into more elementary data. This model is therefore more general than the relational model; it is closer to the object model for which modeling is done by abstraction mechanisms such as aggregation, classification, composition-decomposition, generalization-specialization.

11.5.2 Model for the data entity description

Three essential aspects are used to characterize this kind of data, namely meaning, composition, and type [WARD-85]. The structural model is based on the three fundamental operators: concatenation, selection, repetition (set).

A data entity is represented by a rectangle, particularly when it is a basic data item. The data type is indicated in the rectangle and the data name is placed outside it.

The following graphical and textual conventions are used for the hierarchical composition description:

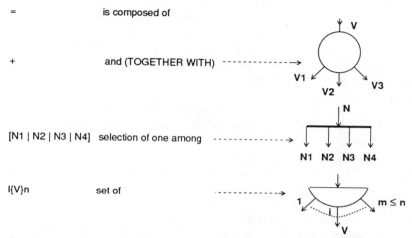

=	is composed of
+	and (TOGETHER WITH)
[N1 | N2 | N3 | N4]	selection of one among
l{V}n	set of

l and n are the minimum and maximum numbers of elements in the set. By default, the limits of a set are 0 and infinity.

The following example in Figure 11.6 shows the hierarchical and graphical model for structured data and shows the equivalent textual notation.

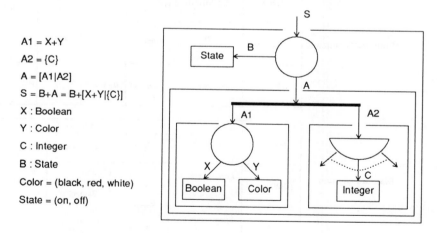

A1 = X+Y
A2 = {C}
A = [A1|A2]
S = B+A = B+[X+Y|{C}]
X : Boolean
Y : Color
C : Integer
B : State
Color = (black, red, white)
State = (on, off)

Figure 11.6   Data entity description example.

For the syntactical notation, the composition and type of a data item are thus defined by the "=" symbol, whereas the definition range is specified by ":". S can also be globally written:

$$S = B\text{:state} + [X\text{:Boolean} + Y\text{:color} \mid \{C\text{:integer}\}]$$

For the structural model, each element designated by a link, has a name and is defined by a data type. A specific data item as part of an entity is designated by the concatenation of path names on the link leading to this data item.

For the above example, an element i of the set (C) is then designated by S.A2.C[i]. When a basic item is involved, the item name and its type name may be confused in a structure. For example, the name B is not mandatory and it is possible to write S = State:(On,Off) + A.

The proposed notation clearly identifies the three data categories. These conventions are classical, and similar symbols are used by other authors [DEMARCO-79], [JACKSON-83], [WARD-85], [HATLEY-87]. Jackson's notation for data is given in Section 8.3.2.

Data considered to be elementary since non-decomposible, have attributes specified on a definition domain. Normal types are those used in programming - Boolean, integer, real, enumeration, etc.

To improve the data specification, particularly related to a specific application, it is useful to consider all information defining each item. Its attributes are properties which particularize this data item in a set of values. A value is associated with each attribute.

Figure 11.7 illustrates a few examples of usual variables.

	Name	Definition	Attributes			
			Unit	Range	Resolution	Period
Continuous signals	POSITION	Trolley position	Meter	0 - 10	0.01	10 ms
	VM	Engine speed	Lap/mn	0 - 6 000	1	Permanent

	Name	Definition	Attributes		
			Nb of values	Value name	Acquis.
Discrete signals	CMD	Engine control	3	Stop Forward Backward	20 ms
	STATE	Speed state	4	Stop Acceleration Constant Deceleration	Permanent

Figure 11.7   Information or data definition examples.

Conventional data attributes in real-time systems are thus:
- the information type;
- the definition domain or limits;

- the precision (or resolution);
- the unit;
- the signal evolution period (for sampled signals).

Example: SPEED = *type: real, limits: 0-200, precision: 1, unit: KPH*;
                VM: SPEED;

11.5.3 Relation description model

Apart from individually identified data, understanding of an entity or a set of entities may require expressing relations. This is particularly true for applications which require the use of databases [WARD-85, MARTIN-88]. Understanding an entity may also necessitate describing relations between entities. For example, a bank customer has an account, writes checks, and regularly receives a statement. These phrases may be translated directly in the form of relations.

A RELATION expresses a fact between entities (see also Section 8.3.2-B). The notation in Figure 11.8 represents a relation. Rectangles are data entity types, and diamonds and links express the relation.

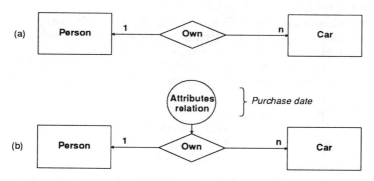

Figure 11.8   Graphical representation of a relation.

The chart in Figure 11.8 shows that a person owns a vehicle. This could also be written using the notation: owns(person, vehicle). Subjects, objects and names are thus entities. The verb expresses a relation. Note that in this notation, each rectangle represents the entity type and not the entity instance. In this case too, there are several graphical models, all meaning the same thing.

Very often, a relation in itself must also possess attributes. These attributes are represented by a circle and are property modifiers for the relation. For example, a purchase date can be added to relation (a) in the figure.

A relation link may concerns several entities of the same type, where each entity is identifiable. If one person has several vehicles, rather than being satisfied by the number, each car will be defined by its registration number, its make, etc. The cardinality of an entity in a relation (according to Chen's notation) is defined by a number on the relation link. In Figure 11.8, 1 means that each vehicle has one and only one owner and then specifies that one person may own several vehicles.

Very recent object-oriented specification methods are based on an approach by relations [BAILIN-89, KURTZ-89, COAD-90, RUMBAUGH-91]. Their objectives are to subsequently facilitate an object-oriented design.

11.5.4 Data modeling technique

Keeping to the data view only, an entity can be described by a static model. It is then characterized by all its specific data items, each possessing values which define its state at all times. The environment can observe the entity state through its outputs, and can modify the state through its inputs by changing values.

This is the simplest model. It is a combinational or operational type description: states always depend only on inputs.

This type of model is obviously the first to be considered. It can be used to deduce the main information and state variables of an entity, and then their relations with the inputs and outputs. Even if it proves to be inadequate, it facilitates more complex modeling later.

As a first illustration, the trolley example given at the beginning of the chapter in Section 11.1 can be modeled by a single variable which is its state, and which can take on three values - right_displacement, left_displacement, idle. The state depends directly on the input command which is defined by three possible values - forward, reverse, stop. The trolley can then be modeled as follows:

TROLLEY_STATE = (case CMD:

      FORWARD --> Right_displacement;

      REVERSE --> Left_displacement;

      STOP --> Idle);

If the possible values of the internal state and the input are the same, we can write TROLLEY_STATE: (forward, reverse, stop) = CMD.

The second example for the automatic speed control and maintenance of a vehicle can be modeled by a state including:

- the number of kilometers;
- the current speed;
- each time the tank is filled, the fuel quantity information.

This is written:

VEHICLE_STATE = KM_NB: integer + speed: integer + Q_fuel: integer;

As a final example, an operator using the centrifuge described in Section 9.8.1. may decide to stop or start the motor or to change the control speed. This is translated into an information item specified by:

COMMAND = [START | STOP | VCONTROL: 0...3000 rpm].

11.6 BEHAVIOR MODELING

The objective of behavior models is to express dependencies between events and actions for an entity. Behaviorally, an entity is in a state corresponding to a phase or a step. An event or input data generates a change in behavior and therefore causes a state change.

When the entity is modeled by data (or state as a special case), a behavioral type model describes the data item evolution under the influence of input events.

A distinction must be made between discrete state models and continuous type models (see Section 8.3.4.). Continuous models describe a permanent evolution whereas discrete models limit the description to specific states which change only at specific instants.

Continuous type models should be used whenever a model cannot be based on discrete states:

- parametric mathematical models: transfer function, recurrent equations, differential equations, etc;
- non-parametric models: signal representations, frequency chart, etc.

These models are used to represent a temporal evolution, but also any other type of representations, for example such as a frequential representation.

11.6.1 The various discrete state models

A state/transition type graph allows discrete state modeling. Each transition is associated with a condition specifying the time at which the transition is true. A condition is defined by:

- the occurrence of an event;
- a specific status for data;
- the combination of an event and states for data (the most general case).

A condition cannot be defined by several events since the existence of several events at the same has no meaning. The only possibility would be an ordered relation between events such as ev1 then ev2, for example. On the other hand, a condition may include any Boolean expression between data. For example, the condition: ON.((STATE=Idle) + (STATE=off)) is true when the ON event appears and the result of the Boolean expression defined by STATE is true.

Since activities have a duration, they are associated with states or steps, whereas actions which are instantaneous are associated with transition. Figure 11.9 shows the recommended notation for a finite state diagram. A bar on the link between two states is used to represent the transition. States or steps are normally represented by circles, or sometimes by rectangles for purposes of clarity.

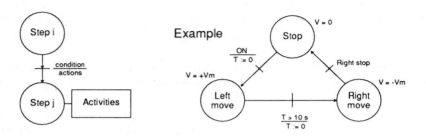

Figure 11.9   Behavior model notation and example.

In the example: ON and Right_stop are events. T > 10 sec is a Boolean condition, T := 0 is an instantaneous action, and V = 0 is a durable action. T represents the current time.

All models derived from this type of state/transition diagram can be used. Known models differ by the addition of complementary meanings. In particular:

- The Finite State Machine (FSM). This diagram limits the model to sequential behavior; only one state is active at any one time. When the number of entity states to be modeled is not finite, an extended version can be used associating variables with states (Extended Finite State Machine). SDL (Specification and Description Language) is an example of this model type, particularly suitable for protocol specifications [ORR-88]. When the number of states or transitions becomes large, it is better to use either a transition table or a transition matrix.

- The Grafcet complies with the above meaning, except for actions which cannot be associated with transitions. On the other hand, pulse activities are possible at the beginning of a state. Compared with the finite state machine, it is able to represent simultaneous evolutions by using the AND divergence and convergence.

- The Statechart [HAREL-87-89] is an extension of the finite state machine to reduce its limitations. In particular, the statechart can represent modularity, a hierarchical description, simultaneous evolutions, and the history concept.

- The Petri net which, with the token concept, can be used to model the temporal behavior of several parallel evolution entities when synchronizations and mutual exclusions have to be specified. Well known as a mathematical tool for extracting properties, this model is more general than the others, but is not hierarchical.

The state/transition model allows refinement. A state can be decomposed to a more microscopic level in a sequence of steps or states. An action can also be described in a sequence of more elementary actions. The statechart illustrates this possibility well, and is particularly useful for gradually writing a specification and allows the understandability of the resulting document. Figure 11.10 shows the advantage of this model.

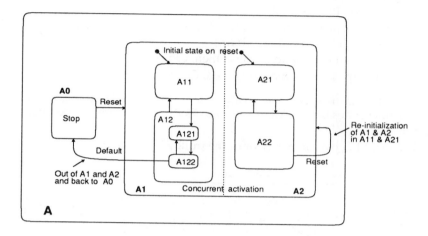

Figure 11.10   Statechart specification example.

Parallel activations (A1 and A2 starting from A0), the refinement of a state (A, A1, A2, A12), and the conditions for activating and leaving a set of states (default, reset) can be shown on this figure.

In the following sections, we will show two model types and will then indicate presentation rules recommended for this behavior model.

11.6.2 State modeling technique

Modeling an entity by its states allows global evolution. It is therefore an external view. Unlike static modeling, expressing an evolution is equivalent to dynamic modeling. The evolution is not simply a function of current inputs but is also a chronological record of the preceding values of them.

For an entity which can be described by discrete states, the behavior is expressed by one or several state/transition charts. States are deduced by analyzing the data and events characteristic of the entity after modeling the data. Mathematical or physical models are more appropriate for continuously evolving entities.

As an example, we will reconsider the trolley model described in Section 11.1 for carrying material. Assume that the trolley has a trap door to empty its contents. In addition, safety limit detectors at P1 and P2 stop movement of the trolley even in the presence of movement commands.

The following list is obtained for a macroscopic model by analyzing data/ events:

- trolley speed V: (0, -VM, +VM);
- position P: (P≤P2, P2<P<P1, P≥P1);
- movement command input: (On right (RM), On left (LM), STOP); hence CMD: (RM, LM, STOP);
- trap-door command events: Open, Close;
- the trap-door position: (Opened, Closed).

Considering the speed and position state variables, the model requires that five distinct states be considered. For P2<P<P1, three states are possible for the speed.

The resulting overall behavior of the trolley is shown below.

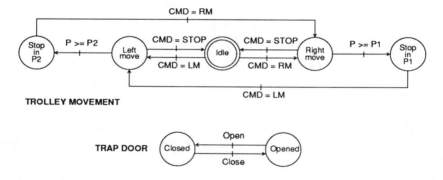

Figure 11.11   Global trolley modeling.

Two variables are sufficient to represent the overall trolley model evolution: trolley_movement_state, and trap_door_state. These variables are internal states and are not necessarily observable states. Sensors are necessary to make these variables available as outputs.

This model shows that the two trolley roles - movement, dumping - are independent, leading to the use of two independent finite state machines for the behavior. A model by states can lead to non-independent activities (or roles or functions or subsets). In this case, finite state charts are coupled by state variables or internal events.

The procedure to be followed to obtain this type of model consists of a search for all successive entity states, and then transition conditions and actions. This modeling technique is particularly useful for describing physical entities characterized by an internal state vector. It is very important for the specification of real-time control systems and electronic systems. This procedure is used by automation engineers who start by modeling the physical process before deducing its control.

11.6.3 Stimuli/response modeling technique

Whereas the previous model is based on the state concept, we now consider the case of an entity rich in input stimuli and carrying out several actions for each.

Rather than search for all entity states, it is easier to model the sequence of actions undertaken on the occurrence of each event. This is equivalent to obtaining a global model of outputs for each event or information input.

This type of model is particularly suitable for so-called reactive systems, in other words systems which produce events following stimuli. These entities have event and information type inputs and outputs. This applies particularly to communicating entities: users and man-machine interfaces, communication systems, etc.

Consider the example of two entities, one transmitting and the other receiving messages. For each transmitted message, the receiving entity must transmit a positive acknowledgement (ACK) if the message is correct, otherwise a negative acknowledgement (NACK). To ensure transfer reliability, if the message or acknowledgement is lost, the transmitter sends the message again until it receives a correct transfer acknowledgement (ACK).

The dialog and modeling protocol for the transmitter and the receiver are shown in Figure 11.12.

The model is based on the finite state machine. The symbols $\triangleright$— and —$\triangleright$ represent receiving and generating an information. States represent wait phases, while waiting for an initiative from the correspondent entity. Actions represent entity reactions. The recommended notation is useful for specifying protocols between communicating entities (see various notations possible in Section 8.3.4-G).

This model is useful since it allows the addition of complementary behavioral characteristics, such as the indication of response times or timing constraints. Such specifications express minimum and maximum times between the occurrence of an input event and the outputs generated as reactions.

The specification procedure for this model consists of expressing all actions to be undertaken when each event appears, and then describing the action sequence.

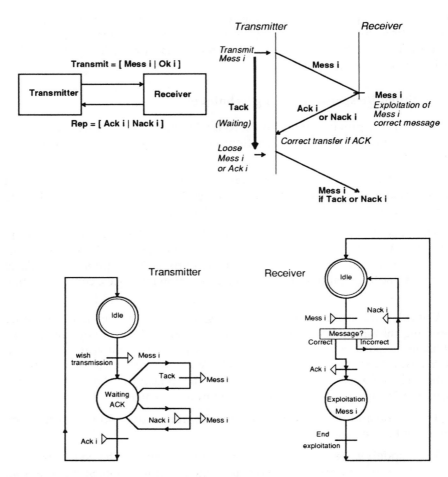

Figure 11.12   Message transmitter and receiver model.

11.6.4 Recommended rules for the finite state behavior model

In principle, all discrete state models can be used. This section summarizes the recommended notation using the finite state machine.

The purpose of this notation is to clarify element categories used in order to facilitate reading and understanding a specification described with a graphical model. The advantage of this notation is that it can be used to express all specifications with a single model rather than using a specific model for each problem category.

This notation is recommended but is not mandatory. A specifier may have to satisfy notation constraints imposed by the issuer of the order. Do not forget either that a specification must be checked and therefore must be understandable by the customer. If the recommended notation is unknown, it can be explained to make documents understandable.

The few essential rules are as follows:

- All elements used (states, events, data, actions) have a name meaningful for the modeled object.
- States are represented by circles (or rectangles), each designated by a meaningful name for the entity to be modeled. The start state is identified by a double circle.
- Possible changes between states are represented by oriented links.
- Transitions are represented by a bar on the oriented link between two states.
- The state change condition is expressed at the side of the transition.
- Instantaneous actions are associated with transitions.
- The transition notation is as follows:

$$\frac{\text{CONDITION}}{\text{ACTIONS}} \quad \text{or} \quad \text{CONDITION / ACTIONS}$$

- Long term actions are associated with states (for example VCMD = +VM). Event or information generation during a state is not correct since the instant is not defined.

There are three categories of input elements used to express a condition: event, information, data. Remember that information means a data-carrying event.

In a condition, one event only is possible; similarly, event and information are exclusive.

To differentiate between the two event and information condition types, we will use:

Ev ⊸⊽⊸ for the event (Ev is its name)

Mess ▷⊽ for information (Mess is its name).

Values of data or states can be used as conditions or complements to an event. The Boolean expression which corresponds to the true condition is then expressed, for example ((T > 10H) and (Day = Sunday)).

For the actions, it is also useful to differentiate between actions in the three categories - event, information, data. The name only is used for the event.

- The symbol ⟶▷ is used to indicate that information is involved;
- the symbol ":=" or "=" means that the value of a data item is changed.

For generated information, the destination can also be named to eliminate any possible ambiguities (M -> entity).

Different actions and states may result from the contents of information. To represent alternatives simply, a long rectangle is used with the question inside it and the various alternatives corresponding to the possible cases outside.

Figure 11.13 summarizes the complete recommended notation.

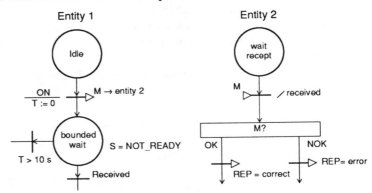

Figure 11.13   Recommended notation for a discrete state model.

The finite state machine may be unsuitable when the model has to be found by successive refinements. It is then recommended that the statechart model be used in preference (see Section 11.6.1.).

11.7 ACTIVITY MODELING

The purpose of activity modeling is to define the relations between data or events/information and the activities of the entity concerned.

An activity means a transformation of input data or information into other output data or information. The model is based on the use of a dependency diagram.

The two most commonly quoted models for this type of model are:

- The SADT model which can be used to model activity/data relations in two views: the actigram oriented towards the specification of functions or activities, and the datagram oriented towards data and information specifications [IGL-83, ROSS-85] (see Section 7.2).

- The data-flow diagram recommended by DeMarco [DEMARCO-79] (see Section 7.3).

These two models represent the information and data-flow, but do not describe the behavior of the whole system. In describing the possible data paths, this type of diagram describes what transforms or produces the data and information but does not specify when. Therefore, these models are structural. An activity can again be decomposed into a data-flow diagram; the model is therefore hierarchical. At the final decomposition stage, an activity can only be described by a specification which characterizes input transformations. This is then a behavior model.

One essential difference between the two SADT and DFD models is that the SADT diagram does not distinguish between data and information in accordance with the terminology used in this chapter. For a DFD, a data item is represented by a file or data store symbol, whereas an item of information is used as a label on a direct link between two activities. MCSE recommends that data-flow diagrams should preferably be used for a specification by activities.

The graphical notation to be used for a data-flow diagram and its meaning [WARD-85] was described in Part 2 in Section 7.3, and we will briefly recall it in Figure 11.14.

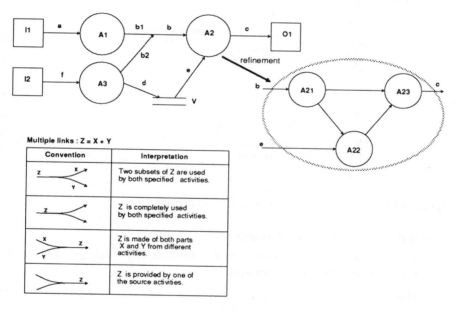

Figure 11.14   Data-flow diagram example.

In the above example:

- I1, I2 are sources and O1 is a sink;

- A1, A2 and A3 are activities;

- **a, b, c, f** are information;

- **d, e** are stored and read data belonging to V;

- A2 is refined by a data-flow diagram.

This diagram states that **C** is the result of a transformation of **b** after using data item **e** belonging to V. **b** results from a transformation of **a** by A1 or from a transformation of **f** by A3, which also produces data item **d** for V. Nothing is said about the times at which **b** and **c** appear from **a**, and the same applies for storing **d** and using **e**.

Figure 11.14 also shows the meaning of conventions for multiple convergent or divergent links. This notation only concerns activities synchronous with information, in other words A1 carries out the transformation of each information **a** at the time at which it appears.

It is suitable for modeling information systems but is not enough for modeling physical systems. We will adopt Ward's double arrow notation to represent a continuous data, thus allowing characterization of activity inputs and outputs for permanent data, as shown in Figure 11.15.

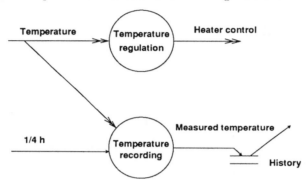

Figure 11.15   Ward's notation for permanently evolving data.

This diagram is interpreted as follows:

- the temperature regulation activity continuously evaluates the heater control based on the temperature;

- the temperature recording activity takes place on each 1/4 h event to update the chronological record data history.

The characteristics of this model are as follows:

- this graphical model is very easy to understand, which is a significant property for a specification;

- it is hierarchical and so facilitates gradual analysis and structuring;

- it describes the data and information point of view and details and entity's global activity;

- however, it is not sufficient to know the global behavior. A temporal specification would have to be added for each activity for this purpose.

To correct the latter aspect, Ward and Mellor, and also Hatley have added a control specification to the data-flow diagram [WARD-85, HATLEY-87].

Evolution times for each activity are specified by a global control specification of all data-flow diagram activities rather than by the activity control description itself. The global control is then specified by a model such as the finite state machine. The following model (Figure 11.16) for the specification of an entity or system is based on this approach [HATLEY-87].

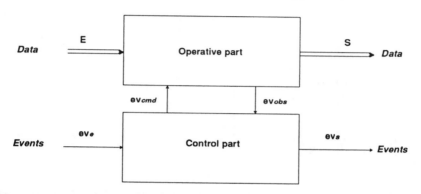

Figure 11.16   Template system specification model.

The operative part which concerns data is described by a data-flow diagram, whereas the control part defining the temporal evolution of activities is described by one or several finite state machines.

Figure 11.17 shows an example of a model using Hatley's notation (see Section 7.8.1).

The behavior in the control part specifies active or inactive states of DFD activities and events produced, based on input events and on events resulting from the DFD. The DFD control activity is represented by a bar which is specified by a finite state machine or a transition table.

Modeling by activities concerns the most general case; an entity is characterized by a data and events set and an activities set.

When the data-flow approach is necessary, which may be the case for fairly complex entities or systems, this type of data + control model is highly recommended. Taking account of the three model views, a description by activities necessitates describing and therefore finding four types of information in the following order:

- all data/information (structure);
- data/event and activity relations (data-flow diagrams);
- the behavior of each activity including input/output definitions;
- global activities evolution by a control specification.

This system modeling strategy is recommended by WARD and MELLOR, and by Hatley.

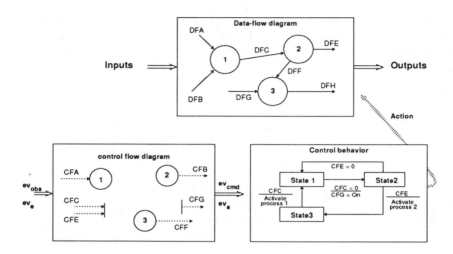

Figure 11.17   DFD + CFD specification example. (Figure 6.9 p92, reprinted with permission from Dorset House Publishing. Copyright © 1988, 1987 Dorset House Publishing, 353 W. 12 Street, New York, NY USA. Reprinted from *Strategies for Real-Time System Specification* by Derek J. Hatley and Imtiaz A. Pirbhai.)

11.8 MODELING GUIDE

The three-view model complexity (data/information, activities, behavior), and the modeling method, depend on the nature of the entity to be described and the required level of detail.

Based on the three model types described in the previous sections, it is easy to explain the procedure to be followed for each entity. It can be described as the trajectory to be followed in a three-dimensional modeling space (Figure 11.18).

Modeling must start by an analysis leading to a description of data, events and information for each entity. The approach is to start from its inputs and outputs while expressing dependencies. This model may be sufficient for the problem to be treated (case 1); in this case it is a static model.

If this is not sufficient, the model must be extended when the dynamic aspect is essential. If the entity evolution can be globally characterized, from an external view stating dependencies between inputs and outputs, a stimuli/response type model or state model must be used. The model is then complete (case 2).

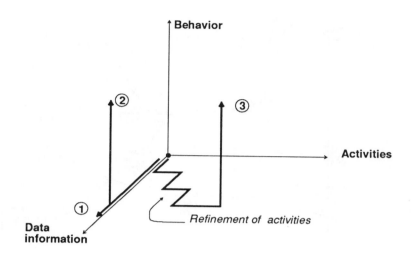

Figure 11.18   Modeling strategies.

When an entity is complex, the above global approach is difficult. The procedure (case 3) then consists in developing a model by activities using the refinement technique. At the final stage, each activity is described by its behavior. The behavior for the global system or for subsets is defined by a control flow diagram. Many methodologies use this specification procedure (see Chapter 7).

In some problems, even if the approach case 2 is possible, it is not desirable to individually model each entity since this approach would not lead to a sufficient description for the application. In this case, the approach by activities is more appropriate. As an example, consider the case of a room heating management application for a school. The problem is to control heating based on timetables and the description of available rooms.

Using the modeling approach by entities, the various users are defined: the studies department responsible for timetables, and the general department responsible for building and room control.

An analysis of each entity category does not give an adequate view of the problem. Therefore, instead of following this procedure, we will search for the global data-flow diagram for this application. A typical diagram is given Figure 11.19.

This global approach is better able to take account of the various activities, events and application information and data, without the need to previously assign them to a specific entity. It is also useful to decide upon a task distribution, and in particular it is easy to delimit the role of a computer system (for example, the part surrounded by dashed lines).

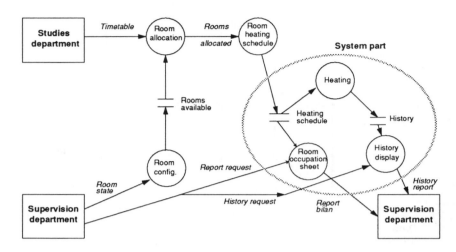

Figure 11.19   Data-flow diagram for room heating management.

In justifying the proposed guide, note that modeling by activities tends to result in a too elementary decomposition for simple entities since the specifier is guided in his analysis by a data-flow diagram, and has no clear criteria when to stop his decomposition. This is observed on examples considered by Ward and Hatley [WARD-85, HATLEY-87]. In particular, the vehicle speed regulation system specified by a data-flow diagram becomes more complex than when a modeling by states approach is used. The specification for this example respecting the point of view described in this chapter was given in Part 1 Chapter 6.

11.9 SUMMARY

This chapter is essential for understanding the recommended procedure for producing specifications; it justifies the modeling basis which will be used in the next chapter. The main concepts are:

- System specification starts by delimiting its environment and characterizing the entities which compose this environment.

- Entities may be characterized by an explicit model, whereas the system can only be described using an external view. The system model can thus be based on the required behavior of its environment.

- An entity is described by a set of characteristic elements - events, data, actions or activities - and by relations between them.

- The model is based on a three-view description: the data space, the state space and the activity space.

- Depending on the nature of the required characterization, the specifier may use:
  - data modeling for a static description,
  - data/event and state modeling for a global dynamic description,
  - data/event and activities modeling in the more general case when the previous modeling techniques prove to be inadequate.

12

THE SPECIFICATION PROCESS

The objective of the specification step is to describe the complete system specifications in the form of a structured, understandable and checkable document. Although a significant time investment is required to produce this document, there is significant gain in subsequent phases, particularly the operation and maintenance phases since there will be few errors.

Previous chapters described the concepts of system modeling. The specification document is essential later for design, and earlier to check that the stated problem has been well understood, and must comply with a description model. The role of this description model is to explain all necessary components, and the meaning and interpretation of each, in order to obtain a complete specification. If a set of rules is respected, the specification will have properties and qualities such that it can be checked with the customer and can be used for the design.

This chapter describes the contents of a specification and the procedure to be followed to produce the specification document. The proposed process consists of sequences of analysis and decisions, and is firstly based on an understanding of the "world" in which the system will act, followed by a progressive description of the role played by the system for the application. Each step produces a component of the specification.

The specification process is illustrated by the two examples given at the end of Chapter 9. To facilitate reading and understanding the method, the first example is considered during the description of each phase, and the second example is worked out fully at the end of the chapter.

12.1 SPECIFICATION COMPONENTS

First, remember that the design will be done according to:

- the functional approach, to define functions internal to the system and relations between these functions;
- the operational approach, to express the behavior of functions and actions;
- the technological approach to define a hardware solution and the implementation of the functional solution on this hardware, satisfying all technological constraints.

In each approach, it is helpful if only one subset of the specifications needs to be used. This implies the advantage of the decomposition into three categories expressing functional, operational and technological aspects.

An application is made up of the system to be designed and its environment. A specification must therefore contain:

- a model of the system environment;
- input-output definition;
- required behavior for the system;
- description of its use.

The environment model concerns all its entities and relations between them.

A detail specification contains two parts and includes for the environment model:

- description of all entities including for each:
  - data and event definition,
  - description of global behavior or, if necessary, the data-flow diagram and then the behavior of all activities;

- functional description of the environment representing all relations between entities without the system.

and for the system description:

- input/output description;
- functional specification including:
  - system function list,
  - specification of these functions;
- operational specifications;
- technological specifications;
- a preliminary document for installation and use.

The necessary information sets are represented in Figure 12.1.

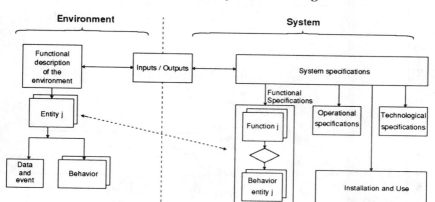

Figure 12.1   Specification composition.

The hierarchical description already suggests the specification process described in the next section:

- bottom-up process starting from entities for analyzing the existing;
- top-down process starting from inputs/outputs and functionalities for the system.

For a complex system, this results in a large amount of information, so it is better to modify the structure. In this case, the solution is to first decompose the problem into functional subsets and then to specify each part. The system specification is then a collection of subset specifications. This structure considerably facilitates the search for information during design and implementation.

12.2 SPECIFICATION PROCESS DESCRIPTION

In our opinion, this first step of the methodology, which produces a complete specifications document, is the most difficult.

As input data, the specifier has the requirements definition document; if there is one. At his request, he can also have access to data relating to the problem and known by the customer (users). Therefore, he has to carry out his analysis efficiently. The process described in this chapter is a guide for questioning and analysis, and then synthesis and verification.

Based on the structure of the specification document to be produced, Figure 12.2 summarizes the phases of this step.

The work is decomposed into two major parts:

- modeling the environment;
- system specification.

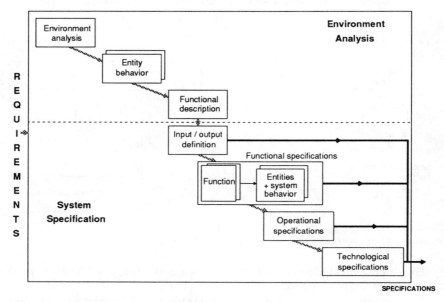

Figure 12.2   Phases for the specification step.

For the first part, the initial phase concerns the environment analysis to identify entities useful to the problem. The next phase produces a model of entities just sufficient for the problem. This first part is completed by a functional description of the environment.

The second part starts by delimiting the system by its inputs and outputs. This is followed by an essential phase describing the functional specifications. The operational, and then technological specifications, are gradually written together with complementary user and installation documents.

There are three steps to each model phase:

- **Analysis**: the objective is to bring out all useful information - data, events, actions - by discussion, reading document and direct observation.

- **Synthesis**: all useful information has to be collected and organized in the form of a model as an abstract description.

- **Verification**: this task is necessary and guarantees the validity of previous work. Omissions and errors are then immediately corrected.

It is essential to note that the starting point, consisting of finding useful entities, is very important since the entire design and implementation will be based on this. An investment in time for this initial work is essential. This time is not wasted although it may seem to be at first. A superficial specification will result in wasting time at various points in later phases with an amplification effect, although it will be difficult to clearly prove the correlation with the poor specifications.

The following sections describe the characteristics of each specification component and the process for producing it. Bear in mind that the specification can only be a result of close collaboration between all customer participants and the specifier(s).

12.3 ENVIRONMENT ANALYSIS AND MODELING

The objective of this first part of the specification is to describe the existing world for the application. How to describe the existing world is the first quality every designer must have.

The environment model is an abstraction, in other words a more or less macroscopic partial description of parts useful for the problem.

The environment is a temporal world within which one or several entities evolve and which may or may not be interrelated. This existing world must be delimited and understood first. Therefore, the initial objective is to find elements in this environment which have a direct influence on the system. The second objective is to characterize necessary and sufficient details for each entity.

Therefore, the first job is to summarize characteristic elements of the environment, ending up with a definition of useful entities. If the environment is complex, the analysis may end with a hierarchical decomposition. Obviously, the analysis can only be carried out if the application objective is well known. The process to be followed has been described in the previous chapter in Section 11.8 in the form of a modeling guide.

Necessary information is obtained from the customer. The customer can probably give a great deal of information about his need. But this may be given in uncorrelated sequences. The specifier will have to guide the discussion so that he can progress efficiently in his analysis. A site visit will be very useful to give an overall view of the problem, together with a physical representation of the installation such as, for example, an organization chart for a production workshop.

12.3.1 Modeling each entity

By considering a single entity in particular, the specifier must produce a model sufficient for the problem to be solved. The useful description level depends on the objective of the system. The specifier is also expected to know how to determine the degree of model refinement necessary, based on the requirements definition.

Based on the concepts described in the previous chapter, the procedure consists of making a list of all characteristic functional elements of the entity, and then to classify them to determine structural and temporal relations. The analysis will classify the functional elements into the following categories:

- data/events:
  - data
  - state variables
  - events
  - information
- activities:
  - actions
  - activities
- relations:
  - relations between data/events and actions/activities,
  - inputs and outputs with its environment.

In order to model it, an entity may be understood by presenting its information in the form of tables for example, as shown in Figure 12.3. The first describes the characteristics of variables, data or information for each entity, whereas the second describes relations between entities by actions.

Entity	Input	Internal variable	Output	Type	Definition
TROLLEY	CMD			MD | MG | AR RM LM STP	Motion control
		Position		P2 ... P1	Absolute position of the trolley
CONVEYOR BELT	CT			Belt_on or Belt_on	Conveyor belt control

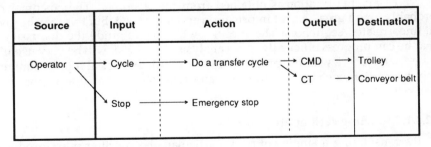

Figure 12.3   Examples of modeling tables.

Modeling according to the three views - data, activity, behavior - then becomes possible. The technique to be followed depends on the nature of the entity: static model for data/events, global behavioral model for an entity carrying out one or a small number of functions, stimuli-response model for a communicating or reactive entity, data-flow model for an information transformation-oriented entity (see usable models in the previous chapter).

The procedure to be followed consists first, of considering a data/event model. If this proves to be sufficient, in that it can define all system inputs and outputs, a more complex model will not be necessary. Otherwise, a global model should be considered to describe the dynamic behavior of the entity. Modeling by activities is only necessary for relatively complex entities (several simultaneous activities), or when decomposition of the environment into entities is not appropriate. An approach in the form of a relational diagram may facilitate the modeling work as suggested by a number of people [WARD-85, BAILIN-89, KURTZ-89].

As an example to illustrate the procedure, consider the case of a system for the management of books in a library. This is an information system rather than an electronic system, but the specification process is similar.

Entities in this system will be at least books. Every book is an instance of the book type. Each book (obviously existing for the library) is characterized by:

- title

- author

- number

- state

Possible book states are: present, reserved, loaned, lost. Characteristic events for each book are: purchase, reservation, loan, return, loss. Each event leads to a status change. This static model is apparently sufficient. It is written (see syntactical notation in Section 11.5.2):

BOOKS = {BOOK};

BOOK = TITLE + AUTHOR + NUMBER + STATE;

STATE : (present, reserved, loaned, lost);

This model may be completed by a description of the book state evolution as a function of events, such as given below.

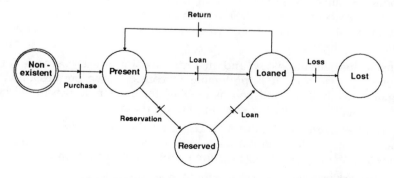

Figure 12.4   Modeling book states and transitions.

For the information system responsible for managing books, the books as environment entities are not related to the system (no direct observation of the state of each book). In the lack of this observation, the librarian must update the state of each book in the system based on related events. The system must therefore have the above evolution model internally and the current state for each book.

This type of problem is different from electronic system problems considered in this book since the entities are not directly observable, but the specification process is the same.

Modeling the user as an entity is a special case. His behavior is unpredictable; he generates events and information as and when he wishes. When he sits behind a keyboard or a workstation, there is nothing to stop him from doing anything he wants. There is thus no point in using a dynamic model for the user. Modeling by data/information is sufficient, by expressing user actions and observations available to him.

12.3.2 Functional environment description

The purpose of the functional synthesis is to show relations between entities in the environment. It is only useful for coupled entities.

The first advantage of this phase is to give a synthetic graphical view of the entire environment. A second possible advantage is to be able to group entities so that subsequent determination of functional specifications is simplified.

To illustrate this point, consider the next application for producing concrete. Concrete results from a quantity of aggregates (PA1 + PA2 + PA3), a quantity of cement (PC1 or PC2 depending on the choice), and a quantity of water QE calculated on the previous values.

The following description (Figure 12.5) of the plant is sufficiently clear for the reader to understand how the concrete is made.

This application contains 12 entities. Each entity is very simply modeled by an inputs --> states --> outputs relation, once all inputs, outputs and internal variables have been identified. The resulting functional description of the environment shows coupling between all entities except the user. It is represented by Figure 12.6.

Considering this topology and in order to simplify the search for the functional specification, it is preferable to consider five entities only. The aggregate silos, balance and belt assemblies form a single functional entity producing aggregates, and the same applies for the cement silos.

As another example, Figure 12.7 concerns the description of zones for heating and shows the notation used to describe a collection of entities and relations of a single type (differentiation between type and instance).

For abstract entities, the environment may be described by a relational diagram using an approach by entity relations.

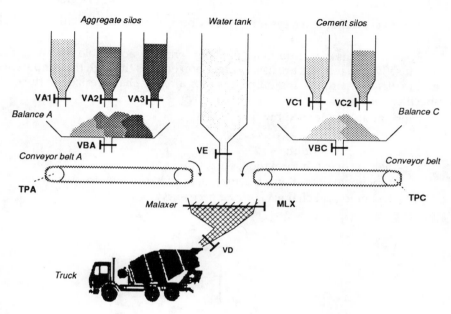

Figure 12.5   Concrete mixing plant.

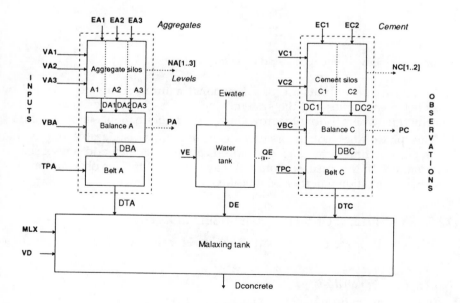

Figure 12.6   Functional description of the environment.

12.4   DELIMITATION OF SYSTEM INPUTS AND OUTPUTS

This phase delimits the system by describing its functional relations with the environment.

System inputs are information about entities accessible through their outputs. System outputs are used to act upon entities through their inputs. The nature of system inputs and outputs is thus already characterized in the entity specification.

Each variable is defined by:

- name;
- use: input, output;
- nature: event, information, data, state;
- functional definition: structure, definition domain, frequency, etc;
- technological characteristics if necessary.

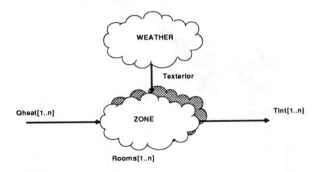

Figure 12.7   Environment description for room heating.

System inputs-outputs are of a functional nature and are represented by links between entities and the system. Single arrow links refer to an event or information, whereas double arrow links concern permanent states and data.

This phase does not necessarily determine all indispensable inputs and outputs. Sometimes, the functional specificationphase may add non-observed information. In this case, sensors will have to be added for observation. The system delimitation will then be modified by looping back.

12.5   EXAMPLE 1: CENTRIFUGE SPEED CONTROL

We will illustrate this first part of the specification work by the centrifuge example.

-A- Environment analysis

The system environment contains two entities:

- the motor, for which the speed is a characteristic state variable;

- the user, who can act upon the system by pressing one of the push buttons whenever he wishes.

-B- Motor model

The motor speed, which is the characteristic variable, is a function of the applied command and the load to be driven:

$$\text{Smotor} = f_t \, (\text{CV, load});$$

The model must be global. It therefore includes the control power electronics. CV is therefore the control value applied as an amplifier input. If a more detailed model, which takes account of the inertia and possible non-linearities becomes necessary, the motor can be modeled, for example, by a first order transfer function or by differential equations.

-C- Behavior for the user

The user observes the state of the centrifuge: observation of the speed set point and state - rotation or no rotation. He may wish to act upon the centrifuge at any moment:

- define speed setpoint;
- request a cycle;
- request stop.

The user's behavior is not useful for this problem. However, input and output information may be specified as in Figure 12.8. All user actions are expressed by the order event, since actions are not simultaneous.

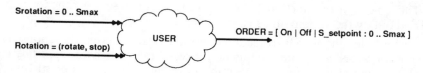

Srotation = 0 .. Smax

Rotation = (rotate, stop)

USER

ORDER = [On | Off | S_setpoint : 0 .. Smax]

Figure 12.8   Model of the user entity.

-D- Delimiting system inputs and outputs

If there is no system, there is no coupling between the user and the motor. The system will take account of user requests and will act upon the motor. The delimitation for this example is shown in Figure 12.9. It assumes that the motor speed is observed. Remember that there is a difference between links with a single arrow and those with a double arrow.

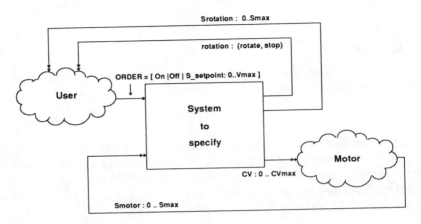

Figure 12.9   Delimiting system inputs and outputs.

12.6 FUNCTIONAL SPECIFICATIONS

Functional specifications are essential information to clarify the problem to be processed and the objective of the system.

The design starts from this category of specification. Consequently, a bad specification and any inaccuracy will inevitably cause problems. To facilitate understanding, we will first define what is meant by functional specifications, and then we will describe the procedure to be followed to express them correctly.

12.6.1 Nature of functional specifications

The objective of functional specifications is to describe functions to be carried out by the system on its environment.

The only functions to be considered are so-called "external" functions. They are not concerned with internal functions necessary to satisfy the specifications, since this would already be a description of the solution. External function means a global function of the application which is a result of the collaboration of the system with entities in its environment.

For example, consider the case of the material transport trolley: the global function for the application is to "perform an automatic material transport cycle". To satisfy this external function, one or two trolley and belt-loader control functions are necessary internally in the system.

It is not sufficient to list system functions; each function has to be characterized to prevent any interpretation ambiguities. As these functions are application functions, so their direct specification is often difficult without refering to entities.

To illustrate the meaning of a functional specification, consider the figure below which shows an application including two entities and a system to be designed. The system is also an entity, which will not exist before its development.

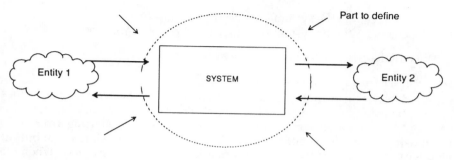

Figure 12.10   Application example.

Since every entity can be modeled, the functional specification of the "system" entity is equivalent to modeling it. Before its design, the system is considered as a "black box" since its internal structure is not yet known, and therefore the model can only be global and described from an external point of view. A functional specification is therefore an expression of actions carried out by system outputs on entities in its environment, and controlled by its inputs which supply observations from this environment. Models and modeling techniques described in the previous chapter can therefore be used to express these specifications.

Therefore, the following rules have to be respected for a specification expressed by a state/transition chart:

- states are significant for the application;
- actions concern system outputs or internal events necessary to express the functional specification;
- conditions use system inputs, specification states and internal events exclusively, in particular the absolute time or relative time (durations).

12.6.2 Approaches for producing a functional specification

The objective is therefore to describe the system from an external point of view expressing only relations between its inputs and outputs. For design purposes, the system will be considered later alone without the need to refer to entities.

The difficulty lies in selecting the model type to be used. Unlike environment entities in which an existing object has to be described, internal knowledge does not exist for the system, and therefore only a global model is possible. But since a more complex system carries out several functionalities, it is rarely possible to produce a single model expressing the global system behavior. The system therefore has to be characterized by subsets and according to different projections. Based on the three model types described in Chapter 11, three non-exclusive approaches are possible:

- characterize the system starting from evolution of its inputs and/or outputs;
- characterize the system starting from evolution of entities;
- characterize the system starting from the global application.

We will describe each of these three approaches.

-A- Approach from system inputs/outputs

For each system output, successive states dependent on system input values have to be expressed using a global model. The description may be made for each output separately, or for many outputs,or globally starting from each input using a stimuli/response model. This approach is possible when output values can be described by a data/information model; this is the case when the behavior of entities which use these outputs is not essential. To illustrate this approach, consider the example of a simple serial transmitter function. The system is delimited as shown in Figure 12.11.

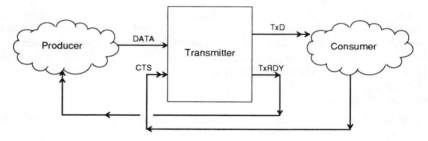

Figure 12.11   System delimitation with its inputs and outputs.

The transmitter stores the data item DATA when it appears, but only when the transmitter is available (expressed by TxRDY).

The transmitter produces the data stored on its TxD output in a serial form (start bit + 8 bits + parity + 2 stop bits). This is only possible when CTS is true.

In this example, the approach by outputs consists of expressing the successive states of the two outputs TxD and TxRDY (see Figure 12.12).

TxRDY takes only two values, leading to a two-state model. The transition conditions depend on inputs (DATA) and states or internal events (data being transmitted). TxD changes only during the transmition state. This state may be refined to represent the successive states: start bit, data bit (i), parity bit, stop bit.

The representation of the behavior of the producer and consumer entities is here not necessary, but facilitates understanding. The completeness of this specification is easy to show because all output states are defined and all input values are used.

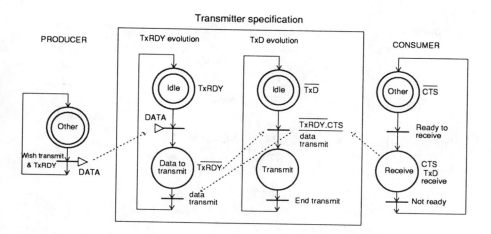

Figure 12.12   Transmission function specification.

-B- Approach from entities

When entities are essential to describe the role of the system, we recommend an approach by entities. This approach is easier by the fact that the first phase of the specification procedure characterizes entities, each taken in alone.

Rather than attempting to describe each system output separately, it is preferable to express the successive required states for application entities. The method recommended by MCSE is therefore **to characterize the behavior of each entity controlled or constrained by the system**. The states of each entity are then used to determine actions and controls to be generated by the system, leading to a definition of system outputs. This rule is very important. In describing the effects of the system and the conditions which produce them, we indirectly specify the functions. This leads to an external description of the system since state names are related to entity states and are not therefore thought of as internal system states.

We will illustrate this point of view using the material displacement trolley example (see Section 11.1).

The three environment entities without the system are specified in Figure 12.13. Entities are not interrelated if there is no control system. The required system is delimited as shown in Figure 12.14.

The R_stop and L_stop inputs were added immediately since they are necessary to carry out the function. This is determined from the functional specifications by the conditions $P \leq P2$ and $P \geq P1$.

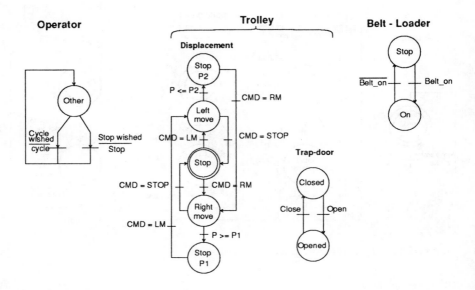

Figure 12.13   Application entity modeling.

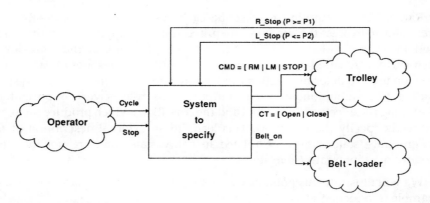

Figure 12.14   System delimitation.

For the application, the system carries out only one function, namely performing an automatic material displacement cycle. To characterize this system function, the actions of the system on its environment have to be described as a function of events or observations. For this purpose, we will start with controllable entities and will describe the evolution of each of them under the control of the system. The behavior of the two entities to perform an automatic cycle with the system is shown in Figure 12.15.

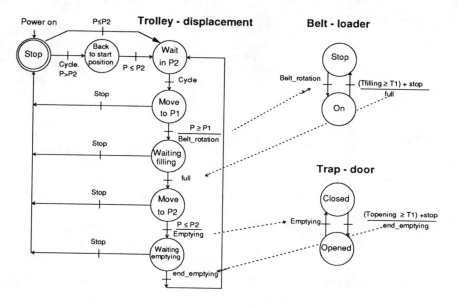

Figure 12.15 Global modeling for controllable entities.

The system can act only on the two entities: the trolley and the belt-loader. The third - the user - is not controllable since he is always able to press push-buttons whenever he wants to. The two coupled application subsets which can be modeled are therefore the system + the trolley and the system + the belt-loader.

The above finite state machines describe the successive states of the two entities. The transition conditions are those of the application. Some are produced by the entities and these are necessarily system inputs. Other conditions - duration of a state and events such as belt_rotation, emptying, end_emptying - will be internal to the system because they are necessary to express temporal relations.

Starting from this type of global description, and taking account of the previous model for each entity without the system, actions on entities and therefore system outputs can easily be deduced for each state. This describes the system role by a global model of the evolution of its outputs as a function of its inputs. The decomposition of the global model into two parts - the system behavior model and entity behavior model - is shown in Figure 12.16 for two application states.

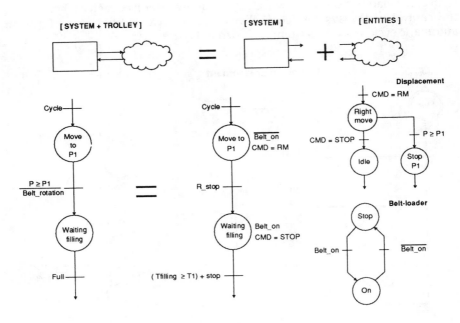

Figure 12.16   Relation between global model and system specification.

The system functional specification has to be found. To express input --> output relations, the specification is obtained by subtracting the part carried out by the entity from the system + entity model. This is normally equivalent to adding input values for each entity state to put the entity into this state, or adding actions generating the necessary events as entity inputs on each transition.

This is always an external definition since description states are for entities, and evolution conditions depend on system inputs and therefore on entity states.

There are two advantages to this approach. First, it remains understandable and therefore checkable by the customer since the description is based solely on knowledge of the environment. Second, when the entity's behavior is to be modified, it is only necessary to modify the part related to this entity.

-C- Approach for the global application

When the two above approaches do not give a correct and complete expression of functional specifications, the global approach will be necessary. This is the case for complex entities or when decomposition of the application into entities is not sufficient (see Section 11.8).

In this case, global modeling of the application by an activity diagram is used as a basis to demonstrate the role and therefore the functionalities of the system.

Subsets to be provided by the system are then specified in more detail by describing the data specifications and activity specifications. The two previous approaches can be used at this level, after some refinement.

12.6.3 Functional specification method

Functional specifications include an expression of system functions followed by a specification of these functions.

-A- System function list

This is the first essential part of the functional specification, and firstly lists all functions which must be provided by the system for its environment. The analysis can be made by searching for application activities.

Each function is described by:

- a title;
- a brief description of its role;
- the environment entities concerned by this function.

It is very important not to confuse internal and external functions. Experience with the method has shown that this distinction causes some difficulties and it is naturally easier to evoke internal functions; for example, the very frequently evoked dialog function is an internal function. To avoid this type of error, an effort must be made to consider the application level and not the system level.

-B- System function specifications

The previous section showed that three approaches can be used to fully describe system functions. These three approaches are not exclusive, but each corresponds to a different view of the system. The objective of a specification is to reduce the entire description to input/output relations for the system. The input/output approach is the most direct when it is possible, and entity modeling is then reduced to specification of their inputs and outputs.

The approach by entities is specifically suitable for real-time control applications. The expression of the behavior of each entity under the constraint of the system is easier if a model of it exists without the system. Normally, the same kind model can be used for the specification.

It has been demonstrated that the description of a system function is obtained indirectly by describing the system + entities set. Therefore, the basis for the specification method is normally to explain the behavior of each entity in the environment under the constraint or influence of the system for each considered function.

In order to clarify relations between functions and entities concerned, a relational diagram may be used as an analysis basis for this specification phase. We have noted that when entities (or entity models) are relatively simple, each is concerned by one function only. Characterizing functions is then equivalent to modeling the required behavior of all entities. Input/output dependencies are then deduced for the system. Models to be used are the same as those recommended for entities.

When this specification technique is insufficient, a global data-flow type model of the application has to be used, delimiting system activities and data. Starting from this global approach, the specification can be refined into subsets, and then each subset can be characterized using approaches 1 and 2.

The procedure to elaborate specifications by using finite state machines or stimuli/response charts consists of starting from the inactive or idle state for each entity. A new state is then added for each by naming it and then by searching for the transition condition into this new state. The specification is then obtained incrementally by adding states, links, transition conditions and actions.

The specification can be found entity by entity. But when they are coupled by the system, it is better to consider all entities simultaneously.

When the user is an application entity, there is no direct method to oblige the user to follow a given procedure. In any case, a user cannot be prevented from pressing any key when he is in front of a keyboard. However, the system can filter those sequences considered to be correct among all user actions. The system specification for the user then concerns an expression of user event sequences considered to be correct for the application. This part of the specification is usually expressed by a stimuli/response type chart which expresses the system behavior relative to the user. This is explained on the centrifuge example in Section 12.6.4.

-C- Specification verification

The specification work must be checked to ensure that the result is globally valid.

An initial check ensures that "syntactical" rules of the model used are respected. Incorrect use of models will always lead to ambiguities in interpreting the specification.

The "semantics" aspect then has to be considered, and therefore the meaning of all elements used - states, conditions, actions, etc. - together with the coherence of the whole related to the objective.

After this phase, it is sometimes useful to reconsider the delimitation of system inputs and outputs. Some non-observable events or conditions may exist in the environment. If this information cannot be built into the system, sensors will need to be added to access it.

12.6.4 Examples

The functional specification for the centrifuge speed control system is described in Figure 12.17. The only function of the system is to perform a centrifuge cycle at a control speed previously defined by the user. It is specified by describing constraints imposed on the user and on the motor, using the entity approach.

The specification shown in Figure 12.17 is obtained by considering the user and the motor as starting points. The system behavior relative to the user is the one recognized correct by the system. A system - user stimuli/response chart for the order input expresses this behavior. This diagram thus represents filtering of events incoming from the user such that correct events only are retained for the application. For example, note that a ON request can only be taken into account after the end of the previous cycle.

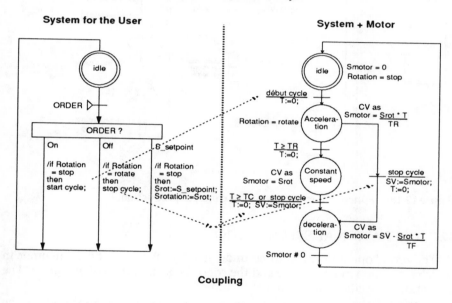

Figure 12.17   Functional centrifuge specification.

As an illustration of the approach by entities, the functional specification for automatically obtaining concrete starting from a user request is shown in Figure 12.18 (see the problem in Section 12.3.2). The specification is again obtained by considering all application entities and constraints imposed by the system.

The states are easy to find for each entity. The reader may think that it is simpler to directly express the global diagram for automation of the whole. This would be a conventional process which would directly describe the behavior of the system; this is more complicated and there is a higher risk of error. The process recommended here is an intermediate stage which can be used to deduce the global diagram. Note also that customer changes to the requirements definition would lead to a modification which would be easy to isolate, whereas it would be much more complicated for the global specification.

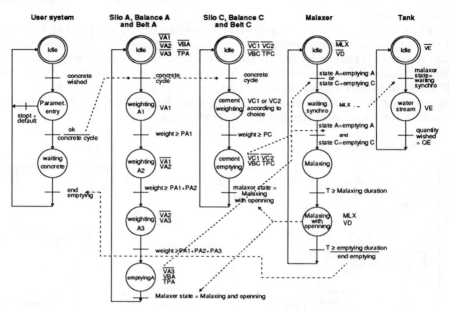

Figure 12.18   Functional specification for concrete production.

12.7 OPERATIONAL SPECIFICATIONS

The term "operational" is to be understood in the sense of the manner in which a function must operate and the conditions and range of operation. The operational specifications therefore include:

- First, all precisions about variables or data which appeared in the functional specifications (type, definition domain). All known information must be indicated. It must also contain operating conditions, accuracy performances and all special operating modes. For example, obtaining a result to 10^{-2} or to 10^{-5} is not the same thing.

- Second, all information which could help designers in selecting solutions to be implemented. Operational specifications may include the way some operations are carried out (for example, calculation methods). These specifications are generally helpful. The customer may have opinions about solutions to be adopted to carry out functions stated in the functional specifications. He will be thoroughly familiar with his domain and, for example, may have had experience with methods and drawn conclusions during previous implementations or during a feasibility study. It is always useful to have these results to increase the chances of success.

These specifications are obtained by analyzing specifications already produced, reading documents, and by discussions with the customer. Depending on the nature of the information, they may be expressed in various ways: natural language, mathematical model, algorithm, etc.

The system performance specification depends on the nature of the problem. For example, it is not easy to characterize performances expected of a fault detection imaging system. One technique would then be to specify the test procedure by defining characteristic objects chosen to validate the product. For example, in a fault detection system, this leads to a definition of good and bad parts that the system must discriminate between to be acceptable.

12.8 TECHNOLOGICAL SPECIFICATIONS

This category is wider since it includes all specifications related to the hardware and software implementation. However, these specifications are more conventional and are easier to produce. We will mention the essential specifications that have to be considered below, as a reminder.

-A- Geographic distribution constraints

When the application is geographically distributed (for example, distance between subsets greater than 10 m), these constraints describe the implementation topology, distances, methods of coupling and usage constraints.

-B- Electrical interface specifications

These concern the characterization of system input and output signals and information, by describing the electrical characteristics of entity inputs and outputs.

-C- Dialog interface specifications

Most systems are directly accessible by operators or by means of a communication device. This specification category describes:

- first, technological elements to be used for man-machine interfaces;
- second, the user procedure. This is equivalent to specifying the man-machine dialog specific to the selected technological device: menu for a terminal, icon system for a microcomputer, buttons and display units for a special panel, etc.

This specification type may be expressed in the form of a paper document, which may be a tedious job, but also in the form of a prototype. The prototyping technique is one way of producing specifications. The customer verification is then greatly simplified.

-D- Temporal specifications (timing constraints)

Up to now, we have not considered system reaction times to external actions. We cannot talk about real-time systems without considering this type of constraint since the environment is a real world which generates events and modifies information at its own speed. Any function interacting with this environment must react at approximately the same speed. Since any implementation involves an execution time or a delay, the designer must determine acceptable reaction times for the various parts of the system with the customer. These decisions are then constraints for the implementation.

Temporal specifications concern the environment only; the system must react globally to input stimuli by acting on its outputs, within a maximum time.

There are several types of timing constraints for the system:

- The activation rate which indicates the system usage frequency for input events (maximum frequency, since this is the worst case), frequency of actions on the environment for outputs (minimum frequency for the satisfactory behavior of the entity concerned).

- Response time characterizing the maximum output modification time after an event or an input condition. A stimuli/response type model facilitates defining these constraints.

- Multiple constraints expressing temporal relations between several signals (minimum time, maximum time). Waveforms are suitable for representing these specifications.

These types of specifications are described in the form of tables or waveforms. Figure 12.19 shows some examples.

-E- Maintenance and operating safety

Functions required for maintenance or diagnostic assistance, such as power-on self-tests, periodic tests during operation, resident maintenance procedures, remote maintenance, etc., are to be characterized.

The objective for operating safety is to characterize various aspects which will influence the implementation:

- system reliability;
- availability in case of fault;
- tolerances to hardware and software problems, etc;
- environment and user safety;
- operation in degraded mode and manual mode, etc.

These are not functional specifications since they depend on the technology used. They may result in modifying or enhancing the solution to take account of these requirements.

Name of event	Type	Constraints
STEP	Internal: regulation period	T < 5 ms
RECEIVED	Input: receive period of characters	9600 bds transfer —> T<=1 ms
ALARM	Input: overheating	Exceptional
C_VALVE	Output: valve closing	Response time < 1 ms after an ALARM

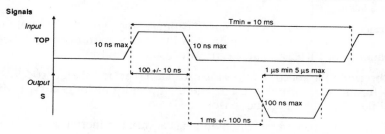

Figure 12.19   Timing constraint examples.

-F- Electrical specifications

These specify the electrical characteristics that the implementation must satisfy such as consumption, dissipation, connections, power supply, component type, etc.

-G - Miscellaneous specifications

This category includes constraints such as:

- Constraints related to the context in which the product will be manufactured (use of specific components, board models, size, cost, development tools, etc.). These constraints are to be considered during the technological solution search phase.

- Environment related conditions (power fail use, disturbances from the environment, sea-water environment, etc.). They may make it necessary to introduce redundancies and special protections.

- Conditions related to the usage phase or the life for an implementation that must be maintained for a long time or that must evolve. Potential possibilities for evolution must be described.

As an illustration, the specifications for the centrifuge speed control system are given below.

For the operational specifications, the initially constant times given in the functional specification will be modified by the supplier to suit customer modification requests.

The times are:

TR = 5 sec
TF = 5 sec
TC = 20 sec

The deceleration slope always remains constant. The speed may vary between 0 and 3000 rpm. The speed accuracy must be better than 10 rpm over the full scale.

Concerning technological specifications, the speed setpoint will be displayed on four BCD display units. A PWM type motor control is used with a frequency of 1 KHz and an electrically insulated output.

Observing the speed requires the use of a 100 pt/rev shaft encoder. An open collector encoder output is used. The motor entity includes a switching type amplifier, the motor and the sensor.

As a timing constraint, the motor has a variable inertia, low when empty (around 50 ms). Therefore, the motor control value must be calculated at least every 5 msec.

12.9 INSTALLATION AND OPERATING PROCEDURES

The description of the system behavior provides an adequate view to allow the reader, and therefore the customer, to determine whether or not the system satisfies his need. It describes what the system is capable of doing. On the other hand, the description does not allow a potential user, or the organization which will use the system, to easily determine if it will satisfy all objectives - usage, installation into the company organization, maintenance, etc. Additional information in the form of documents is therefore necessary, namely:

- A **preliminary user documentation**. This document describes the system as seen by users. It may be structured in parts when several user categories are concerned by the system (for example, specific interface for each category). This document precedes the final user manual.

- An **installation document**. This is a description of how to use and manage the system. For the installation, it may also be necessary to previously install a transition system within the customer's organization to quickly make use of the system, for example changeover from a manual procedure to an automatic procedure. This document must therefore describe how the organization must work, making it possible to modify the system environment.

These documents are gradually written starting from all previous specifications. Prepared at the end of the specification, they give the customer complete information about the product which will be supplied. Users can then take the necessary measures to facilitate installation, start-up and use of the system.

12.10 EXAMPLE 2: WIRE-GUIDED TROLLEY AUTOMATION

To illustrate the specification process and the resulting document, the analysis for the wire-guided trolley automation example is described below. The requirements definition was given in Section 9.8.2.

12.10.1 Modeling the environment

A brief analysis of the problem shows that the following entities must be considered:

- the platforms as command issuers, both have identical behavior;
- the workshop as topology for displacement support: position of platforms, trajectory, obstacles, etc;
- the vehicle for the mechanical part carrying out the displacement and loading/unloading;
- the operator responsible for the satisfactory operation of the plant. He is concerned only by the siren. In this case, he will observe the problem, reposition the trolley and re-initialize its control system.

The transported packets are not used to solve the problem since their presence is not detected. Radar, sensors C1 and C2, the infrared transmitter/ receiver and incremental shaft encoders are only interfaces.

-A- Behavior of a platform

Relative to its environment, each platform carries out two functions:

- dialog with the environment through infrared link: transmit command (COMMAND) and message reception (MESSAGE);
- rotation of its belt in two directions for the displacement of a packet. The belt is characterized by three states which are defined starting from the C_belt command (OFF, FORWARD, BACKWARD).

The platform model is described on Figure 12.20.

-B- Vehicle behavior

The vehicle is composed of two functional subsets:

- the displacement part including the two motors;
- the belt which moves in both directions.

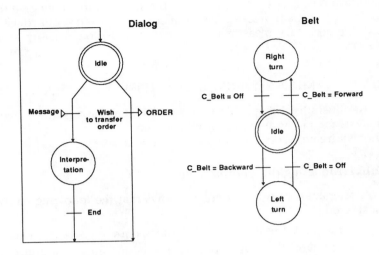

Figure 12.20   Modeling a platform.

Figure 12.21 summarizes the vehicle variable characteristics.

Subset	Inputs	Internal variables	Outputs	Definition
Displacement part	CVM1, CVM2			Motor command 0 .. CVMAX
		P		Two dimensional Trolley position
		VM1, VM2		Speed of each wheel 0 .. Vmax
Belt	C_Belt			Belt command: Forward, Backward, Off
		BELT_STATE		Belt state: stop, loading, unloading.

Figure 12.21   Vehicle analysis.

The model can be deduced from this analysis. A three-state machine (obvious, not shown) characterizes the belt. For the displacement part, we can simply state that the position variation along the direction traveled is proportional to the average speed of the two wheels and therefore of the motors and that the direction change is proportional to the difference between speeds VM1 and VM2. This may result in a formulation which is not helpful in solving the problem.

-C- Modeling the workshop

For the trolley, the workshop defines the trajectory to be followed and the position of obstacles at all times. Information useful to the system about the trolley are:

- OBSTACLE: Boolean information;

- DCA: distance of the trolley from its desired trajectory.

12.10.2 System specifications

-A- Delimitation of inputs/outputs

The system to be specified linked to the entitiesof its environment is shown in Figure 12.22.

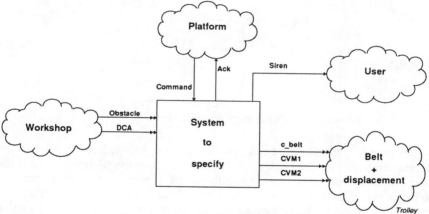

Figure 12.22   The system and its links with its environment.

It is fairly obvious at this stage that some observations necessary to satisfy the objective are missing since the system acts on the trolley in an open loop. These required observations will be determined from the functional specification.

-B- Functional specification

We are concerned here only with the trolley. Its control system must carry out a single function, which is to automatically perform the transfer cycle for each packet. The specification includes the trolley and the two platforms, each of which has a different role. Platform 1 initiates a transfer cycle.

The role of the system is defined by the following finite state machines which clearly demonstrate that the deduction is made starting from entities. Since the belt subset is very simple, the specification shown in Figure 12.23 considers the trolley globally as a single unit.

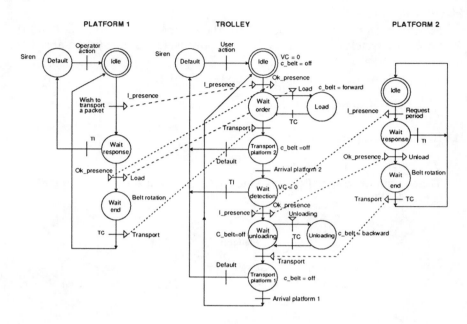

Figure 12.23   Functional trolley control specification.

Commands incoming from platforms are therefore *I_presence* for interrogation and loading a packet, *Transport* to the next platform, and *Unload* packet. The only message from the trolley is *Ok_presence* to satisfy the presence interrogation. The time TC is the load or unload time. TI is a maximum wait time for a response.The trolley speed VC is that imposed on the trajectory defined by the guide wire. The displacement state is identical since it involves moving from platform 1 to platform 2, or vice versa. It is refined by bringing in the start, constant speed and stop phases. With a duration of one sec and of linear speed variation up to 5 kph, the trolley takes 0.7 m to start and to stop as shown in Figure 12.24.

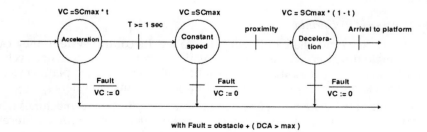

Figure 12.24   Displacement state specification.

Stop due to obstacle detection takes place by cancelling motor control, leading to stop by inertia.

Analysis of transition conditions in this specification shows the necessity for the following observations:

- platform_presence, for stop;
- platform_proximity for the deceleration phase;
- platform_arrival.

A discussion with the customer will define the sensor(s) necessary for determining these variables. In addition, the speed of each wheel has to be observed if the trolley is to move at the control speed VC.

-C- *Operational and technological specifications*

Since this is only an example introducing the procedure, we will not describe the details of the technological specifications here, which consist mainly of the data given in the requirements definition (see Section 9.8.2.).

This problem has no geographic distribution. If we had to deal with the overall workshop control - platforms + trolley - we would have to build a three-site geographically distributed system with the infrared link as communication support.

There is no user interface either, but this is a real-time problem since the motor control function must react quickly (between 1 and 5 msec) to allow the trolley to satisfactorily follow the required trajectory at a speed of 5 kph.

12.11 SPECIFICATION VERIFICATION AND VALIDATION

The objective of the specification step is to obtain a coherent document, checked and accepted by the customer. This validity is obtained by an author/reader cycle. Intervention of the various participants requires task scheduling.

12.11.1 The participants

For the verification, in conjunction with the project manager and at the beginning of the step, the specification author or authors will define which readers will review the specification in order to obtain a quality document. The readers must represent the categories concerned by the result, namely:

- the customer, as purchaser;
- product or system users;
- installers, operating and maintenance personnel;
- product designers;
- if necessary, a specification specialist.

This procedure is efficient since, in this way, all customer's personnel concerned are aware of the product. If the objectives do not converge, a discussion will lead to an accepted compromise. The document will then be validated and accepted as a contractual basis. Any later modification can then be reasonably considered as an additional clause to the contract.

Before starting the work, the design team gradually becomes aware of the objectives to be achieved, the environment and complete specifications. The feasibility can then be evaluated very quickly.

A specification specialist may also carry out a critical analysis of specifications and the process followed. This will improve the quality of the document, simplify models and the specifications, subsequently reducing the complexity of the development.

12.11.2 Scheduling work and reviews

For reasons of efficiency, at least three reading stages are necessary (Figure 12.25):

   - after modeling the environment. This initial reading will correct specifier interpretation errors;
   - after the functional specifications, this stage is essential and justified for a good check;
   - after completion of the specifications to correct and eliminate all errors and omissions.

Before describing the desirable schedule, note that experience has shown that specification lasts considerably longer than the amount of time dedicated to this work. There is about a 3 order factor between the duration and the time allowed.

For the author/reader cycle, each reader must read and comment on every document that he receives. In return, each author prepares a synthesis of all comments and updates his document which he then redistributes for acceptance.

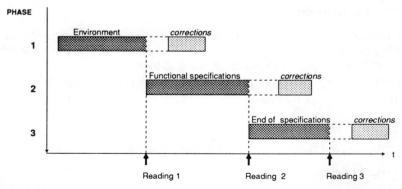

Figure 12.25   Scheduling phases and reviews.

This procedure only gives good results if readers share a responsibility for the quality of the result. This is one way of training specifiers and giving some responsibility to customer participants. This approach to specifications should be participative.

12.12 SPECIFICATION CHARACTERISTICS

To complete this chapter, we will summarize the described process and the advantages of a specification as a model.

The essential characteristics of the recommended specification model are as follows:

- It is a conceptual model which describes what the system must be, and not a physical model which would describe the implementation. Models are abstract which allows elimination of details by a simplified expression of the behavior. Apparently complex to those who encounter a specification method for the first time, the specifier will quickly note its efficiency for assisting with the analysis of all aspects of a system and then its advantage for subsequent design and implementation phases.

- The specification is structured. This quality facilitates a progressive approach to specifications and customer requirements until arriving at the complete characteristics of the system. This structure facilitates reading the document for customers and users, which is essential for verification. The classification of specifications into categories also increases the efficiency of designers in their progressive search for the solution, considering only the necessary information for each phase.

- The specification is complete because it considers all aspects of the system. The reader can thus get a precise and correct idea of the resulting product or system. Since it is complete, it is a useful intermediate point between the customer and the final product. The specification is thus verifiable before starting the design. Similarly, when the product has been made, an exhaustive check of the system against the specifications is possible.

- The specification can be interpreted. Little knowledge is required to understand the various parts of the specification. Some models are graphical, so that we can analyze the information more efficiently. Without using extreme formalism which would complicate understandability for the non-specialist, models remain precise and explicit. The specification document based on this model is thus especially beneficial to readers.

- The specification is verifiable. The model structure and dependencies between components introduce implicit verification rules for the coherence of a specification. The understandability of the document by several readers - customer, users, designers - will eliminate many errors or omissions. In addition, modeling entities without the system, and then including the system constraints, can easily be checked by simulation. Similarly, prototyping for man-machine interfaces is a technique which helps validating specifications.

12.13 SUMMARY

The specification method is a direct result of the recommended description model. The main points are:

- Specification production consists of two main phases: modeling the environment and system specification.

- The environment is characterized based on an analysis of the behavior of application entities. Inputs to these entities are the outputs from the system and entity outputs are available as input. If necessary, this model can serve as a basis for simulation, particularly for the correct system behavior test before on-site experimentation.

- The system itself is considered as an added complementary entity for making a functional coupling. Unlike entities which, since they exist, can be modeled based on reality, the system specification cannot and must not be based on the description of internal system functions.

- The system is specified by an external description which is as complete as possible. Seen from the outside, it performs functions for the environment. These functions are characterized by describing their actions on entity behaviors. The system specification is therefore clearly based on the environment modeling.

- The complete system specification is classified into three information categories - functional, operational, technological - to facilitate its use in all subsequent development phases.

- The method gradually produces a complete specification document. The specification is then analyzed by readers, verified and finally becomes a contractual document.

REFERENCES PART 3

BOOKS

[ABBOTT-86]
> *An Integrated Approach to Software Development*
> R.J. Abbott
> Wiley, Interscience Publication, John Wiley&Sons 1986

[ALFORD-82]
> Distributed Systems. Methods and Tools for Specification.
> An advanced course. *In Lecture Notes in Computer Science.*
> M.W. Alford, J.P. Ansart, G. Hommel, L. Lamport, B. Liskov,
> G.P. Mullery, F.B. Schneider.
> Springer-Verlag 1982

[AMGHAR-89]
> *Méthodes de Développement d'un Système à Microprocesseurs*
> A. Amghar
> MASSON Collection Manuels Informatiques 1989

[BAILLY-87]
> *Les Langages Orientés Objets: Concepts, Langages et Applications*
> C. Bailly, J.F. Challine, P.Y. Gloess, H.C. Ferri, B. Marchesin
> Cepadues - Editions 1987

[CAPRON-86]
> *Systems Analysis and Design*
> H.L. CAPRON
> The Benjamin/Cummings Publishing Company Inc 1986

[COAD-90]
> *Object-Oriented Analysis*
> P. Coad, E. Yourdon
> Yourdon Press Computing Series 1990

[COHEN-86]
The Specification of Complex Systems
B. Cohen, W.T. Harwood, M.I. Jackson
Addison-Wesley Publishing Company 1986

[DATE-86]
An Introduction to Database Systems, Vol 1
C.J. Date
Addison-Wesley, 4th edition 1986

[DAVIS-90]
Software Requirements. Analysis and Specification
A. M. Davis
Prentice-Hall 1990

[DEMARCO-79]
Structured Analysis and System Specification
T. DeMarco
Yourdon Computing Series, YOURDON PRESS, Prentice-Hall 1979

[GALACSI-86]
Les Systèmes d'Information - Analyse et Conception
Galacsi, Nom collectif
Dunod Informatique 1986

[HATLEY-87]
Strategies for Real-time System Specification
D.J. Hatley, I.A. Pirbhai
Dorset House Publishing New-York, 1987

[JACKSON-83]
System Development
M. Jackson
CA.R Hoare Series, Prentice-Hall 1983

[MARTIN-88]
Structured Techniques - the Basis for CASE
J. Martin, C. Mc Clure
Prentice-Hall 1988

[RUMBAUGH-91]
Object-Oriented Modeling and Design
J. Rumbaugh, M. Blaha, W. Premerlani, F. Eddy, W. Lorensen
Prentice-Hall 1991

[VELEZ-89]
The O2 Object Manager: An overview
F. Velez, G. Bernard, V. Darnis
Rapport Altair No 26, Février 1989

[WARD-85]
> *Structured Development for Real-time Systems*
> P.T. Ward, S.J. Mellor
> *Vol.1: Introduction and Tools*
> *Vol.2: Essential modeling Techniques*
> Yourdon Computing Series, YOURDON PRESS, Prentice-Hall 1985

PAPERS

[ABBOTT-81]
> *Software requirements and specifications: A survey of needs and languages*
> R.J. Abbott, D.K. Moorhead
> *The Journal of Systems and Software* No 2 1981, p 297-316

[BAILIN-89]
> *An object-oriented requirements specification method*
> S.C.Bailin
> *Communications of ACM* Vol 32, No 5, may 1989, p 608-623

[BRACON-88]
> *La spécification du logiciel dans l'industrie*
> G. Bracon
> *Bigre* No 58 Janvier 1988, p 12-19

[DAVIS-88]
> *A comparison of techniques for the specification of external system behavior*
> A.M. Davis
> *Communications of the ACM* Vol 31, No 9, September 1988, p 1098-1115

[HAGEMANN-88]
> *Requirements analysis for real-time automation projects*
> M. Hagemann
> *Proceedings of 10th International Conference on Software Engineering,* Singapore
> 11-15 April 1988, p 122-129

[HAREL-87a]
> *Using statecharts for hardware Description*
> D. Harel, D. Drusinsky
> *IEEE International Conference on Computer-Aided-Design*
> November 9-12 1987 St Clara, CA p 162-165

[HAREL-87b]
> *Statecharts: a visual formalism for complex systems*
> D. Harel
> *Science of Computer Programming* North Holland, Vol 8 1987, p 231-274

[HAREL-89]
Using statecharts for hardware description and synthesis
D. Drusinsky, D. Harel
IEEE Transactions on Computer-Aided Design Vol 8 No 7 july 1989,
p 798-807

[IGL-83]
Introduction à SADT
Documentation IGL France, 1983

[JOHNSON-88]
Deriving specifications from requirements
W.L. Johnson
Proceedings of 10th International Conference on Software Engineering
Singapore 11-15 April 1988, p 428-438

[KURTZ-89]
An object-oriented methodology for system analysis and specification
B.D. Kurtz, D. Ho, T.A. Wall
Hewlett-Packard Journal April 1989, p 86-90

[LUDEWIG-87]
Specification techniques for real-time systems
J. Ludewig, H. Matheis
Computer Standards and Interfaces No 6, 1987 p 115-133

[ORR-88]
Systematic method for real-time system design
R.A. Orr, M.T.Orris, R. Tinker, C.D.V. Rouch
Microprocessors and Microsystems Vol 12 No 7 September 1988, p 391-396

[PARNAS-86]
A rational design process: how and why to fake it
D.L. Parnas, P.C. Clements
IEEE Transactions on Software Engineering Vol SE 12 No 2 1986, p 251-257

[RAMAMOORTHY-87]
Issues in the development of large, distributed, and reliable software
C.V. Ramamoorthy, A. Prakash, V. Garg, T. Yamaura, A. Bhide
Advances in Computers, Vol 26 -Purdue (LD-26), p 393-443

[ROSS-85]
Applications and extensions of SADT
D.T. Ross
Computer April 1985, p 36-46

[SHEMER-87]
Systems analysis: a systemic analysis of a conceptual model
I. Shemer
Communications of the ACM Vol 30 No 6, June 1987, p 506-512

PART 4

FUNCTIONAL DESIGN

The objective of this step is to create a complete description of the selected solution, considering purely functional aspects only. It must remain completely independent of technological constraints and solutions, so that it represents the "invariant hard core" for the application.

Using the functional specifications, the designer starts with the preliminary or architectural design work which involves searching for an internal solution.

The selected solution must comply with a model referred to as the "functional model", so that it can be used as a specification for the next step.

This model corresponds to the two dimensions of the global model:
  - the functional dimension which is a spatial or topological model;
  - the behavioral dimension.

To facilitate his work, the designer must have a guide to help him produce quality solutions conform to the functional model.

In this part, Chapter 13 describes the functional model. Chapter 14 then describes the main design principles that every designer must try to respect to produce quality solutions.

Chapter 15 develops the method to be followed, illustrated by examples.

To help designers, Chapter 16 demonstrates the advantages of template solution models leading to general quality solutions.

13

THE FUNCTIONAL MODEL

The functional model, and particularly the functional structure model, were briefly described in Part 1: MCSE Overview (Chapter 5).

The functional model expresses a set of rules which must be respected by any solution developed by a designer to comply with the methodology. If these rules are respected for a solution, it will have the model properties. The solution can then be used as a specification for the next step concerning the implementation specification.

In order to concentrate on the essentials for the application without getting involved in technological type constraints, the functional model concerns:

- the topology of functional constituents;

- the behavior of these components.

This chapter fully describes this model by defining description and behavior rules and then describing its properties. It details the three parts: the functional structure model, the function behavior model and the data description model.

13.1 FUNCTIONAL MODEL COMPONENTS

First, remember that the methodology is based on a three dimensional model. The first two dimensions - functional structure and function behavior - form the functional description model (see Chapter 5).

First, we will propose a definition:

- A **functional model** is a representation of all or part of a system by a component structure. It expresses the semantics of its components and relations between them, and the system behavior towards the application that includes it. Active components are functions.

The functional model described in Calvez [CALVEZ-82] consists of three sets of information:

- the **functional structure**, the first dimension of a global description model;

- an **expression of the behavior** of elementary functions, the second dimension;

- the **data structure** contained in the first dimension.

The functional structure and the data structure describe the organization dimension, and the function behavior expression describes the behavioral dimension very often, but not necessarily, by a temporal description.

The organization dimension explicitly uses a hierarchical model, thus allowing refinement and abstraction operations. A top-down hierarchical approach can also be used to express behavior based on the contribution of structured programming.

The composition of the functional model can be represented as shown in Figure 13.1.

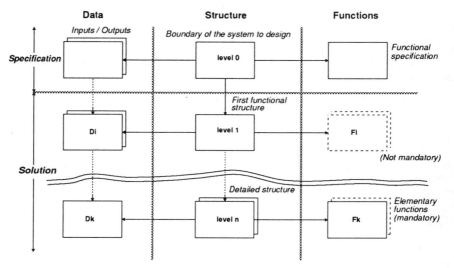

Figure 13.1   Hierarchical functional model decomposition.

The organizational part (or structure) is a tree structure since a non-elementary function is described by a lower level structure. The data part is a collection of trees or terminal elements. The functions part is a collection. Each level contains specifications for data and functions involved in the structures of the same level.

There are no functions for level 0 since there is no refinement. The functional specification characterizes this level.

This hierarchical description already suggests a guide for the solution search process. The rest of this chapter discusses the characteristics of the three parts of the functional model: functional structure, elementary functions and data.

13.2 THE FUNCTIONAL STRUCTURE MODEL

A functional structure is the topological expression of a function implementation by a component network. The abbreviation FS is sometimes used in the following for Functional Structure.

Function usually refers to the conceptual entity carrying out a specific activity.

Since every function can be described by a structure containing more elementary functions, an FS is a refinement tool.

The rest of this section discusses drawing conventions (static view), followed by symbol interpretation for a non-ambiguous understanding of any FS (dynamic view).

13.2.1 Graphical representation

Every function to be described by a functional refinement has inputs and/or outputs. A functional structure is made up of four element types, namely:

- functions (F), each represented by a rectangle,

- state variables (SV), represented by the symbol:

- events (EV), represented by:

- ports (PT), represented by:

Links between these elements have to be added to define relations.

Relations are only possible between functions and necessarily by using an intermediate state variable, event, or port element. The intermediate element between two functions is strictly necessary since the two functions may be asynchronous. Three relation types are allowed:

- the synchronization relation by an event;   ·················→
- the variable sharing relation by a state variable;   ─────────→
- the information (message) transfer relation through a port.   ══════⇒

An example of a functional structure describing the solution for the control of a multi-axis robot is shown in Figure 13.2.

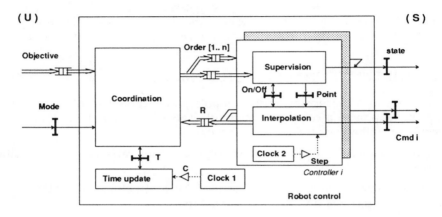

Figure 13.2   Functional Structure example.

A controller is associated with each robot axis. There is therefore the same number of controller type instances as there are axes. The coordination function transmits commands to each ORDER[i]. Each controller sends an acknowledgement R after carrying out each command.

State variables and messages may be of any type: see data specification in Section 13.4. Multiple instances are also shown to improve readability.

All links are unidirectional, except when a variable has to be accessed for reading and updating. Links for a function described by a functional structure start from its inputs (U) and end at its outputs (O).

Every function internal to a functional structure also has inputs and/or outputs. Relation links end at the inputs and start from the outputs of these internal functions. Each function input or output has a nature: event, variable, message. A relation is only correct if all its constituents are compatible: element types for the relation, links leaving and arriving at the element, inputs and outputs concerned.

We can formally state that a function Fi described by a functional structure FSi is defined by a 3-tuple:

$$Fi = (U, O, FSi)$$

13.2.2 FS coherence and understandability

We will express a few common sense rules for representing any functional structure.

-A- *Controlability and observability*

A function is said to be controlable if all its inputs are externally linked to another function.

A function is said to be observable if all its outputs are externally linked to another function.

The graphical representation is coherent if all inputs and outputs of each function described by an FS are used. Finally, all functions of the FS must be controlable and observable, and all EV, SV, and PT elements participate in a complete relation.

-B- *Specification of all elements*

The functional specification must not be ambiguous. Therefore, all elements, inputs and outputs must be named. It is very important for interpretation to make a suitable choice of a concise name with minimum reference to explanatory text.

Some rules to be followed for selecting names are:

- State variables are information or more generally objects used by functions. These elements must therefore have object names only. For example: SPEED, AUTHOR CATALOG.

- Functions transform or use object elements. The name must therefore be a verb followed by a noun. Example: check speed, read authors.

- An event name must be a state change. For example: STOP, TIME ELAPSED.

- The name of messages and therefore of ports which receive them must express the occurrence of data or commands. For example: ORDER, BOOK RECEIVED.

Apart from these rules, always try to choose the most appropriate words since the selected names will probably be used throughout the life of the project and interpretation will be unnecessarily complicated if a bad choice is made.

Input and output names may be different from the name of the connected element. If the name is identical, it is omitted thus clarifying the presentation.

-C- *Presentation*

For reasons of clarity, a functional structure must have a good quality presentation.

First, the number of functions at a level is necessarily limited to a maximum of 5 to 7. A simple presentation rule then consists of showing all inputs at the left and all outputs at the right of functions. If possible, function positions should be such that relations move from the left towards the right, whenever possible.

This is obviously impossible when there are internal loops. Understanding topology can be optimized by analyzing relations participating in loops. A functional relation is shown horizontally. A hierarchical relation is preferably shown vertically. Figure 13.3 illustrates these presentation rules.

13.2.3 Interpretation of an FS

Interpretation expresses behavior rules subjacent to the graphical representation, so as to unambiguously define the specification of all constituents and the behavior for interactions. These rules make it possible to get an understanding of the dynamic behavior of the functional structure to its static view.

It will then be possible to understand the behavior of a functional structure at every description level, without needing to know the detailed and complete behavior of each function and the nature of the data.

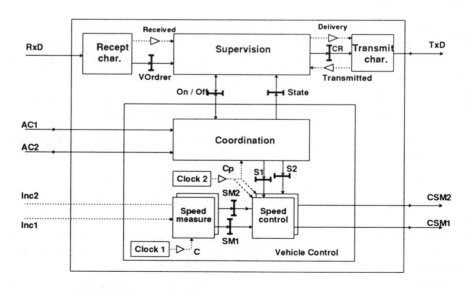

Figure 13.3   Presentation example.

-A- Rules for events

Every event (EV) produced by a function simultaneously affects all related functions.

-B- Rules for state variables

State variables (SV) are used to exchange data between functions which may be completely asynchronous. Any variable may thus be modified or read at any moment, singly or simultaneously by several functions.

Integrity constraints must be respected for the implementation; this means that two simultaneous assignments (d1 and d2) must give a resulting value of either d1 or d2, but not a combination of the two.

-C- Rules for ports

The PORT (PT) is used for the temporary storage of messages during a transfer between two asynchronous functions. They are normally called producer and consumer. Functions submit and remove individual messages at arbitrary times. A removal can only take place if at least one message exists.

Unlike the state variable which can take on only one value at any time, the port is a storage QUEUE of all messages produced and not yet "consumed". The queue is assumed to have an infinite capacity and is of the FIFO type - First In First Out.

As a result of the storage effect, the message transfer time is quite arbitrary by using this method. Figure 13.4 summarizes the behavior for the relation by message transfer.

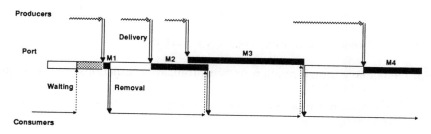

Figure 13.4   Specification for transfer by port.

-D- Rules for functions

A function is a transformation operator acting on input information or data to produce output information or data. Every function is cyclic, in other words it carries out the same transformations but on consecutive data.

Two behavior cases have to be considered, depending on the nature of inputs:

- **Permanent function**: this is a function with no event type or message input. In the absence of any synchronization relation with its environment, the function permanently carries out its transformation role.

- **Temporary function**: one or more inputs are of the message or event type. Transformations are then necessarily synchronous with received messages or events.

During the activity of a function, all variables linked by inputs and outputs can be read and modified. Similarly, events and messages can be produced by outputs, see Figure 13.5.

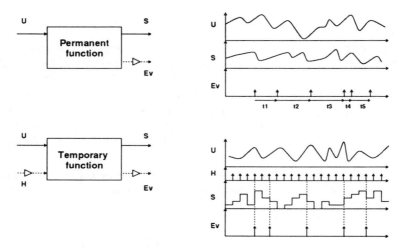

Figure 13.5   Permanent behavior, temporary behavior.

For elementary transformation or synchronization functions, the behavior can be compared with:
- a sequential machine, synchronous to input messages or events, for a temporary function;
- a generator for a permanent function.

Without detailed specifications, transformation times should be considered as null. Using this rule for temporary functions, generated outputs are synchronous with input events. For permanent functions, these generations are specified by temporal features. Figure 13.6 is an example illustrating the above rules.

The LOADING function is invoked by each ORDER message. When its task is executed, it produces a RESULT message.

This function is decomposed into three more elementary functions:
- For each ORDER message, SUPERVISION as a temporary function decodes the message, makes the execution request using the On/Off and REQUIRED QUANTITY variables, waits for the end of execution observed by On/Off, and generates the RESULT message. Therefore, the execution time cannot be null.

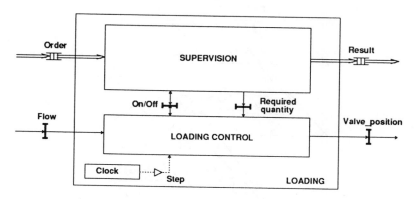

Figure 13.6   Functional structure example.

- CLOCK is a permanent function for generating a periodic event.
- The temporary LOADING_CONTROL function observes the On/Off request and the FLOW input variable, and calculates the VALVE_POSITION control value for each STEP event. When the requested quantity is obtained, it sets On/Off = Off.

Variables are only modified when the SUPERVISION and LOADING_CONTROL functions are active.

13.2.4 Refinement and abstraction of an FS

The FS model is used to describe a function by a structure made up of simpler functions. It is therefore a refinement tool. Conversely, abstraction on a functional structure simplifies the structure. These two mechanisms will be described in more detail.

-A- Refinement

When a function is not sufficiently detailed to be fully specified, it may be described by a functional structure. The use of this top-down procedure for a set of functions leads to a functional structure hierarchized into description levels as shown in Figure 13.7.

Function delimitations for lower levels can be eliminated. They are of no technical use. A "flat" model then results. This is not a good idea for a system, since intermediate levels facilitate readability and therefore understandability.

For identification reasons in complex structures, functions are numbered. The start function considered to be level 0 does not need to be numbered. Any function in a refinement is numbered starting from 1. All instances included in one function have the same number since they derive from the same specification.

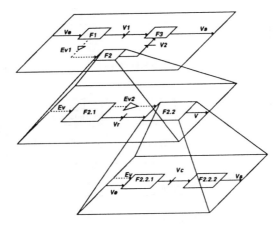

Figure 13.7   Example of hierarchized functional structure and numbering.

Following this rule, the number of an elementary function includes the complete path in the hierarchy tree. The function level can then be found by counting the number of digits.

-B- Abstraction

A functional structure can be built up by associating subsets so as to integrate already known solutions. This procedure encourages reuse. But the solution may become difficult to understand for complex problems. Details must be eliminated to obtain a more macroscopic description. The abstraction process for this purpose consists of:

- choosing a subset of the functional structure internally consistent with the objectives by delimiting it;

- replacing this subset by the specification of a non-refined function obtained by eliminating the entire internal description.

The abstraction approach is not the simplest since it is not immediately obvious that combined functions are coherent. However, this technique should not be excluded since a purely top-down procedure by refinement is not always realistic for complicated applications. Iterations are necessary, and sometimes the best functions to be considered for an application can be found by abstraction.

13.2.5 Maximum decomposition: elementary functions or actions

Using the successive iterations refinement technique, the solution becomes more and more detailed. Obviously, the question arises of when to stop the iteration for each function. A clear criterion must therefore be specified.

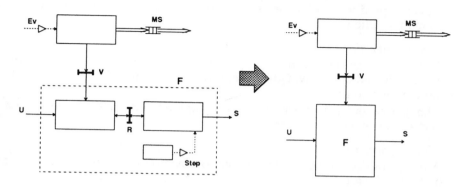

Figure 13.8   Abstraction techniques.

The rule is designed to be simple: a function with a sequential and necessarily cyclic behavior, can no longer be refined. Why? Simply because the advantage of the functional structure model is to show potential concurrency in solution functions. Therefore, refinement is no longer justified, if the behavior is sequential. This type of function is called an "elementary function" or "action".

But how can we know that a function has a sequential behavior because, according to a top-down process, this function is not defined yet? This is a difficult question.

If a functional description is to be complete and therefore checkable, each function must be specified, which means it must be described from an external point of view.

If the function specification is based on a sequential model (for example, a state diagram or transformation model), the answer is available. Otherwise, a refinement must be attempted which may lead the designer towards a functional structure or a specification in which the function is actually elementary.

13.2.6 Behavior rules for an elementary function

We will now describe behavior rules imposed on every elementary function for checking purposes, in order to be able to interpret the behavior of a complete FS with maximum refinement. Without needing to detail the contents of a function, the interpretation will then be unambiguous for all levels of the functional structure.

The following rules were drawn up for their simplicity and because they subsequently facilitate the implementation work.

The internal description rules given in Section 13.3.3.C (function behavior expression) produce a behavior as seen from the outside, in accordance with rules in this section.

-A- Permanent action

Every function which has no message or event type input evolves continuously and cyclically. Otherwise, it would be impossible to indicate the evolution start point.

The permanent action can thus be compared with a continuous data generator or event generator process.

-B- Temporary action

Message or event type inputs are used to synchronize the necessarily cyclic evolution of the function. Transformations carried out by the function normally take place in zero time.

The behavior of the function for several synchronization inputs is specified by the Petri net in Figure 13.9. We consider here a function synchronous to many events (EVi) and message receptions (MESj). Initial marking for EVi and MESj shows the effect of storing events and messages.

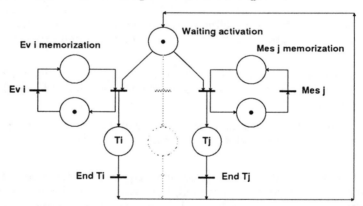

Figure 13.9   Behavior specification for a temporary action.

This Petri net shows that:

- evolution conditions may be due to the emergence of events or the presence of messages;

- transformations or operations (Ti, Tj) are carried out sequentially (due to the presence of a single token) and therefore in mutual exclusion (sequential behavior);

- the evolution ordering for simultaneously true conditions is not deterministic (non-deterministic behavior);

- all events or messages are taken into account (memorization effect).

This behavior is deliberately restrictive. After having applied this model to develop a large number of applications, we have concluded that all solutions can easily be reduced to this type of synchronous sequential machine.

Considering a single macroscopic behavior level, the solution is not always easy to describe since it requires considerable functional decomposition. Specifications sometimes require that waiting periods conditional on events or messages can be described in the cyclic process loop. For example, this applies to protocol specifications.

This is why the behavior model during the evolution of a function was enhanced by a wait statement on a single or multiple event type condition. This means that the conditional wait can be used as one of the operations carried out by the function. The behavior of this wait statement on one or several events or messages is specified as shown in Figure 13.10.

Only one operation, Ti, is carried out when the first event or message for the condition appears. If two or more events (or messages) appear simultaneously, the decision of which branch is used is non-deterministic.

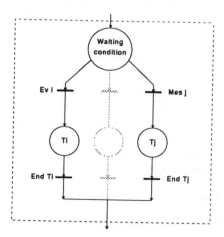

Figure 13.10   Wait statement specification.

This behavior is particularly useful in communication protocols when, for example, it is required to state that the evolution must continue when an acknowledgement message arrives or on a "watchdog" deadline.

-C- Complementary notation

As a result of the imposed behavior described above for a temporary action, not all received events and messages have the same meaning:

- Activation events or messages trigger an activity cycle;
- Condition events or messages delay the activity evolution within a cycle.

To differentiate them, input to the former is shown by a single arrow, and input to the latter by a double arrow. We can therefore state a simple presentation rule: every temporary action has at least one activation input.

13.2.7 Functional structure properties

We will quickly describe the essential properties of the functional structure model.

-A- Structure model

Hierarchical decomposition facilitates a progressive understanding of the description and the solution search. For refinement, each function is described by a structure. For abstraction, a set of functions is replaced by a more abstract function for example, for its reuse.

The structured hierarchical model thus presents the solution as a set of hierarchical structure levels starting from a functional specification (purely external view) and leading to a functional description for the application. Level i+1 is deduced from level i by adding supplementary constraints for the solution.

-B- Interpretable and therefore checkable model

Knowledge solely of behavior rules for all elementary function, variable, port and event elements mentioned in the previous sections can be used to deduce the complete behavior of the functional structure. For a given application, this deduction does not require precise knowledge of the specification of each function.

The model is therefore interpretable, which is helpful when checking conformity against part of the specification.

-C- Synchronous evolution

With the zero time assumption for the evolution of temporary functions, all events and messages produced are synchronous with condition or activation messages and events. The analysis is thus simplified since all evolutions are immediate and simultaneous by category.

-D- Conservation of order relations

Partial order relations from the generator to receivers and from each producer to the corresponding consumer are respected.

-E- Maximum parallelism

The decomposition rule is to continue refinement until elementary functions are obtained. Since by definition these functions have a sequential behavior, the complete functional structure model therefore represents the maximum possible parallelism for its evolution.

It should be noted that for some problems with hard real-time constraints, for example image processing, known algorithms are generally sequential. But for implementation, these algorithms must be transformed to introduce parallelism. This work always takes place after the functional design phase.

-F- Dynamic structure model

Relations between functions and the number and type of functions may also be static or dynamic. Therefore, the structure can also evolve in time but respecting the stated behavior rules.

Therefore, it is possible to describe systems allowing structural evolution (reconfiguration, degraded operation, self-adaptation, etc.) and by deduction to design them. In the following sections of this book, we will restrict ourselves to the design of static structures.

13.3 ELEMENTARY FUNCTION SPECIFICATION

The elementary function specification described in the previous section expresses an external point of view. This point of view is justified to allow checking of the functional solution after each refinement step.

The objective of this section is to formalize description rules for the internal behavior of any elementary function. The description will be made in accordance with external point of view rules, and will act as a complete and unambiguous specification for the implementation phase. This specification will be sufficient for subsequent phases, without needing to refer to the functional structure containing it.

13.3.1 Specification objectives

After each refinement phase, the designer must verify the selected solution against the specifications. He makes the check when he is thoroughly familiar with the way in which he expects the function to behave.

In order to guarantee complete coherence of the functional solution, the behavior of each elementary function must be expressed on paper after the refinement has been completely achieved.

The main objectives for this specification are:
- to eliminate all interpretation ambiguities. This is a necessary condition to guarantee validity of the selected solution. The solution must therefore be concise, understandable, unambiguous, complete.
- to be compatible with the functional model, meaning that this specification adds an additional dimension to the description (very often temporal), with coupling compatibility between function inputs and outputs.
- to express the "WHAT" in preference to the "HOW": specification rather than the implementation. The specification must also be expressed without considering time constraints.

- to facilitate the search for an implementation solution. Apparently incompatible with the previous objective, it must not be forgotten that the final product is an implementation. A compromise must be made between the formal purely external specification and a pure implementation description.
- to facilitate validation. There are two complementary ways of achieving this:
  - by readers who may be specification authors, or even customers;
  - by the use of computer tools which, after translating the description, can check the behavior by partial or total simulation.

13.3.2 Description language choice

The description method must satisfy the above objectives as well as possible. We will discuss the possible solutions by categories.

-A- Graphical or textual description

The graphical description facilitates understanding. It is a well-known communication tool. However, it is difficult to give a complete description, especially for the details. Although it is an essential tool for global specifications, it is not sufficient at this stage if an adequate functional description is required for use during implementation.

A textual description has less global visibility. It has the advantage that the description can be as complete as required. Therefore, we will use this second form, noting that the unit to be described will be limited in size.

-B- Declarative or imperative description

In the strict sense of the term, a specification can only express the "WHAT" and not the "HOW"; in other words it should only give an external view of the described object. This type of description is not procedural. For example, it may be expressed by formal models (mathematical or other) which are expressed by stating pre-conditions and post-conditions for the function. The advantage of this solution is that implementers will subsequently be completely free to find or choose the most appropriate solution to satisfy the specification.

On the other hand, this type of specification is not easy to write; it is easier to express the behavior using an internal model. Validation is also more difficult, or even impossible for complex descriptions. Finally, the description is not suitable for use for the implementation.

An imperative description is based on the use of an internal model and therefore expresses part of the "HOW". The danger of this solution is that a typical implementation solution may be selected. Implementation alternatives will subsequently be limited.

The advantage is that it considerably facilitates implementation and validation by computer tools, resulting in a significant time saving.

To express how the output variables are to be obtained from the input variables, it is practically essential to make use of internal variables which, for example, can be deduced by an analysis of the specifications.

Best satisfying stated objectives, an imperative type description is used with a sequential machine type internal model. The author of the behavior description must find a good compromise between a purely external view and a too strict implementation in order to keep options open for the implementation.

-C- Natural language or "executable" language

After selecting the textual form and imperative type, the syntactical strictness question must be considered.

Natural language is very rich, allowing many different ways of describing the same "thing". Understanding may not be obvious due to redundancies in the text. Similarly, checking its completeness is not easy.

An "executable" language, in other words a computer language, is particularly strict because it is governed by precise syntactical and semantic rules. It has significantly less degrees of freedom. But as a result of its strictness, criteria such as conciseness, completeness, unambiguity and non-redundancy are more easily satisfied.

A positive point for executable languages is the existence of currently available high-level, and therefore structured and structuring, hardware-independent, languages such as Pascal and ADA.

There is no doubt that an executable type language must be used. This type of language satisfies the criteria stated in the objectives, reduces development time since it is almost executable, and finally allows almost complete solution validation by simulation and remains independent of the technology used later.

As a basis, and perhaps also by practice, the Pascal language will be used with a few minor extensions described below. It is obvious that an "If Then Else" type pseudo-language could be used; the disadvantage is that this would not facilitate automatic verification by executing the description and then the implementation.

13.3.3 The description model

After having described the choice of the description type, this section formally describes the description rules to be followed. The description model is described in three levels, each corresponding to a refinement, see Figure 13.11:

- the interface with the functional structure model;
- the body of the behavior description;
- the evolution control description.

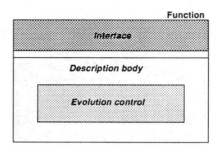

Figure 13.11   Description structure.

Before we start, we will mention a few important points to be satisfied:

- two function types: temporary or permanent depending on whether or not event or message type input or inputs are present;
- nature coherence between inputs and outputs and variables related to the functional model;
- initialization of the functional model variables. Necessary to allow the application to start from a given initial state, these variables can only be initialized by functions related by an output.

-A- Interface with the functional structure model

The functional structure model considers an elementary structure like a graphical symbol representing a "black box" with three types of inputs and outputs: events, variables, messages.

There are two types of messages and event inputs (single and double arrow) depending on whether it is an activation input or an evolution condition input.

A textual description of the interface must be compatible with this symbolic notation as shown in Figure 13.12.

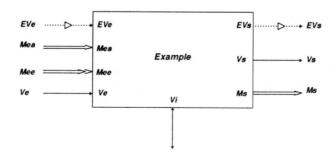

Figure 13.12   Graphical representation of a function.

The syntax used for the above example is as follows:

```
action EXAMPLE on event Eve and message Mea: T_Mea with
                    (inputs message Mee; T_Mee;
                          var Ve: T_Ve;
                    input/output var VI: T_VI;
                    outputs event EVs;
                          var Vs: T_Vs;
                          message Ms: T_Ms);
```

This example can be used to easily deduce the general syntax to be respected. All inputs, events and activation messages are specified after "on", and other inputs and outputs after "with". "On" does not exist for a permanent action.

The nature of each input or output is identified. For messages and variables, the information structure is defined by its type (for example, T_...).

The term "action" is used rather than "function", "process" or "task", to avoid confusion with terminology previously used elsewhere and possibly too close to the implementation. Bear in mind that an action is a task which evolves like a cyclic process, but is limited to a single function, and is therefore relatively instantaneous.

-B- Description body

This part describes the global behavior of any function. The description must comply with the specification used for the functional model. Therefore, every function behaves like a sequential machine, which also implies initialization of all its internal variables. Output variables must also be initialized.

Therefore, the body description must respect the following model:

```
Declaration constants, types, variables; (internal)
begin
initialization of output variables and input variables;
    cycle
            <behavior>
    end cycle;
end action name;
```

The "cycle <behavior> end cycle;" statement expresses the cyclic action of the <behavior> statement.

-C- Action evolution expression

A distinction should be made between permanent actions and temporary actions. There are no activation and condition inputs for permanent actions. The behavior is then expressed as a series of sequential operations.

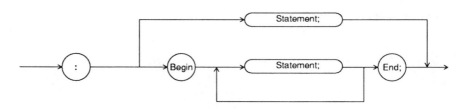

For temporary actions, each activation message, or event input must be associated with an expression of the behavior as a set of sequential operations.

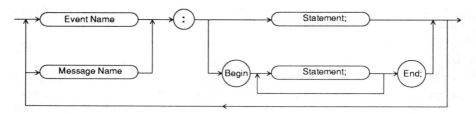

Evolution, implying the execution of operations described in <behavior> takes place only when the activation element appears.

Additional condition message, or event type inputs can also be used as wait condition during evolution controlled by an activation. The syntax is as follows:

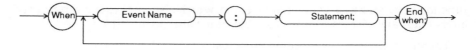

Nested when should be avoided. It is much better to return to the functional structure to simplify the function specification.

To complete this presentation, the behavior at the most elementary level is expressed using structured programming control structures, namely: statement sequence, iteration (while or repeat or do loop), decision (if, case). The syntax is then specific to the language used.

A structured language type syntax is not always the most appropriate form, especially for combinational type behavior in which outputs depend on inputs only. For reasons of clarity and conciseness, it is then better to use:

- a decision table,

- a decision tree.

A search could then be made for the best implementation solution: implementation of the table, translation into programming language, etc.

-D- Example and comments

To illustrate the description model, the details of the example introduced at the beginning of the section are given below. The message Mea contains two information types, CMD and ACK, which is translated by the message type T_Mea = [CMD | ACK].

```
Action EXAMPLE on event EVe and message Mea: T_Mea with
                    (inputs message Mee: T_Mee;
                                    var Ve:T_Ve;
                     input/output var VI : T_VI;
                     outputs event EVs;
                                    var Vs: T_Vs;
                                    Message Ms: T_Ms);
        const K = 10;
        Var STATE: (off, on); MESS: string;
begin
        STATE:= off;
        Vs:= 0; VI:= 15;
        cycle
          Mea:
                Case Mea of
                        CMD:    Vs:=1;
                        ACK:    begin
                                VI:= VI + 1;
                                signal (EVs);
                                end;
                end case;
          EVe:
                begin
                MESS:= "OK";
                Send (MESS, Ms);
                when
                        Mee: STATE:= on;
                        end when;
                end;
        end cycle;
end EXAMPLE;
```

This example has no meaning for an application, but shows extensions not included in the Pascal language. Note three compound statements:

- "action....on....with (...);" for the interface,

- "cycle...end cycle;" for controlling activation,

- "when ... : ... end when;" for controlling evolution.

These two latter control structures implicitly receive input messages and events.

It is also useful to be able to decide upon specific processing for each type of received message. Consequently, part of the message structure description is identical to the data notation in the specifications, thus avoiding the use of variant records, and the meaning of the CASE statement is extended to allow testing the message content type received.

Event generation (SIGNAL) and message generation (SEND) statements are added, together with decision tables and structures when necessary.

Note that we could have chosen the ADA language as a description rule. Cycle and When would then be replaced more or less directly by accept and select. We have deliberately preferred to use a more independent syntax, probably easier to understand for people unfamiliar with ADA. Moreover, the synchronization communication mechanism in ADA is special because of the rendez-vous type requiring synchronization, which in principle, is very different from the asynchronous message exchange through an intermediate buffer recommended by the functional model. Obviously, if the implementation is to be in ADA, the transcription will then be almost immediate (see Section 22.7).

13.3.4 Model interpretation

This section specifies behavior rules induced by the syntax.

-A- Initialization - Evolution

The system described by the functional model must start from a fully defined state, independent of an execution order introduced by the implementation. Initialization sequences for all functions are then to be considered to execute before the evolution part delimited by "cycle". The start state is therefore defined correctly if all system variables and internal variables are initialized. This is one of the description check rules.

-B- Access to state variables

State variables (or shared variables) are always accessible for display or updating. Every state variable can then appear in an expression evaluation or assignment instruction. Access is assumed to take place in zero time.

The use of these variables assumes that they are always coherent and therefore that integrity constraints are respected. The implementation must provide a solution to ensure that this coherence is respected. For simultaneous assignments by several functions, state variables must be defined such that the application is insensitive to the sequence in which a single variable is accessed.

-C- Exchange by messages

A port acts as an intermediate element for a transfer by message. The SEND (A, B) instruction submits message A generated by the action into the port linked to output B. B may be understood as the communication channel for accessing the port. No assumption is made about the capacity of the port. Every SEND operation thus immediately makes a deposit, and the remove operation may take place at any instant when a message exists.

-D- Action activation

Events or messages have a stored effect for temporary actions. The port carries out this role for messages. All activation messages will thus be taken into account by the action, and there will be no losses.

Operation sequences associated with each activation condition are mutually exclusive as indicated in the FS model. For two or more simultaneous activations, sequences are executed in a non-deterministic order. Therefore, the function behavior specification must be created such that it is unaffected by the order. The advantage of this activation control structure is to carry out mutual exclusion on all internal action variables.

-E- Conditional evolution in an action

Events or messages can be used to delay evolution. These evolution conditions have no storage effect.

If there are several conditions, only the first event to appear will be taken into account. This will cause the execution of a single branch. Events or messages for other conditions which appear later will be eliminated. This behavior has been described by the Petri net in the functional model (see Section 13.2.6.B).

-F- Evolution time

Apart from technological features, the only realistic assumption is that the action takes place in zero time. For temporary actions, all outputs are then produced synchronous with evolution conditions. For permanent actions, temporal specifications are necessary for defining the output rate.

13.4 DATA SPECIFICATION

The functional model, internal to the system, uses data in the form of state variables or messages intermediate between the functions which carry out transformations on them.

This data must be fully specified if the functional description is to be complete.

In this chapter, we are not considering the question of what order should be followed - should we start by specifying functions and then variables, or the inverse? This question will be considered in the description of the solution search method. However, we can state that it is difficult to completely specify a function linked to data inputs and outputs without previously defining their nature.

In this section we will describe the objectives of this specification and then describe the recommended description rules followed by the rules for using data.

The data specification model recommended for the functional design is very similar to that described for the specifications (see Section 11.5). However, only internal data is characterized in this case.

13.4.1 Data specification objectives

Consider the essential points that the proposed specification model must satisfy:

- define the nature of the data, which requires describing the category (state variable or message), the meaning of the data, the data structure, and the type of each basic constituent;

- decide upon necessary and sufficient constituents for the functional model and for each data item. This implies that the model must facilitate orthogonality of constituents, to avoid redundancies;

- completely, concisely and unambiguously express all necessary characteristics;

- be suitable for a large class of data: from Boolean to relations between entities;

- be independent of the implementation, hence the use of a conceptual model which always facilitates the search for an implementation.

13.4.2 Description model

To satisfy the above objectives, the description form must be textual for reasons similar to those for the function description choice. In addition, graphical aids used for the specification phase can act as a complement or solution search aid.

Three essential aspects have to be defined to formalize the model [WARD-85], namely: the meaning, the composition, and the type. The model will then be detailed based on the fundamental operators.

-A- Meaning

Every data item is referred to by a name. To avoid ambiguities, it must be defined in different words. The problem is the same as the need to define a word in a dictionary.

The meaning of a data item is obtained by analyzing the role of this item in the system, and therefore in the functional model.

Example: MILEAGE = * distance covered by the vehicle in miles *

-B- Composition

A data item may be elementary or composed of more elementary data items. For example, the position of an aircraft may be defined by three data - latitude, longitude, altitude.

The composition is obtained by expressing constituents and operators used for the composition. Refinement and abstraction techniques are therefore usable to produce a structured description. Data structuring is based on the three fundamental composition operators:

- **concatenation**, or Cartesian product, or the AND (TOGETHER WITH). This is the combination of at least two more elementary components, in a given order (+ symbol);

- **selection,** which expresses the choice of a structure from a set (EITHER OR)(| symbol);

- **repetition,** which defines the set of a single type of constituent, for 0, 1 or more times ({} symbol).

Therefore, the same syntactical and graphical conventions will be adapted as for specifications (see Section 11.5). The example V =[A + B | {C}] means that the variable V is the selection of one of two types of data - (A + B) which is the concatenation of A and B, or {C} which is a set of type C elements.

-C- Element type and attributes

Data considered as elementary is information specified on a definition domain. Conventional types are those known in programming - Boolean, integer, real, enumeration, etc. To improve data characterization, attributes are added such as the information type, the definition domain or limits, the precision (or resolution) and the unit.

13.4.3 Data categories: structures

After summarizing data characteristics, we will consider fundamental types of data obtained by composition and usable for the internal data specification of a system. Apart from individually identified data, more complex descriptions can be obtained using coupling relations. These relations lead to data structures.

-A- Data categories

We have already stated in the specification part that the two data categories to be specified are:

- data entities
- relations

An entity is a physical or logical "object", or other type (we then refer to an abstract object) which has its own identity - a person, a department, an aircraft flight, etc. It can be modeled as a data item, defined by its type for a basic element, or a composition of types for a more complex object. Information characterizing the entity are Attributes which define the specific properties of the entity [ABBOTT-86].

A relation expresses a fact between entities.

With relations, data becomes data structures resulting from a set of data and coupling links between them. The function structure <-> data structure duality is fully equivalent to the functions and relations <-> data and relations functional structure model.

How can all data structure types be specified for data ?

To satisfy objectives, the specification to be used should facilitate subsequent implementation. Implementation of complex structures is facilitated if relational or object type databases are used. For the relational model, entities of any one type are stored in a table, and the same applies for relations. A table is a collection of data of the same type; it is therefore a set. Links expressed by a relation are equivalent to references to the entities concerned. Data entities and relations can thus be expressed by data structures. In defining the specification technique, we can therefore start from this essential point which will facilitate implementation.

-B- Data structure specification

We still have to define the syntax to be used to specify entities and relations, in accordance with the description concept described in the previous section.

Entities and relations are both defined in the form of data. Analyzing the categories makes it necessary to distinguish between two data levels:

- individualized data;
- collection of a defined data type (also called a SET).

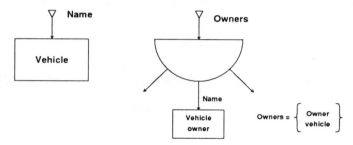

Figure 13.13   Individualized data and collection.

An individual data item is referred to by a name specific to it, see Figure 13.13. For several instances of the same type, each instance has its own specific name. For example, V1, V2: vehicle; means that objects V1 and V2 are of vehicle type.

In a collection, all data are of the same type, but are not designated individually. However, since each data item must be identified without having to associate a name with each, several designation techniques could be imagined: first, next, last in the collection. These mechanisms are special techniques which concern the implementation phase.

Another possible solution, which is used here, is accessing by content. Part of the information contained in the data is used to identify a specific data item in the collection. This minimum information is called the KEY.

Using this principle, a collection of data can only contain data with different keys.

As an example, assume that registration number and social security number could be used as keys for vehicles and persons, where the two collections, vehicles and persons, are defined by:

vehicles = {vehicle}

vehicle = <u>registration number</u> + make + color + ...

persons = {person}

person = $\underline{SS\ Nb}$ + job + name + address + age + ...

The information used as a key is underlined. The notation used here is that given by Ward [WARD-85].

Specifying a relation necessitates designating the entities concerned. This is carried out by references to entities. A relation may be considered as an individual data item, or part of a collection. An individualized relation for a person owning one or more cars could then be written:

Owner N = $\underline{Owner\ Ref}$ + $_1\underline{\{vehicle\ Ref\}}_n$ + date

This specification expresses all vehicles for a given person. The suffix "Ref" specifies that it is a reference. The limits 1 and n define a minimum and maximum number of vehicles. The relation is therefore of type 1-n. Date is an attribute of the relation.

A collection is then used to express all owner type relations:

Owners = {Owner}

Owner = $\underline{Person\ Ref}$ + $_1\underline{\{vehicle\ Ref\}}_n$ + date

Each special relation in a collection is then identified by a key of the relation formed here from the two designated items. If we want to include the purchase date for each vehicle, we would have to write:

Owner = $\underline{Person\ Ref}$ + $_1\underline{\{vehicle\ Ref}$ + date$\}_n$

13.4.4 Data decomposition: minimization and standardization

Data must contain the minimum information necessary for the system. This is obtained by choosing so-called independent information. Modifying one piece of information does not then necessitate modifying others. We refer to minimization of data redundancy.

The same criterion must be applied for specifying entities and relations by data. A specific item of information must be defined once only.

Rules are defined for the relation model to produce a so-called normalized database by analyzing functional dependencies. If the application requires more precise information, the reader should refer to specialized books on databases [DATE-86, ROLLAND-88, GALACSI-86,-89]. Briefly, the method recommends several steps:

- Producing the list of relation and entity fields or attributes.

- Transformation using the first normal form, in other words the definition of a primary key for each entity type. This is carried out by searching for the smallest set of attributes which uniquely identify each entity in the collection.

- Transformation using a second normal form. For relations with a primary key, all attributes other than the primary key for the entity must functionally and elementarily depend on this primary key.

- For example, for (A, B, C, D, E) and the following dependencies which must be the minimum coverage of functional dependencies:

$$(A, B) \quad\quad \longrightarrow C$$

$$A \quad\quad\quad \longrightarrow D$$

$$B \quad\quad\quad \longrightarrow E$$

the following three entities have to be considered:

($\underline{A}$, B, C)

($\underline{A}$, D)

($\underline{B}$, E)

For example, assume an order defined by:

CDE (<u>ord Nb</u>, <u>product code</u>, date, quantity)

The second normal form is:

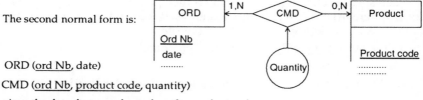

ORD (<u>ord Nb</u>, date)

CMD (<u>ord Nb</u>, <u>product code</u>, quantity)

since the date does not depend on the product code.

- Transformation using the third normal form. This representation must not include dependencies between attributes which are not keys (no transitive dependencies). If this is the case, an additional decomposition must be made. For (A, B, C, D) with B -> D, use: ($\underline{A}$, B, C) and ($\underline{B}$, D).

- Transformation using Boyce-Codd's (BCNF) normal form [DATE-86]. In this form, every field which is determinant (the left part of a functional dependency) for other fields must be a key. This eliminates redundancies.

13.4.5 Use of data

After having defined the description model, we will discuss how to describe how data is used. Variables in a functional model are available for reading or updating providing that integrity constraints are respected. The nature of possible operations on data is defined by the link direction. A variable may be used entirely or in part. This is specified by the link description as indicated in Figure 13.14.

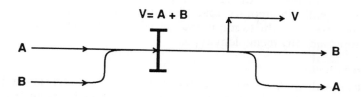

Figure 13.14   Example of labeling links to a variable.

A complete or partial individualized data item can be used directly at the left of an assignment or in an expression. A data item defined as a collection requires that the element or elements concerned be designated.

Some operators available for manipulating a set or collection (A) are given below:

- assignment of a data attribute: A [key].field:=value;
- read attribute of data name N: V:=A[N].field;
- add elements: A:=A + {entity};
- remove elements: A:=A - {entity};
- update a field for a set: field:= value for {entity};
- select elements from a set A: A where <selection criterion>

Adding, removing, updating and selection concern a set of entities. A set of entities may be the result of a selection using a criterion on field values.

Examples:

A:= A +{owners where

owner.vehicle_ref.registration_Number > ???M144};

STATE:="Retired" for {persons where person.age > 60 years};

For a relational database, these operators are available in the SQL interrogation language by the select, insert, delete, update statements. Relational model tables and SQL are one between several implementation solutions for specifications described using the proposed model.

13.5   GLOBAL FUNCTIONAL MODEL PROPERTIES

To conclude the functional model description, we will mention a few interesting aspects about this model.

-A- Technological independence

The functional model is general. No assumption was made about the nature of the data. It may be continuous or discrete. In the continuous case, the transformation function may be permanent or temporary.

The permanent case refers to a continuous function. Operators such as operational amplifiers, multipliers, frequency converters, etc., can be modeled in this way. In the temporary case, the function acts synchronously with event(s) and uses or produces continuous variables at discrete times. The model can thus represent any technology type.

-B- Hierarchical model

Unlike so-called "flat" models, the hierarchical model facilitates any incremental procedure. Using this type of model, a procedure may be:

- purely top-down: starts from the highest level and defines the lower levels by decomposition;

- purely bottom-up: each level description is obtained by combinations of subsets at the previous level;

- mixed: the level of detail can be increased or reduced starting from any intermediate level.

-C- Refinement and abstraction

In the top-down procedure, refinement enhances every element (function, variable) by adding complementary details. Refining an element is equivalent to showing a more microscopic view. These details act as solution constraints. These details which may be imposed or selected contribute to the expression of an implementation (in the solution sense) for the element considered, thus eliminating any other implementation at the outset. Correctly designing by refinement therefore requires consideration of all plausible implementations and then selection of the best based on specific criteria.

Building increases complexity by adding constituents. In the bottom-up procedure, it must be possible to reduce this complexity, allowing the abstraction operation.

The abstraction operation consists of:

- first, delimiting or "encapsulating" a part of the set considered;

- then replacing this part delimited by its specification.

The abstraction operation can thus eliminate information specific to an implementation of the abstracted element. This technique facilitates the definition of objects in order to reuse them.

-D- Independence and redundancy

Independence or orthogonality is an essential design concept. In general, a set of elements is said to be orthogonal, if modifying one of them does not modify any other element in the set.

When the elements are functions, we refer to the function space. For data type elements, we refer to the data space. The judicious choice of an orthogonal space minimizes the number of variables for data, and complexity and interfunction coupling for functions.

Obviously, in an orthogonal space, "defectiveness" of a variable or a function will lead to a loss of information, thus leading to an incomplete implementation therefore incapable of satisfying all its specifications. If necessary, additional elements should be added to correct these faults. The space then becomes redundant. Redundancy is obtained:

- by copying some critical elements one or more times;

- by adding elements representing compositions starting from basic elements.

Redundancy contributes to improving operating safety, and is obtained by increasing the complexity.

-E- Graphical representation

There are a number of possible syntaxes or representations for a textual-graphical model, and the functional model is mostly graphical.

This makes it simple, concise and efficient. Due to its simple interpretation rules, its use enhances readability of documents produced by designers.

-F- Preservation of properties

By respecting description rules, any solution expressed by a designer is a special solution of the functional model. The solution thus inherits all properties of the model.

13.6 SUMMARY

The main points in this chapter which describe the formalization of the functional model are:

- the functional model is composed of three sets: the functional structure, the function specification and the data specification;

- the functional structure model is a hierarchical model which facilitates refinement and abstraction;

- there are three types of functional relations: variable sharing, synchronization by event, message transfer;

- graphics notation greatly improves readability;

- a function cannot be decomposed if its behavior can be expressed by a sequential model;

- every elementary function is cyclic and permanent (no activation) or temporary (activations);

- specifying a function in algorithmic form facilitates its checking and implementation;

- the data model is relational and hierarchical. It facilitates the implementation (relational databases and typed data);

- the functional data expresses the maximum possible amount of parallelism for the solution;
- the functional model expresses the problem solution without defining its technological characteristics.

14

DESIGN PRINCIPLES

Every solution developed by a designer must comply with the functional model. It can then be used as a specification for the next detailed design stage. Respecting the model also results in obtaining properties, some of which improve quality, others implementation, testability and safety. The purpose of the previous chapter was to formalize this model.

But knowledge of the model is not sufficient. A solution may be conform with the model and yet not satisfy the specifications or have no simplicity, understandability or maintainability qualities. In addition to knowledge of a model, the designer must have a guide which will help him sequence his process: questions to be asked, decisions to be taken and on what criteria. This is the objective of a method.

A method is based on some main principles which will give intrinsic qualities to any solution. Globally, these qualities are intended to improve the entire product life cycle.

Before describing the details of the method associated with the functional model, this chapter gives an overview of the principles which facilitate the search for a functional solution. These principles will be used as a basis for the method described in the next chapter. Some of the essential questions that the designer must ask are:

- How should the decomposition be made to propose a solution? - what principles should be followed?

- What elements should be searched for to lead to a good decomposition?

- What criteria are used to evaluate the quality of a solution?

14.1 SUBJECT-ORIENTED DESIGN

Real-time systems to be designed are essentially dedicated systems for a specific application. Every system is the result of associating a number of components. If an analysis of the various components used in this type of system is made, we find: functions close to the specific nature of the application (regulation, observation function, etc.) and more general functions which may be found in many applications (database, dialog manager, multi-task executive, etc.).

Therefore, designing is searching and then selecting the necessary components to express a solution. This search must start from the application subject(s).

Alford defined the characteristics of dedicated systems starting from a global view of an application [WARD-85]. In general, all systems have a "perception" space and an "action" space. Entities in the environment which are "subjects" of the application enter into the perception space, are observed, the system acts on them, and then they leave the action space, see Figure 14.1.

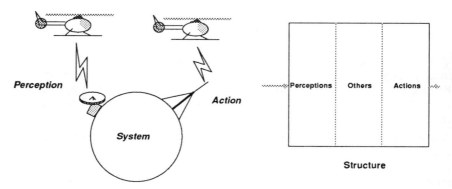

Figure 14.1   The perception/action model for a control system.

This view of the system to be designed in global objective terms, helps to guide the analysis process towards a search for the essential components in the three categories:

- perception

- action

- use, transformation, evaluation, etc., as intermediate steps between the above two categories.

This approach is subject-oriented since it starts from the essential WHAT, unlike an implementation approach which consists of searching for the elements which could be used to satisfy the specifications. Different authors have different terminologies to express the same idea: logical rather than physical approach, separation between the essential and the implementation.

Morever, a design must satisfy the problem specifications. The designer must therefore make his analysis based on the specifications. A subject-oriented design is simplified if the specifications are based on a model of the environment and therefore of the subject. The proposed process in Part 3 is appropriate for producing functional specifications. Consequently, input data for the design phase, in other words the functional specifications, facilitate the development of a subject-oriented solution.

This process makes it necessary to first solve the very specific application problems before considering more general problems encountered in most applications and for which solutions are known. The following temperature control example shows the difference in results between a subject approach and an implementation approach.

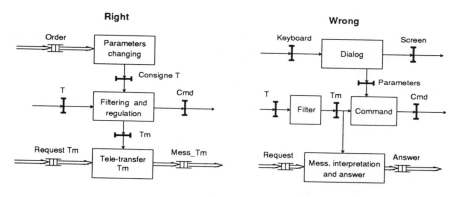

Figure 14.2   Subject approach, Implementation approach.

In the first case, the functions and variables are defined relative to the subject, whereas functions are more general in the second case, see Figure 14.2.

14.2 TECHNOLOGY INDEPENDENT DESIGN

A complete solution includes both functional and hardware components such as sensors, actuators, processors, memories, communication network, etc. The second category is a support for the first category. In design, the functional aspect must be found first and the support is deduced later.

One imposed constraint is that **a functional design must be completely independent of the technology.** The advantage of this approach is that efforts are concentrated on the essential points from the beginning, and technological details are considered only at the last minute. This is similar to the subject-oriented approach. For the subject approach model, perceptions and actions are necessary functions to the system that must not be confused with physical interfaces for sensors and actuators.

An additional advantage is that since the solution is independent of the technology, a single function or design can be used as a starting point for searching for several technological solutions. This is necessary, for example, when the implementation time, development and reproduction cost have to be optimized, or when it is desirable to modify the implementation to incorporate new technological advances.

Respecting this principle necessitates knowing the points that we consider to be technology dependent. Some items are obvious (for example, electrical interfaces), but others much less so. Structured specifications are then necessary concerning the functional part only which is not concerned with technological constraints.

Categories of technology dependent functions or constraints are described in the rest of this section. These categories are the result of long experience applying the methodology to industrial problems and comparisons between developed solutions which include these characteristics as technological constraints and others solutions which do not include them.

14.2.1 Interface functions with the physical environment

Every function which does not transform information, in other words which does not change its nature, is a technology-dependent function. In particular, this is the case for all interfacing functions which have the only objective of changing the representation of information and not its nature.

For instance, when the velocity V is an essential variable for a system and the sensor is of the incremental encoder type, the function which makes V available at all times starting from the INC event is a technological function as shown in Figure 14.3.

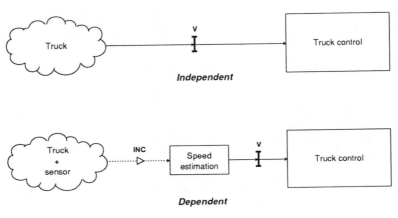

Figure 14.3   Technology independence/dependence.

Remember that a solution is independent of the technology if it is subsequently possible to use any type of sensors or actuators without changing the functional solution. This is true if the variables considered are functional and not physical variables.

14.2.2 Man-machine dialog functions

Dialog functions fall into the interface category. But it is useful to consider them separately from the above functions since the corresponding entity is a user and not a physical process. The system is reactive to user actions. Coupling necessitates an interactive type of function.

A dialog function for a system controls the ease of use of the entire system. This ease of use can be very variable depending on the technology used and the form of the dialog:

- use of potentiometers and observation of dials;
- keyboard and display units;
- terminal;
- question-response dialog;
- command language;
- icon driven menus;
- multi-window manager.

The form of the dialog has obvious implications on the technology (icon-driven menus cannot be used with a simple alphanumeric terminal). Conversely, a given technology delimits the possible dialog forms.

If a functional solution for the man-machine interface is to be completely independent of the technology, it must allow a choice of any possible form of dialog. The technology will be deduced later after selecting a form.

A suitable solution can only be obtained for the dialog aspect if the designer puts himself at a high level. He should thus consider only global information or significant events produced by the user as inputs, and those supplied by the system as outputs. Inputs and outputs must be only of functional type. This point of view must be followed during the specification phase. For example, there is no need to go down to the level at which individual keys typed on a terminal keyboard are managed. On the contrary he must consider the user generated command message level. Figure 14.4 shows that any dialog device such as a keyboard-display unit, terminal, voice recognition and synthesis, etc., can be used without changing the functional solution.

14.2.3 Geographic distribution

Using the microprocessor type technology, systems are more frequently designed as distributed systems, in other words, functions are distributed on different processors coupled together through an interconnection system.

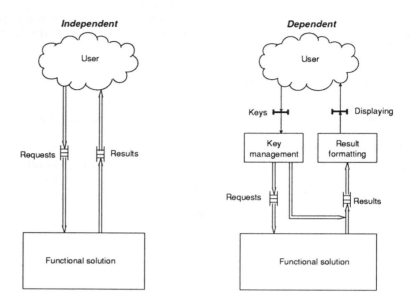

Figure 14.4   Dialog independence/dependence.

When the distance exceeds a few meters, coupling between the processors is necessarily made through a communication line - often through a serial line, or possibly through a local network or a telecommunications network. The use of communication lines imposes coupling between functions by only message transfers.

It may therefore seem natural to include physical distribution constraints at the functional level in order to search for a solution adapted to the topology from the beginning.

For several years, we have adopted this point of view without thinking about any other way. After experimenting with the method by postponing this type of constraint until the next implementation definition step, we observed an interesting solution quality. The result can be explained. If we consider the distribution constraint at the functional level, the solution is based on message transfer- type relations. Messages are difficult to specify because they depend on the function distribution which is not known and has to be found. It is difficult to select the strictly necessary exchanges between functions when starting by searching for functions including the distribution constraint.

On the other hand, if this constraint is not considered, a search is made for a functional solution satisfying the functional specifications. The function distribution can be decided upon later taking account of geographic constraints, and the information to be exchanged and appropriate communication systems can then be easily deduced.

Figure 14.5 shows that it is then easy to introduce the geographical distribution. The selected communication mechanism (serial link) only updates V" after a modification of V'. The solution results from a geographical copy of V.

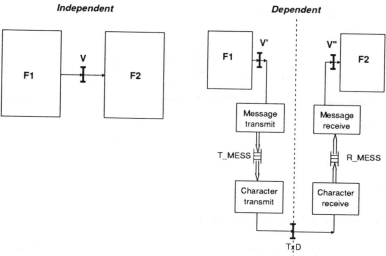

Figure 14.5   Distribution independence/dependence.

14.2.4 Maintenance, operating safety

Functions, which are auxiliary to the application but essential to the system, may appear in specifications. For example, self-tests and maintenance are diagnostic assistance functions and help keep the system running smoothly.

Operating safety, which includes at least the terms availability and reliability, may require the addition of other functions: for example, hardware, software, functional redundancies. All these functions should be taken into account at a later stage since they form part of technological constraints. For safety, they are deduced from the functional solution by analysis of safety characteristics and then by adding the necessary redundancies to satisfy the imposed criteria.

The example given in Figure 14.6 shows the addition of a power on self-test and the duplication of a temperature sensor to increase observation reliability.

Additional functions and states are thus added to the system to satisfy the technological type specifications.

14.2.5 Importance of specification categories

The recommended method for producing specifications leads to include the characteristics of physical interfaces, the man-machine dialog, distribution constraints, and safety constraints in the technological specifications. We have just justified why.

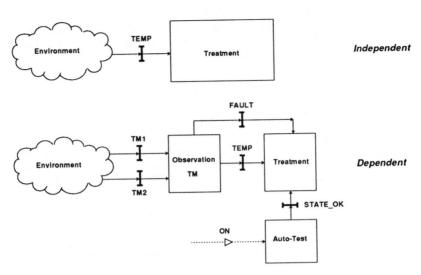

Figure 14.6   Safety and maintenance independence/dependence.

The exclusive use of functional specifications thus facilitates the design of a technology independent solution. However, detail levels and technological dependence should not be confused: a solution may be very detailed functionally without expressing technological dependencies.

14.3 MINIMUM COMPLEXITY AND INDEPENDENCE

A solution for a system or for each function is obtained by refinement. Each decomposition must be made respecting a maximum complexity rule which facilitates readability and therefore understandability. The rule of 7 plus or minus 2 recognized by several authors is applicable here. It simply means that if more than 8 to 10 elements are introduced into a refinement (functions + variables + ports + events), the solution becomes difficult to understand.

But since refinement is iterative, an extremely complex solution can eventually be obtained by using a large number of levels. Therefore, a solution quality evaluation criterion is also necessary when the solution is completely "flattened", in other words after removing the levels. The complexity must then be minimized. How can this be obtained? There is no unique answer.

14.3.1 Orthogonality or function coherence

Complexity is reduced by searching for an orthogonal set of functions, each with a specific functionality independent of the others. Each function then uses and produces data independently of the others. Independence is a result of the encapsulation principle of coherent subsets which leads to defining objects with specific functionalities.

The complexity for a given problem also depends on the nature of the problem. For a control problem, for example automation, an approach based on data may lead to a more complex solution than an approach based on events.

14.3.2 Reducing couplings

The design analysis may lead to a set of functions and data. The construction of a functional structure starting from any or all of these elements produces various solutions which depend on the groupings made.

A satisfactory functional solution for a given refinement level would appear to be that which minimizes couplings and therefore interfaces. This minimization applies both to the number of couplings and to the complexity of each coupling.

Minimizing the number of couplings converges towards parts independence. Understanding a part of the solution becomes simpler when it is less linked to other parts.

The complexity of each coupling depends partly on the coupling nature (state variable or event), and second on the structure of the exchanged information. Coupling by event or by message transfer is more complex than coupling by variable, since it implies function synchronization subsequently in the implementation. This is not the case for variables.

Finally, an implementation becomes simpler when the organizational part representing couplings between the functions other than by variables is weak. The best solution is that which leads to the smallest organizational part. This point of view will be discussed in the next part dealing with the implementation specification step.

Information complexity defined by a variable or a message also has an influence on solution understanding.

14.4 SOLUTION DEDUCTION PROCEDURE

When starting a refinement work, the designer is faced with a function defined solely by its specifications. At this stage, this function (more or less complex) is equivalent to a "black box" as far as its internal structure is concerned: no internal information is known. Refining is finding an internal description as a solution satisfying specifications. This solution must also have qualities. Some have been described in previous sections.

This is therefore a creative task. How must the designer proceed?

Several approaches are possible - intuition or analysis, approach by functions or by data, refinement or abstraction.

14.4.1 Analysis rather than intuition

Design is a creative process. Therefore, intuition can be used to propose a solution. This must then be checked to ensure its conformity to specification. Many errors will probably have to be corrected and it may be difficult to justify choices. When using this method, experience is extremely useful since this represents a knowledge of solutions for typical problems. Intuition and experience tend to do not use the specifications very directly, which inevitably leads to design problems.

Analysis is the opposite of intuition. It is based on careful reading and "fine" interpretation of specifications, and the use of a method. In most cases, the relevant information which has to be found to propose a solution is in the specifications. Specifying is describing the details of the application, but these details are essential internal in the system since part of the system is an image (entity models) of the application (mirror principle).

Analysis thus reduces the creative features, but will give a high probability of a quality solution independently of the designer quality. When specifications are correctly produced, most of the thought and synthesis work has already been undertaken during the specification phase. Obviously, well-defined specifications are necessary for an analysis-type procedure, and may not be so necessary for intuition.

14.4.2 Data-oriented approach rather than function-oriented approach

What should be searched for first in the specifications document during the analysis?

There are two opposed approaches:

- search for functions, then relations;
- search for data, then functions.

The functions approach is more frequently used and is more natural. This is explained by the fact that, to describe a task our reasoning would naturally lead us to bring out a sequence of activities. This is undoubtedly exaggerated with computers since programming requires that we decompose an objective to be reached into more elementary sequential operations.

We have had a large number of opportunities to check that designers, without any particular recommendations, invariably propose decomposition based on functions. To determine whether this type of procedure has been followed, simply look at the proposed function or structure. The following example in Figure 14.7 reflects this type of approach.

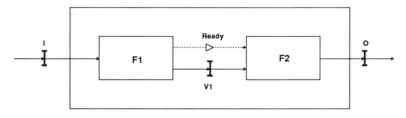

Figure 14.7   Functional structure example based on functions.

In this solution, as a result of analysis work, the designer has found that two functions are necessary to obtain O from I: F1 carries out part of the processing and F2 completes the transformation. Since F1 and F2 are sequential, V1 is produced at the end of processing by F1. The READY event is strictly necessary in order for F2 to take V1 into account when it is available after its submission by F1. The sequential relation here may also be expressed by transferring a message containing V1 through a port.

The essential comment to make is that this approach invariably leads to synchronization between functions. This mark in the functional structure reflects the procedure followed by the designer.

The procedure by variables, and therefore by relations rather than functions, gives a very different result. For the function to be refined, the designer must search for one or more internal variables strictly necessary to express a solution. These variables are deduced by reading and interpreting specifications.

When at least one variable (event or information) has been found, at least two functions have to be deduced - otherwise this variable adds nothing to the functional refinement. The functional structure normally found using this approach is similar to the one in Figure 14.8.

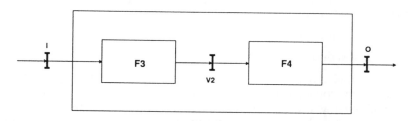

Figure 14.8   Functional structure example based on variables.

There is no correlation between the variable V2 and the variable V1 of the previous figure; the same applies to F3 and F4 compared with F1 and F2. In this case, the variable has a permanent meaning, which is not the case for V1. Since V2 is permanent, the two functions F3 and F4 are asynchronous. No synchronization appears which facilitates understanding, and subsequently implementation.

This approach does not lead to a sequential solution but rather to a solution which expresses natural concurrency; this is the objective of a functional structure, otherwise the decomposition is not strictly necessary. Therefore, the decomposition based on a data approach must be used to lead to a simpler solution.

14.4.3 Refinement rather than abstraction

The functional model is hierarchical. A solution can also be obtained by the composition of more elementary functions rather than by decomposition.

Even if the purely top-down procedure is difficult, the search for solutions by refinement is preferable to the bottom-up procedure by combinations. The solution searched for must satisfy a specification. In the top-down procedure, each function to be decomposed is defined by a specification; by analysis, the decomposition work is simple and the check is also possible.

Using a bottom-up procedure, abstraction ends up in identifying a function by combining more elementary functions. It can then be described by its specification. This approach does not start from the objective but attempts to converge towards it, this is more complicated and probably produces more hesitations and therefore more work.

It is therefore recommended to work more by refinement, however being aware than some loopbacks will be necessary to correct analysis errors detected later on.

14.5 VERTICAL OR HORIZONTAL DECOMPOSITION

The functional model is hierarchical. Each non-elementary function is thus described by a functional structure. In this refinement work, the selected functional structure may be one of two decomposition types [ROTENSTREICH-86]:

- an horizontal decomposition;

- a vertical decomposition.

The so-called horizontal decomposition is most frequently used. This is equivalent to considering that all refinement functions act at the same functional level as an implementation of the higher level function. Relations between functions have the same meaning as the functional organization in companies. Each function contributes on the same level to obtain the result. Relations express transformations of inputs into outputs.

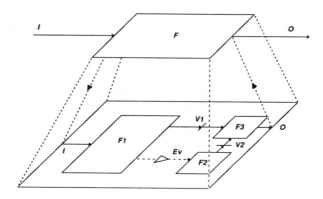

Figure 14.9   Representation of an horizontal decomposition.

All functions of F are represented in the same horizontal plane. Function classes for this decomposition lead to:

- structuring by enhancement (addition of new functionalities) or deduction of more elementary functionalities;
- the introduction of less abstract solution views.

Vertical decomposition represents a hierarchical relation. To carry out its role, a function may need the services of a lower hierarchical level. Lower functions are rather of the adaptation type to satisfy a constraint. For example, a message transmission function must use a character transmission service. This decomposition can be represented as shown in Figure 14.10, demonstrating that relations are represented in a vertical plane.

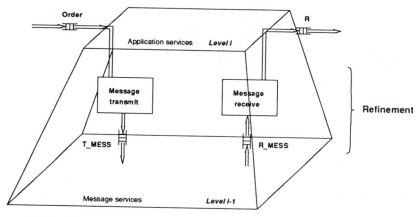

Figure 14.10   Representation of a vertical decomposition.

Do not confuse refinement levels which are only meaningful for presentation thus improving understandability, and the levels in a vertical decomposition which represent different natures of services.

14.6 SOLUTION TEMPLATE MODELS

Even after analysis, when faced with the refinement task, the designer has a large number of degrees of freedom to propose a solution. As the analysis progresses, he may also experience difficulties in extracting the main elements. The approach by variables is not entirely natural either. Can the quality of the design work be improved more than by simply using the principles stated above?

There is no doubt that the designer naturally works by analogy. When he has already solved a similar problem or when he knows solutions, he attempts to use whatever is already existing, which is very praiseworthy. This is a form of what could be called "experience".

Starting from this point of view, we wondered if it would be possible, by analyzing a wide variety of solutions obtained by the application of the MCSE methodology, to define a number of general solutions. These solutions should be understood as template solution models. A model is suitable for a problem class and a given functionality level. It can be used to induce a collection of solutions, each customized to the specific features of the application being processed, but each having all the properties and qualities of the model.

The objective of this section is not to describe defined template models, since these are dealt within Chapter 16. However, to explain the template model concept, we will take the example of the Moore's machine which is useful for the design of digital functions.

Faced with the problem of designing a digital function specified by a finite state machine, rather than searching for an intuitive solution, the designer will take inspiration from the structure of the Moore machine. The model suggests to him that he searches for the strictly necessary internal variable which is the internal state. This internal state is directly defined by the specification: for example, state of the finite state machine.

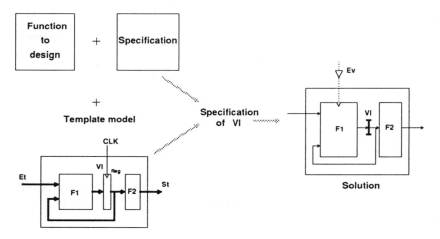

Figure 14.11 Example of the benefit of a template model.

Since the functional structure is defined by the template model, after this internal variable has been found the design work is reduced to solving two combinational problems: input or receptivity combinational function, output or action combinational function, each being specified by a transition table.

We have succeeded in formalizing several of these models and have had groups of designers experiment with them. The results comparison procedure is simple. It consists of comparing solutions produced with and without knowledge of template models. We have compared solutions proposed for the same problems before and after these models were used. The results obtained were judged on the criteria of satisfying specifications, simplicity and understandability, and were clearly in favour of the use of template models. This is logical since these models are generators of good ideas and "right" questions to be answered.

14.7 SUMMARY

This chapter has discussed various functional design alternatives and the main recommendations are:

- The design must be guided by the application subject. This approach facilitates the decomposition procedure from inputs towards outputs (horizontal decomposition).

- A functional design must be independent of the technology. Therefore, functional specifications only must be used. Interfacing problems with the environment and with users, and physical distribution constraints should not be taken into account at this stage.

- The functional solution must be simple to facilitate its understanding and its implementation. Attempt to reduce the number and complexity of functions and relations. Use an approach based on orthogonality and coherence of functions and data.

- A solution must be deduced by analyzing specifications and searching for the strictly necessary internal information (variables, events) to express the solution, using a top-down procedure by refinement.

- The designer can make use of template solution models as a guide for the analysis and synthesis work.

15

THE FUNCTIONAL DESIGN PROCESS

The objective of the functional design step is to propose a complete solution in accordance with the specifications and with qualities which will benefit the entire product life cycle.

Applications to be developed, described by their specifications, are necessarily varied. Solutions for a given application, described by a precise specification, may also be very varied. Since the design work is essentially a creative process, the result is an expression of the designer's thought process. A solution is not immediately produced using an automatic process; the production rules have to be completely formalized beforehand.

The important result of the design must be a document describing the solution and not the process followed by the designer [PARNAS-86]. To a certain extent however, the result is the principles and process to be followed. Thus, the designer's competence and logical thought capability remain important factors affecting the quality of the result.

The objective of this chapter is to describe the recommended procedure to help the designer acquire this competence and logical approach. This process describes the sequence of decisions to be taken to give a quality result.

Using the functional model, the design process is a combination of phases, each used to deduce a component of the model. The design principles stated in the previous chapter are used to define recommendations for each phase.

It is impossible to formally prove that a design process is well founded. It is a result based more on experiments. This requires dealing with a variety of industrial problems and deducing advantages and disadvantages by analysis. Therefore, creating a design method is very slow and is the result of a synthesis using a bottom-up type process.

15.1 OVERVIEW OF THE DESIGN PROCESS

The objective of the second step, the functional design, is to produce a complete functional description of the system to be designed. This description must comply with the model and must include:

- a functional structure;
- behavioral specifications of all elementary functions;
- specifications for all data.

The documents to be used as input are the functional and operational specifications. The following figure (Figure 15.1) represents this step.

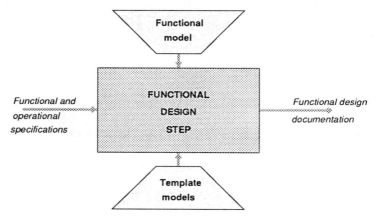

Figure 15.1   The design step.

The recommended process makes use of successive refinements of each function with the starting point being the entire system delimited by its functional inputs and outputs. The refinement process stops when each function can be described by a sequential behavioral model. Data is specified as it appear for each refinement level.

The process shown in Figure 15.2 thus consists of the following phases:

- delimitation of system inputs and outputs;
- search for a first functional decomposition;
- refinement of each function (iteration on this phase);
- behavior of each elementary function;
- synthesis of the global solution.

Since the functional model is hierarchical, the first functional decomposition level is very important since it will subsequently influence the entire solution structure. This first solution approach should therefore be given special care.

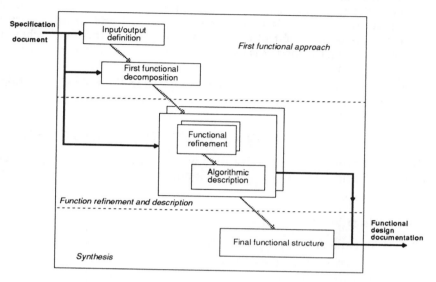

Figure 15.2   The functional design process.

The functional refinement of each function is an iterative process which can be carried out in any order of the various branches of the hierarchy. However, it is always recommended that the most difficult functions be considered first. The solution found for a complex solution may have repercussions on its environment.

When all decompositions have been carried out, a global synthesis is justified to check the coherence of the whole. It is true that a purely top-down process is very difficult to follow. Loopbacks and corrections are inevitable during the design; hence the necessity to reconsider the whole. The final document is a result of this synthesis.

The designer must consider three steps in each refinement phase:

- **Analysis**: this brings out the essential elements starting from the specifications.

- **Construction**: this synthesis work proposes a solution based on elements defined during the analysis. Several solutions may be considered and selection is then based on various criteria.

- **Verification**: this consists of checking that the solution selected for the function satisfies the system specifications. The checking work is simplified if a complete specification exists before the refinement.

The verification phase may show up omissions which are to be corrected by returning to the previous construction step. If the process is too incremental or too intuitive, the solution is more a result of a trial and error correction procedure. This is the result of a bad analysis work. In this case, when all problems have been clarified, it is useful to reconsider the overall construction and then recheck it in order to improve the solution.

Each phase of the method is described in detail in the following sections, after describing information input into the step and the results expected from it.

15.2 INPUT AND OUTPUT DOCUMENTS FOR THE DESIGN STEP

The design work, like the specification work, consists of producing a paper document. Consider first the contents of input and output documents for this step.

15.2.1 Specification document

The useful parts of the specification document for the design step are:

- the system/environment delimitation;
- the functional specifications;
- the operational specifications.

Delimitation of the system context helps to deduce a delimitation of the system with its inputs and outputs. Exchanges between the two parts may be logical or functional, but not physical.

The functional specifications describe the system functions for the application subject. These are therefore subject-oriented information, and therefore facilitate a subject-oriented design. The role of each function is described by one or more specification models expressing the behavior of entities in the environment (therefore related to the subject).

Operational specifications describe information, data and their attributes. If a problem solution method is suggested or imposed, it will be described in this part of the specifications.

These three information categories do not include any physical or technological type of information. This type of document therefore facilitates a subject-oriented approach, and a data rather than function-oriented approach, since application functionalities alone are considered excluding internal functions.

15.2.2 Design document

The process will probably not be completely linear and top-down. The design document must express the result linearly and in a top-down manner. The result only is important for subsequent use, understanding and acceptance of solution relevance.

The design document thus does not follow the temporal progress of developments undertaken by the designers. It is a hierarchical and logical document describing the solution which will not be coherent until the global synthesis has been completed.

Each refinement must also be associated with the complete solution description, the analysis which led to various alternatives and the decision criteria which were used to accept one among the various solutions.

The document is therefore also a trace of the designer's thought process. This facilitates reuse of the work for other applications for the designer himself and, perhaps more importantly, for training new designers.

Although the document results from a synthesis of all the design work, it should necessarily be produced gradually throughout the development. Disorganized before the final stage, the important points are written down as and when they are found. Otherwise, time leads to forgetfulness, limited vision and consequently a valueless document.

Therefore, the synthesis work consists of putting all design elements into order, eliminating useless parts and loopbacks which were necessary for corrections and introducing an overall coherence.

15.3 FUNCTIONAL INPUT AND OUTPUT DELIMITATION

First, the separation between the system to be designed and the entities in its environment must be clearly and accurately defined.

Entities are represented by "cloud" shapes, whereas the system is represented by a rectangle. Coupling between the two parts takes place uniquely by the three functional model relation types as shown in the example below.

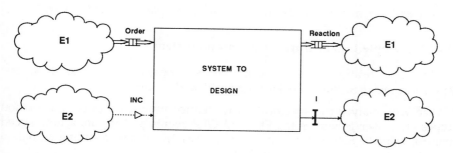

Figure 15.3   System delimitation example.

15.3.1 Process

Possible observations on entities may be used as inputs for the system. Similarly, control information for entities will correspond to system outputs.

Observations and control outputs are given in the specifications. These relations are functional and not physical when specifications have been correctly written.

The relation type then has to be defined. The choice depends on the nature of the link in the specification. The following simple rules should be followed:

- when only the state of a variable change is useful, the relation is of the event type;

- when the occurrence and contents of information are to be considered simultaneously, the relation is of the message transfer type;

- when the value of some information is necessary regardless of the time, the relation is of the state variable type.

The implementation nature is also deduced from the specification. For example, a data- flow type link leads to a relation through ports.

To complete the delimitation, each state variable and each message type must be specified.

Note that some input observations necessary to satisfy specifications may be forgotten in this phase. Normally, these observations are used in specifications, for example as transition condition. This type of omission will probably be detected before the end of the functional decomposition. A correction can then be made by looping back.

To improve understanding, all system inputs are shown at the left, and outputs at the right. Inputs and outputs of the same nature derived from different instances of a single entity type can be shown by a array of inputs an outputs.

We will illustrate this phase with the two examples specified in Part 3.

15.3.2 Example 1: Centrifuge speed control system

The specification for this example is repeated in Figure 15.4. See specifications in Section 12.6.4 for the problem description.

We will analyze the specification to deduce inputs, outputs and relation types. The user generates the ON and OFF events and inputs a new speed control value (S_Setpoint) whenever he wishes. Event type coupling with data transfer is necessary for the control value.

The user is also a permanent observer of the current speed control value and an indication whether or not the motor is rotating. This information is of the state variable type.

The rotating assembly for centrifuging is characterized by its CV control and its rotation speed SMotor. These are state variables.

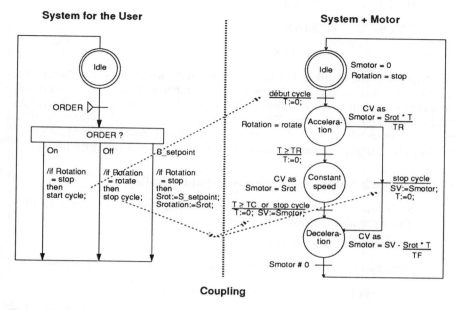

Coupling

Figure 15.4   Motor control functional specification.

Therefore, the system input-output delimitation is as follow7z in Figure 15.5.

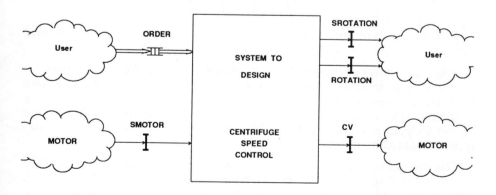

Figure 15.5   Delimitation of the speed control system.

All variables must be specified to complete this phase:

ORDER   = [ON | OFF | S_Setpoint: 0..SMAX];

SROTATION   :0..SMAX;

ROTATION	:(Rotation, Stop);
SMOTOR	:0..SMAX;
CV	:0..CVMAX;

The nature of the coupling between the user and the system is functional and not physical. The physical interface available to the user to act upon the system can be considered from the beginning: ON, OFF, MORE and LESS push buttons for adjusting the control value. The advantage of the selected solution is to be able to subsequently change the nature of the dialog: replace the MORE and LESS keys by a digital keyboard or even by a serial link for remote control.

15.3.3 Example 2: Automation with a wire-guided trolley

The specifications for this problem were also described in Section 12.10.2. Four entities were identified in the environment:

- the platform as issuer of commands;

- the trolley as a mechanical assembly for displacement and loading;

- the workshop as the support on which the trolley moves;

- the operator responsible for the smooth operation of the installation.

For this problem, we are interested only in the trolley and its control electronics. The only function of the trolley control system is to carry out packet transfer cycles between the two platforms. The reader should refer to Chapter 12 to familiarize himself with the problem specifications.

Starting from entities, we will analyze the specification in order to deduce the inputs and outputs for the electronic system to be designed.

The platform is an information generator for the trolley commands. In response, it is sensitive to trolley reactions. The necessary commands and acknowledgements are shown in the specification: platform actions and trolley conditions for commands, trolley actions and platform conditions for acknowledgements. The coupling relation is therefore of the message transfer type (COMMAND and ACK).

The mechanical part of the trolley which carries out the displacement is controlled in displacement by the two motor speed controls CVM1 an CVM2, and in belt rotation by a Boolean variable C_BELT defining the two possible states. For the moment, trolley observations are not specified.

The workshop defines the trajectory that must be followed by the trolley between the two platforms. The trolley control takes account of the distance of the trolley from this trajectory (DCA). The workshop also contains a number of mobile obstacles which must be avoided. The obstacle information is necessary for correct operation.

During normal operation, the operator does not directly act upon the trolley control system. This is controlled only by the platform. However, the operator is informed by a siren if an incident arises, that is obstacles: no response from the platform or the trolley. He then repositions the trolley and reinitializes the control system.

An additional analysis should be made starting from the specification, namely that all transition conditions other than possible evaluations by the system must be supplied by the environment and therefore by entities.

In particular, there are the states or events: platform_presence, platform_proximity. These two observations are necessary for developing the system. They are obtained from the workshop. All other conditions are commands, or acknowledgements, or temporal conditions. The system delimitation with its inputs/outputs is given in figure 15.6.

To complete this phase, all variables and messages have to be specified.

COMMAND = [I_PRESENCE | LOAD | TRANSPORT | UNLOAD];

ACK = [OK_PRESENCE];

OBSTACLE, SIREN: Boolean;

C_BELT: (Off, backward, forward);

DCA: -Dmax, +Dmax;

CVM1, CVM2: 0..VCmax;

It is obvious that coupling information between the trolley and the control system are missing. The procedure deliberately followed in this chapter will show that these omissions show up during the design stage.

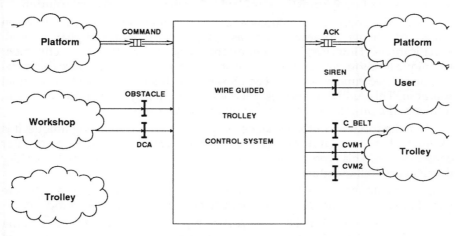

Figure 15.6   Delimitation of the trolley control system.

15.4 SEARCH FOR AN INITIAL FUNCTIONAL DECOMPOSITION

Up to this stage, no internal system information is known. The designer must start to propose the first necessary functional elements to solve the problem.

Remember the essential points for undertaking this work. First, the proposed solution must comply with the functional model and particularly with the functional structure model, since decomposition will almost certainly be necessary. Since the model is hierarchical, each decomposition must be limited to an understandable solution.

The approach must then be subject-oriented. The proposed procedure consists of searching for the strictly necessary internal variables, information, events, rather than searching for internal functions. Also, the solution must remain independent of the technology.

But special care should be taken with the first decomposition which is very important and has a very significant influence on the rest of the development and consequently on the overall project cost. We will consider this point in more detail before describing the three phases of the solution search method - analysis, construction, verification.

15.4.1 Importance of the first functional decomposition

The recommended process is globally top-down. Each description level is thus detailed by refining each function in the previous level. This is a result of the hierarchical nature of the model.

This technique is applicable for the functional design, but also in part for the implementation specification step, particularly for introducing interfaces and to satisfy the geographic distribution. Hardware and software implementations are the result of transformations applied to the detailed functional solution.

Obviously, solution corrections and loopbacks are always possible when faults or errors appear such as incoherence, non-compliance with specifications. However, it is important to be aware that the refinement technique tends to maintain the initial structure. Consequently, once the initial functional decomposition has been chosen, it will still be present in the final solution. This initial choice is therefore particularly important and will influence the project complexity and therefore its cost.

Since the solution for the initial decomposition is far from being unique, it is useful to have a quality evaluation criterion which takes account of later consequences. This type of criterion is not simple to express. We will consider the final product to outline it.

Implementation in most cases comprises a hardware part and a software part. The cost of the hardware part depends on the quantity to be produced:

- many systems: it is better to reduce reproduction costs by minimizing material. This is obtained by transferring a maximum number of functionalities to the software part.

- a few installations: it is better to reduce the development time both for hardware and software.

Minimizing the functional complexity thus tends to minimize hardware cost. The cost of the software part can be broken down into two parts:

- the **operational part**, which contains all operations necessary to satisfy the application. This operational part is minimized if function algorithmic descriptions are produced carefully and with no redundancy. In this case, it may be considered that this part is relatively incompressible.

- the **organizational part**, which provides coupling between all modules, functions and software procedures. This part results from transformations applied to the functional structure and will therefore reflect the functional complexity.

Software development essentially involves minimizing the organizational part, implying that the functional complexity at least should be minimized from the beginning. The complexity depends on the nature of functional relations. Relations by variable sharing do not generate any organizational "cost" unlike relations by synchronization and message transfer, which generate temporal dependencies.

The objective for the quality criterion thus consists of using variables for coupling between functions, in preference to the use of synchronization and message transfer through ports.

This reasoning should be maintained for all refinement levels. The repercussion is even greater for the very first levels defining the global architecture of the solution.

15.4.2 Decomposition process

Rather than trusting one's intuition, a three-step procedure is suggested: analysis, creation of one or more solutions by construction and verification.

-A- Analysis

The analysis consists of using specifications and extracting from them essential elements which may be useful for the solution. Careful reading can lead to extract words, phases, actions, events and data. The analysis can be refined by an order of element importance classification.

Analysis models are also used for this task, in particular, the "Structured Analysis" method based on data-flow diagrams. This type of model is then used to express successive transformations from inputs to outputs. Intermediate data can then be used to express the solution.

The analysis should be carried out so as to first search for the strictly necessary data and events, rather than activities, operations and functions which are derived from the former.

-B- Construction

A solution is created by placing characteristic elements in the part to be refined. If the analysis is data-oriented, elements to be placed are variables or events with or without information. Since elements must necessarily belong to relations, functions have to be placed around them, some to produce and update and others to use them.

The functional structure then has to be completed so that all input and output variables are used. If some appear unnecessary, the higher level should be modified. Finally, all used components must be correctly named and then specified. In particular, the specification of each function will then be used as an input document for its refinement.

This incremental construction procedure by variables is simple and leads to not too much complexity for each refinement. Only one variable, one event or one item of information has to be found to express a solution. This single element will necessarily induce at least two functions related to it. Therefore, the choice of the right element is essential hence the importance of the previous analysis phase.

Since the solution is far from being unique, it is recommended that several functional decompositions be considered. The choice of one solution among a set is then based on the criterion described in the previous section. If the choice is not easy, it is desirable to refine each solution up to the stage at which it becomes clear that one solution is better. Do not hesitate to reconsider the solution during the functional design since the benefit for the remainder of the development can be very significant.

-C- Verification

After a solution has been found, a check has to be made that it will satisfy the specifications. It is impossible to confirm that the solution satisfies specifications since not all solution elements have been identified and specified during the refinement. The complete verification which can provide a guarantee, then referred to as validation, is only possible at the end of the functional design step.

The verification recommended here consists of eliminating flagrant errors that must not be propagated. Make sure that all inputs and outputs are used, that relation types between functions are correct, that each function allowing for its permanent or temporary nature is capable of producing its outputs starting from its inputs.

A verification made by a person other than the designer himself is also useful to reduce errors. This justifies the advantage of the author/reader cycle applicable to all documents.

We will illustrate the three-phase procedure on the two examples to be considered.

15.4.3 Example 1: centrifuge speed control system

-A- Analysis

The analysis considers the observation of the characteristics that entities in the environment must monitor (subject approach). This applies to the motor that will be constrained by the system, and not the user who will issue commands.

The motor must respect a speed profile, regardless of the driven load. The speed setpoint value defined by the user is therefore essential information for the application. The coupling between the user and motor entities takes place by the "On" and "Off" events in one direction, and by "Rotation" or "Not rotation" state of the motor in the other direction.

-B- Construction

The analysis has shown the essential elements that can be translated by three variables:

- SROTATION: 0...CVmax, for the requested speed setpoint,
- ON/OFF: which will induce the two events On and Off,
- STATE: (ROTATE, STOP), as observation of the motor state.

The following functional structure, in Figure 15.7, is developed around these three variables.

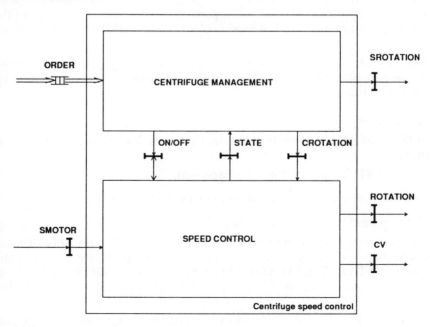

Figure 15.7   First functional decomposition.

-C- Verification

This involves reading the functional specification and checking that all transition conditions exist and that all actions are possible.

For CENTRIFUGE_MANAGEMENT, the two event orders On and Off from ORDER are used to modify the ON/OFF state. The S_Setpoint value from ORDER will result in modifying the display SROTATION and updating CROTATION.

Observing the motor state by STATE validates a new cycle and informs the user when rotation stops.

On request when ON/OFF = ON, the SPEED_CONTROL function is capable of controlling the motor within the imposed profile with a constant speed equal to CROTATION.

The solution to this example remains relatively macroscopic, since the three phases, acceleration, constant speed, and deceleration, do not appear. Refinement must remain very incremental to provide quality.

15.4.4 Example 2: automation with a wire-guided trolley

-A- Analysis

Starting from entities, there is some behavioral similarity between the trolley and the motor in the previous example. A speed profile has to be respected with an acceleration phase, a constant speed phase and a deceleration phase. But the constant speed value here is not modifiable. Therefore, this information is not essential.

Analysis of the behavior imposed upon the trolley shows two phase categories: displacement and others. Each displacement is characterized by start and end times.

-B- Construction

In the light of the previous example, two variables are necessary for this analysis:

- ON/OFF: to start or stop a displacement,

- STATE: to synthesize all information about the displacement.

The proposed functional structure is shown in Figure 15.8.

The partition into two functions is not unique. The functionality of these functions varies depending on the inputs used for each: for example, the variables OBSTACLE and PLATFORM_POSITION at the SUPERVISION level rather than being linked at the control level leads to a different role of the functions.

The C_BELT command is related to SUPERVISION. Otherwise, additional coupling information is necessary.

-C- Verification

Due to the simplicity of the interface between these two functions, checking is easy.

When displacement is blocked as a result of a variation from the trajectory or due to an obstacle, a signalization is given to SUPERVISION by the variable STATE. This variable is therefore defined by STATE: (DISPLACEMENT, IDLE, BLOCKED).

The trolley must follow a speed profile. The functional structure shows that this is done with an open loop control because the trolley speed is not observed. To ensure satisfactory displacement, the speeds of the two wheels VM1 and VM2 are strictly necessary information. They should be added as system inputs. This shows possible loopbacks to adjust input/output delimitations. Similarly, stopping the trolley in front of the platform requires that the position of the trolley relative to the platform is known. Three states are sufficient - distant, approach, presence. This input is called PLATFORM_POSITION and therefore has to be added.

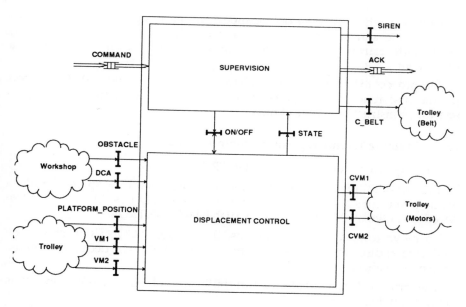

Figure 15.8   First functional decomposition.

15.5 FUNCTIONAL REFINEMENT

When the first level of the functional structure is obtained, each function should be decomposed. Sufficient refinement should be carried out to produce simple elementary functions, considering the necessary functions only.

15.5.1 Refinement stop criterion

Remember that a functional structure expresses the parallel evolution of its constituents. When a function no longer necessitates parallelism to express its behavior, it must not be decomposed. This is the stop criterion to be used for the functional refinement.

Analysis can be used to deduce whether or not refinement is necessary. This deduction is generally fairly simple based on the specification for the function. If this specification is expressed by a sequential model - finite state diagram, mathematical model - the response is immediate.

15.5.2 Refinement process

The order of decomposing functions is not very important since functions are independent and each is justified by a generally informal specification.

However, it is suggested that the more difficult functions be detailed first. This is because surprises are not expected for simple and therefore obvious functions.

However, when functions do not appear simple, it is possibly due to the fact that the role and specification were not clearly defined. In this case, it is desirable to clarify these functions with an analysis which then leads to a refinement.

The process to be followed for each refinement is the same as that described for the first functional decomposition. Proceed following the three steps - analysis, construction, verification.

15.5.3 Example 1: centrifuge speed control system

First, we will refine the SPEED_CONTROL function.

Independent of the load, the motor must follow a speed profile - acceleration, constant speed, deceleration. This is only possible if the control speed is known at all times. Let this variable be SCONTROL.

To move towards digital solutions, the variable SCONTROL should be evaluated at discrete intervals at a sampling step (CK) to be deduced from the precision obtained.

The proposed functional structure built around SCONTROL and CK is described in Figure 15.9.

The CLOCK function is necessary to produce CK. The two functions CONTROL_SPEED and SERVO_SPEED are temporary functions synchronous to CK, which is justified for a completely digital solution.

The SMOTOR input is necessary for the CONTROL_SPEED function to indicate the state ROTATE or STOP to CENTRIFUGE_MANAGEMENT. The SERVO_SPEED specification is a proportional type regulation, or proportional-integral-derive type if necessary. The specification of CONTROL_SPEED corresponds to the specification finite state machine (see Section 12.6.4) specifying the behavior imposed on the motor. All functions thus have a sequential behavior. Refinement is therefore completed.

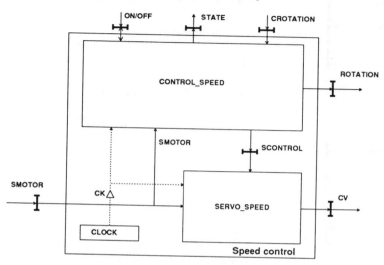

Figure 15.9   SPEED_CONTROL refinement.

The specification for the CENTRIFUGE_MANAGEMENT function can be expressed starting from the behavior imposed on the user (finite state machine given in Section 15.6.4). The behavior is sequential. Therefore refinement is no longer necessary.

15.5.4 Example 2: Automation with a wire-guided trolley

Once again, we will start with the DISPLACEMENT_CONTROL function.

The two trolley motors are mechanically independent. But the trolley must follow its trajectory and simultaneously respect the acceleration, constant speed and deceleration cycle. Coupling is therefore necessary between the two motor speed controls.

Essential information is the speed control value for each wheel at all times. Let these two variables be VC1 and VC2. The controls to be applied for each wheel are also generated at discrete intervals defined by STEP.

One refinement solution is as shown in Figure 15.10.

It is obvious that several solutions exist depending on the coupling variable considered. The difference between the various solutions is that the operations to be carried out can be located in different functions. This affects the organizational part and not the operational part.

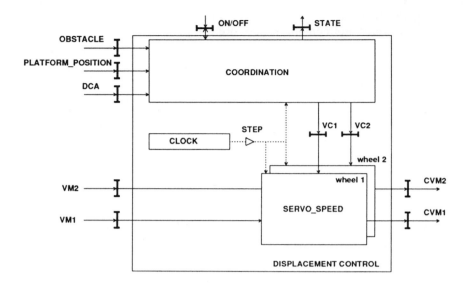

Figure 15.10   Refinement of DISPLACEMENT_CONTROL.

In the selected solution, coupling between the two wheels to follow the wire based on DCA is located in COORDINATION, which also allows consideration of fault cases. If the selected function coupling variable is the trolley control value VC, and the trajectory is maintained by servo control functions, they would be more complex; it would also be necessary to return an error indication; for example, offset from a too high trajectory.

In this example, the COORDINATION function is specified by the behavior imposed by the trolley during each displacement phase (see the specification in Section 12.10.2). Refinement is therefore not necessary.

Similarly, the SUPERVISION function is specified by the global behavior of the trolley, which is sequential. However, duration type conditions exist which also necessitate access to the current time value. Let T be time remaining before the start of the wait phase. The SUPERVISION function must therefore be refined as shown Figure 15.11.

The Timer function generates the END_T event. This solution is strictly necessary to comply with the functional model. SUPERVISION is activated on the occurrence of each COMMAND. The activity execution time is not zero since there are temporal waits. Therefore, to respect the zero time assumption for operation execution, temporal waits must take place on the condition type END_T event (passive wait instead of active wait). END_T is a condition event input shown by the double arrow on the event link.

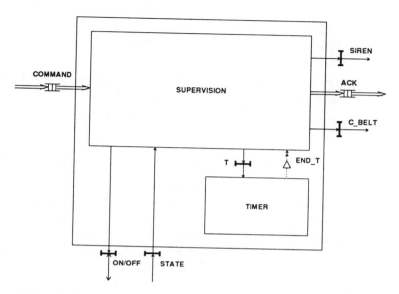

Figure 15.11   Refinement of SUPERVISION.

15.6 BEHAVIOR OF ELEMENTARY FUNCTIONS

To achieve the complete functional solution, all elementary functions have to be fully described. The same applies for all functional structure variables.

Initially, the order of descriptions can be arbitrary. However during a refinement, the proof appears after producing the behavioral description by an algorithm since the question of knowing whether or not a function is elementary has to be asked. Second, expressing the algorithmic description is more difficult than creating a functional refinement, since it is more severe but is consequently more useful for checking the completeness of the solution.

Data should be described as and when it appears during the refinement steps.

The logical order suggests that data should be described before the functions which use or produce it. This attitude is justified, first because the functional design principle is data-oriented, and second because it would not be possible to describe a transformation function without knowing the input and output data.

15.6.1 Method of obtaining an algorithmic description

The algorithmic description expresses the internal behavior of the function. This description is one possible solution for the function to behave externally like its specification.

The solution is not unique and does not necessarily represent the solution which will subsequently be used for the implementation. A transformation may be undertaken to satisfy various criteria such as optimization, simplification, etc.

The description is obtained starting from a specification. The translation work depends on the nature of the specification:

- for a very informal specification, the task is fairly long and verification is difficult;

- for a formal specification, the work consists of a simple translation only.

Consider the example of a specification expressed by a finite state machine. This specification expresses the external behavior of the function by a set of states which characterize outputs starting from inputs. This type of model is very helpful for obtaining the internal description. The description can simply be built around an internal variable which uses the specification states as values. This variable can then be used to express transition conditions and output states. The example in Figure 15.12 shows the simplicity of the translation.

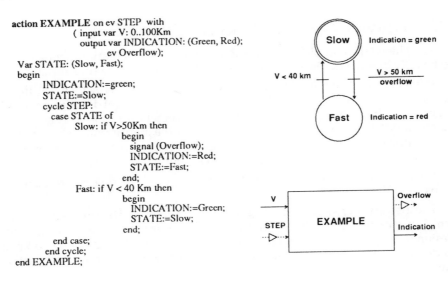

```
action EXAMPLE on ev STEP  with
            ( input var V: 0..100Km
              output var INDICATION: (Green, Red);
                   ev Overflow);
     Var STATE: (Slow, Fast);
     begin
            INDICATION:=green;
            STATE:=Slow;
            cycle STEP:
              case STATE of
               Slow: if V>50Km then
                        begin
                          signal (Overflow);
                          INDICATION:=Red;
                          STATE:=Fast;
                        end;
               Fast: if V < 40 Km then
                        begin
                          INDICATION:=Green;
                          STATE:=Slow;
                        end;
            end case;
            end cycle;
     end EXAMPLE;
```

Figure 15.12   Translation example of a diagram specification.

This writing technique is illustrated by the two examples dealt with in this chapter.

15.6.2 Example 1: centrifuge speed control system

Three elementary functions, one of which is permanent and two temporary, result from a refinement of the SPEED_CONTROL. CENTRIFUGE_ MANAGEMENT is a temporary action and has not been refined. The four algorithms are described below.

```
action CLOCK with (output ev CK);
        const PAS_CK = 5 ms;
        begin
          cycle: begin
                   wait(PAS_CK);
                   signal(CK);
                   end;
          end cycle;
        end CLOCK;
```

For the proportional-integral_derive type servo-action, the fact that the variable CV is limited has to be taken into account. If the control calculation gives a magnitude exceeding the maximum value, then CV has to be limited to this maximum value.

```
action SERVO_SPEED on event CK with
                    (input var SCONTROL, SMOTOR: def_speed;
                      output var CV:0...CVMAX);
        Const KP =..; KI = ..; KD = ..;Servo_speed coefficients;
        var C, I: real; ERROR,SM_PREC : def_speed;
        begin
          CV:=0; I:=0; SM_PREC:=SMOTOR;
          cycle CK: begin
                   ERROR:=SCONTROL-SMOTOR;
                   C:=KP*ERROR + I - KD*(SMOTOR-SM_PREC);
                   I:=I + KI*ERROR;
                   SM_PREC:=SMOTOR;
                   if C>CVMAX then CV:=CVMAX
                           else if C<0 then CV:=0
                           else CV:=C;
                   end;
          end cycle;
        end SERVO_SPEED;
```

Since the CONTROL_SPEED function plays a supervision role for motor variations, this function must impose a behavior described by the functional specification on the motor. The function simply has to behave like the specification. This leads to directly writing the algorithmic description by simply translating the finite state diagram.

```
action CONTROL_SPEED on event CK with
                    (input var CROTATION, SMOTOR: def_speed;
                     input/output var ON/OFF:(On,Off);
                     output var SCONTROL: def_speed;
                           var STATE, ROTATION: (eotate,stop);
        Const
          PAS_CK = 5 ms; Smin = 5 rpm;
                TR = 5 s;
                TC = 20 s;
                TF = 5 s;
        Var
          MOTOR_STATE: (idle, acceleration, constant_speed, deceleration);
          SV: 0...SMAX; T: integer;
```

```
begin
      MOTOR_STATE= idle; STATE:=stop; ROTATION:=stop;
      SCONTROL:=0;
      cycle CK:
              begin
              T:=T+PAS_CK;
              Case MOTOR_STATE of
                      idle: if ON/OFF = On then
                              begin
                                  MOTOR_STATE:=acceleration;
                                  SCONTROL:=0; T:=0;
                                  STATE:=rotate; ROTATION:=rotate;
                              end;
          acceleration: if ON/OFF = Off then
                              begin
                                  MOTOR_STATE:=deceleration;
                                  SV:=SMOTOR;
                                  T:=0;
                              end;
                                  else if T > TR then
                              begin
                                  MOTOR_STATE:=Constant_speed;
                                  SCONTROL:=CROTATION;
                                  T:=0;
                              end
                                  else
                                  SCONTROL:=(CROTATION*T)/TR;
        Constant_speed: if (ON/OFF=Off) or (T>TC) then
                              begin
                                  MOTOR_STATE:=deceleration;
                                  SV:=SMOTOR; T:=0;
                              end;
          deceleration: if SMOTOR < Smin then
                              begin
                                  MOTOR_STATE:=idle; ON/OFF:=off;
                                  STATE:=stop; ROTATION:=stop;
                              end
                                  else
                                  SCONTROL:= SV - (CROTATION*T)/TF;
                  end case;
                  end;
          end cycle;
    end CONTROL_SPEED;
```

The centrifuge management function must comply with the specification given as a constraint for the user. The algorithmic description is deduced directly.

```
action CENTRIFUGE_MANAGEMENT on message ORDER: def_order with
                        (input var STATE: (rotate,stop);
                         output var SROTATION, CROTATION: def_speed;
                              var ON/OFF:(On,Off);

type def_order =      record
                      kind: (On, Off, setpoint);
                      speed_value: def_speed;
                      end;
begin
      ON/OFF:=Off;
      CROTATION:=0; SROTATION:=0;
```

```
    cycle ORDER:
            case ORDER.kind of
                On:      if STATE=stop then ON/OFF:=On;
                setpoint:if STATE=stop then begin
                                CROTATION:=ORDER.speed_value;
                                SROTATION:=ORDER.speed_value;
                              end;
                OFF:     ON/OFF:=Off;
                end case;
        end cycle;
end CENTRIFUGE_MANAGEMENT;
```

15.6.3 Example 2: Automation with a wire-guided trolley

The two examples are functionally very similar. Some functions described for example 1 can also be used in this example. This applies to the CLOCK and SERVO_SPEED actions. We can therefore reuse functional developments.

The COORDINATION function monitors the environment during the displacement phase: wire position and obstacle detection. It also imposes the acceleration, constant speed, deceleration pattern and manages coordination of the two wheels.

In this case, the speed profile is obtained by adding or subtracting a speed increment at each step. Speed control also has to make use of the two trolley positions relative to the platform: approach and presence.

```
Action coordination on event STEP with
        (inputs: var OBSTACLE: boolean;
                 var PLATFORM_POSITION:(distant, approach, presence);
                 var DCA: -Dmax..+Dmax;
         input/output var ON/OFF: boolean;
         output var STATE: Def_state;
                 var VC1, VC2: def_speed);
const
      Tstep = duration; VCmax = maximum speed;
      km = coeff; Dmax = maximum distance;
      INC_VC = 0.75*Tstep m/s;
      DEC_VC = 0.7*Tstep m/s;
type
      Def_state=(idle, acceleration, V_constant, deceleration, fault);
var
      VC: def_speed;
begin
      VC:=0; VC1:=0; VC2:=0; STATE:=idle;
      cycle STEP:
              begin
              case STATE of
              idle:  if ON/OFF and not OBSTACLE then
                            begin
                              STATE:= acceleration;
                            end
                            else VC:=0;
              acceleration: if VC+INC_VC >= VCmax then
                            begin
                              VC:=VCmax;
                              STATE:=V_constant;
                            end
                            else VC:= VC + INC_VC;
```

```
                    V_constant: if PLATFORM_POSITION = approach then
                                begin
                                   STATE:=deceleration;
                                end;
                    deceleration: if PLATFORM_POSITION = presence then
                                begin
                                   VC:=0;
                                   STATE:=idle;
                                   ON/OFF:=false;
                                end;
                                else VC:= VC - DEC_VC;
                    fault: if ON/OFF = false then STATE:=idle;
                    end case;
                    if OBSTACLE or abs(DCA)>=Dmax then
                                begin
                                   VC:=0; VC1=0; VC2:=0;
                                   STATE:=fault;
                                end
                                else begin
                                   VC1:= VC + km*(DCA);
                                   VC2:= VC - km*(DCA);
                                end;

                end;
          end cycle;
    end COORDINATION;
```

This algorithm assumes that the two platforms are at least 1.5 m apart, which is realistic. A more robust solution is not difficult to write.

```
action SUPERVISION on message COMMAND:Def_order with
                  (input var STATE:def_state; event END_T;
                   output message ACK: def_cr;
                          var ON/OFF: boolean; T:integer;
                          var C_BELT:def_C_belt; SIREN: boolean);
const
      TC=3s; TI = 10s;
      TD=4s;
type
      def_order = (I_presence, load, unload, transport);
      def_cr = (OK_presence);
      def_c_belt = (off, backward, forward);
begin
      ON/OFF=false;
      SIREN:= false; C_BELT:=Off;
      cycle COMMAND:
        case COMMAND of
                 I_presence:   send(OK_presence, ACK);
                 load:         begin
                               C_BELT:= forward;
                               T:= TC;
                               when END_T: C_BELT:=Off; end when;
                               end;
                 transport:    begin
                               ON/OFF:=true;
                               Repeat
                               until (ON/OFF=false) or (STATE=fault);
                               if STATE = fault then SIREN:= true
                                  else begin
                                  T:=TI;
```

```
                            when
                            END_T: SIREN:=true;
                                    I_presence: send(OK_presence, ACK);
                                    end when;
                            end;
                         end;
            unload:      begin
                         C_BELT:= backward;
                         T:= TD;
                         when END_T: C_BELT:= Off; end when;
                         end;
            end case;
          end cycle;
    end SUPERVISION;
```

This function uses a T decrementer for the TC, TD and TI delays.

15.7 DATA DESCRIPTION

Data is used in two relation types: variable sharing and message transfer. Each variable type and each message type must be specified and then described during the development of the functional structure.

As the data has to be correctly described, it is important that the logical description, useful only for the functional level, is not confused with the physical description necessary for the implementation (see description model in Section 13.4). The terms used here are different from the levels used for the databases; the term logical description is fairly similar to the term conceptual model.

15.7.1 Data description method

Data in its most general form is a structure. Consequently, the recommended process for the functional structure search - analysis, construction, verification - is also applicable for producing data descriptions.

-A- Analysis

A variable or a message type appearing in a functional structure after refinement is the result of analyzing the specifications. The specification of each data item to deduce its description is dependent on its complexity. The model described in Section 13.4 discusses four complexity levels:

- The elementary data item: its specification and the corresponding description are direct, since it is comparable to basic types - Boolean, integer, enumeration, etc.
- Structured data: its specification is expressed by the composition of more elementary data using the concatenation, selection and set operators. Its logical description is a data structure.
- Data collection: each data item is identified by its key.
- Relation type data: specified by Chen entity/relation diagrams. It is logically described by one or several data collections. Each individualized relation is designated by keys.

The analysis task must first define the complexity of the data. It is a result of an interpretation of the functional specifications.

In the most general case, the analysis demonstrates the conceptual outline using the entity/relation diagram. This outline is the result of interpreting specification wording, translating names into entity types and verbs into relations. Each entity is then specified by identifying all constituents and the structure linking these constituents. This specification must result in obtaining the basic constituents.

-B- Construction

This phase starts from the specification and ends with a logical structured description of the data. This results from a transformation of the specification. Remember that the description must remain logical and must not translate the data implementation.

Each entity is described based on the three model symbols described in Section 13.4: composed of, selection among, set of.

Entity and relation sets are transformed into collections. Relations are described by links between entities. Use translation rules for this purpose to obtain the third normal form. A KEY is selected to identify each entity (see Section 13.4.4).

-C- Verification

As for a functional structure, check that each data structure satisfies the specifications.

This check deals with the completeness, coherence, orthogonality of fields or attributes. It also has to consider the function or functions which produce the data and use it. The check can thus only be completed after all functions in the functional structure, which produce or use the data, have been described.

15.7.2 Illustration by an example

The chosen example is a building programmed heating control system. Each room belongs to a heating zone. There are less zones than rooms.

The following information must be available for each room:

- the state: fault, off, heating;
- the control temperature;
- the current temperature;
- the outside temperature.

The outside temperature is determined from the position of the zone containing the room relative to the four sides of the building.

Programming for a room and the observation of room states are in accordance with the following screen in Figure 15.13.

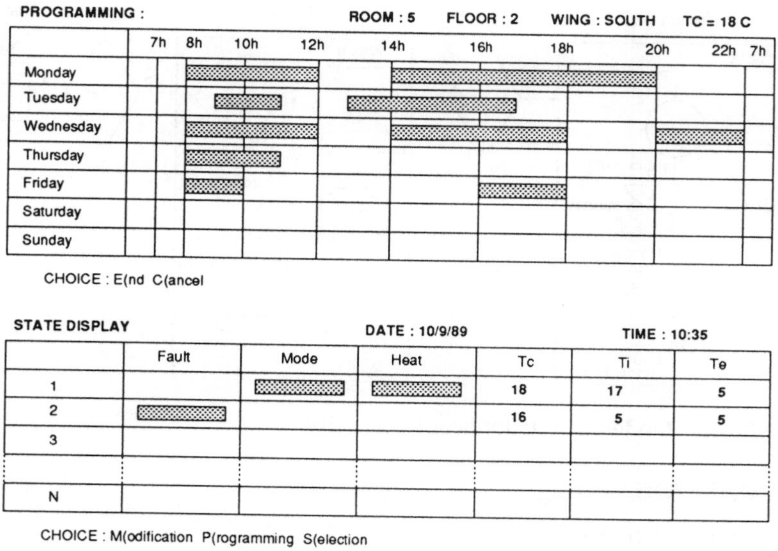

PROGRAMMING :				ROOM : 5	FLOOR : 2	WING : SOUTH		TC = 18 C	
	7h	8h	10h	12h	14h	16h	18h	20h	22h 7h
Monday									
Tuesday									
Wednesday									
Thursday									
Friday									
Saturday									
Sunday									

CHOICE : E(nd C(ancel

STATE DISPLAY			DATE : 10/9/89		TIME : 10:35	
	Fault	Mode	Heat	Tc	Ti	Te
1				18	17	5
2				16	5	5
3						
N						

CHOICE : M(odification P(rogramming S(election

Figure 15.13   Screen presentation example.

Heating is also programmed by individual rooms, to a weekly program. The resolution is 1/4 hour, except between 10:00 pm and 7:00 am within which the temperature is constant. This gives 60 programming periods.

All rooms in any one zone are characterized by the same state. Programming for each zone is deduced from room programming as the union of heating periods, and the control temperature is the maximum value of control values for all included room.

The state of each ROOM is deduced from the ZONE definition and the belong relation between ZONES and ROOMS. The model described in Figure 15.14 is used for data.

Variable descriptions are deduced from this model.

facades = {facade};

facade = <u>name</u> + TO: -30°C..+50°C;

zones = {zone};

zone = <u>name</u> + facade_Ref + zone_state + zone_prog;

zone_state: state + Tc;

state: (fault, off, heat);

Tc: 0..30°C;

Zone_prog = 60 {mode} 60 (there are necessarily 60 periods);

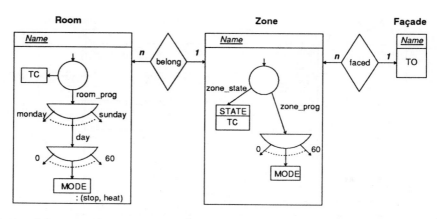

Figure 15.14   Modeling data for heating description.

Mode: (Off, heating);

rooms = {room};

room = <u>name</u> + zone_ref + TC + room_prog;

room_prog = 7{day}7;

day = 60 {mode}60;

Heating_description = facades + zones + rooms;

This data description remains functional. The functional structure is deduced from it, followed by the implementation description. For example, the functional structure may be as follows:

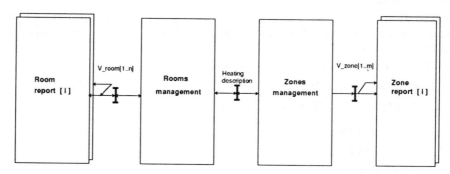

Figure 15.15   FS for heating control for each room.

For *n* rooms and *m* zones, the variables V_ROOM and V_ZONE for each zone are defined as follows:

V_ROOM[i] = TC + room_prog + state;

V_ZONE[j] = zone_state + zone_prog;

15.8 SOLUTION EVALUATION CRITERIA

Several solutions can be found to satisfy any one specification. Therefore, criteria must be used to evaluate which is to be considered the best. The following criteria are usually used for structural analysis:

- coupling analysis;

- coherence analysis;

- complexity analysis.

Coupling concerns the relation created per pair of functions. Coherence and complexity deal with internal aspects of each function. These analyses can be carried out for all refinement levels. The readability criterion applies in addition to the previous criteria.

15.8.1 Coupling analysis

The structure functions are coupled by type relations: variable, event, port for messages. The coupling complexity is related:

- to the number of relations per pair;

- to the complexity of each relation for variables and messages.

Couplings can be reduced by grouping various data within a single data structure.

Couplings acting on evolution control may be reduced by carrying out a data-oriented approach rather than a function-oriented approach.

The complexity of a coupling can also be measured by the implications of modifying the intermediate element. What modifications have to be made if the nature and/or structure of the variable are changed? Coupling is high when a variable is used by many functions.

15.8.2 Coherence analysis

Coherence is the measure of the functional unity of all included elements of a component. This analysis is equally applicable to functions and data.

Observation can be made from the outside or inside. External coherence means that the name is appropriate to the function or data. Coherence reduces as a name becomes more general. Good external coherence facilitates readability. Internal coherence is observed by analyzing the internal structure and relations between constituents. Coupling by variables leads to a better coherence than coupling by event or message since the latter expresses a temporal relation. If the data acting as links between functions has unity related to the functionality, the considered subset has a high degree of coherence.

15.8.3 Complexity analysis

The problem is to express the complexity of each function decomposed by a functional structure or described by an algorithm.

The complexity of functional structure for each refinement level is measured by the number of internal functions and the number of relations. The refinement technique recommended in this chapter limits the complexity to between 5 and 10 elements which allows good understandability.

Complexity can also be observed vertically. Into how many levels can a function be decomposed? This analysis demonstrates the number of subordinate functions. The higher this number is, the lower the understandability will be.

The complexity of an algorithmic description is measured by:

- the complexity of the function inputs and outputs, (fan-in, fan-out);

- the description length;

- the operation sequence complexity.

Qualimetry tools now exist for measuring this algorithmic complexity [ROUVE-88].

15.8.4 Solution understandability

Understandability is essential for the rest of the development and for all forms of maintenance.

Understandability of the functional structure is particularly visual. The form used for the presentation is an important factor for understanding. To a certain extent, it indicates the process followed by the designer and the logic he used. It is recommended that all inputs be at the left and outputs at the right. As far as possible, relations should progress from inputs towards outputs. Relations expressing an internal loop only should be shown in the reverse direction.

Understandability is a result of the previous criteria: weak coupling, strong coherence and low complexity.

Algorithmic descriptions are made understandable by respecting program understandability criteria: description length limited to one page, otherwise use procedures and functions; the use of structured programming control structures, limitation of the number of nested control structures, reduced interfaces with procedures and functions.

When the complete solution has been formulated, it is recommended that all solution details be reconsidered based on the above criteria. Modifications may appear desirable to improve understandability and simplicity.

For the functional structure, interfaces between functions must be reduced; this is achieved by grouping variables, grouping functions or displacing some operation parts from one action to another.

15.9 DOCUMENTATION

Finally, the essential part of the design step is the document produced. This design document plays several roles, and is useful for:

- checking that the solution matches the specifications;

- the transfer of knowledge of the solution developed for the problem;

- the development of an implementation.

The verification is carried out by an author/readers cycle correcting, modifying and improving the solution. This same cycle allows readers to become familiar with the problem and its solution. This document is also used as a reference document for the product. This facilitates application maintenance and evolution tasks.

For the next implementation specification step, the document will be used as input data together with the detailed specification document. Hence, the chronological order of thoughts and developments should not be described. Only the selected solution should be described using a top-down process to facilitate understanding.

A guide must facilitate global understanding of the solution - hierarchical description of functions, data, etc.

15.10 SUMMARY

The functional design process was presented making use of two examples which initially appeared very different. Similarities were noted when developing the solution: speed servo control, speed profile generation, coordination, etc. The process thus naturally facilitates the reuse of subsets developed in other projects. Problems to be treated include general classes of subsets for which the solution is identified by a functional process.

The essential points of the procedure proposed in this chapter are as follows:

- First, a good functional design cannot be undertaken unless input documents are complete, validated and are of high quality. The functional and operational specifications are used.

- The first phase consists of delimiting the system by its inputs and outputs. These must be functional related to environment entities and not technological.

- The first functional decomposition must be carefully considered; it will induce the architecture of the entire solution. The best is that which minimizes the organizational part of the implementation.

- The solution search by refinement is carried out in three steps: specification analysis, construction of one or several solutions, verification.

- Functional refinement must not be excessive. Refinement for a function is complete when it has a sequential behavior.

- The algorithmic description of actions must be well prepared: consider the strictly necessary only, improve understandability, comply with the model for permanent and temporary actions. If possible, this description must be no more than a simple translation of specifications.

- The description of all data must be complete before undertaking the algorithmic description. A data structure is produced in a three-step procedure: analysis, construction, verification.

- The complete solution must be evaluated based on criteria which help judge quality: coupling, coherence, complexity, understandability.

- The documentation must be structured and complete. It must describe the final solution using a top-down approach in order to facilitate understanding. This result is obtained if the method is applied.

16

TEMPLATE MODELS FOR DESIGN

In the functional design stage, developers have to search for a solution as a refinement to each function. This work is related to the creative design process. The quality of the designer is therefore still an important factor influencing the nature of the solution. The first functional decomposition is essential for the quality of the entire project. The previous chapter showed how this decomposition is the result of an analysis phase.

Carrying out experiments on a diverse population of designers faced with the same design problem (for example a group of students from different origins), it is easy to observe that, starting from the same design principles, there is a wide variety of proposed solutions. This means that designers do not find the same essential variables. However, one solution is more appropriate than the others.

Having observed this, we made an effort to find a technique for improving solution homogeneity.

The starting point for this thought was to consider that designers tend to work by analogy. If a designer has experience with a similar problem or if solutions are available, he will naturally be tempted to reuse this experience.

Since problems are different, it is not enough to have a wide range of solutions available, since one solution does not always correspond very closely to the problem to be treated. If solutions are available, the design technique is an assembly work using a bottom-up procedure. This method of proceeding is contrary to the design principles described in the previous chapters.

In this chapter we will propose the concept of template solution models for design. A very small number of these models are particularly useful for solving a wide class of problems.

16.1 TEMPLATE MODEL ROLE AND BENEFIT

A solution template model is an expression of a general functional architecture as a solution outline adapted to a problem class.

A template model suggests internal functions and specific couplings between these functions. Thus, instead of searching for the essential internal variables with no guides, when starting from a template model the designer searches for the essential variables which will provide coupling between the model functions. The variety of possible variables is then much reduced. Having defined the essential variables, the designer then simply needs to specify the model functions for the application.

Experience has shown that using an imposed template model for a given problem, there is little variation between proposed solutions even with a varied population of designers.

Is uniformity a good thing? Not necessarily, since it could prevent the best solutions from appearing. A template model must also intrinsically possess quality properties if it is to lead to the best solutions. The benefit of the template model in a top-down design process is then considerable since it improves the solution produced, thus globally reducing the project development cost.

How can we find a template model? Creation starting from scratch is not very promising. It is necessary instead to start from observing the principles and architectures of solutions thought up by designers. The general character is deduced from this observation and the approach as a template model is then formalized. The model must then be validated by numerous field trials using the model to solve industrial problems. These experiments lead to modifications, quality measurements and conclusions.

Finding, formalizing and validating a template model requires a great deal of experimental work that the designer can save if he uses already validated models judiciously. The objective of this chapter is to make these results available to designers.

The rest of this chapter describes a few template models useful to know for functional design. Note that this template model concept can also be used for the next detailed design stage. These models are then oriented more towards hardware architecture such as Moore's machine, the operative part/control part decomposition, or the software architecture such as the object model.

16.2 CONTROLLER/PROCESS MODEL

16.2.1 Principle

This initial model simply reuses the automation engineer's view of a process or an entity to be controlled. All controls must be closed loop. Since the process behavior cannot be perfect - sensitivity to disturbances or other effects. A control applied to the process will only approximately produce the required effect. To improve the result and satisfy an objective precisely, observations have to be made on the process to correct faults. This initial principle is shown in Figure 16.1.

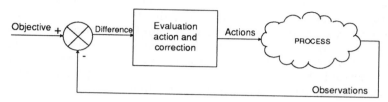

Figure 16.1   Closed loop control.

16.2.2 The model

We will now consider the contents of a control problem specification. The specification process recommended in MCSE suggests that environment entities be modeled first. The approximate behavior of the process or processes therefore has to be expressed. The behavior imposed on each entity in the system is then expressed by the functional specification. The conclusion, based on the closed loop principle, is that each entity monitoring the imposed evolution must be driven by an action evaluation function which must behave as described in the functional specification.

This reasoning has to be made for each entity. Since temporal dependency relations must very often be respected for entity evolutions, couplings are necessary between the internal check functions.

The process/controller modeL is then as follows.

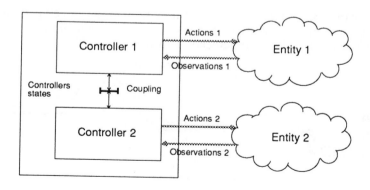

Figure 16.2   Process/controller template model.

Each entity is internally associated with a controller function coupled to its entity by action relations and observation relations.

The behavior of each controller function is expressed by the functional specification for the corresponding entity. For example, if the specification is of the finite state diagram type, the algorithmic description of the control function behavior is obtained by simply translating the finite state machine.

Controller functions may be coupled together by state variables if there are synchronizations in the specification. A simple unidirectional temporal dependency between two controllers, for example expressed by a condition, makes use of an internal variable which stores the current state of the controller which generated the condition. This variable is then placed outside this controller function to make it accessible for reading by the other controller.

16.2.3 The method

This model can be used as follows:

- firstly, analyze specifications to determine if this model is suitable;

- draw controller functions, each coupled to its entity to be controlled through system inputs and outputs;

- analyze specifications to search for couplings between the necessary state variables to satisfy temporal ordering relations;

- place coupling variables and complete functional relations;

- write controller algorithmic descriptions by translating specifications;

- check the coherence of the complete solution respecting all specifications.

16.2.4 Example

We will illustrate the use of this model by the simple example of a handling trolley.

The following figure shows the automation to be developed using an electronic system. The objective of the system is to automate the cycle - move the trolley from P1 to P2, dump bucket, return trolley to P1.

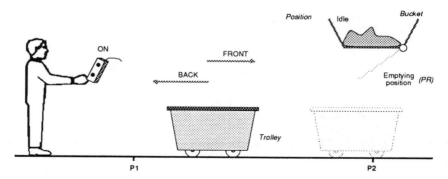

Figure 16.3   The three application entities.

The specification for this automaton is described below using three coupled finite state machines. Positions P1 and P2 are detected by end of travel detectors FCL and FCR. The two bucket positions are controlled by events C_idle and C_dump. The FAULT variable is generated by the trolley. The cycle can only start if the trolley is at P1. Otherwise, it returns to this position. The operator generates the ON event by pressing the push button, see Figure 16.4.

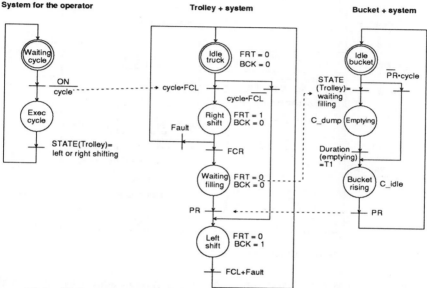

Figure 16.4   Finite state specification.

The input and output delimitations can be deduced from this specification as shown in Figure 16.5.

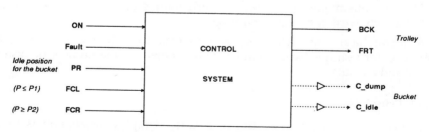

Figure 16.5   System input and output specifications.

The designer must then propose a refinement. Since the behavior imposed on each entity is described in the specification by a sequential diagram, we will use the controller template model for each entity.

The solution is then organized around three controllers. The necessary coupling between the controllers must then be found. A unidirectional coupling exists between the user controller and the trolley controller, another bidirectional coupling exists between the trolley controller and the bucket controller.

The functional structure obtained is as shown in Figure 16.6.

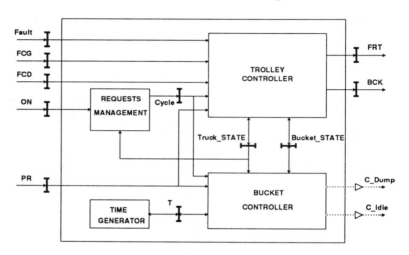

Figure 16.6   Automation functional structure.

The solution is completed by a time T generation action to perform the timing necessary to control the dump state duration.

16.3 SUPERVISION/CONTROL MODEL

The previous model is suitable for fairly simple applications: few entities and relatively weak functional coupling.

A hierarchical approach is to be preferred for larger applications, as measured for example by the number of functions and the number of system inputs and outputs.

16.3.1 Principle

The concept is that the control of a fairly complex installation is to be globally handled by the system. The user or operator simply defines objectives to be satisfied and observes the installation behavior at a macroscopic level.

Operator control is a high-level functionality compared with the control of each entity in the installation.

This type of system may be structured on at least two levels:

- a supervision level which forms the interface with the operator for overall control of the application;

- a control level which manages all physical entities in the application so that they contribute to satisfy the highest level objective.

The two levels are therefore coupled together: in the top-down direction for assigning objectives, and in the bottom-up direction for reporting on progress towards objectives.

16.3.2 The model

The proposed model follows on from this structuring principle. Decomposition is made in two functions: Supervision and Control. To specify the model, the general coupling between the two function categories has to be detailed in order to propose an analysis guide to the designer to help him in his search for the internal essential variables, see Figure 16.7.

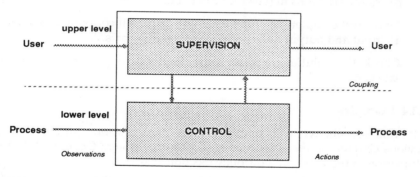

Figure 16.7   Supervision/control model.

Top-down coupling from Supervision towards Control requires two categories of information:

- parameters, which will qualify objectives to be achieved for the physical part: for example, temperature control value, response time, etc;

- commands, which are events with or without associated information to designate operations which must be handled by the control part.

Bottom-up coupling from Control to Supervision also requires two categories of information:

- observations which, when synthesized by the control part, will monitor operation progress;

- reactions, to inform the top level of special situations to be taken into account.

Operation inputs and outputs are associated with supervision. Other inputs or outputs are associated with the control part.

16.3.3 The method

The first step necessary before using this model is to decide whether or not it is suitable. Experience has shown that many applications, especially those involving any form of operation (users, others, etc.) and physical entities, can be developed based on this model.

When this choice has been made, proceed as follows:

- Identify entities linked to each of the two levels.

- Analyze specifications to search for the necessary coupling variables: parameters in one direction, observations in the other direction.

- Then, search for coupling events, in other words commands in one direction, reactions in the other direction.

- Draw and complete the functional structure - all coupling relations and all input and output links with one of the two parts.

- Check the solution to make sure that all specifications have been satisfied.

16.3.4 Examples

In this section, we will simply analyze the solutions proposed in the previous chapter for the centrifuge speed control system (Section 15.4.3) and automation of the wire-guided trolley (Section 15.4.4).

After determining the internal variables essential for the solution in the first functional decomposition, two functions were found. The proposed functional structures comply with the supervision/control model. Thus, rather than searching for the necessary internal variables with no specific guide, this type of model facilitates this task by proposing four coupling categories.

Moreover, it is interesting to observe that for the four examples, the control part is again decomposed into two functions. This decomposition also conforms with the supervision/control model.

Thus, the model can be used for different functionality levels. When it is no longer suitable since it is too close to the entity to be checked, it is very likely that the previous controller/process model is suitable. This is the case for the SERVO_SPEED function.

There are many pedagogic type examples such as automation with a wire-guided trolley, heating control, elevator control, which were handled in both ways a few years ago without knowing the model and then making use of this model. The quality of solutions based on the model is unquestionable considering understandability, simplicity, coupling and coherence criteria.

For larger industrial examples - for building control by centralized technical management with 500 inputs and outputs - this type of model can be used to carry out an initial global data-oriented approach essential for the application, and then to approach the detailed solution by successive refinements of each subset using the two models described.

16.4 CLIENT/SERVER MODEL

16.4.1 Principle

To describe this model, we will consider the case of distributed applications.

The OSI (Open Systems Interconnection) model was formalized by ISO (International Organization for Standardization) to facilitate the interconnection of heterogeneous computers as implementation support. It suggests decomposing coupling between functional entities into seven hierarchical levels shown in Figure 16.8.

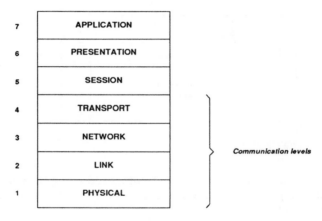

Figure 16.8   The seven levels in the OSI model.

The Application, Presentation and Session levels are oriented towards obtaining application functionalities. The Transport, Network, Link and Physical levels are communications-oriented.

This model specifies that each level must be able to make use of services in the lower level for its operation. Each level is responsible for a set of specific functions. This principle, and the concept of seven levels are the basis for the client/server model in Figure 16.9.

16.4.2 The model

Although particularly suitable for the implementation specification of distributed functionalities, we felt that it would be useful to include this model in this chapter due to its general nature.

This is a vertical type of functional model. To carry out its functionality, a function must be able to use services. The function to be decomposed is then broken down into two subsets: the function to be carried out and the necessary services. Coupling between the two parts is then of the event driven type with information transfer, translated by relations by message or data transfer.

The proposed model is shown in Figure 16.9.

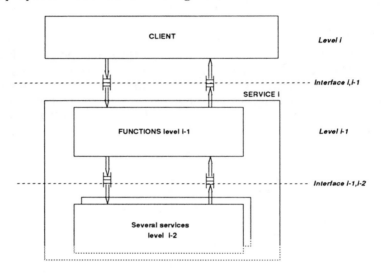

Figure 16.9   The client/server model.

The service function may itself be decomposed using the same model. It is thus possible to go down from level to level until existing, available or known services can be identified.

The OSI model suggests the nature of services for each level, each carrying out a different functionality from the other levels.

16.4.3 The method

First, the advantage of this method for the problem to be dealt with has to be identified. In general, it is suitable when resources have to be implemented to satisfy the required functionality. These resources are accessible by services or made available in the form of services.

The suggested method is as follows for this problem class:

- Identify the services strictly necessary for the function to be implemented. For example, based on the OSI model for a communications problem.

- Specify the behavior of the requesting client function based on the existence of the above services.

- Then specify the behavior of the services to satisfy the requests from the higher level.

- Specify the coupling information necessary to request services and the information expected in return. This will have to define the interface between the two levels.

- Based on the decomposition model, describe the functional solution and information passing through the interface.

- Check the solution coherence and its suitability for satisfying the objectives.

The same procedure can be used again to decompose the function providing services. Prior to this, it may be desirable to carry out a refinement of the level based on a functional horizontal type model.

16.4.4 Example: message transmission through a serial link

This example is only useful to illustrate the model and the method. This problem type would normally be dealt with during the implementation specification step.

Assume that an application requires two functions F1 and F2 coupled by a MESS port for message transfer as shown in Figure 16.10.

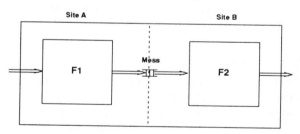

Figure 16.10   Distributed application example.

As implementation constraints, F1 and F2 are remote. The transfer between F1 and F2 can no longer take place directly through MESS.

The solution requires that a message transfer service from site A towards site B is available. Based on the client/server model, the functional structure is as shown in Figure 16.10.

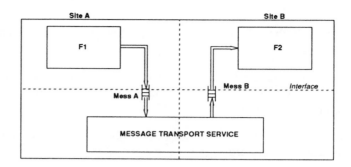

Figure 16.11   Solution refinement based on the model.

It is interesting to note that the process here leads to refining the MESS port.

The functional decomposition is continued by searching for the solution to carry out each message transfer. Since each message is a sequence of characters, the necessary services are send character and receive character. Similarly, continuing the refinement, each character transmitted on a communication support is a sequence of bits.

The complete solution detailed down to the support is given in Figure 16.12. This solution remains purely functional, since no assumption has been made about the size of the ports. During the next implementation specification step, each port will have a limited size. It is probably necessary to servo control the producer to the consumer, imposing a feedback coupling between receiving and sending characters.

The solutions for these problems are simpler to deduce from a purely functional solution as shown below than by using an intuitive approach.

16.5 INTERACTIVITY MODEL

Many applications require the development of a man-machine interface for coupling the system with users, maintenance, etc.

One such interface is different from interfaces with physical entities. The user is specific: first, his actions are uncontrolled and therefore it is essential that actions considered to be correct for the application are filtered and second, the information exchanged may be very complex and presented in a variety of forms.

16.5.1 Principle

There are several forms of man-machine dialog, for example:

- the command language: for example MSDOS or Unix;

- a question/answer dialog: dialog controlled by the system;

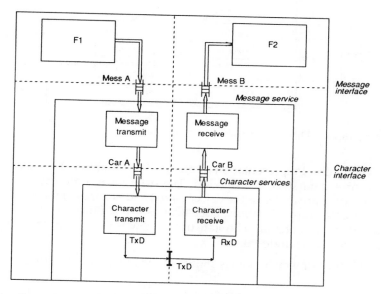

Figure 16.12   Complete solution for message transfer

- dialog by menus: all presentation types including pop up menus and icon menus;

- direct manipulation. This is the most sophisticated form.

Direct manipulation consists of representing application objects which concern the user. Objects are acted upon by directly selecting the object followed by the action to be performed.

This principle is now available in a multi-window graphic environment using a mouse as pointer on workstations or microcomputers.

The implementation of this type of interface is based on work undertaken by Xerox about the Smalltalk object language. In this language, interactivity by direct manipulation is easily installed based on the MVC (Model-View-Controller) Metaphor [MEVEL-87].

This metaphor suggests that every application object must first be represented by an internal model. This model can then be shown in the form of one or several views. Manipulation of the object involves the use of a controller inserted as a filter between user actions, the model and the views. Figure 16.13 summarizes this metaphor.

16.5.2 The model

The interactivity model described in this section is derived from the MVC metaphor.

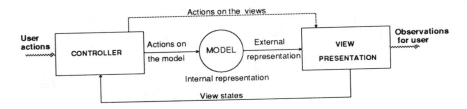

Figure 16.13   The MVC metaphor.

The internal representation of an application object is translated by a data item or a data structure (model). The external representation or view uses information attributes of the object model and additional information defining the external representation. User actions are a function of selection on the external representation. The state of the view is thus necessary to decide upon the actions to be undertaken.

This type of view model is shown in the functional structure in Figure 16.4.

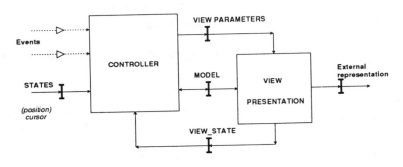

Figure 16.14   The interactivity model for a view.

Events may be pressing keys or mouse buttons. States may be the position of the mouse on the screen.

The variable VIEW_STATE allows the controller to differentiate between requested actions depending on the position of the pointer on the screen and therefore relative to the object shown.

Possible controller actions deal with modification of the model, for example attributes and even the structure and view parameters.

The VIEW_PRESENTATION function calculates an external representation of the internal model at all times, taking account of display parameters. Therefore, if the model is modified in real-time, its display will follow.

This template model is only functional. It does not express the implementation technique which will be deduced later from this model. In particular, the VIEW_PRESENTATION function should be triggered solely if the model or view parameters are modified.

16.5.3 The method

Starting from the specifications, the required interactivity form has to be found first. If it is required that the direct manipulation principle is used to simplify use, the following phases are suggested:

- first, search for the application objects involved in the interactivity;

- specify these objects by searching for characteristic attributes and then define an internal representation;

- specify the view(s) desired for these objects. Then deduce the representation parameters and the external representation states;

- specify the behavior of the VIEW_PRESENTATION and CONTROLLER functions. Use them to deduce an algorithmic description.

16.5.4 Example

We will illustrate the use of this model with a simple example.

The contents of two tanks need to be represented in real-time; one spills over into the other through a closed or open valve with a variable flow. The user observes the level in each tank in real-time. He can change the state of the valve and can also adjust the flow. The application objects are:

- the two tanks, each of which can be modeled by its diameter and height;

- the valve with its state and flow when it is open.

The required presentation is as follows in Figure 16.15:

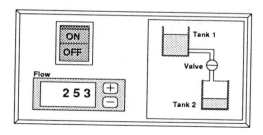

Figure 16.15   Required presentation for the man/system interface.

The On/Off switch fixes the valve position, and the position is changed by pressing it.

The flow is indicated by its numerical value. This value can be modified in two ways - by changing the numeric value or by pressing the + or - keys after selecting the field containing this value and then clicking the mouse.

The state of the two tanks is represented by a graphic display. The valve is shown open or closed depending on the position of the switch.

All objects in the view - the switch, flow adjustment and tanks - can be displaced by clicking on the object and displacing it. Releasing it fixes the final position.

The internal model deals with:

- - the state of the switch;
- - the flow rate;
- - the quantity in each tank.

The view parameters are:

- - the switch position;
- - the flow adjustment position;
- - the position of each tank.

The view state is characterized by:

- - the field containing the switch;
- - the numeric flow rate modification field;
- - the fields for the + and - buttons;
- - the fields for each tank.

The functional structure is therefore as follows in Figure 16.6.

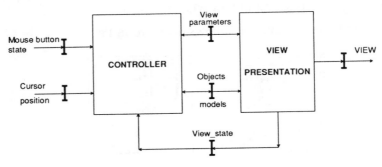

Figure 16.16   Functional structure for the application.

The mouse push state must be observable at all times to allow modifications by pressing + or - for object displacements. This variable can also be replaced by the two events Press and Release.

16.5.5 Generalization of the model for a multi-window environment

In a multi-window environment, a window represents a logical screen. Several objects and views can then be displayed. Two levels should be differentiated - window management, and the management of the display in each window.

The above model can be used as a structuring base. Each object must be checked, and its view must be produced and checked in a window. All views then form a logical modeling of objects, which must be translated into a physical presentation.

The functional structure extended to multi-windows is then as follow in Figure 16.17.

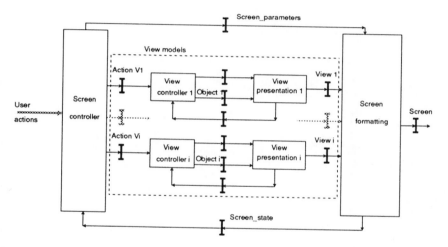

Figure 16.17   Functional structure for a multi-window presentation.

This type of model must facilitate the implementation of interactive graphics application which makes use of a multi-window manager.

16.6 SUMMARY

This chapter introduced template models which can provide significant assistance to the designer in carrying out a functional decomposition. The list of models is not very long and extensions would be welcome.

However, the template model could not be confused with the solution for a specific problem. Solutions developed for other applications have the advantage of being directly reusable. But the template model concept seems essential since few problems are similar.

The main points discussed in this chapter are:

- a template model helps the designer to propose a quality functional decomposition;

- since each model is suitable for a problem class, the first step is to search for the most suitable model starting from the specifications.

REFERENCES PART 4

[ABBOTT-86]
> *An Integrated Approach to Software Development*
> R.J. Abbott
> Wiley, Interscience publication, John Wiley&Sons 1986

[CALVEZ-82]
> *Une Méthodologie de Conception des Systèmes Multi-microordinateurs*
> *pour les Applications de Commande en Temps-réel*
> J.P. Calvez
> Thèse de Doctorat d'Etat, Université de NANTES, Novembre 1982

[DATE-86]
> *An Introduction to Database Systems* Vol 1
> C.J. Date
> Addison-Wesley 4th Ed. 1986

[GALACSI-86]
> *Les systèmes d'Information - Analyse et Conception*
> GALACSI, Nom collectif
> Dunod Informatique 1986

[GALACSI-89]
> *Conception de Bases de Données - Du Schéma Conceptuel aux Schémas*
> *Physiques*
> GALACSI, Nom collectif
> Dunod Informatique 1989

[MEVEL-87]
> *Smalltalk-80*
> A. Mevel, T. Gueguen
> Eyrolles 1987

[PARNAS-86]

A rational design process: How and why to fake it
D.L. Parnas, P.C. Clements
IEEE Transactions on Software Engineering Vol SE-12, No 2, Febuary 1986,
p 251-257

[ROLLAND-88]

Conception des systèmes d'information - La méthode REMORA
C. Rolland, O. Foucault, G. Benci
Eyrolles 1988

[ROTENSTREICH-86]

Two-dimensional program design
S. Rotenstreich
IEEE Transactions on Software Engineering Vol SE-12, No 3, March 1986,
p 377-384

[ROUVE-88]

LOGISCOPE: Contribution à la maitrise de la qualité des logiciels
C. Rouve, M. Viala
Génie Logiciel et Systèmes Experts No 12,   juin 1988, p 36-44

[WARD-85]

Structured Development for real-time systems
P.T. Ward, S.J. Mellor
Vol 1: Introduction and Tools
Yourdon Computing Series, Yourdon Press, Prentice-Hall 1985

PART 5

IMPLEMENTATION SPECIFICATION

The purpose of the third step in the methodology is to determine all specifications for the implementation necessary to satisfy the system objectives. The work consists of refining, detailing and enriching the functional solution to satisfy the new constraints expressed by the technological specifications. This step is also called detailed design.

The starting point is the functional solution generated during the previous step, which has the special property of being technology independent. The implementation resulting from this step will involve the complementary use of a hardware part acting as execution support and a software set specifying the imposed evolution of the microprocessors for the application.

The procedure recommends:

- *introducing technological interfaces;*
- *taking account of all real-time system constraints;*
- *determining the hardware/software distribution;*
- *specifying the characteristics of the hardware part and the organization of the software part.*

This part first describes the executive model, the third dimension of the global description model for all solutions (Chapter 17).

Chapter 18 describes the integration model which deals with the correspondence between the functional level and the execution level, and rules to be respected for the software development.

Chapter 19 presents the objectives to be achieved, the various criteria for the implementation, the principles and process to be followed in developing the solution. The two examples are considered for illustration purposes.

17

THE EXECUTIVE MODEL

The brief introduction to the general solution description model in Part I showed that an implementation eventually comprises two parts: a hardware part which causes the evolution of system functions, and a software part which customizes the behavior of the equipment so that the global evolution complies with the detailed application specifications.

The hardware part must be specified. This means that a detailed description of the hardware to be used must be prepared, but not including board schematics and equipment references. The description must be limited to expressing characteristics and constraints of necessary hardware functions, and links between these functions. However, this description must be sufficient to allow a specialist or a team to produce the schematics, select the equipment (subsets, boards, components) and complete the work during the next implementation phase.

The objective of this chapter is to describe the executive model as a specification tool for the hardware part of a system. It first describes the executive model by characterizing its global behavior and then the specifications for each type of component.

17.1 EXECUTIVE MODEL CHARACTERISTICS

The executive model expresses a set of rules that must be respected by any specification of the hardware part of an implementation. For the description of existing hardware known by its schemas, subsets and boards, this model facilitates a macroscopic view of this hardware by abstraction.

When the hardware part is to be designed, this model defines the hardware assembly from a purely external view, thus leaving the choice open to any technical solution satisfying the constraints. Obviously, this external view is no longer independent of the technology in the functions sense, but should be independent of market components.

17.1.1 The executive model and its constituents

The executive model is based on the assumption that every implementation for a system is composed of:
- **processors** as information transformation systems;
- **memories** for saving and storing data;
- **communication nodes** between intermediate elements for information transit.

These three types of technological elements are necessarily interrelated. This model uses three types of links:
- **interprocessor signalling** for direct coupling between processors;
- **memory sharing** between processors for indirect coupling without order relation;
- **interprocessor communication** as indirect coupling with order relation through a communication nodes network.

The executive model is therefore a structure referred to as the executive structure. The following example in Figure 17.1 gives an idea of this graphical type of model.

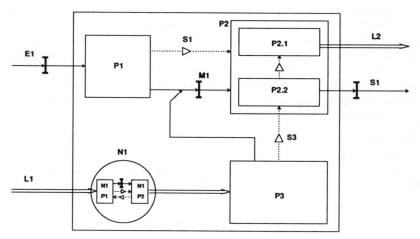

Figure 17.1   Executive structure example.

This example shows that processors and communication nodes may themselves be described by an executive structure.

An executive structure is characterized by:
- a topological description in the form of an element interconnection network;
- a specification of each element type and each relation type formed by links.

This is a structural type model which allows a hierarchical description. The executive model is shown as follows in Figure 17.2.

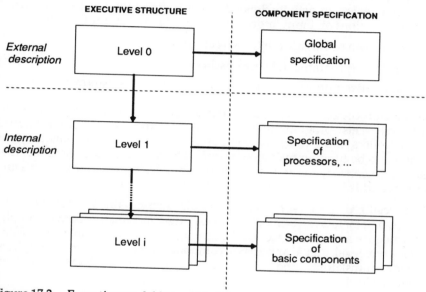

Figure 17.2   Executive model hierarchical decomposition.

The organizational part is a tree structure, since each element - processor, communication node - is decomposable to an executive structure. Terminal elements are basic technological elements. Level 0 delimits the application executive support.

The specification part of constituents characterizes all element types in the executive model: processor for each refinement level, communication node and memory for the user level, and the relation role for the executive structure decomposition level.

17.1.2 Meaning of elements and relations

Before considering the model rules in detail, we will mention the element types and relations and their meanings. The previous example showed the graphical notation and the description level allowed by an executive structure. It is helpful to bear in mind the similarity between a function structure and an executive structure, particularly when interpreting the role of each constituent.

This characteristic can be explained since the executive structure is the motor for the evolution of a functional structure. Functional level actions thus evolve by means of processors, and functional relations are carried out by means of signalling, memories and communication nodes.

-A- Processor

The term "processor" is used here in its most general sense. It is firstly a dynamic object which has its own independence. It is thus able to carry out its role when it wishes. Its activity depends on its functionality: globally, it carries out transformations on input information to produce output information.

Processors can be classified into two categories:

- **general** (programmable) **processors**;
- **specialized processors** (which may or may not be parametrable).

General processors are programmable so that their functionalities can be customized. This programming is done by software. Microprocessors, microcontrollers, mini and microcomputers and computer systems are thus considered to be programmable processors. The term processor here includes all elements necessary for its operation: for example, local memory, inputs and outputs are added to the microprocessor for programs and data.

A specialized processor has a specific non-modifiable functionality. However, parameters can be modified to vary the functionality. Some examples in this category are: specialized VLSI components, programmable controllers- and at a lower level: digital and analog components such as adders, multipliers, frequency translators, and all types of interfaces: PWM generator, programmable clock, etc.

-B- Memory

A memory is a passive object. It stores any type of information transmitted by a processor and provides its value on request.

-C- Communication node

A communication node is an active object acting as an intermediary between a set of communication channels linked to processors. Its role is to direct all information that it receives towards the right destination.

Information received in the form of messages are temporarily stored, analyzed and then retransmitted through output channels. For a given message, there may be a delay between its input and output.

The complexity of a communication node may be very varied. The simplest case is a single link with one input and one output with no memory. In more complex cases, for example the Transpac network, a node itself is a communication node network.

-D- Interprocessor signaling

Each processor decides upon its activity at all times. Some activities necessitate coupling with the environment respecting order relations. Interprocessor signaling allows synchronization between activities distributed on different processors. For the hardware, they are implemented by control signals and interrupt lines.

-E- Memory sharing

A processor may use an external memory to submit or read data. Data exchanges are possible using this relation type when memory is accessible by at least two processors.

Thus synchronization and message transfer are possible using this mechanism, but since memory is a passive object, temporal relations are only obtained as a result of regular reading by processors.

-F- Interprocessor communication

This relation type is suitable for message transfer between processors. A message produced by a processor through an output channel will be directed by the node or the communication node network towards the destination processor named in the message.

A communication node can be used for point to point (single destination) or broadcasting (a set of destinations).

17.2 THE EXECUTIVE STRUCTURE MODEL

An executive structure is the topological expression of hardware support elements by a network (the notation ES is sometimes used). This section firstly describes graphical conventions (static view) and then describes the interpretation of each symbol specifying its behavior relative to its environment (dynamic view).

17.2.1 Graphical representation

The representation of an executive structure describes the decomposition of a processor or a communication node type element.

Each element to be described has inputs and outputs. The refinement of an element is described using four element types:

- processors, each represented by a rectangle:

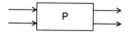

- memories, represented by the symbol:

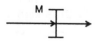

- signaling, represented by:

- communication nodes, represented by: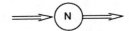

These following relations are all between processors. They are only possible by using an intermediate signalling, memory or communication node type element.

The three authorized relation types use special symbols for links:

- for signaling: ....➤

- for access to a memory: ─────────────➤

- for message transfer.   ══════════➤

The figure below gives an example of an executive structure showing the hardware support for a distributed application requiring a multiprocessor architecture on one of the sites as shown in Figure 17.3.

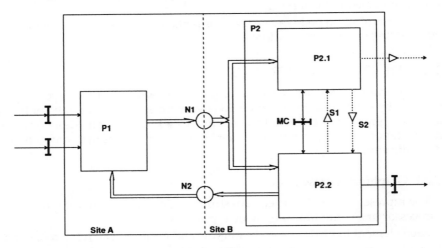

Figure 17.3   Executive structure representation example.

Links are unidirectional except for the access to memory MC.

There must be a link between each processor and node (N1 --> P2.1 and also N1-->P2.2). A signal may be produced and used by several processors.

An executive structure processor can be refined by an executive structure (P2). The same applies for a node.

The common sense rules given for coherence and understandability of a functional structure are also applicable to an executive structure:

- Controlability and observability of all elements: the use of all inputs and outputs, participation of all elements in an relation.
- Choice of a meaningful name for all constituents: the name must have an explicit relation with the functionality and the role played.
- Presentation quality: limitation of the complexity of each refinement level, relations showed from the left towards the right.

17.2.2 Interpretation of an ES

We will explain the role played by each constituent of an executive structure below, so that a representation can be understood without ambiguity. This is equivalent to modeling the external behavior of each constituent type.

-A- Behavior for processors

The following rules characterize the behavior of each processor:

- A processor is always active in working condition. Breakdown and power-fail situations are translated by removing the processor from the executive structure.

- Unlike the assumption used for function execution times in the functional model, the execution time for operations within a processor is finite and not zero. These times are defined by the processor specifications.

- A processor may read or modify contents of memories connected to it at any time. It specifies the information concerned for each access.

- A processor can generate signals at its outputs at any time and transmit messages through its output communication channels.

- When it wishes, a processor can modify its activity on detection of a signal or the existence of a message available on one of its input communication channels. The processor is thus always master of its activity.

-B- Rules for memories

Each memory identifies whether or not the variable concerned by the designation at the time of an access belongs to it. If so, it either stores it or reads it depending on the access direction. The time taken for each access is not zero but is generally low. It is assumed that integrity constraints are respected for simultaneous access requests. These potential conflicts must be solved by the implementation.

-C- Behavior for communication nodes

A communication node may have several inputs and outputs. Each input is linked to a processor to provide a communication channel. The same applies for each output.

Every message output by a processor is accepted in its entirety by the communication node. Every requested message is thus completely accepted. A message for communication is therefore indivisible. Each message carries routing information, namely the destination and the sender. Two communication types are possible through a communication node:

- Point-to-point transfer: each message concerns one destination only.
- Transfer for broadcasting: a message concerns a set of destinations. In this case, the node generates a message to each destination. The communication type is also identified in the message.

There may be a delay of arbitrary duration between the reception of a message and its sending by the node. The transfer type is thus not known in advance. A node is always active. If it becomes defective, it disappears from the executive structure.

A communication node does not perform any information transformation. However, it can change its presentation.

-D- Rules for signalling

All signals sensitize all connected processors. But it is only taken into account if the called processors want to take it into account.

17.2.3 Executive structure refinement and abstraction

The executive structure model is hierarchical. An element can be described based on simpler elements. Conversely, a usable element may result from a structure. We then refer to a logical or virtual communication node or processor.

Refinement and abstraction are used for processors and communication nodes. The example in Figure 17.4 shows several description levels.

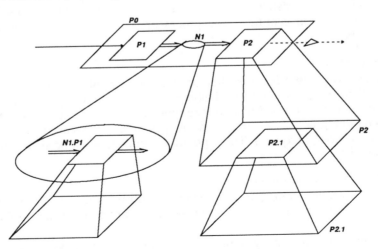

Figure 17.4   Hierarchical levels of an executive structure.

We can very easily show that at the most microscopic level, any executive structure can be constructed simply by using processors, memories, signals and two relation types. The relation by communication node added to the model and constructed using a memory and signals has the advantage of a specification at a more macroscopic level.

-A- Processors

All element and relation types can be used for a processor decomposition. Refinement must stop when constituents are clearly and sufficiently specified for the implementation phase. Knowledge of functional features provided by components, subsets and systems is necessary to avoid excessive refinement.

By abstraction, the designer can define a processor or a communication node. For the second case, functionality is defined by behavioral rules described in the previous section. Second, all links with the environment must be communication type links.

-B- Communication nodes

The decomposition of a communication node can be translated by:

- a network of communication nodes;

- an executive structure including processors.

In the second case, the role of the structure is restricted to acting as a support to satisfy node communication functionalities.

The objective of the abstraction is to construct communication nodes starting from a set of processors.

The refinement or abstraction technique for a communication node is illustrated in Figure 17.5.

17.3 SPECIFICATION OF COMPONENTS FOR THE IMPLEMENTATION

After describing the behavior of each element type in order to give an unambiguous graphical representation, we will now describe the specifications necessary for each component so that the implementation can be deduced. The executive structure cannot be used as a specification for the hardware implementation unless all components are described by their external characteristics. A specification must be sufficient to determine a hardware solution for its implementation.

A review of each component category is given below to define its specification.

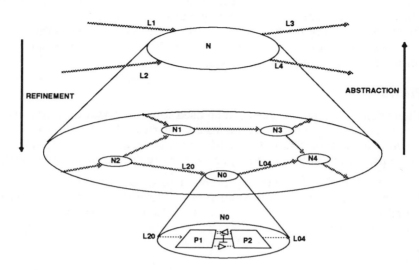

Figure 17.5   Description levels for a communication node.

17.3.1 Processor specification

Processor specifications can vary a great deal due to the very general character of the term specification.

A specialized processor is characterized by:
- its input and output specifications, describing the type and nature of the information;
- its functionality: all specialized models described in this document are obviously usable. For example, a frequency diagram for an analog filter, precision and conversion speed for a digital/analog convertor.

A general programmable processor is characterized by:
- its input and output specifications;
- the specification of all processor attributes, namely: the memory capacity for instructions and data, the processor class (8, 16, 32 bits), the performance for typical operations;
- the specification of internal functions necessary for the application: programmable clock, counters, floating point calculation, and the functions necessary for inputs/outputs: analog/digital conversion, serial asynchronous/synchronous receiver- transmitter.

A programmable processor can be defined by very diverse specifications. In this way it is possible to reduce the refinement work for an executive structure. This is consistent with technological evolution making available more and more powerful processors with a variety of specialized functions in a single component, in addition to the typical microprocessor function as a central processing unit.

17.3.2 Memory specification

A memory is characterized by:
- - its capacity in number of data items (using bytes as unit);
- - the size of each information item handled per access;
- - the number of simultaneous read and write accesses;
- - the maximum time for each access and the memory cycle time.

17.3.3 Communication node specification

A communication node is characterized by:
- - the number of inputs and outputs and the type of information exchanged. A specific type can be related to each input and output, but it is more realistic to use one message type only;
- - the node storage capacity, in number of messages. This capacity may be global or specific to each input/output pair;
- - Message processing performances. This performance may, for example, be expressed by a mean transit time or a minimum number of messages sended per unit time.

17.4   PROPERTIES OF THE EXECUTIVE MODEL

The objective of the executive model is to act as a guide for producing hardware support specifications for an application. We will mention the essential properties of this model.

-A- Structure model

Like the functional model, the executive model is hierarchical. It therefore facilitates understanding or the gradual search for a solution. For the functional model, refinement and abstraction techniques allow introduction of additional constraints for the hardware implementation, and for the executive model they facilitate reuse in the logical or virtual processor specifications.

-B- Interpretable model

Knowledge alone of component behavioral rules and their specifications is sufficient to deduce a technological solution for the hardware implementation. Therefore, this document is sufficient as interface between the implementation specification step and the subsequent implementation step. As a result of its simplicity, it increases understandability which is beneficial for checking and use.

-C- Scale invariability

This simply means that the model can also be used to describe solution specifications at a level very close to components, and even the internal structure of components, registers, combinational networks, clock, etc., or system specifications at a very macroscopic level: distributed applications using computers, local network, telecommunications network.

-D- Similarity: functional model/executive model

These two models are represented in a similar manner. This characteristic is particularly helpful for passing from step 2, functional solution, to step 3, implementation structure specification. In the most direct case, for the executive structure, a topology similar to the functional structure can be used.

-E- Maximum parallelism

When an executive structure is fully detailed, assuming that each processor executes only one operation at a time, the maximum degree of parallelism is equal to the number of elementary processors. If performances are inadequate, the executive structure has to be revised by increasing either the number of processors or the performance of some processors.

-F- Introduction of redundancies and tests

An executive structure can be enhanced by additional components to satisfy some constraints such as safety, testability, maintainability, etc. This would be translated, for example, by doubling up processors (or the use of three to take the best out of three), or by doubling up information paths.

The necessary additional components are deduced by considering probable failure situations which must not degrade the application characteristics.

17.5 SUMMARY

This chapter introduced the description model used to specify the third, or executive, dimension of the global model.

The main conclusions are:

- The executive model is composed of two information sets: the executive structure, the specification of all components used for the implementation.

- Refinement and abstraction techniques are usable to define specifications for a processor or a communication node.

- Decomposition must not be carried too far. It must simply facilitate the search for the detailed hardware solution without imposing additional selection constraints compared with the technological specifications.

- The executive model is not sufficient for the implementation since it concerns the hardware part only. The software specification has to be added for programmable processors. This is the objective of the integration model described in the next chapter.

18

THE INTEGRATION MODEL

A functional description expresses a solution independent of the technology for the application considered. An executive structure describes the hardware support. To complete an implementation specification, the functional --> hardware correspondence or allocation and the software part organization have to be added. The software organization is a result first of the functional description which expresses the objective to be satisfied, and second of the executive structure used as the operational support.

The objective of the integration model is to completely specify the mapping of a functional description on an executive structure.

Although the purpose of the design process is to deduce an executive structure and a mapping from a functional description, for the purposes of describing the integration model we will consider the case in which the functional description and the executive structure are given.

As shown in this chapter, integration concerns two levels: the executive structure level or global level and the processor level. For the global level, the complete functional structure must be located on the executive structure. For each programmable processor, the functionality is expressed by a software organization type scheme.

18.1 THE INTEGRATION MODEL AND ITS COMPONENTS

The integration model specifies two implementation levels. First, given an executive support, each of its components is the operational support for one or more components of the functional structure:

- a processor for a partial functional structure;
- a memory for state variables;
- a communication node for ports.

This FS --> ES correspondence is called the "allocation" or "configuration".

For each programmable processor <--> partial functional structure type association, the functionality is then obtained by software. In this case, the rules for the organization of the functional structure on the processor have to be expressed.

The integration model thus comprises two parts:

- the **allocation model** which describes the correspondence between a functional structure and an executive structure;

- the **implementation model** which describes the implementation rules for each subset of the functional description performed by software on a programmable processor allocated as support.

The integration model composition is shown in Figure 18.1.

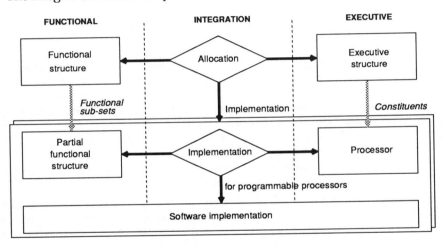

Figure 18.1   The integration model.

For a given application, there is only one allocation definition: this expresses all relations between components of the functional structure and of the executive structure. But there are as many implementation definitions as there are programmable processors.

18.2 THE ALLOCATION MODEL

The similarity of the functional structure and executive structure models facilitates correspondence between the two structures. Each structure is composed of elements and relations between these elements. The allocation model thus details correspondences between elements in the two structures and correspondence constraints to be respected.

18.2.1 Correspondence between elements in the two structures

The correspondence between elements is as follows:

partial functional structure (SF)	-->	processor (P)
variables (VE)	-->	memory (M)
events (EV)	-->	signalling (S)
ports (PT)	-->	communication node (N)
links: function <--> EV, VE, PT	-->	link: processor <--> S, M, N.

The following rules must be respected for all correspondences:

- An elementary function is a description and distribution unit. Consequently, it is indivisible for the implementation. Its activity will be the result of using one processor only. If this assumption is impossible, the functional decomposition must be continued. This situation may arise for high-performance or severe timing constraint applications.

- State variables and messages are also indivisible objects.

- The processor, memory, and communication node can each support several functions, state variable and port elements respectively.

- A general processor is the support for a partial or complete functional structure.

The first two rules above indicate that the functional decomposition has been carried out far enough to allow integration.

The last two rules indicate the possibility of reducing the complexity of an executive structure. A programmable processor is generally too powerful as a support for an elementary function only.

The same applies for the capacity of a memory or communication node. Reducing the cost of the hardware support involves reducing the number of processors, memories, communication nodes which also reduces the number of physical links to be made. The essential reduction is obtained by installing the largest functional structure possible on each processor.

The example in Figure 18.2 shows two forms: the first graphic, the second textual to describe correspondence between elements.

For elements:

S1	<====	(E3)
P1	<====	(SF[A1, A2, E1, V1])
M1	<====	(V2, V4)
P2	<====	(A3)
P3	<====	(A4, A5)
N1	<====	(PT1)

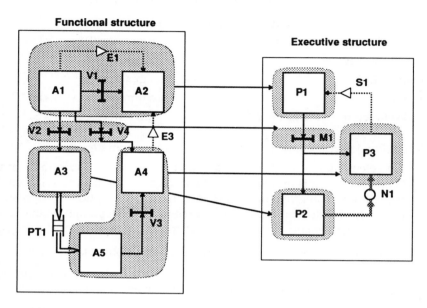

Figure 18.2   Description of correspondence between elements.

and for links

P1->M1	<====	(A1->V2, A1->V4)
P2->N1	<====	(A3->PT1)
N1->P3	<====	(PT1->A5)
(M1->P2)	<====	V2->A3
(M1->P3)	<====	V4->A4
(P3->S1)	<====	A4->E3
(S1->P1)	<====	E3->A2

This example shows that all elements of a functional structure must have a correspondent on the executive structure. However, given an executive structure, all elements are not necessarily used for the application.

18.2.2 Allocation constraints

An allocation is only correct for the application if rules are guaranteed for the selected correspondences. Two types of rules have to be respected:

- First, since a processor can act as executive support for several functions, it must be suitable to involve the required function behaviors, respecting all timing constraints. Respect of this rule expresses the fact that each processor is operational for the selected allocation.

- Second, the correspondence between elements in the two structures is only correct if all functional structure relations can be carried out by the executive structure. In this case, it is said that the functional structure is accepted by the executive structure.

This section describes the checking rules for each category.

-A- Operational processor

A processor acts as executive support for one or several actions. In real-time applications, timing constraints are associated with each action: activation rate, maximum executive time or deadlines for temporary actions, performances for permanent actions.

A processor is said to be operational for a given allocation if all actions are carried out and if all timing constraints are satisfied for the implementation resulting from this allocation. The operational character depends on several factors:

- the complexity of the functional structure to be supported: number and nature of actions and operations;

- timing constraints to be respected;

- the processor performance.

An allocation is modified by changing correspondences and/or changing the processor specifications.

Verification rules are described in the next chapter in Section 19.5. For the moment, two essential rules will be considered:

- The maximum processor utilization rate for all its temporary actions $(i=1,n)$ must be less than 1: $Tocc = \Sigma i\ FAi*TEi < 1$. For an action, the maximum utilization rate $(Tocci)$ is the product of its maximum activation frequency (FAi) and its maximum execution time (TEi). The rate therefore depends on the processor performance expressed by the term TEi.

- Maximum execution times, deadlines, reaction or response times on external events are always satisfied.

Figure 18.3 shows the execution of two concurrent actions on a single processor when execution A1 has a higher priority than A2.

B- Functional structure accepted

For the implementation, the functional relations internal to a processor are carried out by the processor. However, the relations between two processors require hardware links between these processors.

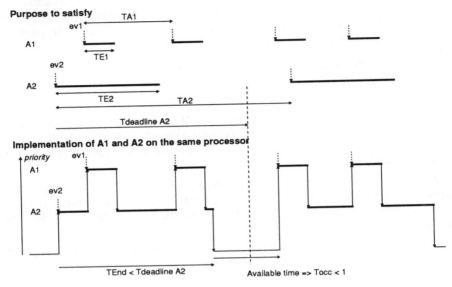

Figure 18.3 Illustration of the two rules for an allocation.

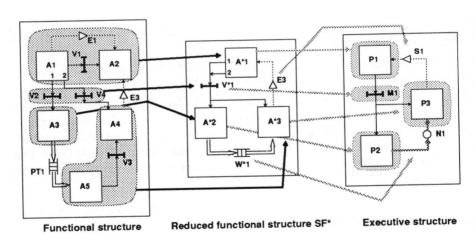

Functional structure **Reduced functional structure SF*** **Executive structure**

Figure 18.4 Global FS, reduced FS and ES correspondences.

To check that a functional structure is accepted by an executive structure, correspondences between elements have to be used to define a reduced functional structure. Reduction is obtained by an abstraction operation which consists of grouping all components (functions, variables, ports) located on the same processor. The structure thus obtained must be included in the executive structure in the graph sense. This means that there must be at least one link at the executive level to support each functional link. Figure 18.4 shows this checking procedure.

18.3   THE SOFTWARE IMPLEMENTATION MODEL FOR EACH PROCESSOR

For programmable processors, the allocation defines the functional subset to implement on each processor. The software implementation model defines the presentation rules for components of this functional subset to express the organization of software.

The software located on a processor can be decomposed into two levels:

- the **task level**: a task is an entity composed of instructions and data with its own autonomy. For the processor, the task is manipulated as a whole: activation, stop, suspension. A task generally carries out a function or an action of the application. Its behavior is sequential. The state of a task defined by a variable called a state vector is stored between two successive activations. A task therefore has a storage effect for its internal variables.

- The **module level**. A module is a set of instructions activated as a unit by a task to satisfy a function or an operation. Since the task is sequential, one module only is active at any one time. A module has no storage effect, meaning that its internal variables exist only for the execution time of the module.

The task level concerns a set of tasks. Evolution is therefore potentially concurrent. But a processor is normally sequential. Therefore, a scheduling strategy for sharing the processor by tasks is also necessary so that the evolution of all tasks appears concurrent as seen by the application.

For the module level, each task is decomposed as a hierarchy of modules.

The objective of the software implementation model is to propose a description method for the tasks and modules levels for each programmable processor. The model decomposition is shown in Figure 18.5.

18.3.1   Task implementation model

The task level explains the selected implementation for a given functional structure on a processor.

The concurrency inherent to the functional structure (normally equal to the number of functions) is generally higher than that for the processor which is often one. Second, relations between functions - by event, by state variable, by port - are mechanisms which are not directly supported by the processor. Finally, the processor coupled to its environment must use hardware links to satisfy functional relations existing between the functional structure subset that it supports and the function structure remainder which is located in the processor environment.

The software organization is represented graphically by a task network. Tasks are interrelated by state variables and control transfers and are linked with the environment by input and output variables and events.

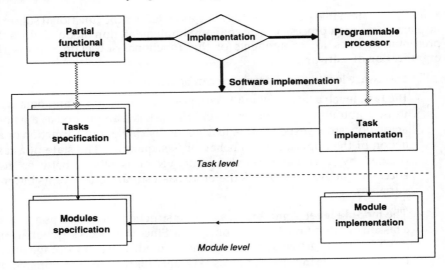

Figure 18.5   Decomposition model for software implementation.

Since one task only is normally running at any one time by a processor, a criterion is necessary for task scheduling. Each task is thus given an execution priority. In the chart Figure 18.6, the vertical axis is the increasing priority axis. Since the processor is always active, it executes a special background task when no temporary tasks have to be executed. Figure 18.6 is an example of a software implementation diagram.

Tasks related to input events (hardware events and therefore tasks activated by interrupts at the left) are activated on occurrence of each event. This type of task evolves when the processor is available to it, which is the case when an activated task has a higher priority than the current task being executed by the processor. This summarizes the scheduling technique used: fixed priority and processor assigned to the highest priority active task.

In the vertical axis, the transfer of control between two tasks and therefore the processor allocation is shown by a double line link. This transfer type, which will be of the procedure call type (call, return) is only possible in the increasing priority direction. The behavioral rule is described in Figure 18.7.

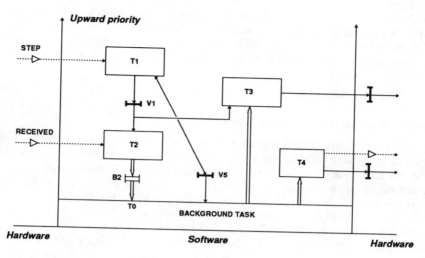

Figure 18.6   Example of task implementation.

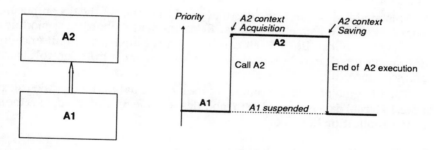

Figure 18.7   Behavior for control transfer of a processor between tasks.

When A1, currently executing on the processor, decides to transfer control to A2 (for example, synchronization of A2 on an event generated by A1), the processor is transferred to A2. A2 keeps the processor until its execution is completed. The reverse transfer returns the processor to A1 which then continues its activity. Therefore, A2 is necessarily temporary and A1 may be permanent or temporary as shown in Figure 18.7.

This transfer of control mechanism is simply a procedure call mechanism, A2 is implemented as a procedure and the transfer is made by a CALL instruction saving the A1 reactivation point. Return is made by the RET instruction to come back to the saved return point. This simple mechanism implemented in all microprocessors very naturally induces execution sequence relations for tasks.

However, take care since the A2 implementation model is still a task and is not simply a procedure. It has its own internal variables which have a life time longer than that of each activation. Execution of A2 by a procedure call therefore implies that execution by the processor starts by recovering A2 state vector context and terminates by storing its state vector ready for the next activation.

This model is also hierarchical. A task may be refined by a network of tasks.

18.3.2 Implementation of each task

An elementary task is considered to be non-decomposable into tasks when execution of its operations is purely sequential. The complexity of this type of elementary task is very variable depending on its functionality. For some operations, an additional decomposition is not necessary since the code is written directly. However, decomposition is desirable for a functionality which requires a complex program to facilitate a modular and structured implementation. The module structure model, or Yourdon and Constantine's structure chart is recommended here as a model for the description of each task (see Section 7.4).

Remember that the basic elements in this model are the module and shared data.

This model is hierarchical. It can be used to represent the decomposition of a task into more elementary units. Relations with subordinate modules are represented by call links. Each call link is associated with input and output arguments which may be one of two types - data or control. Control structures are: sequence, call, iteration, alternate.

The life time of data internal to a module is equal to the module execution time. External data is accessible to modules. The life time of this data is the same as the application life time.

18.3.3 Specification of each element

In addition to task and module structures, the implementation specification is not complete until all elements have been specified. We will now review each category.

-A- Tasks

Each task must be specified: inputs, outputs, activation conditions, the role for the application expressed by the function(s) in the functional description to be carried out by the task, the description of its state vector.

Timing constraints must also be specified: performances, maximum execution times, reaction and response times.

-B- Shared data

These are first state variables, which provide coupling between tasks, and second, external data necessary for modules.

The specification for this data is deduced from the functional description: structure, domain, accuracy, etc. Some implementation information may be added: definition of data representation, data scheduling and access mechanism.

-C- The modules

Each module must also be described by a specification. This specification must subsequently allow correct coding, but it should not be necessary to write the programs.

Most module specifications are inferred from the functional description; complete functions or parts of functions are implemented as modules.

18.4 SOME RULES FOR DEDUCING A SOFTWARE IMPLEMENTATION

A software implementation diagram results from a translation of the functional structure used on the processor. All functional structure elements must exist in this implementation specification . The objective is also to reduce the complexity of the resulting implementation.

Therefore, rules must be respected to obtain this translation. We will discuss these rules useful for element categories and relations between them.

18.4.1 Function --> Task correspondence

In defining the software implementation, a task is an execution unit. It corresponds to an elementary function or a group of several functions of the functional structure.

First, a grouping normally concerns several functions simultaneously activated by the same event. Figure 18.8 illustrates this grouping type, with the decomposition being expressed by a module structure.

The task is activated by the step hardware event. The main control module sequentially executes the three modules resulting from a transformation of each function into a procedure.

Permanent actions are then necessarily grouped in the background task. The processor is then shared by regular switching for allocation of the processor to the various task functions. The background task thus plays the role of scheduler as indicated in Figure 18.9.

18.4.2 Translation of relations by variable sharing

These relations are kept in the implementation diagram. As tasks have different priorities, internal coupling by variable is represented by vertical links.

Function grouping in a single task may induce groups of variables accessible for input and output. Second, for a group of actions in any one task, action state variables become the internal global variables for the task.

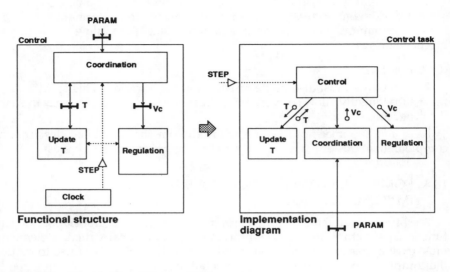

Figure 18.8   Translation with function grouping.

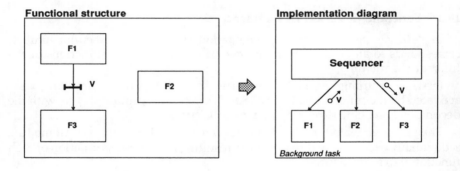

Figure 18.9   Implementation of several functions in the background task.

18.4.3 Translation of synchronizations by event

The source of the event may be hardware (input for the processor) or software (internal to the processor). Three principles apply to translation, depending on the case.

— **First principle**: an event can be transformed as a Boolean variable. In this case, the temporary function which depends on it is no longer activated by the event. It must then observe the evolution of the equivalent Boolean variable to decide on activation times. In this case, the function is then transformed into a permanent action and is integrated into the background task.

– **Second principle**: an internal synchronization (therefore software) is transformed according to the priority of the two related functions:

- lower generator priority: procedure call;
- higher generator priority: use of a Boolean variable indicating the event generation. This variable must be observed regularly to imply the correspondent activation. This role is assigned to a third function, generally the background task.

These two transformation cases are illustrated in the following example in Figure 18.10.

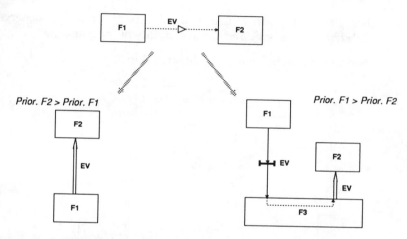

Figure 18.10   Illustration for a software synchronization implementation.

– **Third principle**: a synchronization by an external event is efficiently implemented using the processor interrupt mechanism. In this case, no transformation is necessary. The task simply has to be associated with an interrupt level corresponding to its priority relative to other tasks implemented under interrupt.

18.4.4 Translation for message transfers

A message is the association of an event and a data item. The principles stated for synchronizations are therefore applicable. Again, three principles may be used depending on the case.

– **First principle**: a port internal to the processor (therefore software implemented) is transformed into a shared variable commonly called a mailbox (symbol ⊨) and is composed of two parts:

- an area to deposit submitted messages: this area necessarily has a finite capacity (buffer);

- an indicator specifying the number of messages available in the area.

To make use of this mailbox, the producer and consumer functions must then test the value of the indicator before starting a submission or withdrawal operation. In this case, the consumer is necessarily transformed into a permanent action. If the mailbox is full, the producer must wait for a withdrawal, if it is empty, the consumer must wait for a submission.

– **Second principle**: a message transfer between two software functions is transformed depending on its relative priorities:

- lower producer priority: use of the procedure call to activate the consumer;

- higher producer priority: use of a third party action to observe the availability of a message and the availability of the consumer.

These two transformation cases are illustrated in Figure 18.11.

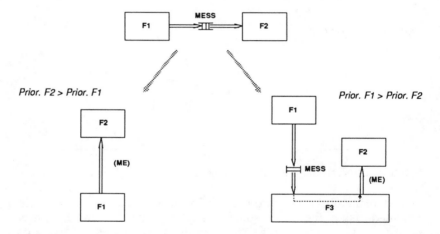

Figure 18.11   The two software implementation cases for a transfer by messages.

– **Third principle**: the message transfer must take place with the hardware environment. By preference, element by element transfer will be used (for example, character by character). The coupling mailbox then has a capacity of 1. This is not a mandatory rule (for example, use of a FIFO), but it is technologically simple. Coupling between the hardware and the software takes place by transforming the mailbox into a shared variable for message submission and the use of two events for the bidirectional synchronization. An event can also be transformed into a Boolean variable, particularly in the direction software towards hardware. The two events can also be transformed into a single bidirectional Boolean variable. Figure 18.12 shows a translation for both cases: incoming from hardware for M1, towards hardware for M2. Pt is transformed according to the second principle.

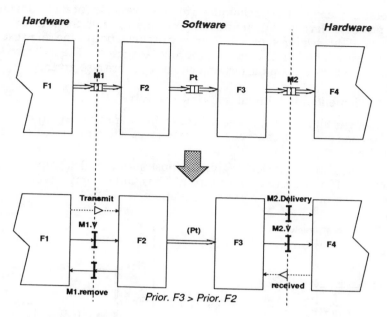

Figure 18.12   Translation example.

This translation shows usual hardware solutions for satisfactory coupling between producer and consumer: exchange by an handshake technique.

18.5 IMPLEMENTATION WITH OR WITHOUT A REAL-TIME EXECUTIVE

A programmable processor may have very variable complexity levels. Essential differences already exist between 8-bit type 8085 processors or microcontrollers and advanced 32-bit processors such as the T800 transputer.

Every microprocessor is sequential for the execution of instructions. It thus executes only one task at a time. If necessary, concurrency is only obtained at a macroscopic level by switching the processor between tasks by means of hardware mechanisms such as the interrupt system or by adding software for managing processor sharing.

A computer system, considered globally as a processor for software functions to be implemented, has mechanisms for the simultaneous or pseudo-simultaneous execution of tasks. These mechanisms are provided by an executive core called a real-time multi-task system or real-time executive or real-time kernel. The availability of these mechanisms facilitates the implementation work. Since the objective is to reduce the organizational part to be developed, this part is directly translated in the form of calls to the real-time executive.

Several implementation techniques are thus available for tasks depending on the processor level and therefore its specifications or its characteristics. The remainder of this section shows the software organization of the same example in both cases: with and without real-time executive. The criteria to be considered to decide upon the technique to be used are also given.

18.5.1 Implementation without real-time executive

In this case, all relations between actions in the functional structure to be located on one processor must be transformed respecting the rules described in the previous section.

The example in Figure 18.13 is given to illustrate a complete implementation with priority T0 > priority T2 > priority T1. This same example will be used to describe the solution with a real-time executive.

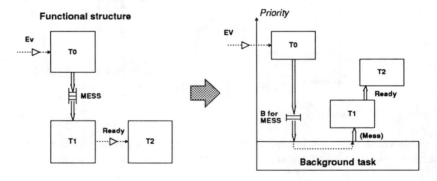

Figure 18.13   Software implementation diagram without real-time executive.

Task T0 is activated by hardware event EV. It thus unconditionally recovers the processor. T0 therefore has a higher priority than all other tasks.

T0 and T1 are synchronized with a decreasing priority using the mailbox B and the background task.

The background task behaves as follows:

```
cycle: if B.No_message>0 then
                        begin
                            message_removal(B, Mess);
                            T1(Mess);
                        end;
            end cycle;
```

The background task thus regularly scans to see if a message is available in B. If so, the first message is removed and sent to T1 for execution and B.No_message is decremented.

The background task scanning period depends on the processor load to run temporary tasks (T0 only in this case).

This example shows the simplicity of the implementation method and the simplicity of the resulting organizational part.

18.5.2 Implementation with a real-time executive

In this case, the real-time executive should be seen as the highest priority task invoked by all other tasks through procedure calls. The highest priority is justified so that this executive can request the processor when it wants to in order to carry out its scheduling role correctly.

Figure 18.14 shows the software implementation diagram for a functional structure using four real-time primitives: SIGNAL and WAIT for synchronization, SEND and RECEIVE for message transfer.

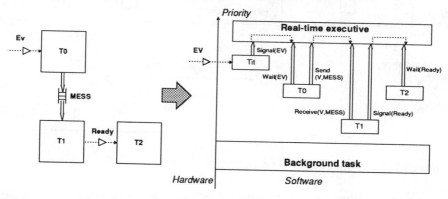

Figure 18.14   Software implementation diagram with a real-time executive.

The above implementation diagram clearly shows the scheduler role played by the real-time executive. External events taken into account as interrupts by the processor are managed by a very short task (Tit) which simply signals received events to the real-time executive.

All requests made by tasks to the executive are made by a procedure call. If the request involves a wait, the time of the return to the calling task is decided upon by the executive. The return order and therefore the processor allocation to the calling task is entirely under the control of the executive. This is another reason why this task should have the highest priority.

To help understand the implementation diagram, Figure 18.15 shows an execution trace for the three actions T0, T1, T2. In this case, the executive is seen as a special unique task invoked by all processor tasks for every special action. The executive therefore has multiple entry points. It manages sequencing returns for calling tasks, based on internal variables, which represent the state of all tasks, relations, requests, etc.

Although the executive may consist of a single task for a simple case, an executive is normally composed of a set of tasks in order to handle the mechanisms provided (time, periodic activation, synchronization on external events, etc.). Coupling between these tasks may be described by the implementation model described in this chapter. The method described can then be used by real-time executive designers.

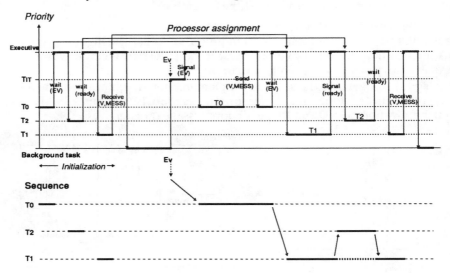

Figure 18.15   Example of an execution trace.

For applications using a real-time executive, the implementation diagram described in Figure 18.14 is unnecessary. It was given simply to explain the role played by an executive. For applications, simply:

- determine the priority of each task;
- translate each functional relation by the available and suitable executive mechanisms.

Figure 18.16 shows a sufficient representation for this implementation.

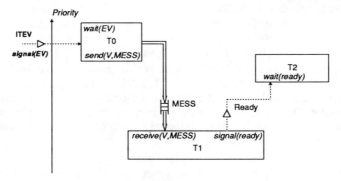

Figure 18.16   Software implementation diagram based on a real-time executive.

Some processors have synchronization and data exchange mechanisms in their standard instruction set. For example, this is the case for the Inmos transputer. If such mechanisms are available, the processor will carry out the task scheduling itself. The designer's work is then simplified (see Section 22.8).

As far as the application designer is concerned, the only difference between this type of processor designed for concurrency management and a more conventional processor associated with a real-time executive is that the executive has to be added as software in the second case. Performances are reduced due to the time necessary for executing monitor functions.

18.5.3 Software implementation technique selection criteria

It is obvious that it is preferable to have an executive, in order to reduce the application development time. The software solution is more expensive in terms of memory and request processing time (switching time or overhead) and in terms of price when the executive is a standard commercial product (VRTX, PSOS, iRMX, SCEPTRE core, VxWorks kernel, etc.).

The executive built into the processor functionality is the best solution and corresponds to a tendency which will probably become generalized. It allows the designer to see the processor as a direct multi-task executive, thus reducing the implementation work. In this case, the designer does not need to go down to the task scheduling level. However, the relative priority of tasks always has to be determined.

In the current state of technology, most of microprocessors do not have this functionality. A choice always has to be made between the use of an executive or the complete implementation specification. The designer has to decide upon the best solution based on technical and economic criteria.

The criteria to be considered are:

- Timing constraints for the application. For very hard real-time constraints, a complete implementation has to be defined without an executive since this solution minimizes task-switching times (overhead).

- The number of product copies. If a few copies only are necessary, the use of an executive reduces development time. For many copies, the cost of each copy will have to be reduced with the probable resulting of doing without a standard executive.

- The application complexity. For small, well-specified and dedicated applications, a direct implementation will remain simple and efficient. For complex applications with evolutionary specifications, a real-time executive is most useful.

18.6   INTEGRATION MODEL CHARACTERISTICS

The description model for a system is based on the association of three dimensions or three views: topological, behavioral, executive. The executive dimension represents the "hardware" or "resources" support which causes evolution of the application.

An operational application is a result of a correct association of the functional dimension with the executive dimension. The objective of the integration model is to specify correspondence rules between these two sets, and then the implementation structuring for the software part.

The essential characteristics induced by the integration model are given below.

-A- Structured model

This model comprises two complementary parts. Firstly, the allocation model defines the functional --> executive correspondence, and the implementation model then defines the organization of the functional structure on each processor. This last model is hierarchical with two organization levels: the TASK level and the module level.

The implementation specification in hierarchical subsets with completely specified interfaces facilitates distribution of implementation work into several teams.

-B- Allocation as an abstraction result

The allocation model describes partitioning a functional structure into subsets. Each subset is associated with a processor for execution. This type of transformation is obtained by the abstraction technique based on the grouping criteria - connectivity, timing constraints and processor utilization rate.

The allocation is correct if each processor is operational and if the complete functional structure is accepted by the executive structure.

-C- A software organization model to specify the implementation

The software implementation model is used for each programmable processor, thus defining its software functionality by describing element organization and mechanisms used for relations between these elements.

Each processor is the execution support for a functional structure as a subset of the complete structure.

The software implementation diagram is the result of a transformation of the functional structure according to a set of rules. The objective of a good implementation is to minimize the software organizational part.

The two organization levels - tasks and modules - can simultaneously represent the sequential execution and pseudo-parallelism execution.

-D- Dependency between implementation and processor characteristics

The implementation model takes account of the processor functionalities. This can be seen by the user as a single task processor, or for some processors as being multi-task. The process to be adopted for each of these two cases is equivalent to continuing the implementation using a top-down procedure until processor features are obtained.

The model is therefore adaptable to future technological evolution. We could imagine in the longer term that processors will directly accept a functional description. The work involved in searching for a implementation would then be very simple.

18.7 SUMMARY

This chapter is complementary to the previous chapter and describes the integration model used for the implementation definition as a tool describing the association of the functional structure and an executive structure. The latter implies the evolution specified by the functional solution. The main points are as follows:

- The integration model includes the allocation of the functional structure on the executive structure, and a description of the software implementation actions on programmable processors.

- An allocation is only correct if the functional structure is accepted by the executive structure and if all processors are operational and respect all timing constraints.

- The implementation model is structured in two levels: the task level for the implementation of functional structure relations and actions, and the module level to describe the decomposition of each task.

- Simple transformation rules are used to decide upon an implementation based on the functional model.

- The implementation to be used depends on the processor functionality level. The two approaches, with or without a real-time executive, are possible.

19

THE IMPLEMENTATION SPECIFICATION PROCESS

The objective of the third step in the MCSE methodology is to propose a complete, detailed solution taking account of all technological constraints.

As input for this step, the designer can make use of:

- a complete document describing the functional solution;
- the specification document containing in particular the technological specifications.

The result is that the detailed solution forming the implementation specification document must contain:

- a description of the executive structure with all its specifications;
- the implementation description of all functional description elements on the executive structure.

Chapters 17 and 18 describe the model that must be respected by the solution for it to be used as an input document for the implementation.

The most appropriate solution for the problem was developed during the functional design without taking account of technological constraints and peculiarities.

The implementation will be the result of a combination of two parts: a hardware part as the executive support and a software part for customizing the equipment to satisfy the application specifications.

At the present time, there is no solution for directly obtaining an operational application from the functional design. Thus, the transition from the functional design to an implementation requires three types of operations:

- adaptation, to take account of the system environment with all its interfacing constraints;
- technological support selection for the application. In some cases, the support is imposed and a verification will then have to be carried out, in other cases it is to be determined;
- transformation, to model the functional solution in order to make it operational on the selected or imposed technology.

This chapter starts by describing complementary or contradictory objectives to be satisfied, and then goes on to describe the recommended procedure used by the designer to efficiently determine the solution maintaining functional approach qualities and minimizing the development cost. Unlike the functional design, the implementation specification is the result of successive transformations made based on the functional description. The process is therefore more systematic.

19.1 OBJECTIVES TO BE ACHIEVED

The implementation solution must satisfy several types of objectives:

- technical and technological objectives;
- economic objectives.

These objectives are normally described in the technological specifications for the problem. The solution must also respect general quality rules which will have repercussions on its cost.

We will first summarize technical objectives to be satisfied, and will then consider economic objectives.

19.1.1 Hardware specifications

This part of the specifications describes the constraints to be satisfied by the implementation.

-A- Geographic distribution constraints

This constraint does not exist in all applications. It indicates whether or not the solution lies entirely at a single physical location. When many locations are imposed, the implementation is a result of combining several subsets linked together by physical links for information exchanges. The solution depends on several factors, namely the distance between subsets, the information flow rate to be exchanged, and available support types.

Since the functional solution was developed without this constraint, subsets are now delimited based on distribution constraints which express the location of the data. Delimitation defines coupling and therefore information to be exchanged. The necessary communication service is specified after an analysis of the nature of this information and the exchange rate.

-B- *Interfaces with the environment*

The system to be implemented is linked to its environment by physical interfaces. These interfaces must satisfy the physical nature of signals exchanged. The nature depends on entities in the environment. We will use two different categories:

- Physical entities which may be industrial processes, machines and others. These entities provide electrical signals from sensors. Conversely, electrically controlled actuators are used to act on these entities. It is assumed here that sensors and actuators, even if they were selected by the designer and included in the service, do not form part of the system to be developed.

- Other entities and especially users. The interface is very variable for this type of coupling - conventional control panel, keyboard-screen, voice analysis and synthesis, etc. The solution must satisfy the easy to use constraint required for the application. Characteristics are described in the technological specifications.

-C- *Implementation constraints*

Rules may be imposed by the customer which limit techniques or technologies possible for the implementation - types of resources, memories and processors.

In addition to these rules, a description of the characteristics of the environment in which the system will operate and the imposed operational reliability and safety.

19.1.2 Timing constraints

We are concerned by real-time applications. Constraints exist and express reaction and response times after the emergence of events and performances expected from the system.

A powerful enough hardware support has to be deduced to satisfy these timing constraints. Rules must be clearly stated to guarantee that constraints are respected.

19.1.3 Reducing development costs

The economic objective for every project should be to design it so as to reduce its cost. The cost is dependent on some data items which can be used to select a criterion for the product development. The essential data to be taken into account for this step is the number of copies to be produced.

The cost of each copy is:

$$CT = CRm + (CDm + CDl)/N$$

where:
- CRm   reproduction cost of each copy,
- CDm   development cost of the hardware prototype.

- CD1   software development cost,

- N   number of copies to be produced.

The following table shows the objective to be achieved for each term as a function of the quantity to be produced.

NUMBER	LOW	MEDIUM	HIGH
CRm	high (equipment purchase)	medium	to be minimized
CDm	very low	to be minimized	fairly high
CD1	to be minimized	to be minimized	to be minimized

This table shows the two extreme cases:

- for a low quantity: it is essential to minimize development time. This is done by avoiding a hardware development and minimizing the software development time.

- For high production: the development time necessary to minimize the reproduction cost per product unit must be spent: material cost + implementation cost + testing cost + maintenance cost.

For the designer, the difference between these two cases is that in the first case, he uses an unoptimized executive structure, whereas in the second case he searches for a minimum optimized executive structure for the application. This induces two development strategies which will be described in this chapter.

In all cases, since the relative amount of the software development cost is continuously increasing, an effort should be made to reduce this cost.

19.1.4 Reducing the organizational part

Globally and on average, the implementation cost is about 50% of the total cost of developing a prototype. Reducing the overall cost means reducing the implementation cost and therefore its complexity during the design and detailed design steps.

For a given application, the design complexity is mainly dependent on the solution selected as the first functional decomposition. The use of template models facilitates the production of simple and appropriate solutions.

The implementation complexity depends on the work carried out during the implementation specification step. The hardware solution may be minimized to reduce the production cost. The software part must also be minimized so that it is simple to write and then to validate.

Continuing the analysis a little further, it can be seen that the software part comprises two parts:

- the operative part, in other words the part which expresses all operations to be undertaken. This is the typically algorithmic part.

- the organizational part, which organizes operations of the operative part at the task and module levels (but not control structure at the basic algorithmic level).

When algorithms are correctly written, the operative part cannot be reduced. The organizational part is the result of a transformation of the functional structure to define its implementation on the processor. The complexity therefore depends on the solution selected for the functional structure, but also and especially on transformations made during this implementation specification step. The purpose of the proposed process for deducing the software implementation diagram is to minimize the organizational part in order to reduce the development time and therefore cost. This point of view justifies the transformation rules proposed in this chapter and is important for real-time applications.

19.1.5 Quality rules

As a more general objective, respect for quality rules leads to a cost reduction for the entire product life cycle.

The result of this detailed design step is a document which plays at least two roles:

- it acts as a specification document for the next implementation step;
- it will also be used later for the maintenance phase: error correction, product adaptation and improvement.

The essential quality rule for this document is its readability. Good readability facilitates understanding of the solution. Technicians responsible for the implementation can then use this document without many discussions with the designer authors. Good understanding also facilitates maintenance. Evolutionary maintenance leads to modifications. It must therefore be possible to deduce solution limits and why choices were made from this document. This quality rule also reduces the overall product cost.

19.1.6 Contradictory objectives

The previous objectives are relatively contradictory:

- reducing reproduction costs lead to minimizing hardware;
- reducing development costs lead to minimizing hardware, software and documentation;
- a good documentation and all technological constraints to be satisfied (timing constraints, adaptation to the environment) make it necessary to spend enough time on the development and implementation of a solution satisfying minimum performances.

The principles described below and the process proposed in this chapter help to find the best compromise between these contradictory objectives. The general idea is to first introduce the necessary interfaces for the technological constraints, then to search for the minimum executive structure and finally to define an implementation which reduces the development time.

19.2 PRESENTATION OF THE IMPLEMENTATION PROCESS

The objective of this third step is to produce a detailed description of the implementation to be undertaken. In accordance with the implementation model, it must comprise:

- an executive structure with specification of its constituents;
- integration composed of:
  - the allocation of the functional structure onto the executive structure,
  - the implementation of software constituents on the programmable processors.

Before determining the executive structure, the functional structure must be modified and completed to take account of technological environment constraints. The executive structure is then deduced taking account of the economic criterion to be optimized. The implementation diagram defining the software and data organization is then produced for each processor.

The process therefore consists of the following phases:

- introducing geographic distribution constraints;
- introducing interfaces:
  - physical interfaces,
  - man-machine interfaces,
  - test, maintenance, safety functions;
- determination of the executive structure:
  - evaluation of timing constraints,
  - hardware/software distribution;
- software implementation diagram for each processor,
- hardware implementation specification.

Figure 19.1 shows the sequence of these phases, documents to be used and the output result.

In the remainder of this chapter, we will describe each phase in detail and illustrate them by the two examples considered for the design.

For an introduction to adaptation to the environment, if necessary, the reader should review the principles given for functional design in Chapter 14 which justify delaying technological details to this step.

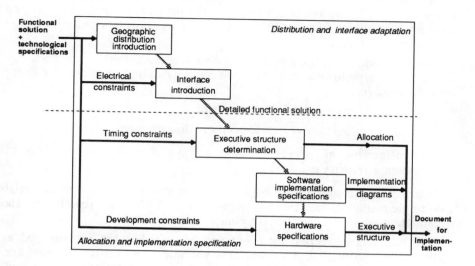

Figure 19.1   Phases for the implementation specification step.

19.3 INTRODUCTING GEOGRAPHIC DISTRIBUTION CONSTRAINTS

As a result of technological evolution, implementations can now be developed more in the form of weakly coupled electronic and computer subsets, which can be easily geographically distributed. For electronic implementations further apart than a few meters, we have geographic distribution. Although the natural tendency is to take account of this distribution constraint at the design stage, Chapter 14 showed the difficulty involved in this approach. The recommended procedure is preferably to search first for functional couplings, then after analyzing distribution constraints to search for necessary transformations. This strategy helps to keep to the strict minimum for the application.

Geographic distribution constraints given in the technological specifications deal with:

- Information or events in the environment. Entities concerned by this information are then distributed, implying distributed inputs and outputs for the system.

- Information or functions internal to the system which must respect specific location constraints.

With the distribution constraint, some functional relations cannot be directly implemented using an available hardware support for transferring information between two remote sites. Functional structure transformations are therefore necessary.

The main principle to be respected consists of considering that any exchange between two remote sites can only take place by information transfer in the form of messages.

The resulting process therefore consists of:

- delimiting function subsets located on different sites;

- transforming all synchronization and variable sharing relations by message transfer relations.

If several choices are possible for delimiting subsets, in order to minimize the implementation complexity, it is recommended to search for the delimitation with the minimum couplings.

The two relation types, by event and by variable, are transformed as indicated in Figure 19.2. An event or a variable is separated into two and coupling is carried out by a unit transfer function. This function is then refined by considering an internal port for the message transfer. The event Ev' or the variable V' is coded by a transmission function in the form of a message. The message is decoded by a reception function.

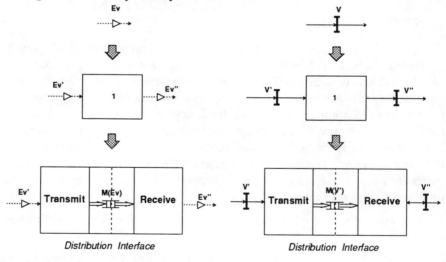

Figure 19.2   Principle for introducing distribution.

For the Ev' transfer, the transmission action is temporary, whereas for the transfer from V' to V", the transmitting action is permanent. The permanent action solution is obviously not satisfactory for the implementation.

Transmitting V' is only useful when it is modified. This may be achieved either by the transmitter being responsible for this observation or by the producer of V' signalling every modification to the transmitter.

We will illustrate the recommended procedure by an example other than those dealt with in design, since these do not have any distribution constraints. Consider the following functional structure in Figure 19.3.

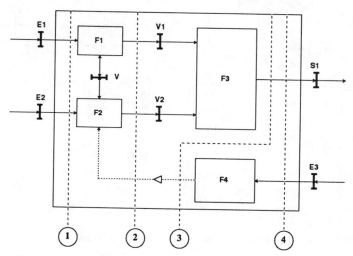

Figure 19.3   Functional structure example.

The distribution constraint is specified by the geographic position of environment entities. Assume E1 and E2 are on site A, and E3 and S1 on site B.

Initially, draw one line in Figure 19.3 to separate the two sites. Several choices are possible, four are shown. The two extremes: 1 and 4, assume all functionalities on one of the two sites, whereas 2 and 3 consider a distribution of system functions. The solution is then obtained by replacing all links crossing the separation line by a single message transfer link for both directions. The following four solutions as shown in Figure 19.4 are obtained for the above example.

After considering the resulting functional structures, the designer can select the simplest solution. Case 1 seems preferable here since the solution involves one unidirectional link only. Site A simply acquires data E1 and E2 and is responsible for transmission to site B. For case 4, site B is used for acquisition and transmission of information E3 and reception of S1. Case 2 is the most complex since the message passing between site A and B concerns the transfer of V1 or V2. The message itself has to include a code for the transferred variable type. On reception, a switching function carries out selective updating of V1 or V2.

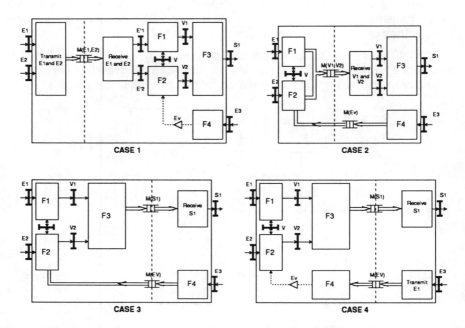

Figure 19.4   Four possible solutions depending on the delimitation.

19.4 INTRODUCING INTERFACES

The functional solution developed independently of the technology must be modified to take account of technological constraints. How should the necessary interfaces be introduced?

In the design step, starting with no initial knowledge about the solution, the designer produces a proposal. This is creative work. It is not the case for the detailed design because the work to be carried out deals with adaptations and selections. This is therefore a much more deductive procedure which starts from the functional solution and eventually produces a detailed solution satisfying each category of technological specifications. Introducing additional elements by deduction reduces the deformation of the functional structure which must remain the stable "hard core" of the application.

19.4.1 Template model for introducing interfaces

Interfaces have a technological role of adapting the system functionalities to its environment. These interfaces therefore form a concentric layer between two parts of the application.

The interfaces can be classified in two categories depending on the environment entity type:

- physical interfaces for physical entities;
- man-machine interfaces for dialog.

Due to the very different nature of these two categories, it is better to deal with them separately. In addition to interfaces, there are technology specific functions such as tests, maintenance procedures, redundancy for operating safety.

Hatley proposes the following template model for introducing interfaces. In this book, we have used the concept of this model as shown in Figure 19.5 [HATLEY-87].

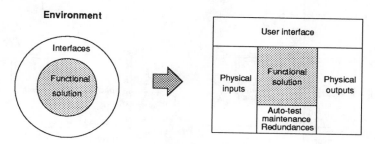

Figure 19.5   Template model for introducing interfaces.

The procedure for introducing interfaces is identical to that described for the functional design. Each of the four parts is a function with defined inputs and outputs, some by the physical nature of the observed or controlled information, others by the functional nature of the input and output variables.

A functional structure, therefore, has to be found for each part, to change the representation of exchanged data. Inputs and outputs thus have to be specified together with the role of each interface. When these specifications have been expressed, the functional design method can then be used to deduce a solution. The same method is applicable for introducing self-tests, maintenance functions and for introducing redundancies.

19.4.2 Introducing physical interfaces

The only purpose of these interfaces is to change the representation of information.

Since the coupling variable used functionally is an essential variable for the environment and system parts, and if this variable cannot be directly observed, a unit transformation is necessary which will result from combining the sensor and the interface. The principle therefore consists of refining this coupling variable.

When all interfaces have been specified, the technique consists of using the functional design process to define the solution which must be found from a functional point of view, knowing that it will now be dependent on the technology since it was selected to satisfy this type of constraint.

Figure 19.6 shows the process for observing a mobile position P with an incremental shaft encoder and for an analog control output CMD.

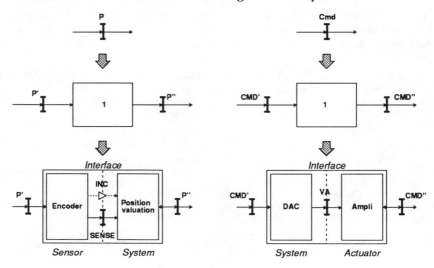

Figure 19.6   Introducing physical interfaces: examples.

Each variable requiring an interface is separated into two. The intermediate function must be unitary to maintain equality of the two variables. The interface is then introduced as the essential internal variable. An inverse function to the sensor or actuator function then has to be represented.

This same technique can be used for coupling by message transfer. It is complementary to the distribution introduction phase. Once the distribution constraint has been satisfied, it is necessary to adapt to the technological characteristics of the support. This support is actually a physical interface between subsets. Normally, the support is not equivalent to a mailbox capable of storing several messages. It is rather a support for serial bit transmission of the sequence of bytes in each message.

Communication is seen here as a service available for the application. The technique to be used is similar to that used for physical interfaces, but by carrying out a communication service decomposition at individual levels. It is recommended that the template client/server model (see Section 16.4) be used as a starting point for searching successive communication levels based on the OSI model.

Figure 19.7 shows an illustration of this process in which each message transfer is decomposed into a transfer of characters and in which each character is sent on the physical support as a sequence of bits.

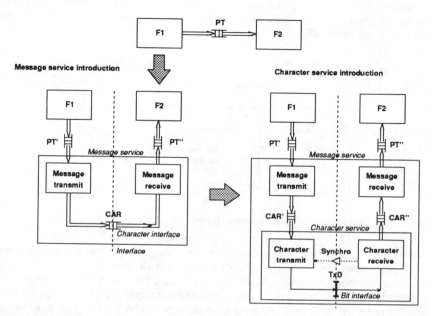

Figure 19.7   Introducing communication levels down to the support.

Finally, the necessary or imposed capacity in number f messages for each port has to be decided upon for the communication service. If the capacity of a receive port is not sufficient to store all transmitted messages, a consumer to producer servocontrol will be necessary. This is carried out by a return line: for example by an RTS / CTS connection for a hardware synchronization protocol, or by a TxD line in the reverse direction for an XON / XOFF type protocol.

19.4.3 Introducing man-machine interfaces

During the functional design, all necessary messages will be used for coupling with users. The user does not directly generate these messages. Similarly, direct message interpretation is impossible. Therefore, an adaptation interface is necessary. This must take account of the user-friendliness type described in the technological specifications, which by deduction induces the technological interface.

Assume that the user interface consists of a keyboard and a screen. The man-machine interface is represented by the function shown in Figure 19.8 which observes the keyboard state, updates the screen, produces and interprets messages exchanged with the functional solution.

The function refinement is based on the specifications for this interface which express the use procedure. The process to be followed is that described for any functional design, but this time taking account of the technological characteristics of the inputs and outputs to the interface. For example, it will be possible to start from a template model such as the interactivity model described in Section 16.5.

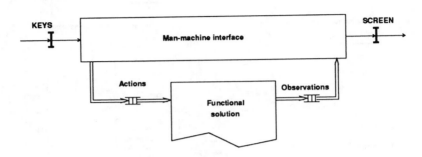

Figure 19.8   Introducing a man-machine interface.

Although the solution consists of adding a single function as an interface, every designer must know that the development of this type of interface, in other words programming to satisfy the objective, is very expensive in implementation and debugging time. These interfaces are the source of time estimate errors which can vary by a factor of between 1 to 4. The evaluation error may depend on the difficulty of defining the specification, but also the inaccuracy of the user's requirements. If the customer is to be happy with the product, the dialog should be specified by prototyping. The interface should be quickly developed with suitable tools which will simplify modifications. Interface generation applications are very useful for this problem class, together with object-oriented languages.

In the following, we will illustrate the introduction of two interface categories: inputs/outputs and user interfaces on the two examples studied in the design part.

19.4.4 Example 1: centrifuge speed control system

In this problem, the interfaces to be satisfied concern the speed measurement carried out by a shaft encoder, the PWM type motor speed control, and the user interface composed of a set of push buttons and a digital display unit.

-A- Introducing physical interfaces

For the motor control, the variable CV has to be transformed into a two-state variable of period 1 kHz and a cyclic ratio proportional to CV. This is carried out by an interface function called PWM_GENERATION.

Similarly, to obtain the speed SMOTOR at any time, the event produced by the shaft encoder has to be used.

F igure 19.9 shows how these two interfaces are introduced.

Each function is refined by the method recommended for the functional design. The characteristic internal variables or events have to be found.

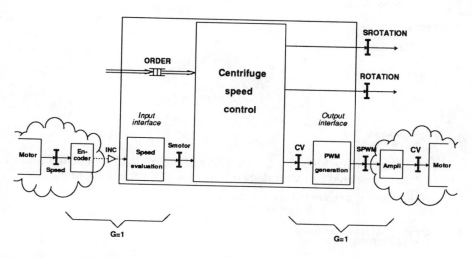

Figure 19.9   Introducing physical interfaces.

To generate the PWM signal, it is first necessary to produce a positive transition at a fixed period. Let CPERIOD be the corresponding event. The negative transition then has to be produced after a time which is a function of the value CV. Evaluation of this time requires an event FC with a high frequency compared with Cperiod (ratio 1000 defined from the PWM signal precision). Figure 19.10 shows a functional structure which can be used for this function.

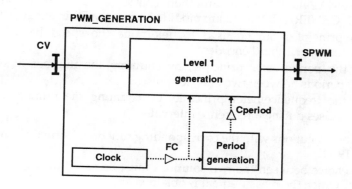

Figure 19.10   Functional structure for PWM_GENERATION.

The algorithms are easily described.

```
Action PERIOD_GENERATION on event FC with
                              (Output event CPERIOD);
  const NMAX = 1000;
  Var N: integer;
  begin
        N:=NMAX;
        cycle FC:begin
                N:= N - 1;
                if N = 0 then
                              begin
                                N:= NMAX;
                                Signal(CPERIOD);
                              end;
                    end;
          end cycle;
  end PERIOD_GENERATION;
```

This is a two-state behavior for the LEVEL1_GENERATION action; state 1 has a duration related to CV, and state 0 occupies the remaining time.

```
action LEVEL1_GENERATION on evs FC, CPERIOD with
                          (input var CV: integer;
                           output var SPWM: 0,1);
  const K = ....; adaptation coefficient;
  var REMAINDER: integer;
  begin
        SPWM: = 0;
        cycle
          CPERIOD: REMAINDER: = K*CV;
          FC:            if REMAINDER > 0 then
                              begin
                                SPWM:= 1;
                                REMAINDER:=REMAINDER-1;
                              end
                           else SPWM:=0;
        end cycle;
  end LEVEL1_GENERATION;
```

These two algorithms can obviously be combined to form a single action only: REMAINDER and N are then considered as internal variables to LEVEL1_GENERATION and are modified when the FC event appears.

Two principles can be used to determine the speed based on events transmitted by the shaftl encoder:
- the periodmeter principle, by counting the number of elementary periods between two encoder pulses;
- the frequencemeter principle, by counting the number of encoder pulses during a reference interval.

The two solutions with the corresponding functional structure are shown in Figure 19.11.

The choice between the two solutions must be based on the precision and speed at which the measurement is obtained.
- periodmeter: low precision at high speed, but low measurement time, long measurement time for low speeds;

- frequencemeter: low precision at low speed, high precision at high speed, measurement time constant but fairly low.

For the frequencemeter solution, with a period T equal to 5 ms corresponding to the required step for regulation with a 100 point/rev encoder, the maximum number of encoder events is ten at the maximum speed of 3,000 rpm. This solution would therefore not be sufficiently accurate. The periodmeter principle will therefore be used.

The period C is defined based on the required precision at the maximum speed. According to the specifications, this should be between 10 rpm and 3000 rpm. Therefore, at least 300 periods of C are necessary between two encoder events 0.2 ms apart. The maximum period of C is therefore 0.66 μs. With a 16-bit counter, the minimum measurable speed is 13.8 rpm, and 10 rpm is necessary throughout the range.

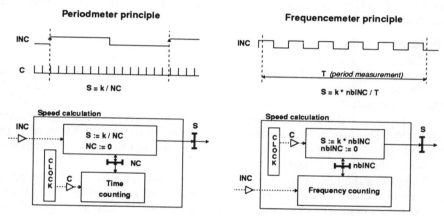

Figure 19.11   Functional structures for speed measurement.

To solve this precision problem, the principle of a self-adaptive periodmeter can be used. This means that the next INC event is awaited if the number of C pulses counted is not sufficient. The period of C is then calculated such that the 16 bits overflow fits to a speed less than 10 rpm. The period of C must therefore be 0.915 μs. The SPEED_CALCULATION algorithm is then written as follows.

```
Action SPEED_CALCULATION on ev INC with
               (input/output var NC: integer;
                Output var V: def_speed);
 const
       NCMIN = 1000; NCMAX = 65535; (16 bit overflow)
       K = 659340; (60/nb_pts/rev * C_period (s))
 Var
       N, NB, N1: integer;
 begin
       S:=0;
       N:=0;
       NC: =0;
```

```
cycle
   INC: begin
            N:=N+1;
            if NC > NCMIN then
                       begin
                         NB:=NC; N1:=N; N:=0;
                         NC:=0;
                         if NB > NCMAX then S:=0;
                                       else S:=(K*N1)/NB;
                       end;
            end;
      end cycle;
   end SPEED_CALCULATION;
```

This algorithm is interesting because it reduces the speed calculation frequency (which requires at least one division) to a value sufficient for regulation, by making an appropriate choice of NCMIN. It is assumed that the TIME_COUNTING action stops NC incrementing when the maximum value is reached.

-B- Introducing the user interface

The output variables are SROTATION which indicates the control speed setpoint at all times, and ROTATION, an indicator specifying whether or not the motor is rotating. These two variables are considered to be compatible with the physical interfaces which are a four digit decimal display unit and a LED.

As input for the functional level, the user was considered as an event generator. The functional interface justifies the use of an ORDER port. If the control speed is adjusted, this value is transmitted in the message which thus indicates the change setpoint event.

The physical interface for the user, described in the specifications, comprises four push buttons: ON and OFF for rotation control, and MORE and LESS for speed adjustment. The user interface to be developed is shown in Figure 19.12.

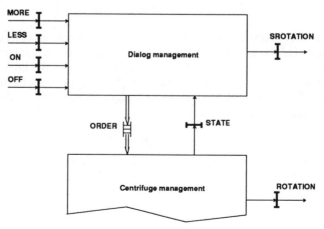

Figure 19.12   Delimitation of the function to be designed.

The functional specification indicates that the speed setpoint can only be modified when the centrifuge is stopped. A state variable (STATE) is necessary as input to the dialog management function. This variable is directly the STATE variable output from SPEED_CONTROL. In order to make an adjustment using the MORE and LESS push buttons, the user must also be able to display the current speed value during the modification. SROTATION must be coupled to DIALOG_MANAGEMENT and is no longer necessary for CENTRIFUGE_MANAGEMENT.

The DIALOG_MANAGEMENT function can be described directly by an algorithm assuming that this function continuously scans the states of the four input push buttons and thus detects the corresponding events. The function specification is given in Figure 19.13.

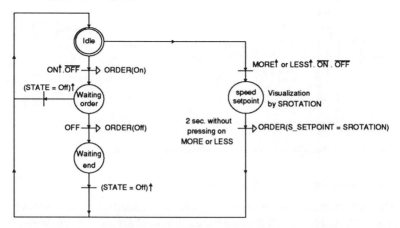

Figure 19.13   Specification of the DIALOG_MANAGEMENT function.

19.4.5 Example 2: automation with a wire-guided trolley

In this case, the trolley is a component of a distributed application. A message transfer type coupling is used between this trolley and the platform with which it has dialog. The functional design thus complies with distribution rules. The interfaces to be introduced are used only for coupling with physical entities and the trolley cannot be directly controlled by the user.

-A- Introducing interfaces for communication

Coupling for the communication is provided by a bidirectional infrared transmission. This support is similar to a serial transmission on a wire. The necessary interfaces are shown in Figure 19.14.

Each message is simple and one byte suffices. The reception and transmission functions are conventional and are decomposed to show the physical components used for the transmission, for example a UART.

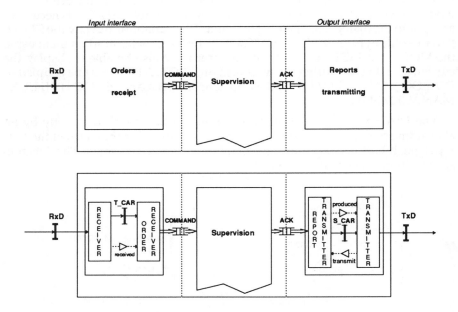

Figure 19.14   Introducing interfaces for communication.

-B- Introducing input and output interfaces

The information to be observed are the speeds of each wheel and the distance DCA. The speed control for each wheel are analog variables.

The distance DCA will be deduced as the difference between data items AC1 and AC2 given by two sensors in the front of the trolley at each side of the guide wire.

The solution shown in Figure 19.15 shows the use of a single conversion function to give DCA as the difference AC1-AC2. The analog/digital conversion is synchronous to the periodic START event. At the end of the conversion, EOC causes VCAN to be used for the DCA calculation after the measurement of the two channels.

The speed of each wheel will be measured using the periodmeter principle in order to give fast observation of the speed for fast displacements (see Figure 19.16).

The number of increments provided by the encoder at the maximum speed is:

$$128 \times (5000/3600)/0.94 = 189$$

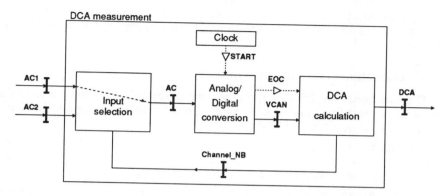

Figure 19.15   Solution example for DCA measurement.

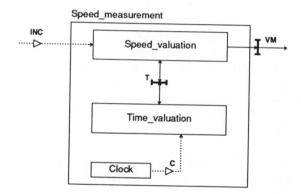

Figure 19.16   Solution for each speed measurement.

The minimum period for INC is therefore 5.3 ms. For a precision of 5%, TC must be 0.26 ms.

Generation of the two analog variables CVM1 and CVM2 requires the use of analog to digital convertors as permanent functions.

19.5 CONSTRAINTS FOR AN EXECUTIVE STRUCTURE

The objective of allocation is to determine the executive support necessary for evolution of the application. Several procedures are possible depending on the nature of the expected results. This depends on the development strategy to be followed and has an influence on the cost: low reproduction cost or low hardware development cost.

To be satisfactory, an allocation must lead to a system which respects all timing constraints. Check rules are discussed first, followed by a description of three executive structure search techniques (by grouping, by refinement and by abstraction).

19.5.1 Evaluation of timing constraints

The functional model uses the zero time assumption for the execution of elementary function operations. This assumption is no longer applicable when an executive support is involved.

Operation execution times (processor power not infinite) introduce a time distortion in the form of delays. Some distortions are not serious, but others may make it impossible to respect timing constraints.

When there are timing constraints for an application, they are expressed in the technological specifications in the form of a time separating the moment at which a request occurs (as an event) and the time at which the resulting action is completed, which must remain below a given maximum time. If these constraints are not respected, the application may go into a state similar to a hardware failure.

Second, to reduce the technological support, several actions are implemented on the same processor whenever possible. Processor sharing for actions can also lead to intolerable execution times.

In the allocation model, a processor which satisfies all timing constraints for the actions that it supports is considered operational. A processor is said to be operational if its utilization rate always remains lower than one, and if all timing constraints for actions have been respected.

Two parameters have to be evaluated for each temporary action in order to check that timing constraints are respected when a solution is defined, or to choose a solution which respects these constraints [CALVEZ-82]:

- the maximum activation frequency FA;
- the maximum execution time TE.

These two parameters are independent. The first, the activation frequency, defined by the action input events or messages, is determined from the problem specifications and the analysis of the functional description. This parameter is independent of the executive structure. However, the execution time is a function of the operation execution times for the selected processor, the operations involved in the algorithm for the action and therefore on the power of the processor used.

To satisfy timing constraints, the designer can modify:

- the number and nature of actions associated with a processor;

- the execution times for each action, either by modifying the algorithm or by changing the nature and therefore the power of the processor.

Only the worst values of the two parameters FA and TE are useful initially for checking timing constraints. We also consider here the case of actions with several input activation events.

-A- Procedure

Problems arise when evaluating timing constraints for at least two reasons:
- Actions carried out by software are unknown at this stage. However, the decision to use a hardware or a software solution for each action is made based on this timing constraint evaluation.
- The processor type is not known. It is therefore difficult to evaluate the execution time.

Despite this difficulty, the following procedure is proposed to facilitate deciding upon the hardware support:
- Analyze the complete functional structure and classify actions into three categories: those which must necessarily be carried out by a dedicated processor (hardware solution), those which can be carried out by a programmable processor, and actions which can be carried out using both techniques.
- Evaluate activation and execution times for the actions in the latter two categories based on a processor category (preferably 8 bits, otherwise 16 or 32 bits).

The analysis starting point is the complete functional structure including interfaces. This represents all actions in the system. All functional transformations have been made: introduction of the geographic distribution and the interfaces, maximum discretization of permanent actions to reduce their number, reduction of the number of clock type generators to increase event synchronization.

Evaluation produces a table of maximum values. The activation frequency is determined from the specifications, whereas the execution time is deduced from the length and nature of the action algorithm.

These times are then compared with timing constraints given in the technological specifications. Actions which deserve special attention are those which have a high utilization rate $T0 = FA*TE > 0.2$ to 0.5 and those for which the maximum execution time is of the same order of magnitude as the end of execution time constraint.

-B- Evaluation of maximum activation frequencies

The worst case for the maximum activation frequency, FA, is equivalent to the maximum value of action activation event occurrences. These events are directly related to events generated by environment entities or by other actions. Therefore, specifications can be used to determine their values.

For permanent event generating actions, the output generation function is only a function of the action behavior. FA is also deduced from the specifications.

It should be noted that the message production frequency is not used in evaluating maximum frequencies. The port is used as a buffer between the producer and consumer. However, if constraints such as a limited port capacity exist, the same evaluation as described above must be carried out, assuming that production of a message is equivalent to the generation of a "message existence" type event.

-C- Evaluation of the maximum execution time

The maximum execution time for each action is directly linked to the processor used for execution support. The evaluation is more difficult if the processor itself is one of the elements to be selected, and similarly if the algorithmic description --> program transposition is only imposed during the implementation phase. The transcription work can be reduced by using automatic translators, which justifies preferring the use of high-level languages.

In the absence of constraints on processors to be used, the execution time is evaluated for a so called "reference processor", which is typical of a performance category. We could take an 8-bit, 16-bit or 32-bit processor type as necessary.

The analysis (performance analyzer) or simulation of a temporary action can be used to determine the maximum execution time for each action activation (temporally undecomposable procedure) for a reference processor. Since processing sequences associated with each event are hardware exclusive, the worst case for the action is when all activation events appear simultaneously. The maximum execution time is equal to the sum of maximum execution times for each sequence. The following figure shows this case and shows the sequential execution to satisfy exclusion of T1 and T2.

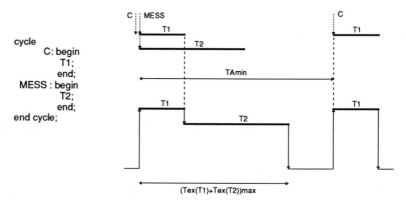

Figure 19.17   Worst case for execution time.

To be correct, the execution time evaluation must include the context switching time which may appear when several actions share a single processor. The maximum time would then be obtained by considering that the processor is using another context before execution, and is returned to the same state after the end of execution. In this way, the cost in time of processor sharing management (overhead) is taken into consideration.

When the algorithm is written in a high level language (for example, Pascal), a first approximation of the execution time is given by the following formula:

Tex = nb_program_lines * expansion_factor * Mean_instruction_time;

The expansion factor is for the transformation of a Pascal instruction into assembly language instructions. It is about five for an 8-bit processor, and three or four for a 16-bit processor. Mean_instruction_time is the mean assembler instruction execution time. It is about 2 µs for an 8-bit processor and about 1 µs for a 16-bit processor.

Obviously, this is only an approximate formula, but with a little experience can be used to isolate constraining actions.

-D- Maximum processor occupation rate for several actions

For each temporary action, the maximum activation frequency is FAi and its maximum execution time is TEi. The maximum processor utilization rate for n actions executed on a processor (suspension of one action for another with a higher priority) is then:

$$T0 \text{ max} = \sum FAi*TEi$$
$$i = 1...n$$

This ratio must always be less than 1, a strictly necessary condition but not sufficient for the processor to be considered operational.

-E- Respect of activation constraints

The task sequencing policy on the processor has an effect on whether or not timing constraints can be respected. For a periodic action, execution of the action must be completed before the next activation event appears.

Two sequencing cases are shown below in Figure 19.18 for different priorities of the same two actions A1 and A2.

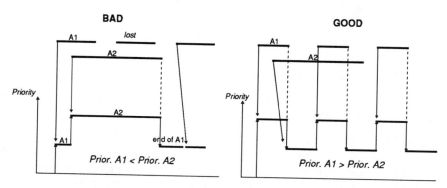

Figure 19.18   Influence of sequencing on timing constraints.

In the first case, an A1 activation event is lost since the processor is assigned to A2 at that time.

As a rule for sequencing, a simple and sufficient strategy will be used based on a fixed priority sequencing. The processor use for this criterion is then optimized by choosing:

$$\text{priority Ai} > \text{priority Aj for FAi} > \text{FAj} \; \forall \; \text{i and j};$$

This strategy is particularly suitable for microprocessors which, due to their low cost, do not necessarily have to be used at their maximum power, unlike mainframe systems. However, care must be taken since this method does not take account of critical sections which may exist due to the use of shared variables. A conflictingl situation may exist between fixed priority scheduling and mutual exclusion [KAISER-82].

-F- Respect of execution deadlines

Deadline type constraints are more severe than the above, since the deadline is normally earlier than the time at which the next event appears. The end of execution time for each action has to be determined in order to check that this type of constraint is respected. Determination is iterative starting from the highest priority action. For fixed priority sequencing, assume priorities such that:

$$\text{priority A1} > ...\text{priority Ai} > ...\text{priority An}$$

The most critical case rises when all activation events are simultaneous.

Let:

- RD_i be the maximum delay for start of execution of Ai;
- RF_i be the maximum delay for end of execution of Ai;
- TO_i be the processor utilization ratio for action Ai and all higher priority actions;
- TE_i be execution time for Ai on the processor when 100% available.

The following result are obtained for the various actions:

$$RD_1 = 0 \qquad\qquad RF_1 = TE_1$$
$$RD_2 = TE_1 \qquad\qquad RF_2 = TE_2/(1-TO_1)$$
$$...\qquad\qquad\qquad ...$$
$$RD_i = TE_{i-1}/(1-TO_{i-2}) \quad RF_i = TE_i/(1-TO_{i-1})$$

These values can be used to check that end of execution deadlines are respected for each action.

-G- Very hard real-time constraints

A situation may arise in which it is impossible to satisfy the timing constraint for a single action: current processors may be not fast enough, or an action may be unusually complex. In this case, it may be better to return to the previous design stage and look for a functional solution to the action using concurrency.

The idea is then to transform a sequential algorithm into a concurrent evolution structure. This is achieved by using the data-flow diagram describing order relations.

-H- Permanent actions

Normally, each permanent action requires an execution processor. Two solutions can be used to reduce the hardware complexity:

- Transform permanent actions into temporary actions. This is equivalent to discretizing the action behavior. Define a discretization step, with the period equal to the maximum tolerated value such that the behavior of the temporary action is sufficiently close to that of the initial permanent action such that specifications are always satisfied. When the period has been defined, the activation event generation action has to be added. This is a classic technique for transforming continuous type functions into discrete functions.

- Group several permanent actions in the background task. This background task is actually the only permanent task possible for a programmable processor. It is then used as a sequencer to periodically allocate the processor to the permanent actions that it includes.

In the second case, checking that timing constraints are satisfied requires the evaluation of:

- the utilization rate of the processor available for the background task and the actions that it includes;

- the execution frequency for each action resulting from the available utilization rate;

- the maximum execution time.

To explain this, assume a background task including the two actions A1 and A2. It is written as follows:

```
cycle: begin
          P(A1);
          P(A2);
       end;
    end cycle;
```

P(A1) and P(A2) are procedures built up by retaining from A1 and A2 only the operation sequence included in the cycle statement.

Let TE1 and TE2 be the execution times for each procedure on a given processor. Assume also that the processor supports other temporary actions. The maximum processor utilization rate for these temporary actions is TOmax.

The minimum available utilization rate for the background task is:

$$TU = 1 - TOmax$$

The minimum execution period for P(A1) and P(A2) is therefore:

$$Tbackground = (TE1 + TE2)/TU$$

The maximum execution time (average) for A1 and A2 is:

TE1/TU or TE2/TU

This simple calculation shows that the background task has a processor for which the power factor is reduced with temporary actions from 1 to TU.

19.5.2 Techniques for deducing an executive structure

An executive structure will result from the procedure followed to determine it which depends on the development time - many of few copies. Independent of these two cases, an executive structure may be obtained:
- by grouping predefined structures;
- by refinement;
- by abstraction.

-A- Grouping predefined structures

This technique consists of using existing executive structures to build up more complex structures.

Existing structures are the result either of previous developments, or are obtained from products available on the market, such as processor boards in STD, VME, Multibus format, etc.

This technique of using existing solutions leads to a significant reduction in the hardware solution development cost together with a relatively high reproduction cost. It is good for the development of a small number of units.

-B- By refinement

Every specified processor which cannot be made directly using current or imposed technology can be decomposed into the form of a more elementary executive structure.

This technique can be used by circuit or card designers and by technicians responsible for developing the hardware necessary to satisfy the executive structure specifications. This is possible since the executive model is a hierarchical model which can be used to describe all architecture levels, complex systems including basic digital components.

-C- By abstraction

It may be useful to replace a subset of a given executive structure by a single processor. In this case, the implementation is simplified since the number of components is reduced and interconnections become internal to the processor. Using this technique, make sure that the abstract processor will be operational for the functional description that it must support.

The abstraction operation consists of :
- delimiting a set of processors;
- eliminating all elements internal to the set;
- replacing the delimited set by a processor defined by its specifications.

The choice of groupings must take account of couplings to minimize the complexity of the resulting structure. Coupling between two processors is a function of the following factors:

- the number of interconnection links;
- the amount of information exchanged;
- the frequency of exchanges;
- the exchange cost in time.

19.6 DETERMINATION OF THE EXECUTIVE STRUCTURE

According to the analysis made in Section 19.1, the designer would prefer to use existing products for a small number of units. He then needs to check that a functional description allocation is possible on the required executive structure.

On the other hand, for a large number of units, the objective is to minimize the hardware reproduction cost. This leads to a search for a minimum executive structure. The abstraction technique should be used. The designer starts from an executive structure similar to the functional structure. This means that he associates a processor for each action, using programmable processors as much as possible. He then progressively reduces the executive structure by abstraction by locating several actions on a single processor, constantly checking the operational character. The search for groupings is carried out by pairs of processors, using coupling as a guide. This is obviously only possible for programmable processors.

In practice, this type of solution search is fairly simple starting from the temporal characteristics of functional description actions, since experience has shown that there are very few actions with hard real-time constraints for any given application.

19.6.1 Choice of the hardware/software distribution

The solution to be selected therefore depends on the development criterion - few or many systems to develop.

For a low number, a hardware solution has to be found which is able to support all system functions. In this case, general expandable executive structures available on the market will be preferred. Special interfaces or functions may be missing. They can be added as extensions.

When the hardware reproduction cost is reduced, the minimum executive structure has to be found.

There may also be choices between a hardware or a software solution. The software solution is preferable since it is more evolutionary and also less expensive for reproduction, provided that the development time is not excessive and that performances remain acceptable.

The procedure for deducing the hardware/software distribution starts from an evaluation of all the action times.

All actions with a low processor utilization rate and with no timing constraints, which is the case for at least 80% of all actions if not more, are grouped together to be located on a single processor. The processor utilization rate is calculated each time an action is added. Even if the method is general and the determination can be made incrementally by considering actions in pairs, experience has shown that the solution is found fairly easily since in most cases, all actions which can be implemented in software can be located on the same processor.

Sometimes, when some actions are especially constraining, they should be given special consideration. Several solutions are then possible:

- implementation by a hardware solution;

- modification of execution specifications (activation frequency);

- modification of the functional approach to reduce constraints;

- choose a higher performance processor (for example 16 or 32 bits instead of 8 bits).

These two phases (constraint evaluation and distribution choice) are illustrated using the two design examples.

19.6.2 Example 1: Centrifuge speed control system

When all useful actions have been considered as temporary functions and then after reducing periodic event generators, the complete functional structure given in Figure 19.19 is obtained.

-A- Evaluation of timing constraints

For SERVO_SPEED function, it is assumed that a sampling period of 5 ms is satisfactory, considering the low inertia of the motor. Event periods are therefore:

$$T\_C = 0.915 \ \mu s \ \# \ 1 \ \mu s$$

$$T\_CPERIOD = 1 \ ms$$

$$T\_INC = 0.2 \ ms$$

$$T\_CK = 5 \ ms$$

-B- Hardware/software distribution

The PERIOD_DIVIDER, CLOCK, TIME_COUNTING, LEVEL1_GENERATION actions must be carried out by hardware. Other actions can be carried out by software.

Since the microprocessor type (for example Motorola 68000) was imposed in the specifications, the maximum execution time can be calculated for each temporary action. The following times are approximate:

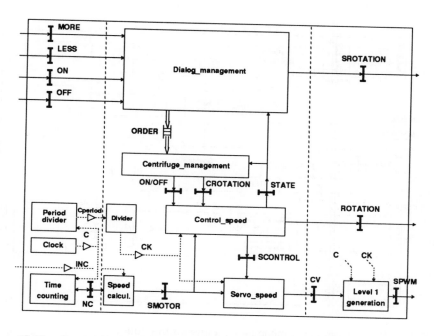

Figure 19.19   Complete functional structure for the centrifuge control system.

DIVIDER Time < 20 μs

SERVO_SPEED Time < 100 μs

CONTROL_SPEED Time < 100 μs

SPEED_CALCULATION Time < 100 μs

We can thus check that all timing constraints will be satisfied even in the worst case of allocation on a single microprocessor:

Tcpu use = 0.020/1 + (0.1 + 0.1)/5 + 0.1/0.2 = 0.56

A dashed outline on the functional structure delimits the hardware and software parts. The central software part (Figure 19.19) shows the role assigned to the microprocessor. The hardware part represents the interfaces between the microprocessor and the system environment.

19.6.3 Example 2: automation with a wire-guided trolley

The complete functional structure is shown in Figure 19.20. This is a synthesis of interface introduction and after reduction of event generators.

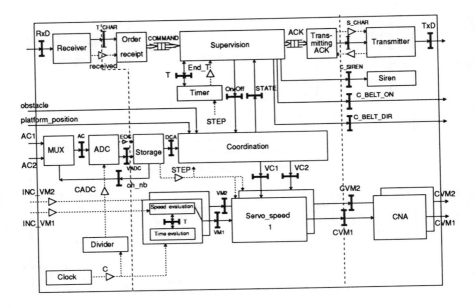

Figure 19.20   Complete functional structure for the trolley.

First, the probable execution frequencies and times for a software implementation are summarized.

Tinc = 5.3 ms   Tspeed_evaluation = 500 μs

TC = 260 μs   Ttime_evolution = 50 μs

Tstep < 15 ms ==> 10 ms   Tcoordination < 200 μs

TCADC = 5 ms   Tservo_speed < 200 μs

Teoc = 5 ms   Tstorage = 50 μs

Treceived = 4 ms (for COMMAND)   Ttimer = 50 μs

If SUPERVISION is excluded, since this is an action with no constraints, the 8-bit processor utilization rate is very approximately:

$$Toccmax < 0.5/5.3 + 2*50/260 + (0.2+0.2)/10 + 2*0.05/5 = 0.32$$

Thus, all actions can be implemented by software on a single microprocessor, except for the serial link management function to be performed by a serial transmitter-receiver component, and the multiplexer and AD convertor function.

19.7 SOFTWARE IMPLEMENTATION DIAGRAM FOR EACH PROCESSOR

The subsets of the complete functional structure to be located on each programmable processor were determined in the previous phase. The software implementation diagram defines the software organization for each processor.

The following have to be decided:

- possible action grouping in order to make up the tasks to be implemented;
- a priority for each task;
- an implementation technique for each functional relation.

In Chapter 18, rules for the implementation model were described. The objective is also to reduce the organizational part in order to reduce the size and complexity of the software and consequently the development, testing and debugging times.

The recommended sequencing strategy for tasks is to use a priority proportional to the activation frequency. The more frequently a task is activated, the less time is available for it, and therefore it should be executed correspondingly faster.

For relation implementations, it is desirable that the procedure call be used as much as possible, simplifying the organizational part. This solution is only possible between actions with increasing relative priorities.

Tasks activated by a hardware event are activated by the processor interrupt system. Permanent actions and some cyclic actions without timing constraints are implemented as procedures in the background task.

When it is desirable to use a real-time executive or the services of an operating system, tasks call these services by a procedure call.

A module structure describes the program structure for complex tasks.

Some translation rules were described in the previous chapter (see Section 18.4), and the reader is advised to review these rules which are essential for this phase. The main rule, which must be thoroughly understood, is first reminded, then special attention must be paid to transformation rules for miscellaneous structures and to transformations applied to data. The technique described is similar to the inversion technique recommended by Jackson (see Chapter 7) [JACKSON-83].

19.7.1 Translating a temporal dependence between two actions

A temporal dependence results from a relation by event or by message transfer. The two actions concerned by the relation are implemented in software and therefore the same will apply for the relation.

The solution to be used depends on the priority of the two actions:

- lower priority to the source action: procedure call;
- higher priority of the source action: use of an intermediate task to assign the processor to the lower priority dependent action.

These two solution cases are shown in Figure 19.21.

The transformation process is used for each pair of actions, starting with the highest priority actions. The advantage of this technique is that it minimizes the software organizational part.

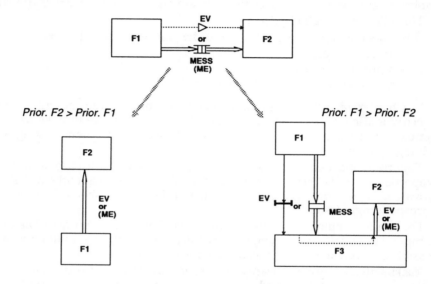

Figure 19.21   The two implementation cases for software dependence.

This phase is illustrated by the two examples.

19.7.2 Example 1: Centrifuge speed control system

On the complete functional structure described in Section 19.6.2, the central subset delimited by dashed lines is to be implemented on a programmable processor.

The INC and Cperiod events are necessarily in hardware since they are generated by hardware implemented actions. The CONTROL_SPEED and SERVO_SPEED actions are combined (executed in sequence) to form a single task activated by DIVIDER. Two actions - SPEED_CALCULATION and DIVIDER - are therefore implemented under interrupt.

The DIALOG_MANAGEMENT function is implemented as a background task. For each ORDER event it calls the CENTRIFUGE_MANAGEMENT action implemented as a procedure. The choice of priorities and functional couplings are shown in Figure 19.22.

The action triggered by the Cperiod interrupt is written as follows:

```
action DIVIDER on event Cperiod;
  Var
        N, SCONTROL: def_speed;
  begin
        N:=5;
      cycle CPERIOD:
                  begin
                  N:=N-1;
                  if N=0 then begin
                              N:=5;
                              CONTROL_SPEED(SCONTROL);
                              SERVO_SPEED(SCONTROL);
                              end;
                  end;
        end cycle;
  end DIVIDER;
```

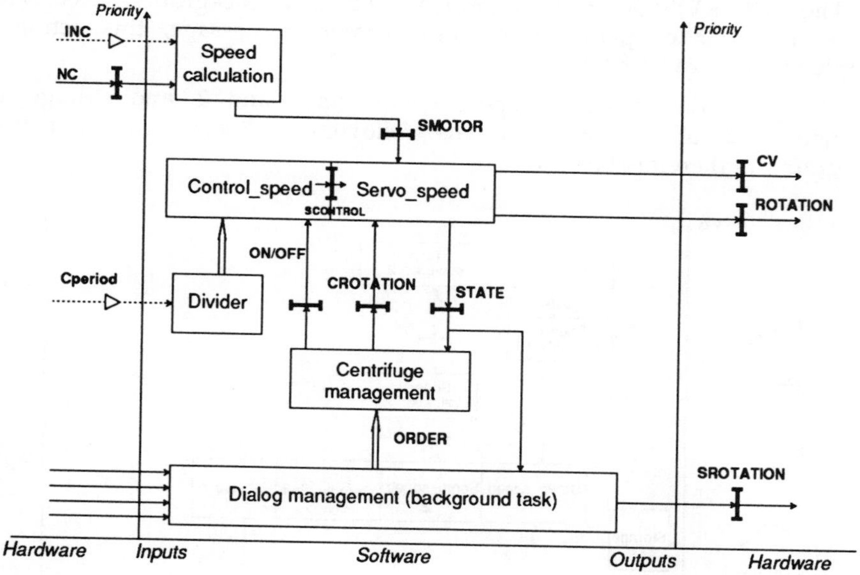

Figure 19.22   Software implementation diagram.

The two actions synchronous to DIVIDER - CONTROL_SPEED and SERVO_SPEED - are thus transformed into procedures. To obtain a satisfactory precision during arithmetic calculations, the expressions must be calculated in a specific order.

The statement SCONTROL := CROTATION*T/TR; must be calculated with the * first and the / second. CROTATION, T and TR are represented as 16-bit integers. Multiplication gives a 32-bit result. The divide operator to be made is then 32-bits/16-bits, giving a 16-bit result.

The result thus obtained shows that the software organizational part is reduced to procedure calls and the programming of two tasks under interrupts.

19.7.3 Example 2: a wire-guided trolley automation

The complete functional structure and the subset to be implemented in software was shown in Figure 19.20.

Since there is a large number of actions, start by grouping all actions activated by the same event.

An initial task is the task activated by C. Similarly for all actions activated by STEP: COORDINATION, TIMER and both SERVO_SPEED functions.

The hardware events are: C, INC_VM1, INC_VM2, EOC, RECEIVED. All associated tasks are activated by the interrupt system. Synchronization by STEP is transformed into a procedure call.

The SUPERVISION task is implemented as a background task. Since transmission takes place by a single character message, this action is implemented as a procedure.

Time_evolution 1 and 2, speed_evaluation 1 and 2, and storage are implemented under interrupt. The following software implementation diagram can therefore be used.

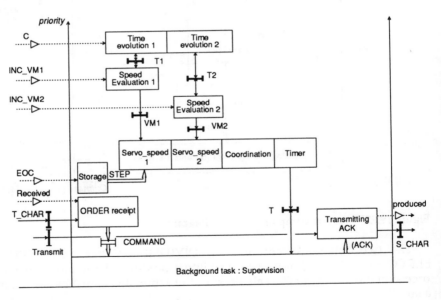

Figure 19.23   Software implementation diagram.

ORDER receipt can also be implemented as a non-blocking procedure. In this case, it is periodically called by SUPERVISION and to test if a character exists. If so, the action corresponding to the received message is undertaken, otherwise SUPERVISION continues its activity.

19.7.4 Implementation of an action sequence

Assume actions coupled by ports for message transfer. The sequence is initially assumed with no loop. Two opposing implementation strategies are possible: the pushed technique or the pulled technique. These are shown in Figure 19.24.

In the first implementation, A1 acts as a monitor and the complete set of actions behaves like a single action which sequentially processes each message output from A1. In the second implementation, A4 acts as a monitor by requesting a signal from A3 and so on down to A1.

The first solution is more appropriate when the system is driven by its inputs (event or message taken into account by A1). The system is then in a slave position related to the environment. This is the case for real-time applications and transactional applications (online operation).

The second solution is more appropriate when the system is driven by its outputs (information request). The system is then a producer and therefore in a master situation. This is more of a "BATCH" type operation.

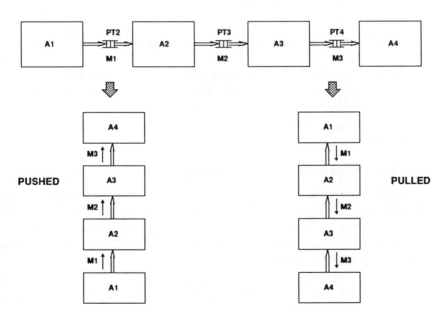

Figure 19.24   Two opposing implementations for a sequence.

19.7.5 Implementation of a looped action sequence

Now assume the case of a functional structure with a loopback (see Figure 19.25).

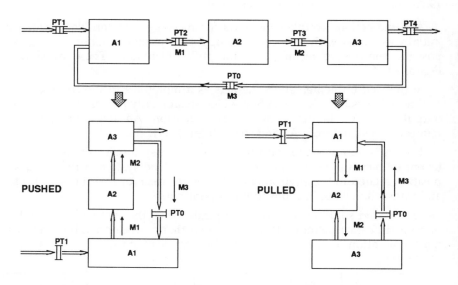

Figure 19.25   Implementation using the two techniques for a looped sequence.

Neither of the above two techniques can be used directly. First, the loop has to be broken, mandatorily by keeping a buffer in the loop. Let PT1 be the port acting as buffer. The push or pull technique can then be used.

In both cases, A1 decides upon the input to be taken into account between PT0 and PT1.

19.7.6 Implementation of several action sequences

Consider the following example composed of three sequences: one main sequence, one convergent sequence, one divergent sequence (see Figure 19.26).

The link from A5 to A2 is similar to the return from A3 to A1 in the previous example. The same applies for the link from A3 to A6. A buffer is thus necessary between pairs of sequences.

For the first solution, A2 acts as monitor thus deciding on the data to be taken between PT1 and PT5. This monitor role is played by A4 in the second solution.

19.7.7 Port capacity

For the functional description, ports are assumed to have unlimited capacity. This assumption is no longer realistic with a hardware support. Therefore, the buffer capacity necessary for the implementation must be determined.

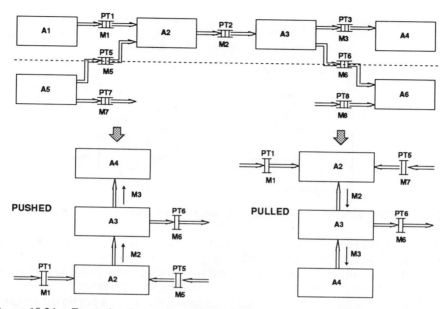

Figure 19.26   Example of several action sequences and solutions.

This determination is based on relative speeds of actions. A buffer may be kept to satisfy arrivals by packets (bursts). The maximum capacity for each buffer is then determined from the application specifications and execution performances.

In some situations, the capacity is still high which may be undesirable for the installation. In this type of case, an acceptable operation can be obtained with a limited capacity buffer provided that the producer can be slowed down. A servo-control mechanism must then be implemented to allow the consumer to slow down the producer. The technique consists of controlling the producer by an event or a state variable set by the consumer. Figure 19.27 shows two solutions.

For the first solution, the producer only submits a new message in V_Pt after reception of the event "consumed" for the previous message. This event can also be transformed into a Boolean variable. For the second solution, the XON/XOFF variable is modified by the consumer as a function of the number of busy places in the mailbox BPt. This specification leads to the use of the XON/XOFF protocol transmission technique.

19.7.8 Using the services of a processor

A processor may make services available to the application in order to reduce the development work. For example, this is the case for a processor with an operating system.

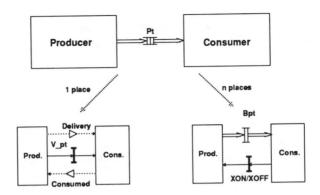

Figure 19.27   Implementation with consumer --> producer feed back control.

The technique is then similar to that developed for the use of a real-time executive. Services are considered, grouped or not grouped, as high priority procedures compared with application tasks. These services may themselves be managed by an executive responsible for sharing the processor.

The following example in Figure 19.28 shows the use of a keyboard for input and a data display screen for output. The system used makes Read(char) and write(Mess) procedures available.

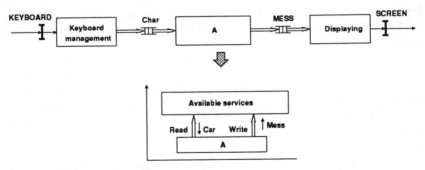

Figure 19.28   Implementation using system I/O management services.

In this implementation, the keyboard management service restores the processor to A only after a character has been read. For writing, restitution of the processor to A depends on whether or not the "with buffer" service is used.

19.7.9 Module implementation

For a complex task, a hierarchical module structure may be necessary. The "Structured Design" method to be used (see Section 7.4) is well known and is described in many books: DeMarco, Jones, Yourdon and Constantine, Ward and Mellor, Martin and McClure (see References Part 2). Rather than describe this method in detail, it is preferable that the designer refers to these works. We will simply recall the main concept that the designer should bear in mind.

A module structure is obtained from a specification expressed by a data-flow diagram. The first phase consists of finding the first decomposition level: the main module and called modules. This deduction is carried out by identifying three parts on the data-flow diagram - the inputs, the central transformation and the outputs. This facilitates positioning the two interfaces to minimize coupling between parts.

This procedure can be reused for each lower level. The technique is illustrated by the following example in Figure 19.29.

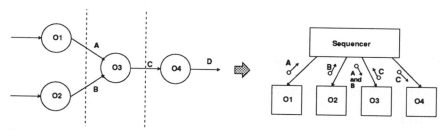

Figure 19.29   Transformation example to obtain a structure of modules.

The example shows that a main module is used as monitor to sequence activities.

19.8 IMPLEMENTATION OF DATA

Data is used to provide coupling between tasks and to store information for the application.

The functional description contains the description of necessary data. It is modeled in the form of individualized data or collections of data. Each variable is described by a data structure which may be very small or complex, static or dynamic. Relations between data are also expressed by references to this data. The description model used for the functional level should be independent of the implementation.

The objective of this section is to show data structure transformations used to facilitate data implementation. We therefore change from a logical description to a physical description.

19.8.1 Data implementation criteria

Two objectives may be considered important for data implementation:
- independence
- efficiency

-A- Independence

Consider shared data used by several tasks in a single processor as shown in Figure 19.30.

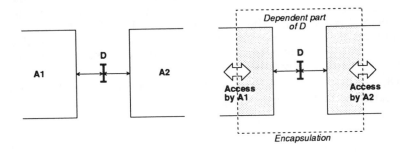

Figure 19.30   Dependence/Independence from D.

Although the implementation is a simple translation of the functional structure, three essential comments have to be taken into consideration [WARD-85]:

- Lack of protection: data D is globally accessible by linked actions. Errors can easily be made.
- Action dependence: any modification to the definition of D results in modifications to all related actions.
- Specific access mechanism for each action: an access technique is developed for each, increasing the development effort.

Obviously, these comments are particularly applicable if D is a structured and complex data. To correct these disadvantages, the objective is to produce a data-independent implementation of tasks and modules. This result is obtained by placing software around data D, thus encapsulating it. This layer provides the actions necessary to tasks in the form of services.

Independence also implies that the position of an item of information in data D is only known at the time of its use, which is a more difficult constraint to satisfy.

-B- Efficiency

Efficiency is very often a necessary condition for real-time systems. It is obtained by using the most direct data access mechanisms. This is the case when the position of information in data D is known for a given access.

The two objectives, independence and efficiency, are thus contradictory. The purpose of the implementation specification is to decide on the best compromise between these two aspects in order to satisfy the specifications as well as possible by proposing an internal structure and the necessary access mechanisms.

19.8.2 Implementation for structured data

Referring to the functional model for data, a structured entity is built based on three structures. An implementation technique is used for each case.

- The composition: all data composing this structure are contained in a contiguous area.

- Selection: all data types are located in the same area, together with the current data type.

- The set: the size of this kind of data is variable. In general, the solution is a list or file structure with an access mechanism to each element. When the maximum size is known and relatively limited, the array structure is better.

The internal structure is therefore deduced by transforming the logical structure produced during the functional design into a physical description.

19.8.3 Implementation for collections and relations

Collections can be used to represent an arbitrary number of data of the same type. External references used in the data can also be used to describe relations. A specific data in a collection is identified by its key.

The most direct implementation for this data category is the use of a relational database. Each collection is then implemented in the form of a table. In this case, access to this type of database is independent of the implementation technique for each field: for example, use of the SQL language as a standard interrogation language. On the other hand, the efficiency may not be satisfactory for hard real-time constraints.

If efficiency is an important objective to satisfy, transformations should be undertaken based on data collections:

- collections are implemented in file structures or arrays;

- external references for relations are direct links by pointers to the selected entities;

- access by a key must be developed to obtain a good efficiency: index table, hash technique, etc.

Figure 19.31 gives an indication of the transformation in the form of tables for a relation.

Knowing the room or zone number, the characteristics of the zone can be efficiently deduced. On the other hand, if all rooms belonging to a single zone are to be found, the access method is more complicated since the room table has to be scanned. Access can be improved by adding a chained list of rooms starting from each zone table entry (part in dashed lines).

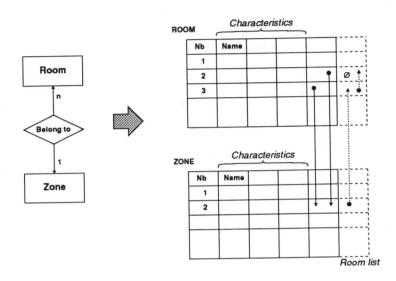

Figure 19.31   Implementation example for a relation.

19.9 HARDWARE IMPLEMENTATION SPECIFICATION

This is the last phase in this step. It consists of fully characterizing the executive structure resulting from the hardware/software distribution. It should preferably take place after the software implementation has been defined since some decisions made for the implementation have an effect on the hardware support, particularly for interrupts. A hardware event may be used to activate a task under an interrupt, but it may also be transformed into a logic input periodically tested by a task.

The executive structure is a result of an abstraction operation carried out starting from the complete functional structure. It consists of replacing each subset performed by software by a single function. An interpretation then has to be given to obtain the executive structure. The name of each function or action is thus replaced by the name of the processor which will be used as an executive support.

Each processor is specified as well as possible by all its characteristics to facilitate subsequent implementation.

Some optimizations can then be made to simplify the hardware and software implementation.

We will first illustrate this phase using the two examples and will then describe the process to determine coupling between processors for more complex architectures.

19.9.1 Example 1: centrifuge speed control system

The executive structure is obtained using the abstraction technique starting from the detailed functional structure given in Section 19.6.2 by replacing all software actions which form a single subset by a function for which the executive support is a programmable processor. The result is shown in Figure 19.32.

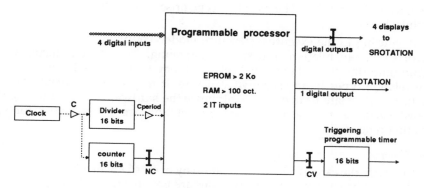

Figure 19.32   Specification of the executive structure.

This executive structure may be used to fairly easily deduce a suitable hardware structure in the VME format, as imposed in the technological specifications.

19.9.2 Example 2: automation with a wire-guided trolley

In this example, the following execution structure (Figure 19.33) is obtained by abstraction, resulting from the detailed functional structure shown in Figure 19.20 on which the software part performed by a programmable processor is shown in dashed lines.

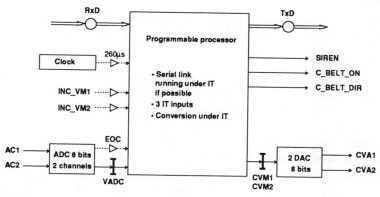

Figure 19.33   Executive structure specification.

A serial link is necessary, represented here by communication nodes RxD and TxD. Depending on which microprocessor is selected, it may be included or have to be added (use of a UART component).

19.9.3 Coupling between processors

When the processors to be used have been defined, couplings between them have to be determined. This problem type arises especially for multiprocessor architectures.

According to the executive structure model, coupling between processors involves three relation types: by signalling, by shared memory, by communication node. Functional relations may be not directly supported by the relation types in an executive structure. It may also be advantageous to make transformations in order to minimize the hardware complexity. Possible transformations facilitating the implementation are given below for each relation type.

-A- Events

Consider the case of a synchronization by events between functions located on different processors. Several solutions are possible for their coupling:

- Events may be directly translated by signalling.

- Events are transformed into Boolean variables. Coupling between processors then involves two digital signals (1 bit memory), M1 and M2 (Case 1).

- Several exclusive events may be coded as a digital information. A single signals is then sufficient (Case 2). The function G using VE provides suitable synchronization.

- A set of events can be translated by transferring messages each encoding the generated event. This solution is useful for the physical distribution (Case 3).

Figure 19.34 shows the three possible transformations, by superposition of the functional relations obtained by transformation and the executive structure.

-B- State variables

State variables to be used for coupling between processors can be located directly in a shared memory. Maximum grouping of state variables is desirable to reduce the number of shared memories (Case 1, Figure 19.35).

Memory sharing may lead to complex technological solutions.Therefore, it may perhaps be preferable to consider that a state variable is located in a processor, generally on the consumer side.

Provision for update must be added, consisting of a communication by message system used whenever the variable is modified. This then gives a solution identical to that resulting from a geographic distribution (Case 2).

In this example, the choice between one of the two solutions is made by analyzing the size of variables, the access frequency, and the cost of each technological solution.

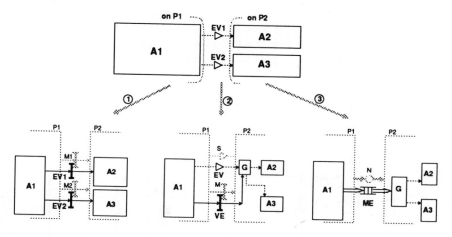

Figure 19.34   Event transformation facilitating implementation.

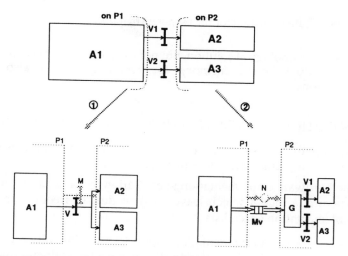

Figure 19.35   Transformation for state variables.

-C- Ports

Coupling by port is naturally implemented by a communication link.

When the transfer rate is very high or the port capacity may be reduced to 1, a port can be translated in a shared variable and two synchronizations. The two synchronizations Ready and Consumed are also replaced by a single Boolean variable BF. This is then equivalent to the exchange between two asynchronous processors with handshake type synchronization as shown in Figure 19.36.

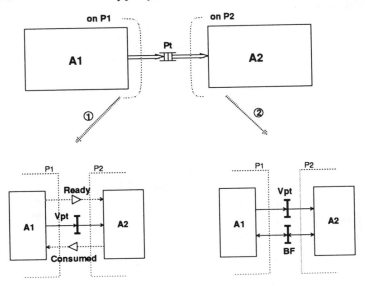

Figure 19.36   Transformation for the exchange by port.

The easiest technological solution, but not the most economical one, consists of using a dual access memory for coupling, which also manages synchronizations.

19.10 SOLUTION DOCUMENTATION AND CHARACTERISTICS

A the end of this step, the designer will have a complete document describing the implementation specification, including:

- The hardware implementation specification in the form of an executive structure, a model which leaves a great deal of freedom to hardware implementation specialists.

- The software implementation specification for all programmable processors. The implementation diagram for the software describes the organization of software components, but not the programs themselves. This will therefore be useful as a programming guide.

This document plays an interface role between designers and implementers. It is deduced from the functional structure and takes account of the technological specifications. The solution is obtained by a series of transformations, and the process to be followed is relatively systematic.

Verification is carried out as the work progresses, particularly by the implementers at the beginning of their implementation since they must first understand the specification to be used, which naturally leads to its verification.

In addition to technical objectives to be satisfied, the solution developed takes account of economic objectives, particularly the cost. The solution depends on the quantity of systems to be produced. This involves either reducing the development cost for unitary systems, or reducing the reproduction cost for production line items.

19.11 SUMMARY

The detailed design procedure described in this chapter was illustrated by the two design examples. The results, the executive structure and the software implementation diagram on each processor, follow on from transformations applied to the functional structure. This is therefore a deductive process based on principles and rules.

The main points of the procedure for this step are summarized below.

- The executive structure must conform with all technological specifications: distribution, interfaces with the environment, respect of timing constraints. This is achieved starting by enhancing the functional structure with all necessary elements to satisfy this conformity.

- The first phase consists of introducing the geographical distribution, since this then brings out the necessity for physical interfaces to be conform with this support.

- A template model is proposed for introducing interfaces with the environment. The solution search is made for each subset following the functional process described in Part 4.

- Physical interfaces are introduced taking account of the nature of sensors and actuators used for coupling with the environment.

- The man-machine interface must satisfy, as far as possible, the user friendliness required for the application.

- Finally, redundancies, maintenance and test functions are necessary to satisfy specifications or to facilitate product debugging.

- The executive structure is deduced by selecting the hardware/software distribution. This choice is based on analyzing characteristic times: probable activation frequencies and execution times relative to the application timing constraints.

- The hardware support differs depending on the number to be produced. For a low number, the development cost has to be reduced, starting whenever possible from existing subsets. However, the objective for large production quantities is to minimize the hardware part.

- Several techniques can be used to determine the executive structure: use of existing structures, minimization of the structure. Coupling between processors must also be simple, but must support the functional relations.

- Experience has shown that few applications require a complex search for the executive structure. There are few timing constraints and they are very confined. Second, by introducing physical distribution, a breakdown into several processors is necessary. The proposed process is thus much more useful as a check method to guarantee that all real-time constraints are respected.

- The software implementation diagram on each processor is determined by transforming the functional structure to be implemented. The criterion to be used consists of aiming to minimize the software organizational part in order to reduce the development cost.

- A software implementation may also be based on the use of a real-time executive or services available on the processor. This technique reduces development times but does not reduce the reproduction cost nor execution performances.

- The implementation of each complex task must respect the model for decomposition into modules, and the data implementation must give a good compromise between independence and efficiency.

- Finally, an executive structure is specified after deciding upon all software implementations.

- Executive structure and software implementation diagrams must be completely specified in the document produced at the end of this step so that teams of technicians can then undertake the implementation of the two parts without ambiguity.

REFERENCES PART 5

[CALVEZ-82]
: *Une Méthodologie de Conception des Systèmes Multi-microordinateurs pour les Applications de Commande en Temps-réel*
J.P. Calvez
Thèse de Doctorat d'Etat, Université de Nantes, Novembre 1982

[HATLEY-87]
: *Strategies for Real-time System Specification*
D.J. Hatley, I.A. Pirbhai
Dorset House Publishing New York 1987

[JACKSON-83]
: *System Development*
M. Jackson
C.A.R HOARE Series, Prentice-Hall 1983

[KAISER-82]
: *Exclusion mutuelle et ordonnancement par priorité*
C. Kaiser
Technique et Science Informatiques No 2, 1982 p 59-68

[WARD-85]
: *Structured Development for Real-time Systems*
P.T. Ward, S.J. Mellor
Vol 3: Implementation Modeling Techniques
Yourdon Computing Series, Yourdon Press, Prentice-Hall 1985

PART 6

IMPLEMENTATION

Essential since it is the final step, Implementation produces the system or the required application in accordance with the customer's objectives.

It is the most expensive step in the development cycle, both in time and resources. The objective is therefore to minimize this cost. Consequently, specifications should be very detailed at the beginning of this step. The MCSE methodology satisfies this objective.

In this part, Chapter 20 describes the process to be followed for the implementation, emphasizing both hardware implementation and software implementation parts. The meaning of refinement in implementation is also discussed to show that implementation may require new design work but in a more restricted field and that the functional design process can be reused.

Chapter 21 describes techniques for hardware implementation, including the conventional technique of using manufacturing catalog circuits, and the development of special components. Like the functional design, template models suitable for the hardware function design are described together with the associated processes.

Chapter 22 deals with software implementation techniques, describing software engineering techniques and methods. This chapter emphasizes the need for reuse, even in industrial data processing, involving the use of the object concept and real time languages supporting this concept.

20

THE IMPLEMENTATION PROCESS

After completion of the three steps described in the previous parts, use of the MCSE methodology leads to a complete solution document. Implementation of a prototype or mass production is a result of this document.

Implementation of electronic and computer-based systems includes two parts: a hardware part and a software part. The product or application is operational only when the two parts are correctly associated. This association results from an integration operation which consists of testing the software on the hardware.

The implementation step is expensive in time and resources since it almost always exceeds the sum of the previous three steps. The objective of MCSE is to substantially reduce this cost. In addition to having complete implementation specifications, the implementation team must respect rules and use techniques and tools which efficiently lead to an operational implementation.

The objective of this chapter is to describe the organization of tasks, the process to be followed and rules and tools for implementation.

20.1 IMPLEMENTATION OBJECTIVE

Before starting the description of each phase, it is useful to restate the main role of the implementation step, the last step which finalizes the product. It is also necessary to be aware of the variety of implementation strategies which depend on at least three factors - input specifications, techniques to be used, available tools and methods.

20.1.1 Implementation step characterization

First, we will give a general definition: implementation is producing the required object described by a set of characteristics.

An implemented object (or an implementation) is therefore a material object. However, the characteristics describing the object represent an abstract model of the real object. In the terminology of the MCSE methodology, this model is a specification of the object. Implementation therefore involves transforming an implementation specification into a real object.

The material object must be operational - this means that it must satisfy all requests and constraints expressed by the customer. This step is therefore essential for the success of the development since it finalizes the project, although it is entirely dependent on previous steps since it is the last step.

The following figure (Figure 20.1) locates the implementation step within the product development cycle.

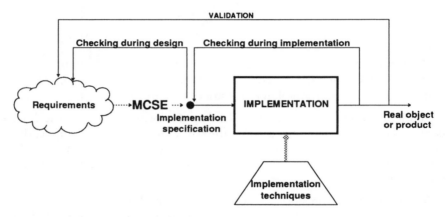

Figure 20.1   Implementation step characterization.

The three MCSE methodology steps already defined start from a requirements definition and lead to an implementation specification which is as complete as possible, and checked against the objective to be achieved. However, it must be assumed that it still contains some errors.

Since the implementation work cannot be completely automatic nor can the solution be unique, errors may also be introduced during implementation. A check is therefore necessary to confirm that the real object complies with the specification.

Since the specification used as input to the step itself probably has some errors in it, a global check of the characteristics of the final object or product against the initial general specification is essential. This check leads to product validation followed by its certification.

The implementation step thus forms part of the complete development cycle. This cycle is generally represented as a V-shaped diagram in the form of a double triangle as already described (see Figure 5.6).

The first three steps in the MCSE methodology form part of a top-down process which, by successive enhancements using the three-dimensional model, leads to a more and more detailed description of the application.

The objective of the implementation is to gradually develop the solution part by part, by building more and more abstract functionalities. The implementation process is therefore a bottom-up process. There is a solution description level for each validated implementation level. Verifications and validations ensure that the implementation satisfies its specification.

20.1.2 Variety of implementation methods and tools

Implementing is also making use of implementation techniques. Each technique is associated with one or more methods and transformation tools or transformation-aided tools [AMGHAR-89].

The implementation efficiency depends on several major factors:
- the specification nature;
- the technique used;
- tools and methods available for transformations.

The ideal would be to have an automatic production tool generating all types of electronic systems with no errors and making use of a wide variety of implementation techniques, and would start from very abstract specifications in order to reduce the work necessary after the requirements definition. It is always nice to dream, but we have a long way to go before reaching this ideal. During the next few decades, specifiers and designers will always find development material for attempting to solve this problem.

To illustrate the objective of this step and the variety of techniques and tools, consider two examples, each of which uses a specific class of techniques, one dealing with the hardware and the other dealing with the software.

-A- Hardware implementation example

The first example is for a sequential automatic control function to be made with an electronic board (hardware solution alone).
- First, specification nature? Several models are possible - Grafcet, finite state machine, waveforms, transition tables, etc. The nature depends on the prior work carried out by the designer.

- Technique or technology to be used? There is a wide variety of possibilities including printed circuits board with TTL type digital components, more complex components, programmable logic devices (PLD), application-specific integrated circuit (ASIC), programmable logic controller, etc. The choice depends on technical, industrial and economic criteria and constraints.

- Tools and methods? Again a wide variety, with each tool appropriate for a specification class and an implementation technique class.

For the last point, we will consider two extreme cases to demonstrate the role of this step and the diversity of the work.

In the first case, the specification is expressed by waveforms and the technique used is conventional SSI TTL type technology. An analysis of waveforms will lead to a solution in terms of digital functions and hence the schematic. The printed circuit board can be developed from the schematic and geometric component models by using a placement-routing tool. Documents produced by the CAD tool will then be used to make the PCB on which components will be mounted later.

Much of the work is carried out by man: analysis and production of the schematic, schematic input, placement and routing which is more complex when it is done manually, PCB implementation and assembly, checking after each phase, error correction.

Implementation errors may be serious: at the start, poor specification, too brief an analysis which results in an incorrect schematic, routing errors, manufacturing and assembly errors, checking errors.

In the second case, the specification is a finite state machine or a statechart. A single programmable logic device type technology is usable and is selected. The specification is provided directly or after a few syntactical adaptations to a PLD programming software. The specification is automatically translated into data compatible with a selected PLD programming system.

The work to be carried out concerns selecting the component and inputting the specification, if the specification produced during the design cannot be used directly. Implementation is then automatic since once programmed and removed from the programmer, the object satisfies the specifications.

However, the implementation may still not be correct due to bad specification, but this is design or input error. In this case, risks of error are significantly reduced.

Does this example show that techniques and procedures leading to automatic implementation should be used? No, not necessarily, the example simply shows that errors, and consequently time and implementation costs, are reduced when using automatic systems. But the economic cost is not necessarily reduced. Firstly, the tools may be expensive. Second, conventional technology may prove to be even less expensive for large production series.

-B- Software implementation example

The second example is for a simple microcomputer software package. We will start this problem by analyzing three factors:

- specification nature? Several specification levels are quite possible: the simple requirements definition (extreme since this is not a specification), data-flow diagram, module structure, structured language description, structured programming language description (PLD).

- Technology to be used? Even if we might think that a microcomputer is automatically a PC compatible, different supports can be used: several types of processors, screen, disk, printer, operating systems.

- Methods and tools? Again a wide variety as a function of the specification and technology.

We will discuss this latter point again by considering two extreme cases.

First case: for input, an idea of the required program. Use of a microprocessor board technology together with the necessary peripherals. The only available software is a symbolic translator, also called assembler program and a debugger. There is a great deal of work to be done - the complete program analysis, processor dependent writing, implementation, and no doubt a lot of tedious debugging and analysis error correction work.

Scope for errors is continuous and the product obtained after a great deal of work is not useful, since it is unreadable and therefore hardly maintainable and not translatable to another technology.

Second case: as input, a specification using a complete algorithmic description in a Pascal-type programming language and a PC-type microcomputer technology. The development tool is the Turbo-Pascal environment and compiler.

The amount of work to be carried out is very low, even more so since the design can be validated using Turbo-Pascal. The only possible sources of errors are the specification, the hardware adaptation, the configuration, and exceptionally the compiler.

In this case, we can see that implementation is the creation of an operational product, in other words the program running on the microcomputer, starting from a specification consisting of a syntactical description. Implementation is performed by the editor-compiler and linker-loader tools.

20.1.3 Time involved in the implementation step

Given a product to be obtained, the time and cost of this step in human resources is a direct function of:

- the nature of the input specification;
- the techniques and tools used.

We will consider the case here in which the specifications are developed using the MCSE methodology. This will therefore be a complete implementation specification document, and technological specifications specific to the implementation. Implementation will concern both hardware and software aspects.

To get an idea of the times involved, we will consider a medium-sized industrial application. The development time is about a year with a cost of about two man-years.

The implementation step will take between 60 and 80% of the total time, and will require 1.2 to 1.6 man-years. On average, the software proportion of this time represents between 70 and 90%.

This shows firstly the importance of the implementation step on the total cost, and second the importance of the previous steps in reducing this relative cost. The organization of teams and working procedures should be managed to improve this productivity and consequently the profitability of companies working in this field.

20.2 IMPLEMENTATION STEPS

Since the three major factors for the implementation are: the specifications, the techniques or technologies to be implemented, and methods and tools -a process must include a working approach which globally optimizes the cost and quality of the result.

There is no point here in reconsidering the specifications since they result from using MCSE and are produced in a structured manner so that they can be used efficiently during the implementation. The proposed procedure therefore considers techniques, methods and tools.

The implementation specification document is used as an input specification for the step and comprises:

- the executive structure specification;

- the integration of the functional solution onto the executive structure;

- software implementation specifications.

This document also includes part of the technological specifications not considered during the detail design step, particularly technical specifications for the implementation - component type, standards to be respected, implementation method, etc., and environmental constraints such as parasiting, hostile environment, temperature range, etc.

The implementation step shown in Figure 20.2 consists of four main parts organized as a three-phase sequence. The process is a three-phase sequence:

1. specification verification and acceptance;

2. hardware and software implementations;

3. integration, tests and validation.

This figure shows the simultaneous development of the hardware and software parts. This is possible since there are two specification categories, and this type of work organization is strongly recommended:

- to reduce implementation times;

- to allow the participation of specialists in both fields at the same time.

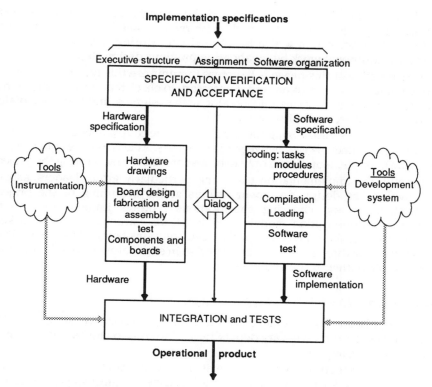

Figure 20.2   Implementation step process.

For complex projects, the number of man-months of work necessary is so high that several teams must collaborate if they are to produce a result within the deadlines. The problems of team structure, task sharing, distribution and sequencing then arise. As a result of its structuring into specified subsets, the document produced at the end of the design facilitates this type of team work organization.

The dialog between the teams, and particularly between the two specialist types of people, is a necessary condition for success to avoid incoherence problems which would otherwise not be detected before the integration and test phase.

The following sections describe each of these four parts.

20.3 SPECIFICATION VERIFICATION AND ACCEPTANCE

The objective of this first phase is to become familiar with the problem and the solution developed during the design. This phase is only useful when the implementation team is different from the design team. It is then used for coupling between the two teams.

The objectives section (20.1) showed the importance of a good, detailed specification in that it should comply with the customer's requirements. Any error in the specification which is detected later during implementation will introduce additional work by invalidating previous design steps.

The objective of this phase is therefore to minimize this type of error in the implementation specification, and if necessary to check that this specification is well understood by entering into a dialog with designers, and starting a dialog between hardware and software specialists.

The method of maximizing the simplicity of the coupling with the design is to have a personnel overlap between the two parts. At least one designer should continue in implementation, if only to be responsible for monitoring the project.

Second, the implementation team, and particularly group leaders, should get involved as design document readers at the beginning of the project. Understanding and checking specifications requires implementers to be familiar with description models used in MCSE. Participants are thus kept informed about the state of the project and solutions being considered. They also participate directly in verification and so in eliminating errors. In this way, they also share their responsibilities.

20.4 HARDWARE IMPLEMENTATION

The hardware solution is deduced from the executive structure. The implementation work will vary depending on the criterion for the development of the executive support.

For a modular structure based on existing boards, development consists of assembling these boards together with the implementation of special interfaces.

When the hardware reproduction cost has to be minimized, all elements have to be considered. The choice of the basic components, the processors to be used, memories, peripheral components, customized circuits, etc. must be made on a cost basis, and ensures that the resulting solution respects all technological constraints.

Every hardware implementation requires technical and recent technology skills. Due to the high speed of technological evolutions, a continuous effort is essential to reinforce this competence - reading technical journals, attending training courses, etc.

20.4.1 Process

There are three phases in the hardware implementation process:
- creation of the implementation schematics;
- location, implementation and assembling of components - printed circuit boards, specific components, etc;
- hardware implementation test.

This process is applicable to the complete system and for each subset or component.

Constituents must be made and assembled as quickly as possible to produce a version which can be manufactured on a production line. In addition, since this phase may be expensive (in time and money), it must work first time. The "ZERO ERROR" quality objective is possible for the hardware. Microprocessor components and VLSI components are suitable for obtaining this result, provided that this technology is well understood, with some experience in the subject and if an effort is made to update knowledge. It is desirable that a model or subset be built for more difficult parts, for example analog parts, in order to guarantee the validity of the implementation schematics.

The third phase for testing is essential. Each component, subset and then the complete product must be tested independently of the application using a bottom-up integration process. The test for boards containing programmable processors leads to the development of test programs subsequently used for checking during the self-test or during the production phase. Some tests require solution extensions; implementers are responsible for this work since the objective is to satisfy constraints given in the technological specifications.

20.4.2 The tools

The hardware implementation requires the use of development-aided tools:

- Electronic CAD tools: used for inputting schematics, simulation if necessary for all verification, layout on printed circuit boards or the implementation of integrated components - gate-arrays, programmable logic devices, ASIC.

- Instrumentation for testing and debugging - analysis and testing instruments such as the scope, logic analyzer, protocol analyzer, emulators, etc.

20.4.3 Rules to be respected

To comply with the executive structure specifications, the hardware solution to be developed must satisfy implementation rules stated for the executive model. The main points are described below:

Each processor is independent, and therefore decides upon its activity at all times. Bearing this specification in mind, the implementation must:

- Ensure that all signals are taken into account.

- Make sure that protection exists against simultaneous memory access conflicts. This applies to common memory in a multiprocessor architecture for which possible conflicts require the use of a bus assignment arbiter, or a multi-port memory.

- Provide protection against simultaneous access to a single communication node input. This is the case for coupling by bus, for which a bus sharing protocol should be implemented.

20.5 SOFTWARE IMPLEMENTATION

The software development consists of implementing the functional description on the hardware respecting software implementation specifications. During this phase, the software implementation diagram defined in the previous step must not be modified. The work to be carried out depends on the nature of specifications and the implementation constraints to be respected.

20.5.1 Process

The general process for the software implementation includes three phases:

- write procedures, modules, tasks in the programming language;
- program translation into executable code;
- test and debug.

When the specification consists of an algorithmic description in a high-level language, the implementation may be produced by a single compilation. Translation can also be carried out manually when programming requires writing in assembly language. This approach should be avoided whenever possible since it is expensive in time. It also significantly increases the probability of errors and is not very readable when the solution has to be corrected or modified during maintenance. However, automatic translation can result in timing constraints not being satisfied. In this particular case, it would be desirable either to carry out a manual translation to optimize execution times, or to modify the specifications to change the solution.

As for the hardware implementation, the software must be subjected to exhaustive tests to minimize the number of errors. Verification makes sure that the behavior required by the specifications, timing constraints and quality rules are respected.

Since any real-time system has physical inputs and outputs, it is not easy to test the software without its environment. Since application inputs and outputs are not necessarily available, the software structure must be such that as many tests as possible can be made without this environment.

20.5.2 The tools

The software implementation is carried out in parallel with hardware implementation. Therefore, the hardware support is usually not available for developing and testing the software. The minimum tools necessary are:

- a program edition tool;
- one or more cross-compilers and linker-loaders producing code compatible with the microprocessors selected for the application;
- test and debugging tools.

These tools are available on computers or microcomputers. For real-time microprocessor based applications, this type of support is called a microprocessor development system. Tools to be used must be compatible with those subsequently used for the integration phase.

Another essential requirement is that software development specialists must fully understand writing techniques and methods, and the associated tools. In addition to these tools, a project monitoring and version management tool should be used for large projects whenever possible.

20.5.3 Rules to be respected

The software implementation must also respect behavior rules given for the functional model and the implementation model. These rules are particularly concerned with the management of shared variables and ports.

-A- Coherence of shared variables

A shared variable plays the role of a common resource for tasks. To respect integrity constraints for this resource, an exclusive access, or in some cases a shared access technique, has to be defined.

The technique differs depending on the size and nature of the variable, and sometimes depending on the application nature.

-B- Access to simple variables

A simple variable is characterized by the fact that the time to read or modify this variable is very small compared with the duration of the task using it. Mutual exclusion is then very easily solved by briefly increasing the task priority during the access. This could be done by disabling the interrupt system, for example.

For bigger variables, and when the priority change may prevent timing constraints being respected, mutual exclusion can take place using the semaphore technique managed by a real-time executive.

-C- Access to complex variables

A variable is considered to be complex when it contains a large quantity of information. This could be, for example, files, centralized or possibly distributed databases.

Access must be such that the corresponding times respect the specifications and therefore, in particular, there is no interlocking or deadlock and privation.

Concurrent access is sometimes necessary to satisfy timing constraints. For a variable composed of disconnected objects, simultaneous access to these objects does not create a deadlock.

A complex variable can be structured into information levels. Each level is a collection of objects. Each object in level i is defined as a level i-1 collection. To access a level i object, simply exclude access to this object, thus preventing the use of all objects composing it down to the most elementary level. On the other hand, simultaneous access remains possible for objects at level i and higher.

In all cases, the conflict resolution algorithm must guarantee that privation does not occur.

-D- Port management

A port accumulates messages sent to it. Conversely, it provides a message to each request. In the most general case for a single port, several tasks can produce messages and several consumers can request messages. For implementation purposes, the port size is necessarily limited in the number of messages.

The software implementation must be such that:
- the message queue remains coherent at all times;
- the exchange takes place taking account of the number of messages in the port: producers locked if the port is full, consumers locked if there are no messages.

The technique consists of considering that a port is a shared variable. File consistency is respected by the use of access exclusion techniques. A port is thus implemented based on two mechanisms - synchronization and mutual exclusion.

-E- Events and messages processing

The implementation must also satisfy behavior rules defined for the Cycle and When statements.

For the Cycle statement, all received events and messages must be processed, and this implies storage. Sequences associated with each case must be executed in mutual exclusion.

For the When statement, several events or messages may be expected. Only one can be used and only the first which arrives. The others must be eliminated if they arrive later.

20.5.4 Error processing

In software, error processing introduces an added programming complexity. A programmer naturally tends to develop a satisfactory solution for normal cases. He then has to add all processing for so-called "marginal" cases and for errors related to the environment.

For instance, when an application requires a communication service, an error may appear at the lowest physical support level, for example a transmission error. The detected error rises through each individual level. A given level may be able to correct the error. If this is impossible, the error inevitably rises to the application level and must be processed here.

Some error procedures have to be solved by designers, other more technological errors must be processed by the implementation team.

Environment-related errors are related to system inputs and are therefore detectable at this level. According to Jackson, inputs can be classified into several categories [JACKSON-83]:

- Valid or invalid inputs. An input is valid if it complies with the specifications.

- True or false inputs. These two types form part of valid inputs. An input is true when it complies with the state expected by the entity which manages this variable, taking account of the action undertaken.

- Desired or mistaken true inputs. These inputs form part of true inputs. But an input may be a mistake and must therefore be eliminated.

Processing errors related to other inputs require the creation of an interpretation software layer to initially detect the nature of the error and then to take the associated action.

Invalid and unanticipated inputs must be signalled and eliminated. The design takes account of these cases if it is initially based on a model of entity behavior.

False inputs are a result of behavior errors of the entity generating the input information or of the interface (sensor).

It is not always easy to detect all these errors. In addition, the processing to be undertaken may lead to complex implementations since the application must never end up in an unsafe state.

20.6 INTEGRATION AND TEST

The objective of this final phase is to assemble all parts of the development in order to end up with an operational system complying with the customer's requirements.

The fully developed and tested software therefore has to be run on the hardware after the hardware has been fully tested. Integration therefore implies coherence of all developments.

Application verification and then validation are carried out incrementally using a bottom-up process:

- module tests
- subset tests
- global test and validation
- global certification.

Validation necessarily implies availability of the environment - machine, processes, etc. However, some processes may be either not available or are impossible to place in test conditions since they are too dangerous. Other methods should then be implemented in order to perform a simulation.

If the specification, design, implementation specification, hardware and software implementations were carried out conscientiously, errors detected at this stage should be minor and easily corrected. For more serious errors, larger loopbacks may be necessary.

Integration and testing require the use of tools used for hardware and software implementations. Development and instrumentation systems are associated for the overall test. Obviously, the two categories of implementation teams cooperate in carrying out this integration and the overall test. Errors may be due to either part, and possibly to a specific point which concerns both parts. A coherent method and understanding are therefore necessary conditions for success.

20.7 SOURCES OF ERRORS

The process proposed for the design is a gradual top-down process. All residual errors are detected at the end of the implementation stage and must inevitably be corrected.

The cost of correcting errors is approximately an exponential function of the time between when the error is generated and when it is detected.

Therefore, errors and omissions made during the implementation phase are still the easiest to be corrected since they do not affect previous steps. But if the implementation technology is expensive, consequences may be serious - for example, a non-operational ASIC or a printed-circuit board to be redesigned. Software errors are generally less expensive than hardware errors. However, a large number of errors, and possible incremental corrections to be made to software, can result in a very high cost which is difficult to control, and also difficult to blame on the implementation team who naturally blame the designers. Hardware developments are easily observed, but the same does not apply for software. Software is like an iceberg - the visible part can be checked, but the submerged part, representing most of the work, is difficult to estimate and check to deduce the stage of progress.

Design errors can affect the hardware solution. This type of error is particularly expensive, and special attention should be given to applications with very hard real-time constraints. They require the implementation of a complex and therefore expensive hardware solution.

Specification errors are also very expensive since they put the entire product development in question.

Therefore, rigorous work is essential in order to reduce all sources of errors. Thorough and detailed verifications must be undertaken after each step, if possible by persons other than the designers themselves (author/readers cycle). These verifications can only be based on documents produced during each step. This confirms the benefit of conscientiously following a methodology.

20.8 REFINEMENT DURING IMPLEMENTATION

Terms do not always mean the same thing to everyone, for example the ambiguity between requirements and specifications. Similarly, others may confuse implementation and design. We have tried to give a clear and unique meaning to terms used throughout the description of the methodology.

However, the implementation step uses specifications as input. We can therefore consider that the design step is intermediate between the specifications and a product when the transformation is not direct. The design work then consists of finding the strictly necessary internal functions to obtain the implementation. Each more elementary function is then expressed by an implementation specification. There is therefore no contradiction between implementation and design since the former may include the latter.

According to this analysis, the implementation work may be refined into three phases shown on the following figure:

- an implementation design phase;
- a parts implementation phase;
- an assembly, integration and test phase.

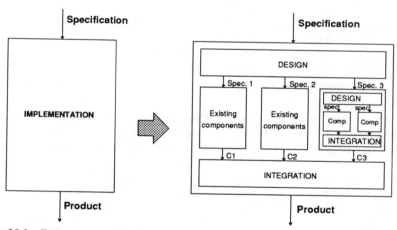

Figure 20.3   Refinement of the implementation work.

Each level thus restricts the technical field concerned by the implementation, and involves specification, design and implementation as shown Figure 20.3.

We will use this presentation and describe the activities for both implementation types, hardware and software in a little more detail.

20.8.1 Hardware implementation refinement

The specification for the hardware implementation level is the same as for the executive structure. The implementation of this part starts by design work to produce the assembly schematic and the specification of each component. It is followed by an implementation phase for each component, and then by the assembly and test phase. The implementation work is completed for all existing elements. Refinement must then be continued for others.

Consider two examples to illustrate this process for the hardware implementation.

First, consider the case of a microcomputer board with real-time signal processing functions. The executive structure includes a 68000 type 16-bit programmable processor and a specialized 16-bit 64 kHz fourth-order digital filtering processor.

Using the above procedure, the question must be asked of whether or not this type of dedicated processor exists, and if so, does it satisfy the economic criteria. If the answer is no, a solution must be found by decomposing the function. The MCSE methodology can then be used for the functional design, this time at the technological level and for a very specific problem class - that of digital filters. Recurrent equations can be used to deduce the algorithmic behavior for the filter. A functional structure is deduced from a suitable template model for this problem class - for example, the operative part/control part model described in the next chapter. The two parts must then be made, assembled and the whole product must be tested.

At this stage, implementation can make use of various technologies - classic components, MSI, specialized microprocessor type components, programmable logic devices, specific components (ASIC), etc.

For an ASIC, by using a silicon compiler, implementation refinement must be continued until a set of configurable blocks such as PLA, registers, adders, etc., can be used directly.

In the second case, an executive structure contains a dedicated processor called a power converter, which has the objective of outputting a sinusoidal 220 V AC voltage at 50 Hz with input from a set of batteries supplying 48 V. The available power must be 5 KW. The problem has to be divided into two problem classes in order to implement this function - the power electronics problem for the power structure and an industrial data processing problem for the power part control electronics. The control part is specified after characterization of the power part based on possible solutions. Control is then designed using a functional approach.

20.8.2 Software implementation refinement

For the software implementation level, the specification includes the software implementation and the task and module specifications. The implementation work for each software component is a function of the nature of the specification and the support used.

We will use two examples to illustrate this implementation field.

For the first case, the implementation is done in Pascal. All real-time tasks are defined by an algorithm written in Pascal and validated. The resulting implementation is automatically translated. In addition, there is a dialog management task for the application, specified by a module structure. The design work consists of using the structured programming method to decompose each module into procedures and functions in order to obtain a completely executable description by compilation. Procedures available in the operating system are themselves directly usable.

In the second case of a prototype, the implementation is to be made in Smalltalk, a particularly efficient language for prototyping. Starting from the specification, the necessary objects for the implementation and the interfaces between them have to be defined. Smalltalk has a large collection of all types of objects, and prototyping is fast because much of the development is obtained by the appropriate use of existing objects.

20.9 ADVANTAGE OF REUSE

As shown in the previous section, during implementation, the specification and design work must be continued until available components are found to satisfy the specifications, and consequently an attempt should be made to use existing components as soon as possible in order to reduce the total time required for a project.

This attitude is not necessarily economically the best for the application. It is desirable that components developed for an application may be used later in subsequent developments. This strategy is called "reusability".

If a component is reusable in other applications, it must be developed with a more global specification than just for the precise problem it was to solve.

Reusability for hardware has existed for several decades. More complex components are available on the market for implementations.

This point of view is more recent for software, but it will become essential in the future in order to reduce development costs and times. Chapter 22 describes this type of objective and a possible procedure.

20.10 SUMMARY

This chapter has described the precise meaning of the term "implementation" by describing its position in the application development cycle.

The main conclusions are summarized below:

- The implementation is a bottom-up process starting from available components and leading to an operational application validated and accepted by the customer.

- The implementation work is a function of the nature of the implementation specifications, the techniques to be used, and the available methods and tools.

- Since this step is predominant in a development, an effort must be made to reduce costs both in preceding steps and in this step.

- The implementation of a system involves three phases - first, becoming familiar with and accepting the specifications, and then the concurrent development of hardware and software implementations, and finally integration, testing and validation of the complete system.

- The hardware implementation consists of producing the application executive structure.

- The software implementation leads to obtain the functionality of the application by programming the processors of the executive structure.

- The integration phase checks the conformity of the various subsets with their specifications, and then the conformity of the entire application is checked.

- The implementation work depends on the variation between the specification of each function and available components useful for this function. The search for available components takes place by successive refinements of each specification through design work.

- The reusability of hardware or software components helps to reduce product development cost and time.

21

HARDWARE
IMPLEMENTATION TECHNIQUES

The previous chapter showed that the work involved in the implementation is a function of the gap between the executive structure specification and the components available for its implementation. When this gap exists, refinement is necessary during this step. This refinement suggests that a design be undertaken first of all for this implementation. Specifications of solution constituents will then be closer to specifications of available components.

Available components, possible techniques and technologies can be very varied. Technical and economic considerations partially included in the technological specifications will reduce the range of possibilities.

The purpose of this chapter is not to give an overview of possible solutions for hardware implementations, since this would be outside the scope of the methodology. However, since implementing well means firstly designing and then checking the solution, it would be useful to discuss the possible strategies and template models and the associated process. We thus show that the MCSE approach can be used for the design of hardware parts.

A summary is also made of the work and attitude similarities and differences between a traditional implementation approach using existing components and the approach of developing specific integrated components.

21.1 IMPLEMENTATION SEARCH METHOD

A hardware implementation is a result of a judicious association of physical components. The term judicious means that components should be selected to reduce the overall cost of the hardware part, respecting technological constraints such as component availability, reliability, reproduction cost, etc.

The association must also be such that interconnection rules and functional and electrical component specifications are respected.

Since a hardware implementation is a topological structure, the method of determining this structure is deduced from that proposed for functional design. The process to be followed is therefore as follows:

- analysis of specifications and search for characteristic variables and events;
- construction of the solution by assembling functions around selected variables and events;
- solution verification and summary of directly implementable parts.

This process can be reiterated in order to continue refinement of each function until existing components only are involved.

It must be constantly borne in mind that minimizing work for the implementation involves the use of existing components as quickly as possible. The search for functions must therefore facilitate finding these components. Implementation designers must necessarily be very familiar with available components, the reference, manufacturer, distributors and a brief specification.

With technological developments, there are more and more components which creates a problem if only to know of their existence. They are also more and more powerful, and more general in the sense that they are configurable without necessarily being qualified as programmable processors. For example, programmable logic devices or analog configurable filters. These configurable components can be used to reduce the variety of components necessary to undertake an implementation: for example, all digital functions can be implemented with a single type of sequential programmable logic device.

21.2 IMPLEMENTATION TECHNIQUES

In this section, we discuss two implementation techniques for systems - the exclusive use of existing components and the development of specific components when necessary.

21.2.1 Implementation with existing components

Conventionally, an implementation uses a set of existing components. For the electronic engineer or technician, this is the only solution since he is unable to manufacture the components he needs at a competitive cost.

Complex and, if possible, the configurable components facilitate his work: implementation of a wide variety of sequential functions with a PLD, implementation of transfer functions with an operational amplifier, signal generation with the PLL.

The cost of each implementation is defined by the cost of components and the support for the interconnections. The size and consumption are difficult to reduce due to the size of each package and interfaces for external couplings.

The designer of an implementation can use computer-aided engineering tools to help him in his work: schematic input, verification by simulation, support production by placing and routing a printed-circuit board.

This type of process is conventional and well known.

21.2.2 Development of specific components

More recently, a new technique has become available which consists of designing one's own components and then subcontracting their manufacture. These components are called Application Specific Integrated Circuits (ASICs).

There are several complementary reasons for this new development:

- this is the only technique which can satisfy consumption and size constraints;
- for a production run, integration reduces reproduction time and cost and reliability is improved;
- the design of integrated circuits is becoming more automated, such that it is possible to design them without being a microelectronics specialist;
- design tools, previously available to manufacturers only, are being more and more developed by third party companies and are accessible to implementers: realistic cost and expertise are fairly quickly acquired;
- the objective of manufacturers is to produce a maximum number of circuits. Hence the economic advantage for the founders of ASICs.

Despite the high cost of an integrated design and without forgetting the cost of errors, the integration technique has a good future. It is therefore useful to define methods and tools to be used at this point.

First, since an implementation is an association of more elementary components, does a good integration consist of going down to the basic components of transistors and diodes? It depends ....

The designer must always continue refining his solution until finding manufactured blocks available to him. This situation is then similar to that for analog components. In most cases, libraries of conventional digital or analog electronic functions are available. The adaptation work is then reduced and the tool is simple to use.

But when the basic blocks are at low level, for example transistors or gates, a great deal of design work is necessary and there is a large risk of errors. In addition, applications with high constraints, particularly requiring high performance, require the use of recent technology which is not yet available to implementers. The design must then be continued to the level of basic integrated structures. In this case, electronic and microelectronic ability is essential for success.

ASICs are now possible, at least for medium series (greater than 500 or 1000 parts), with a fairly low investment in expertise acquisition time. There is little time for design and for producing parts, since customized circuit design tools are construction-based on fairly high level functional blocks, or using a library of functions identical to the components used for a conventional implementation.

For example, a design tool for gate arrays and standard cells makes most commonly used digital SSI and MSI functions available to designers: gates, bistables, counters, multiplexers, adders, etc.

As another example, consider a silicon compiler, thus named because it is capable of producing mask drawings for manufacture, making use of the technology based on block specifications. This type of design tool makes a set of configurable blocks such as PLA, RAM, ROM, counters, arithmetic and logical units, clocks, input and output pads, buffers, etc., available to implementers.

Designing a circuit with this type of tool is equivalent to describing the selected blocks, their specifications and interconnections. Based on this data and the technical characteristics of the founder, a compiler produces masks for each block, positions the blocks, creates the routing between the blocks and input and output pins.

Design criteria differ somewhat from those used in conventional technology. The cost objective is to reduce the area of silicon, and since not all manufactured components will work, it must be possible to test them efficiently. For these reasons, the structures to be used are slightly modified to improve testability.

The first production run is expensive (if a mask is necessary). But is there a guarantee that it will work well? Design tools include verification methods to satisfy this question.

The first tool available to the designer is a simulator which allows him to test and functionally validate each block step by step and then the entire circuit. Additional tools are available to verify times and that the simulator takes proper account of integration parameters such as capacitors, loads, interconnection lengths, etc.

Prototyping is thus no longer necessary. However, the circuit is necessarily modeled to allow its simulation.

In conclusion, the ability to design specific integrated components is identical to that for conventional technology, since the designer uses approximately the same functional blocks. The main difference lies in the validation technique. With the conventional technique using discrete components, implementation involves the development of an incrementally built and tested prototype. Errors are quickly corrected at lower cost. Using the integration technique, prototyping is no longer possible. The complete design is computerized, verification is made by simulation and is the designer's responsibility.

Two types of tests are necessary and are extremely important: the functional test to check that the circuit which will be produced will satisfy the functionalities, and the manufacturing test which will discriminate between good and bad components. The next section will describe the objective of these tests.

21.3 VERIFICATION AND VALIDATION OF AN IMPLEMENTATION

An implementation is developed to satisfy an objective. The logical sequence is therefore objective, specification, design, implementation, production. Two questions have to be asked about this logical progression:

1. At the end, does the implementation conform with the objective to be achieved ?
2. Since any reproduction can introduce errors, how can correct products be identified ?

These two problems are illustrated in Figure 21.1.

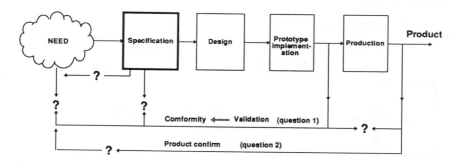

Figure 21.1   Development sequence and validation.

An implementation (prototype or production line product) is said to conform if its functionality satisfies the required objectives. Validation is the action of checking this conformity.

The prototype is validated by a functional test. When the prototype conforms, each item on the production line is validated by a manufacturing test. We will describe the meaning of each of these tests and procedure to be followed.

21.3.1 Functional test

In the MCSE methodology terminology, an objective is not a formal description. Only the specification deduced from it can be formalized. Validation can therefore only take place when compared with the specification. Obviously, it is always possible that a non-conforming product will be obtained due to the specification non-conforming with the objective. Unfortunately, some risk of error remains since these errors are not observable.

To validate the implementation, it has to be operated by applying a sequence of electrical actions. It must be possible to deduce its conformity by observing its evolution. But the observed variation is intimately dependent on the action sequence selected. If this is wrong or incomplete, the observation will be wrong or incomplete, and consequently conformity will also be false.

Therefore, correct validation requires that the test procedure, and particularly the necessary test sequences, be developed in addition to the design. This work is the responsibility of the designer and not the implementer, since a solution which cannot be tested is bad.

Does a prototype necessarily have to be made to guarantee conformity? Not necessarily. Before the existence of simulation tools, a hardware prototype was necessary. It is now possible to develop a "virtual" prototype as a model on computer. The advantages are to be able to validate the design and to develop a test procedure. Testability can then be analyzed. When the solution by simulation has been validated, a prototype is made and checked using the same test procedure.

This process is shown in Figure 21.2.

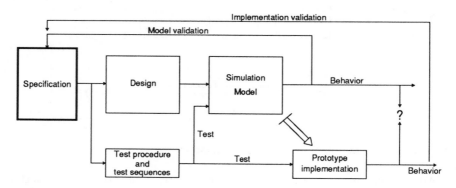

Figure 21.2   Design-validation procedure.

This figure shows that when a model is available, the prototype can be validated by comparing its behavior with the behavior of the model, both under the action of the same test sequence.

A simulation model is not essential. It is justified by an economic cost evaluation. Is validation less expensive by simulation with a good guarantee or by building a prototype?

When using the conventional implementation technique, the prototype is often preferable. However, the simulation technique is only realistic for an integrated component, due to the high cost of the manufacturing process.

21.3.2 Manufacturing test

The purpose of this test is to identify conforming products from the production line. This can be done by comparing with a prototype that conforms rather than checking against the specifications.

Non-conformities, due to production defects or defective components, will be demonstrated by the previous functional test. However, a complete functional test may be particularly expensive in time and resources, especially for cards or complex circuits. Simply imagine the case of a digital signal processing board or a microprocessor component.

The objective of the production test is to use a small number of observations to check that all internal elements behave correctly. For a digital integrated circuit, this means that all nodes in the circuit change state. A different test is developed with the objective of generating and observing all state changes, and comparing them with observations on the prototype for the same sequence. This test can be carried out by placing the implementation in a different situation from the functional test, for example opening the loop of a finite state machine.

An implementation may not be completely testable for two reasons - inputs cannot modify all internal nodes, even with a very long sequence (controllability), and outputs cannot observe node state changes (observability). We then talk about the fault coverage rate of an implementation test.

Again, the designer is responsible for developing an implementation with the largest possible test coverage and the shortest possible sequence.

The manufacturing test procedure is shown in Figure 21.3.

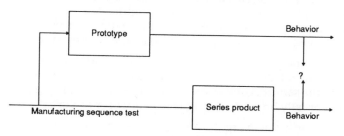

Figure 21.3   Procedure for the manufacturing test.

By combining the two previous figures for validation by simulation, we can see that the manufacturing test sequence can be developed on the model. If this model is realistic enough, the degree of confidence may be such that the prototype implementation can be eliminated. This procedure is used for integrated circuits, obviously knowing that a pre-production batch is made to check functional conformity.

21.4 REUSABILITY FOR HARDWARE

In Chapter 20, we saw that implementation times can be reduced by reusing existing structures. This procedure is visible for hardware. Component manufacturers are gradually making more complex components available to implementers, used simply from knowledge of their specifications. Components developed perform the most frequently required functions for implementations.

The more general a component is, the more it can be used in different applications and hence its economic advantage for manufacturers. The microprocessor is a particularly typical example, and in MCSE we have considered it as the component fulfilling the programmable processor function. The operational amplifier and the PLL are other examples in analog electronics.

Reusability will only be possible if implementers are aware of available components. This competence is acquired slowly and gradually and must constantly be updated. This type of knowledge is facilitated by template models since they provide an analysis guide and a component classification guide based on their specifications.

Does the development of integrated circuits facilitate reusability? Yes and no.

No, since each designer may wish to develop his own circuit, thinking that it will be better than existing circuits. Even at the block level, he may not consider functional blocks already built and which are the property of his company. This tendency already exists in software, and is quite possible for ASICs. A design tool is a fairly individual tool which also hides the designed and unmaterialized object. For these reasons, if there are no constraints, the tendency for individual development is quite realistic. To prevent this, safeguards must be implemented by an information, project coordination and development monitoring policy, similar to a quality insurance policy.

Yes, since if the previously described situations are avoided, each designer develops blocks which can then, after validation, be made available to other designers in the same organization. If these blocks have an even wider interest, they can eventually be made available to every user of the CAE tool.

In this way, in a single organization, after developing a microprocessor core and a set of functional peripheral blocks, a very complex circuit can quickly be developed by combining available functionalities. Understood in this way and if objectives are defined carefully, reusability is an essential economic gain factor.

As shown in the next section, using template models facilitates this reusability strategy; for example, we could consider that the microcontroller core which is a programmable processor is the most highly developed hardware template model.

21.5 TEMPLATE MODELS FOR IMPLEMENTATION

Since implementing from an executive structure may require some initial design work, we will use the same concepts here as for the functional design. Designing is a creative process. The designer's ability is also an important factor influencing the nature of the result. In order to refine a function, the specification has to be analyzed to deduce the essential and strictly necessary internal elements by searching for variables in preference to functions.

Another complementary method would be to make use of template solution models capable of leading to a quality and a solution that is easy to build. A template model thus reduces the analysis work by facilitating deduction of the essential elements.

In order to illustrate the advantage of this type of model, we will describe two template models below, particularly suitable for the design of digital functions. This base is very useful for board and integrated component designers who must search for the solution architecture.

A lot of development work still remains to be done in all electronic fields to bring out essential template structures, in order to improve implementation quality and work using the models. This type of structure probably exists in these fields but is perhaps not clearly visible to designers, probably for presentation reasons. We are thinking at least of the analog electronic, transmission, power electronics and signal processing fields.

To illustrate the benefit of a template model, the next section describes Moore's machine as a typical digital architecture example. This machine structure is a very old template model for the implementation of any sequential function. Its advantage at the present time is that configurable components conform with this model exist (programmable logic devices), and that tools exist for translating directly from a specification (equation, finite state diagram), to PLD programming.

If this design model is not known, the advantage of logic arrays is reduced and consequently associated production tools. Why not think how this type of template model in analog electronics would be of considerable benefit to electronics people.

21.6 THE MOORE'S MACHINE MODEL

21.6.1 The principle

G.H. Mealy and E.F. Moore, two pioneers in the design of digital sequential systems, proposed a mathematical formulation in the 1950s to express the solution of any sequential function [FLETCHER-80].

$$Xt+1 = F(Xt, Et)$$

$$Yt = G(Xt, Et)$$

where:

- Et	the input vector;
- Xt	the state vector at the current time;
- Yt	the output vector;
- F and G	two combinational functions.

This formulation defines the method to be used to solve a sequential problem. If all states of X are known (first design work), the sequential problem then leads to two combinational problems since F and G have to be found.

The above equations are equivalent to an implementation structure called the Mealy's machine. Using the terms considered, four structures are produced by degeneration, as shown in Figure 21.4.

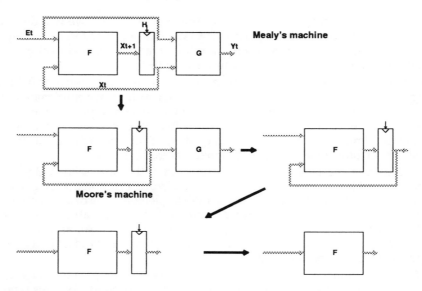

Figure 21.4   Implementation structures based on Mealy's machine.

The latter two structures in the figure correspond only to combinational functions, which are thus presented as special cases of the general model.

The essential difference between Mealy's machine and Moore's machine is that the outputs Yt for the first are asynchronous with Xt since they are directly dependent on Et.

In digital electronics, asynchronous problems are much more difficult to solve. To induce solution quality and simplify the solution search task, it is recommended that synchronous solutions only be considered whenever possible. Therefore, we consider that the Moore's machine is more suitable for the design of sequential structures.

21.6.2 The model

Since Moore's structure is more suitable for designing any sequential function, it is a template solution model. An additional advantage is that programmable logic devices (PLDs) comply technologically with Moore's structure. Therefore, every sequential function can be implemented in a given

PLD if its design allows it. Another advantage is that tools exist for translating a specification into a program and simulating its behavior for verification purposes.

The template functional model induced by Moore's machine and the corresponding implementation structure are shown in Figure 21.5.

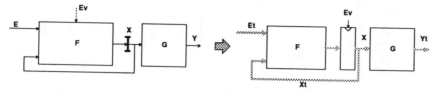

Figure 21.5   Moore's template model and its implementation.

The variable X is translated into a register Y. The event Ev defines X and therefore Y evolution times (operation synchronous with EV). The event Ev may not exist. F is then a continuous action evaluating X_{t+1} at all times. This corresponds to a transparent or non-existing register X. This is the case of an asynchronous sequential machine which should not be used for subjacent hazard problems.

21.6.3 Method

The design method is deduced from the model. The starting point is a knowledge of the internal state vector. The procedure is therefore as follows:

- search for the state variable X strictly necessary to satisfy the specification;
- define the two functions F and G;
- check the solution against the specifications;
- transform the solution into an implementation: encode states of X, and then deduce equations of F and G.

This procedure conforms with the proposed functional design method, and in this case the model helps to find the essential variables to solve the problem initially.

The most appropriate specification model for this method is the finite state machine.

When the specification is more complex - Petri net, Grafcet with concurrency, statechart - it must first be transformed into a finite state diagram, initially with a maximum number of diagrams equal to the degree of parallelism in the specification. Simplifications may appear, and in this case the specification should preferably be transformed before searching for a solution, see Figure 21.6.

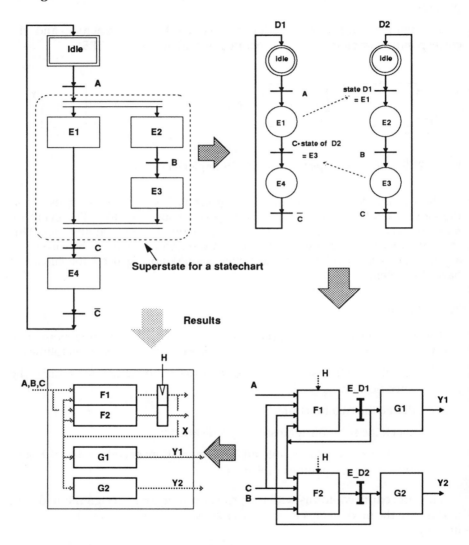

Figure 21.6   Procedure for the design of a sequential function.

A sequential machine thus corresponds to each diagram. The global solution is a result of an interconnection of these machines with coupling through their state variables. The following example illustrates this procedure. The specification is a Grafcet with parallelism. A statechart is also possible. It is translated into two coupled automatons. Moore's model can then be used leading to the hardware solution.

For a specification with concurrency, it may sometimes be possible to avoid decomposition into several sequential diagrams. This is done by attempting to transform the Grafcet with concurrency into sequential Grafcets. This is possible for the above example by separating E1 into two substates E'1 and E'2, with B as transition condition. This preliminary specification transformation work forms part of the analysis which precedes the design.

21.7 THE CONTROL/EXECUTION MODEL

The scope of the previous model is limited to fairly simple cases for which actions associated with states are of the logic type. When it is difficult to express the specification by a finite state machine or a statechart, it is preferable to use an algorithmic type specification. This type of model is still sequential, but actions and conditions may be complex (calculations, comparison, etc.).

Order relations may also be complex. A more general template model is therefore necessary.

21.7.1 Principle

Since the early days of computers, Turing and Von Neumann in particular have demonstrated that every algorithm can be executed by a sequential memory machine with a program and data memory. The structure of most sequential computers follows on from this concept. The structure analysis of processing machines shows that they are based on the association of the two parts - an operative part and a control part. The operative part, commonly called the "datapath",stores data (memory, registers) and transforms data by specialized operators (addition, multiplication, offset, etc.). The control part decides upon transformations to be made by the operative part and determines times at which storage is performed by the operative part.

The corresponding general structure is described in Section 21.7.

Referring to the equations for Mealy's machine, this model assumes that vectors Et and Yt are decomposed into two categories: data and events, and that functions F and G vary as a function of time to define the role of the operative part. The variation of F and G is frozen during design of a programmed machine and can be modified at any time for a programmable machine by instructions.

The vector of observations made on X can be reduced to the conditions useful for the control part alone. These observations are called indicators (flags).

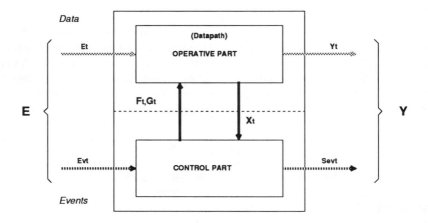

Figure 21.7   General structure for a sequential processor.

21.7.2 Model

The general structure described in the previous section has been used as a guide for data-processing machine architects for more than 40 years and is a type of template model. We call this type of model a control/execution model and the structure is of the master/slave type. This structure can also be compared with the supervision/control template model described in the design part (see Section 16.3). Although both models share the same concept, they are not at the same level:

- the supervision/control model is at a high level (application level) since it is a functional model and is very oriented towards process control type applications;

- the control/execution model is at the most elementary (architectural and technological) level, suitable for the development of hardware solutions.

The functional template model is as described in Figure 21.8.

Inputs E are separated into two parts: Ed for data and Ec for external events considered to be observable digital variables. Similarly, there are two types of outputs: Sd for data and Sc for actions translated by variables or events.

There are also two types of actions from the execution part specified by CMD: states, for example to designate the operation type, and events to define action times. Observations necessary for decision making are transmitted by IND.

The specifications for the control part are defined once and for all for the implementation of dedicated processors. The clock event C acts on the control part and defines variation times: taking account of inputs and CMD changes.

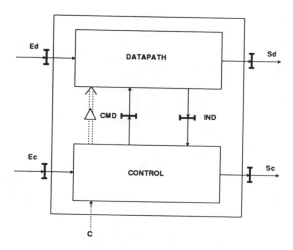

Figure 21.8   Control/execution template model.

This template model facilitates decomposition by encouraging the search for the essential variables or events which are Ed, Sd, Ec, Sc, CMD and IND. The two parts can then be refined to define internal components as described in the following sections.

-A- Refinement of the execution part

This part is responsible for carrying out required transformations on variables Ed, storing variables for subsequent use, and generating output information. The internal structure is deduced from an analysis of the specification in the form of a data-flow graph. The necessary internal variables are extracted from this graph, together with transformation operations. Internal and output variables are obtained by passing through the transformation operators and then storage following a command. This leads to the data-path structure.

The execution part can thus be represented by a functional structure, composed solely of internal variables and transformation functions, driven by control events. The constituents of this functional structure correspond to physical elements - registers or memories for variables, operators for functions, data paths for function <--> variable links, control signals for events.

The following example shows the functional structure for the operative part of a processing unit, and a translation (datapath) in accordance with a hardware structure organized around a bus.

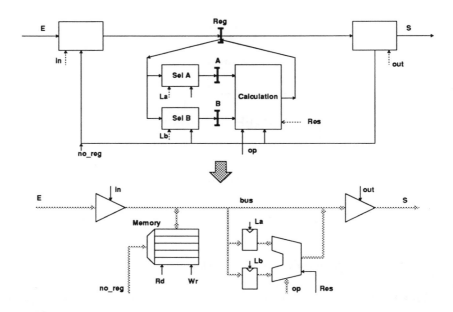

Figure 21.9   Decomposition example for the execution part .

The variable Reg is translated as a memory. The architecture is built around a bus. The CMD variables are No_Reg and Op, whereas the CMD signals are: Rd, Wr, La, Lb, Res, In, Out.

The model based on decomposition into variables and transformation operators is called the operative model. When the design of the execution part is completed, it is possible to deduce the specification of the control part, essential to satisfy the overall specification. This specification is often described in the form of a state diagram.

-B- Refinement of the control part

The control part synchronous with a clock event C produces outputs CMD and Se based on observations IND and Ec. Since this is a sequential model specified by a state diagram, it can be designed using Moore's model. The above template model can therefore be used for refinement.

Depending on the complexity of control specifications - number of states, order relations, conditions, even action concurrency, decomposition may justify the use of several coupled sequential machines. For example, when the state diagram is complicated and includes sequential branches, decomposition may induce one sequential machine for branch control and another for sequence control. This then leads to the following solution in Figure 21.10.

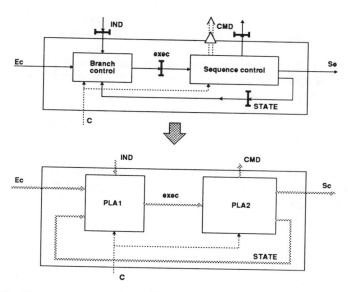

Figure 21.10   Decomposition example for the control part.

The two PLAs are sequential; they include the register corresponding to the EXEC and STATE variables respectively.

21.7.3 Method

The template model induces the design method. Firstly, the necessary internal variables have to be found, followed by the transformation operators to produce these variables. The interface between the two parts is then deduced. The procedure is as follows:

- Design of the execution part:
    - data-flow diagram,
    - search for internal variables,
    - search for transformations and specification,
    - interface specification,
    - translation to a technological solution.
- Design of the control part:
    - control specification starting from the execution part as its environment,
    - structure selection,
    - design of each sequential machine,
    - translation into a technological solution.

The most appropriate specification model for this method complying with the principles of functional design is an algorithmic description.

The data-flow analysis follows on naturally from the specification since the algorithm uses variables and arithmetic, comparison and assignment operators. The datapath structure necessary to carry out all operations in the algorithm must be deduced from this analysis. This structure can be optimized to reduce the necessary elements: for example, use of a common bus for several transfers. This optimization is carried out during the translation phase into a technological solution taking account of timing constraints.

Specification of the control part responsible for sequencing operations is deduced by replacing operations by control actions or observations. It is then translated into a finite state diagram to subsequently deduce the most appropriate structure.

To reduce the implementation time, we have seen that we must try to reuse existing structures. As a move in this direction, integrated circuits also exist for each part in the control/execution template model which have:

- a general data-path structure including a set of registers, an arithmetic and logic unit, counters, etc.;

- programmable universal sequencers.

Slice processors are the oldest illustrative examples (AMD 2901, 2903). The use of this technology justifies severe performance constraints which cannot be obtained with the more general microprocessor model.

The above described procedure can be directly applied for the design of ASICs and dedicated processors. At the present time, this work must be carried out by designers. The objective of silicon compiler research work, and particularly in architectural or high-level synthesis, is to develop automatic architecture production tools down to the implementation starting from an algorithmic specification. These tools are based on both the template models described above.

21.8 SUMMARY

This chapter described implementation techniques and methods for the hardware part of an application. An implementation normally requires an initial design phase. Two template models suitable for the implementation of digital systems were described in order to illustrate the design procedure to be followed, respecting the functional design principles.

Described for the design of dedicated processors, the process presented is also applicable, if necessary, for the design of programmable processors.

This chapter is far from being complete and does not satisfy all classes of functions such as analog electronics, power electronics, etc. It is particularly oriented towards digital electronics, although this does represent most hardware developments at the present time. Obviously, other models and methods will have to be prepared for other fields to encourage acquisition of competence and synthesis work for designers.

The main points mentioned in this chapter were:
- An implementation is the result of a refinement process which involves design at each level until reaching existing usable components.
- The solution is far from being unique. Economic criteria, depending on the quantity to be produced, must be taken into account in selecting the best technology.
- Two opposing implementation techniques may be used: implementation based on existing components, and the development of specific integrated components. Design methods and techniques are very similar. However, implementation and validation methods are very different. Economic criteria control the strategy to be followed.
- Reducing costs involves reusability, regardless of the implementation development strategy, and the organization must encourage this reusability.
- Template models facilitate the solution search during the decomposition work. Components are equivalent to template models for hardware, simplifying the implementation task.
- The implementation team leader has a big responsibility: implementation quality and long life, choice of components to reduce reproduction costs, evolution and reusability policy, etc.
- Validation to ensure conformity is essential; the designer is responsible for developing the implementation to satisfy this objective and for validation procedures.

22

SOFTWARE IMPLEMENTATION TECHNIQUES

Software development takes up an increasingly large part of the total implementation time due to several complementary reasons. Some of them are: the increased performance of the hardware thus making a software solution possible instead of a hardware development, secondly the considerable increase in requested functionalities, and finally the development flexibility possible using software.

Discussing the "software crisis", many authors [ABBOTT-86, M. JONES-88, FREEMAN-87, BOOCH-83, -86, COX-85, etc.] agree that growth in software production remains linear whereas growth in hardware is exponential. More detailed analyses by M. Jones have shown that of all software developed in 1983, probably less than 15% is unique, new and specific to an application. The remaining 85% is used to adapt these applications on computers.

This chapter is intended for software developers. It does not attempt to cover the software engineering field. This book is especially intended for designers and developers of real-time applications, and these industrial computing specialists are probably more electronics-oriented than computing-oriented. Consequently, it is useful to show how software engineering methods and techniques can produce a significant improvement in cost and quality. The objective is to position the various techniques currently available to develop efficiently the software part of a real-time application. The starting point is the software implementation specification with the constraint of running on hardware support developed elsewhere.

This chapter particularly emphasizes that developments must make executive support functionalities evolve towards applications by creating more abstract levels for reuse, rather than systematically conforming to hardware support constraints for all projects.

Real-time high-level languages, real-time executives and object-oriented programming are techniques for reducing the gap between the functional level and the executive support, at the same time encouraging reusability. Knowledge of these techniques proves to be necessary since they have a significant effect on the application development cost.

22.1 FUNCTIONALITY LEVELS AND PROCEDURES

The functional design step of the MCSE methodology results in the development of a so-called functional solution, and one of its main characteristics is that it is independent of the technology and therefore of the executive support. The software part dealt with in this chapter is deduced during the implementation specification step. Therefore, the executive support is an imposed constraint for the software implementation based on a set of technical and economic constraints.

Note that the hardware support may be chosen as a function of the development technique used for the software. The development time and reproduction costs influence the cost of the project, but their importance depends on the number of copies produced.

Therefore, the various possible processes and functionality levels are described in the following sections in order to make all decision elements available.

22.1.1 Functionality levels

Known data for the software development includes the following:

- as specification, the detail description of the software part with the software implementation diagram;
- as constraint, the hardware support consisting of one or several programmable processors.

These two realities are completely opposed. The functional solution is specific to an application and can only be used for this application. However, computer support is potentially capable of satisfying a wide variety of applications, but no application works without adding complementary information in the form of software programs. This difference is illustrated by Figure 22.1.

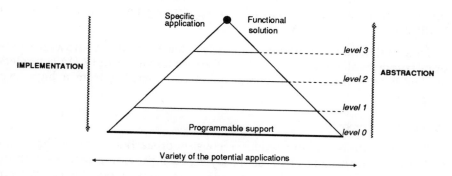

Figure 22.1   Differentiation between two realities.

Considering the gap between these two aspects, it is easy to see the advantage of intermediate levels. Each level is a lower level abstraction made up of a set of services facilitating the development of a specific application, but limiting the possible variety of applications and probably also reducing performances.

For example, consider the case of real-time executives (or real-time kernels). The software layer implemented on a programmable microprocessor support facilitates the implementation of a multi-task application. Task management procedures reduce real-time performance as a result of task switching times, and also because the processor interrupt mechanism is no longer accessible, thus limiting possibilities.

The end result of the software development is to obtain the running of each special application on a programmable support. Potential implementation processes are deduced from this presentation.

22.1.2 Implementation processes

We will consider the case of a specific application and a given programmable support. To fill the gap between the two realities, the two opposed procedures are the top-down procedure, and the bottom-up procedure starting from the support up to the application.

-A- Top-down procedure

The top-down sequence is used to develop all necessary layers by successive refinements. Each layer corresponds to a given abstraction level and the objective is to provide services necessary for the higher level(s). Useful services in the lower level are deduced by analyzing the specifications for each level. The best known normal method is structured programming for programs, whereas the Structured Design method is more suitable for the development of a set of programs. Searching for services is well controlled since the hardware possibilities are well known.

The top-down procedure requires design work (searching for program and service structures) and a level by level programming development down to the hardware.

Note that the transformation from a given level directly to hardware can be done automatically if tools exist. This is the case for Pascal and ADA compilers, etc., with cross-compilers to obtain object code starting from a high level language.

-B- Bottom-up procedure

The opposite bottom-up sequence consists of starting from the hardware and building up a hierarchical set of layers, each providing services with the objective of facilitating the application implementation. Services thus developed can then be used for other applications, which is useful for reducing development times. As a result, more complex problems can be dealt with when more abstract levels are available.

However, for the objective of a specific application, it is obvious that starting from the programmable support, the features of each level and consequently developments will be very much greater than those strictly necessary to implement the application. Consequently, development time, and therefore the resulting cost, will be significantly higher. This procedure can only be justified if the development can then be reused for other applications.

To compare these two extreme procedures, the top-down process is efficient for each application since it considers only the essentials in a systematic development down to the support, but introduces a loss of efficiency for a series of projects.

The bottom-up procedure requires a longer term investment since it creates reusable service levels. Less efficient, and therefore not particularly good for a given application, it is useful for a set of products by reducing the gap between the application and the support once and for all. Improvement in development techniques and tools is a result of a global bottom-up approach, which can only be slow.

-C- Mixed procedure

The two procedures are not at all exclusive. On the contrary, it is more realistic to consider them as complementary and that there is an intermediate level consisting of services useful for the class of applications dealt with. Figure 22.2 illustrates the three types of situation.

The mixed procedure consists of carrying out a top-down procedure starting from the application to demonstrate the necessary services and to make the best use, as quickly as possible, of services already developed. Development times are lower for a high number of service levels.

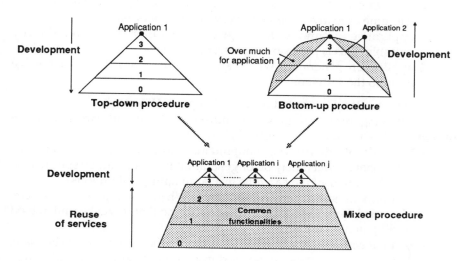

Figure 22.2   Top-down and bottom-up procedures, reusability.

This analysis for software can be compared with the existing situation for the hardware. It is no longer economically possible to develop a hardware system down to the basic component level of the transistor (to be compared with the software instruction). Hardware implementations are based on very complex components which can be used because they are made available by manufacturers. These components are the result of a slow bottom-up advance, a synthesis of developments which lead to technological evolution. Long-term investment facilitates reusability leading to a geometric progression of developments.

A hardware designer, even if he feels that a component is not very efficient, is constrained to use it since it is the only viable economic solution. However, each programmer can write and rewrite procedures with software developed by his colleagues and even by himself since these products are abstract and difficult to measure.

22.2 REUSABILITY FOR SOFTWARE

The above analysis showed that the use of services structured into abstraction levels can reduce the development time for an application. The initial motivation is therefore economic.

According to Freeman [FREEMAN-87], reusability is an activity. For software development, it refers to any procedure using all or part of a prior development. Reuse concerns several levels in the development process:

     1. procedures and modules in the form of executable code, referred to as software components;

2. services collections for satisfying a functional objective. For example, real-time executive, operating system, compilers, etc.;

3. applicative programs, for a given application field and directly reusable. This is the case for program packages;

4. application generators which are configured based on knowledge input to the software.

We are particularly interested in levels 1 and 2 in this chapter.

The following problems must be addressed if the software reusability concept is to become a reality, [HOROWITZ-87]:

- **Methods of identifying components.** How can we determine the components which may be of general interest and can be specified so that they are useful by anyone in a large number of projects?

- **Methods of specifying components.** When a component has been identified, how to prepare its description so that it will be understood by all potential users?

- **Form of components.** In what form should these components be made available so that they can be used in different environments (different operating systems, processors, programming languages)?

- **Component catalog.** How can users become aware of existing components?

A direct analogy can be made with hardware components. The above four points are satisfied. Each designer still has to read about and keep up to date with new products in order to know about and make the best use of components on the market.

For software, if there is too much work involved in combining components, or if it requires special skills, the potential advantage of reusability disappears and the programmer will prefer to develop the components that he needs himself. This is impossible for hardware components. The spirit of reusability and knowledge of components is developed by studying categories and specifications, properties for each [COX-85].

Since 1980, reusability has become the key word for software developments. However many problems related to methodology, organization, strategy, teaching methods, etc., remain to be solved.

The following sections show a few techniques for reusability and useful for real-time applications.

22.3 DEVELOPMENT PRINCIPLES

A software development must satisfy:

- specifications deduced from the functional design work and the implementation specification step;

- quality criteria to respect objectives imposed by quality assurance and to improve the product life cycle.

Quality criteria result in the definition of software object characteristics. These characteristics follow on from the design and development principles [ABBOTT-85].

22.3.1 Qualities

The following qualities are normally mentioned as being essential (Abbott, Tonies, M. Jones, Booch, etc.):

- **Usefulness.** The software satisfies the objective expressed by the customer. This quality depends on the suitability of the specifications to explain the objective and then the product conformity for these specifications.

- **Efficiency.** The software is optimally operational with available resources. Resources used are those imposed and are sufficient for the problem. Performances and all temporal constraints are satisfied.

- **Reliability.** The product objective is satisfied under all circumstances. Qualifying terms used are correct, robust and fault-tolerant.

- **Maintainability:** the software is written to facilitate error corrections, modifications and improvements or developments. This quality is essential, since the maintenance cost is very high, up to 70% of the total product cost has been reported.

- **Portability:** this criterion is for quickly implementing any software development onto other hardware.

22.3.2 Characteristics

In order to satisfy the preceding quality objectives, Abbott recommends two essential characteristics for the software:

- **Understandability.** Software understandability makes it easier to determine if it satisfies the objective (usefulness), checks its robustness (reliability), and makes changes (maintainability). It leads to a global cost decrease.

- **Reusability:** the software is developed based on existing components and its development generates other components used by others. The behavior of existing components is well known (reliability). They are well documented (understandability) and economic.

22.3.3 Principles

Starting from the above two characteristics, Abbott states two essential principles for software design:

- **Abstraction**: abstraction consists of creating a sufficiently simplified representation for a more complex reality. Abstraction leads to the design of levels between the application and the executive support. It satisfies both understandability and reusability.

- **Encapsulation**: encapsulation is grouping all design and implementation decisions for a given function into a single unit (module, object, etc.). By definition, a module which forms a logical entity has high internal cohesion and its intermodule coupling is low. Moreover, internal characteristics are not visible to the user. The hidden information principle is another way of expressing encapsulation. The specification and implementation are thus completely separated.

Abstraction and encapsulation lead to modularity. A modular program is broken down into specific modules, each of which carries out a specific function. A collection of modules can be used to build an abstraction.

Apart from the term "module" which has been used for several decades and is therefore ambiguous, other preferred and more recent terms are used to designate entities resulting from the use of abstractions and encapsulation principles:

- package in ADA;
- software component [ABBOTT-86, COX-85];
- object [BOOCH-83,86, ROSEN-87], in Smalltalk and derivatives.

22.4 TECHNIQUES FOR INDUSTRIAL DATA PROCESSING APPLICATIONS

After describing the development procedure and principles, the objective is to describe techniques available for software development for real-time applications.

Software specifications were determined during the implementation specification step. They consist of the software implementation diagrams and specifications for each constituent: tasks and modules. We will therefore mention all methods and techniques which can be used for the software development in order to make the application operational. Two categories of techniques are considered:

- Techniques for raising the functionality level of the executive support. These techniques tend to reduce the development time.

- Techniques for improving understandability and reusability.

We will consider three solution categories for techniques to improve the functionality level:

- the use of a real-time executive;
- the use of a real-time language (ADA and OCCAM);
- the use of a set of services complying with the functional model.

Figure 22.3 compares solution categories.

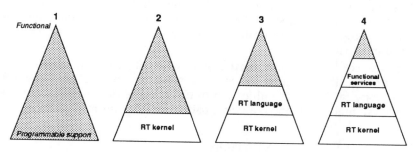

Figure 22.3   Development cost comparison for 4 solutions.

Starting from the top which represents the software specification, the development work for each application is represented by the area in grey.

For a given application, solution 4 is apparently the best when considering the development time criterion. However, we should not conclude that it is the only realistic solution. The following table gives an idea of the costs for each solution, and the circumstances in which it may be used.

	Development cost	Reproduction cost	Applications categories
Solution 1	fairly important	nul	small applications heavy constraints
Solution 2	medium	executive	medium
Solution 3	medium	executive	medium and complex
Solution 4	fairly low	executive+services	medium and complex

Solution 1 is interesting because the number of tasks is low. The software implementation technique described in Part 5 leads to a implementation diagram under interrupts and with a background task. This solution gives the best real-time performances.

Solution 2 is used with a standard C or Pascal language. It is justified for an application consisting of a few dozen tasks and which are evolutive.

Solution 3 consists of using directly a language and its real-time executive.

Solution 4 is identical to the previous solution, but also with a set of reusable services complying with the functional model.

The four solutions are described in the following sections.

Structured programming is the most frequently used technique facilitating understandability and reusability. Well known today, this technique should not be compared with the use of a structured programming language (Pascal, ADA). A program can be written in Pascal without respecting structured programming rules.

We are concerned here particularly with objects and object-oriented programming. In particular, it is interesting to observe that the MCSE methodology facilitates identification of objects. The object technique is thus presented in this document as a very positive strategy for reusability.

22.5 DIRECT IMPLEMENTATION

A conventional programmable processor can only execute one task at a time. Without additional software, only the interrupt mechanism can preempt the processor for the execution of higher priority tasks.

Using the interrupt system only, the technique described in Part 5 dealing with the implementation specification can carry out a set of tasks. The background task plays the role of monitor for processor sharing.

This very simple technique gives good performances since it produces the lowest switching times. It is only realistic for fairly simple dedicated applications. This probably represents about 80% of microprocessor system developments. This tendency will continue to increase with technological advances and the geographic distribution of functionalities. For a medium or complex application, it may be preferable to use several microcomputers rather than attempt to group everything onto a single more powerful computer.

Based on a set of simple implementation rules, the recommended method for software implementation is useful to know and to use because it leads to an implementation with a zero software reproduction cost. It is particularly suitable for 8 and 16 bit microprocessor-based applications and microcontrollers. It also minimizes the organizational part thus reducing development times.

22.6 USE OF A REAL-TIME EXECUTIVE

For larger applications, which have to operated on a single programmable processor, it is better to use a real-time executive to manage scheduling of all tasks. This solution is justified particularly for evolutionary applications: evolution of the functional solution, or when tasks have to be dynamically created.

The real-time executive is a software layer added to the programmable processor to allow management of a real-time application [BEN-ARI-86].

Each task has a priority or deadline. A scheduling process takes charge of allocating a processor to the highest priority task depending on the criterion used - priority or deadline. Scheduling by priority is the most commonly used technique.

The minimum primitives necessary for the implementation of a functional description are as follows:

- **Signal(EV)** and **wait(EV)**: for synchronization by event. All tasks waiting for EV are activated when this event is generated by signal.
- **Alloc(V), Release(V)**; for mutual exclusion on variable V. These two primitives allow exclusive access to all resource types.
- **Send (Mess, Port), Receive (Mess, Port)**: for the asynchronous exchange of messages through a mailbox which corresponds to the implementation of a port.
- **Start (task, priority), Stop**: for creation, activation, and deletion of a task.

All real-time executives on the market (PSOS, VRTX, SCEPTRE core, iRMX, VxWorks, etc.) include all these primitives. They can be used from a high-level language such as C or Pascal, through links with an interfacing library.

Other primitives are available and may facilitate tasks implementation:

- periodic activation or delay for wait, useful for the implementation of periodic tasks or for timers;
- wait for a set of events. This allows efficient use of the WHEN instruction;
- use of semaphores;
- mailbox available for a multi-processor architecture;
- input/output and file management system.

The use of a commercially available industrial executive requires a licence which can significantly increase the reproduction cost of an application. It is therefore not unusual to find companies who, for cost reasons, develop a proprietary executive kernel suitable for their applications. In order to reduce cost, a real-time executive with basic primitives can be developed quickly. In this case, it is useful to know that only two primitives on semaphore - P(sem) and V(sem) are sufficient to implement the three functional model relation types. A semaphore is a variable composed of an integer and a list of waiting tasks. The reader is assumed to be familiar with these concepts.

The minimum primitives for functional relations are implemented as follows:

- Synchronization is provided by V(SEM_EV) for the source function and P(SEM_EV) for the receiver. The semaphore SEM_EV is initialized to zero. This solution allows activation of one task only at any one time.
- Mutual exclusion is implemented by P(SEM_V) before resource use and V(SEM_V) after use. The semaphore SEM_V is initialized to 1, the degree of the resource.
- A mailbox with N places is formed by a FIFO managed buffer variable and two semaphores - SEM_FULL initialized to N and SEM_EMPTY initialized to zero.

22.7 USE OF THE ADA LANGUAGE

The ADA language, first developed in 1979-80, and probably the last imperative (or procedural) language, is the result of the United States Department of Defense wish to make methods and tools for the development of real-time computer applications uniform.

This language is a multi-task language. It is also particularly oriented towards modular programming and object programming. It facilitates the separation between specification and implementation. This section considers only multi-task aspects of the language useful for the implementation of a functional description. The reader is assumed to have a basic knowledge of the language [BOOCH-83, BUHR-84, NIELSEN-88, ALSYS-83, etc.].

An ADA description is translated by compilation into an executable code for the required target processor. Execution requires the use of a real-time executive, generally provided with the development environment as an executive "support". Due to the large number of ADA mechanisms, the real-time executive is large and the compiler and its environment require a minicomputer or super microcomputer type development support.

For these reasons only, this language is justified today only for medium and high complexity applications in which total portability is a strictly necessary condition.

For real-time, the task as a basic unit is syntactically similar to the module, or package. Statements allow activation of tasks concurrently with the current task. A completion statement is inside the task itself (end of description) but may also be controlled by other tasks. These statements are: initiate Ti, and abort Ti. Relations between tasks are all expressed by a single mechanism called the rendez-vous mechanism. This is briefly described below to show its advantages and also its limitations or constraints.

22.7.1 The rendez-vous mechanism

Communication and synchronization between tasks are all carried out by a single mechanism based on the rendez-vous technique.

A client/service type mechanism is used. The client task calls an entry or service of the corresponding task while the server task performs an acceptance on its entries.

This mechanism is shown in Figure 22.4 for two simultaneous calls to two different but exclusive services on a single server.

The entry or service specification is syntactically identical to that for a procedure. Parameters can pass between the two tasks in rendez-vous. Input parameters are passed from the calling task to the called task at the time of the rendez-vous. The calling task is suspended during the execution interval of the client service (between do and end of the accepted statement). At the end of the service, return parameters are transmitted to the calling task, the rendez-vous is completed and the two tasks continue their execution separately.

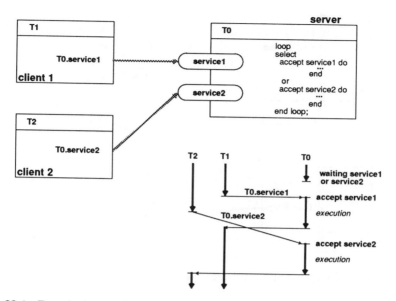

Figure 22.4   Description and behavior of the rendez-vous mechanism.

A rendez-vous cannot take place without a calling and called party. The first to request the rendez-vous is suspended until the correspondent is ready.

The rendez-vous mechanism is asymmetric since the requester or client only names his correspondent. This mechanism is fairly simple to use if it is considered that the requester inserts the service statements sequence in his temporal procedure at the time of the service call, knowing that this sequence will be executed by the called task.

This mechanism alone allows synchronization since it establishes an order relation and bidirectional communication for passing parameters when calling and returning from the service. A server task can be put on wait for requests on several entries by the select statements. When several requests appear simultaneously, they are executed sequentially.

This feature makes it possible to describe indirect relations between tasks such as those used in the functional model. Note that the Cycle statement on several events is automatically translated by a select and accept on these events.

22.7.2 Implementation of functional model relations

To illustrate the possibilities of the ADA language for a multi-task application, we will show in Figure 22.5 the possible implementations for the three functional relation types - synchronization, variable sharing, message transfer by port. The proposed solutions are obviously not the only solutions. For more information about possible techniques, refer to Buhr, Nielsen [BUHR-84, NIELSEN-88] and others.

-A- Variable sharing

The variable to be used in mutual exclusion is encapsulated into a task. Two entries allow access for reading and writing. The object approach for a data item is used here.

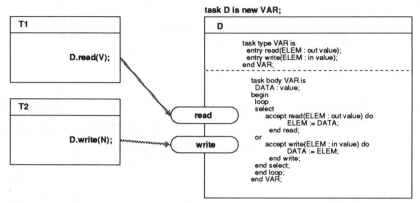

task D is new VAR;

```
task type VAR is
  entry read(ELEM : out value);
  entry write(ELEM : in value);
end VAR;
```

```
task body VAR is
  DATA : value;
begin
  loop
  select
    accept read(ELEM : out value) do
      ELEM := DATA;
    end read;
  or
    accept write(ELEM : in value) do
      DATA := ELEM;
    end write;
  end select;
  end loop;
end VAR;
```

Figure 22.5   Shared variable implementation .

-B- Two-task synchronization

Synchronization can be expressed directly or indirectly. When it is direct, the generating function designates the correspondent, whereas in the indirect case the two tasks to be synchronized designate the intermediate event which in ADA must necessarily be implemented as a task.

In the first case, the generator may be blocked waiting for a rendez-vous (event without memory), which will be probably wrong for a real-time application. This problem does not exist with the second solution.

The implementation is as described in Figure 22.6 for these two cases.

The preceding implementation activates one task only. To conform with the functional model, all tasks have to be activated; this is carried out by using the COUNT variable associated with the WAIT entry which indicates the number of waiting tasks.

-C- Buffer message transfer

As for the shared variable, the variable BUFFER is encapsulated into a task. Two entries SEND and RECEIVE are used to deposit and remove a message. Since the buffer size is limited, "guard" conditions precede acceptances (Figure 22.7).

22.7.3 Interrupts and exceptions

External interrupts are simply generated since they are interpreted as external calls. Therefore, all that is necessary is to declare a task with an interrupt as an entry point. The following example in Figure 22.6 illustrates the simplicity of this system.

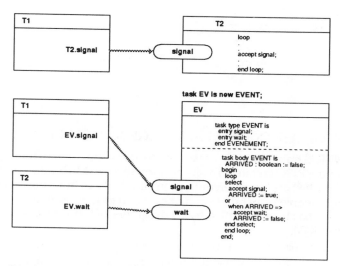

Figure 22.6   Synchronization implementations.

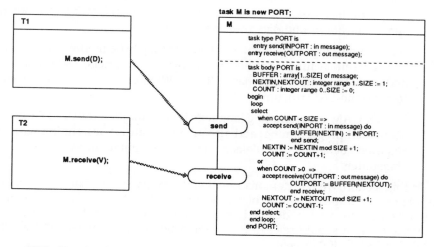

Figure 22.7   Port implementation.

```
for IT use at 4; - - - - - - - - - - - - - - -> accept IT;
```

The exception mechanism was implemented using the ADA language to efficiently process error conditions. An exception implies an ordered time relation between an exception generator when a special condition is detected and the task or procedure responsible for processing the exception. It is written as follows.

```
Task body T1 is              Task body T2 is
   begin
      raise T2.FAILURE;        begin
      ----                     ---
                               exception
                               when FAILURE ==>
   end;                                           .
                                                  .
                                                  .
                               end;
```

22.8 USE OF THE OCCAM LANGUAGE AND THE TRANSPUTER

The INMOS transputer forms part of the new generation of microprocessors. Built around a RISC architecture, its performance (10 MIPS and 1.5 MFLOPS for the T800 in 1988) and its interconnection simplicity in building an architecture with a high degree of parallelism makes it one of the essential components of the future. It has been qualified by its designers as the computing "transistor" for the year 2000.

The transputer is useful for real-time applications for at least four reasons:

- Its performances are useful for hard real-time constraint applications.

- It is functionally able to manage a multi-task application, due to its instruction set. Switching times between tasks are very low. The processor includes a unique rendez-vous mechanism by channel for synchronizations and data transfers.

- It is a single chip component and hence is easy to be mounted on boards. It has essential functionalities internally: RAM, timers, DMA channels and serial links. Its four exchange links with its environment make it easy to build meshed structures.

- The OCCAM programming language is very simple, similar to Pascal for sequential programming, and also allows a natural description with the required behavior parallelism for a transputer or a network of transputers.

In this section, we will demonstrate that the exchange by channel method is usable for the implementation of a functional description. This description is not intended to give a detailed insight into the OCCAM language. The interested reader should refer to books and articles on the subject [INMOS-86, CARLING-88, G. JONES-88].

22.8.1 The exchange mechanism by channel

OCCAM is based on the communication principles recommended by Hoare in *Communicating Sequential Processes* (CSP) [HOARE-78].

In OCCAM, a task is declared as easily as an instruction. The instruction:

```
PAR
      inst1
      inst2
```

indicates the simultaneous execution of two statements. Each statement may be a sequential execution SEQ or parallel execution PAR.

Each elementary statement is either an assignment, an input or an output. An input is used to receive a value from a channel. An output transmits a value to a channel. Therefore, all transmissions between tasks is made by channel only.

Communication between two tasks by channel is synchronous. Data exchanges take place only when both tasks (transmitter, receiver) are ready to communicate through the same channel. The first task designating the channel is thus suspended until the correspondent is ready. This is a rendez-vous mechanism. At the time of the rendez-vous, the value of the producer side variable is copied into the consumer side variable. The two tasks then continue their execution separately. The notation used in OCCAM to describe exchanges is as follows for three independent tasks (see Figure 22.8). T2 receives the value of the variable X in Y.

This is an unidirectional communication. The graphical notation used previously shows the direction of each communication. The same system can be used to program a network of processors. Each coupling, still using a channel between tasks located on different processors, is then made by a physical channel using one of the serial transputer links. So an application can be developed first on a single transputer. Then, by simply changing the configuration (task distribution and channel address definition), the same application can be executed on the network of transputers.

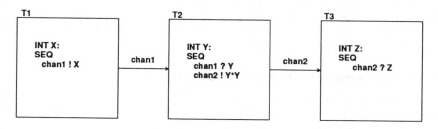

Figure 22.8   Exchange between tasks by channels.

The communication by channel mechanism is similar to the ADA rendez-vous mechanism in fact the latter was inspired by CSP. However, if the client designates the server (unidirectional designation) in ADA only, both communicating tasks designate the link element in OCCAM.

A channel is also different from a port. A port is a mailbox acting as a buffer between two asynchronous tasks. It has one or several places and acts as a memory. However, a channel has no memory. There is no submission or remove in a channel, there is a direct data transfer between tasks. Therefore, a channel is only useful for defining a relation.

Figure 22.9 shows the difference between the two mechanisms.

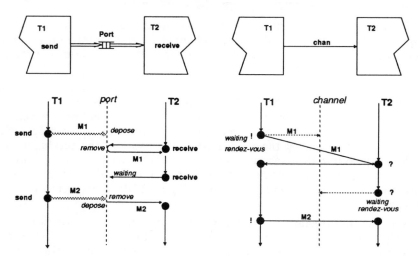

Figure 22.9   Behavior for exchange by port and by channel.

In the transputer, a special channel is dedicated to the real-time clock. It is thus very easy to implement waits for a specific time or time interval. The rendez-vous takes place at the specified time or after the specified time interval.

Another special feature of OCCAM is that a task can wait on several channels simultaneously using the ALT statement. In this case, the first rendez-vous is taken into account. This allows direct implementation of the functional model CYCLE and WHEN statements.

22.8.2 Implementing the functional model relations

As for the ADA language, in this section we show how the OCCAM language can be used for the implementation of functional model synchronization relations, variable sharing and message transfers. This brief introduction gives an idea of the OCCAM language and communication mechanisms. A major restriction is due to the fact that a channel can only be used between two tasks - one producer only and one consumer only.

-A- Task synchronization

In the functional model, the event has a memory effect. The generating task thus never waits for the correspondent, condition which is essential for real-time signalling.

This is why an additional element which can only be an OCCAM task is necessary with the transputers acting as an intermediary between the generator and the receiver. Two channels are therefore necessary for synchronization between each pair of tasks. The solution appears fairly complex; the variable

ARRIVED is used to store the event. The ALT structure allows the EV task to wait on the two tasks to be synchronized. Communication with T2 can only take place when ARRIVED = true as shown in Figure 22.10.

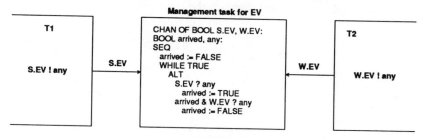

Figure 22.10   Synchronization between T1 and T2 by an event.

-B- Variable sharing

In OCCAM, a shared variable is a global variable which must be accessible by several tasks. However, to respect integrity constraints, this variable type must be considered as a critical resource.

The solution consists of associating the variable with a semaphore. Implementing the two primitives P and V on semaphores then allows allocation and release of the critical section. One possible solution is as shown in Figure 22.11.

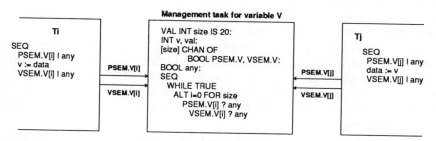

Figure 22.11   Variable sharing with mutual exclusion.

With this solution, several tasks can share the single variable V. Another solution would be to place the shared variable V in a task responsible for its management. User tasks then call this task to obtain or to update this value. This type of solution is similar to the solution for messages.

-C- Use of a port for message transfer

The port is implemented like a mailbox with N places. The data storage area is a global variable managed like a circular buffer. Two indicators are necessary: FIRST defining the position of the latest submitted message, and LAST pointing to the first free place.

The exchange between the two producer and consumer tasks is made through three channels as shown in the following solution in Figure 22.12.

The consumer signals his wish to receive a message through the "Request" channel. The reply is returned through the other "Remove" channel.

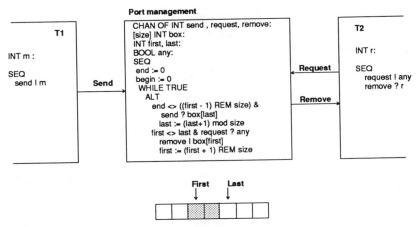

Figure 22.12   Message transfer through a port.

A port implemented as above can only be used between a producer and a consumer due to the fact that a channel is restricted to acting as a link between two tasks. To extend possible accesses to N producers, N send channels must be used and an internal ALT structure must be used on all channels.

Therefore, there are a few difficulties in developing general mechanisms complying with the functional model. In addition, limiting the number of transputer priorities to two is also a restriction which creates a problem in predicting the execution end times of tasks subject to timing constraints. Some precautions therefore, have to be taken to define a correct and efficient implementation.

The availability of an ADA compiler for the transputer is one possible solution to these problems.

22.9   SERVICES FOR THE FUNCTIONAL MODEL

For medium and complex applications, the availability of a functionalities level developed once and for all facilitates the implementation of an application specified by its functional description.

For the above two techniques - direct use of ADA or OCCAM - the implementation of an application requires a fairly thorough knowledge of the language, and particularly of synchronization and communication by rendez-vous mechanisms. The only objective of the description in this chapter is to make the reader aware of these mechanisms.

However, to avoid the need to adapt the functional description to mechanisms (implementation using a top-down procedure down to the hardware) for each application, it is preferable to have services available for the functional model once and for all. These services grouped in a library are then accessible in the form of procedures or generic tasks.

The few useful procedures are as follows:

- **Signal(EV)** and **Wait(EV)** for synchronization;

- **Read(data:def_V,V)**, **Write(data:def_V,V)** for access to the shared variable V;

- **Send(message:def_mess,port)**, **Receive(message:def_mess,port)** for access to a port.

As shown in the previous sections, these procedures use objects as server tasks: event, shared variable, mailbox. These objects are to be created as a function of requirements. The following procedures will be used to create and initialize each instance.

- init_ev (ev);

- init_var (V:type_V);

- init_port (port: type_mess; size: integer);

When built on ADA or OCCAM, these procedures can then be used as primitives for a real-time executive. Portability on various real-time executives is relatively simple and automatic.

These services cannot be used to implement all functional model features. In particular, a direct translation of the CYCLE and WHEN instructions with a wait on several events or messages is impossible. For a wait on a single event or message, translation is immediate using Wait or Receive primitives. We will mention two possible solutions for the implementation of a multiple wait:

- Translation of a task including the CYCLE or WHEN, into as many tasks as required waits. Tasks must then be executed mutually exclusive to conform with the functional model. This technique is shown in Figure 22.13.

- Direct use of the ADA or OCCAM language multiple wait statements. This solution is more efficient but requires a good knowledge of multi-task mechanisms. The T1 and T2 statements are executed in mutual exclusion managed by the SEM_T semaphore.

What solution should be used? That depends on knowledge of the language and required performances. Note however that this type of implementation with multiple waits represents only a small set of cases.

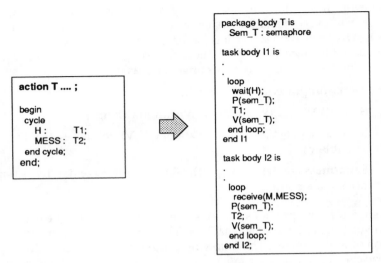

```
                                                 package body T is
                                                   Sem_T : semaphore

                                                 task body I1 is
  ┌─────────────────────────┐
  │                         │                     loop
  │  action T .... ;        │                       wait(H);
  │                         │                       P(sem_T);
  │  begin                  │                       T1;
  │   cycle        ⟹         V(sem_T);
  │     H :      T1;        │                     end loop;
  │     MESS :   T2;        │                   end I1
  │   end cycle;            │
  │  end;                   │                   task body I2 is
  │                         │
  └─────────────────────────┘                     loop
                                                     receive(M,MESS);
                                                     P(sem_T);
                                                     T2;
                                                     V(sem_T);
                                                   end loop;
                                                 end I2;
```

Figure 22.13   Translation of a task including a CYCLE on two events.

22.10 OBJECT-ORIENTED IMPLEMENTATION

Structured programming is the most conventional method to write software for complex problems. As a methodology, it facilitates breaking down a problem into sub-problems: a program is composed of a set of elementary modules, and each module is then refined until simple actions are obtained which can be written directly in the selected programming language. Pascal is a typical example of a language compatible with structured programming principles.

Using this approach, each module is developed specifically to satisfy the requirements of the higher level. The resulting program architecture is very monolithic, similar to a jigsaw puzzle in which each piece fits in a specific location for which it was designed [ROSEN-87]. Consequently, to satisfy functionality modification or improvement requirements, reusability and maintainability become difficult. In addition, structured programming assumes sequential scheduling of actions. The description is therefore not easy for systems with concurrency.

To satisfy the two abstraction and encapsulation principles mentioned at the beginning of the chapter and which can satisfy quality criteria required for the software, many authors agree that the object can be considered as the most suitable basic element [ABBOTT-85, BOOCH-83,86,87, COX-85, ROSEN-87]. The object concept and methodologies were introduced in Chapter 7 (see Section 7.11). We will simply mention object categories here to then show how the MCSE methodology is useful to find application objects.

22.10.1 Object categories

Objects can be classified according to the nature of the resulting composition or the role played by each. Object association may take place:

- in a horizontal composition: an object carries out a functional role in the transformation chain from inputs towards outputs;

- in a vertical composition: an object requests services from objects in more elementary levels. Each service layer forms an abstraction level.

If we are interested in the role played, objects may be classified in four categories [ABBOTT-85, BOOCH-83].

- **Abstract data type**: this object type defines problem variables. It is a static object used for data types, data structures, and storage units such as files and databases.

- **Service** (or operation) type: these objects make the necessary functions or operations available to a higher abstraction level. They may request services from a lower level.

- **Agent** (or transducer) type: this type of object transforms data. It accepts data as input and the result is transmitted through one of its outputs.

- **Actor** (or driver) type: these objects have their own independence and control the activity of other objects.

The four object types are shown in Figure 22.14, representing their respective roles with a specific notation allowing recognition of the object type.

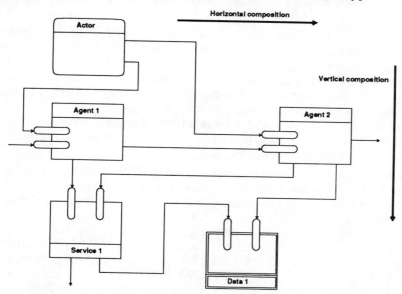

Figure 22.14   Representation of the four object categories.

The two composition axes for objects can be seen on this figure: vertical for a service hierarchy and horizontal for a chain of agents. The actor has outputs only, agents and services are requested and make requests, and data objects are requested only.

22.10.2 MCSE and object-oriented design

Faced with a realistic size of problem, the efficiency of current typically object-oriented methodologies (see Section 7.11) is limited due to the absence of a powerful tool for the construction of objects and the system architecture by problem decomposition [ROTENSTREICH-86].

In trying to use object-oriented programming, the designer is faced with two extreme approaches:

- Very quickly invoking the object concept by preparing a model of the problem reality. Objects found are then specified by progressive enhancement [BOOCH-86].

- The use of an existing conventional methodology in order to follow a top-down design process down to the identification of objects and relations between them [ABBOTT-85, NIELSEN-88].

The first approach shows the natural tendency which reflects the wish to quickly get started with an implementation (for example, prototyping), and builds a solution using an incremental, fairly intuitive approach. Direct bottom-up construction does not guarantee efficient convergence towards the problem objective.

The second point of view considers that design is carried out by a top-down methodology which facilitates structuring into abstraction levels. At each level, the design process displays entities and the necessary relations between them. In order to quickly use an object implementation, the decomposition model must facilitate this convergence. For example, Jackson's JSD method based on modeling data and then design based on a process network appears particularly suitable for object programming. The SDWMC, DARTS and especially Nielsen and Shumate's ADM methodologies (see Chapter 7) are examples of this point of view.

When languages allow multi-task or multi-object description, it is not always obvious to know when to use tasks and objects instead of procedures [D. JONES-89]. A task approach may lead to greater solution complexity. D. Jones indicates in particular that when a problem which can be solved by a single task is specified by a data-flow diagram, the solution leads to a set of tasks which are badly interrelated. As a criterion, he recommends that deterministic problems be differentiated from non-deterministic problems, and the latter only require the use of tasks. We will subsequently show that the MCSE procedure can be used at an earlier stage for the identification and structuring of the objects and tasks in a real-time application.

22.10.3 MCSE for object identification

MCSE is a top-down specification and design process. The implementation specification step produces a partition of the solution into a hardware part and a software part. A software implementation diagram specifies the organization of all software modules. On each microprocessor, the software may be implemented conventionally using structured programming. But can an object-oriented implementation be deduced, and at what stage?

To answer this, consider the software structure diagram shown in Figure 22.15. This is the solution used for the centrifuge speed control example (see 19.7.2). Based on the previously mentioned object categories, several types of tasks can be seen on this figure:

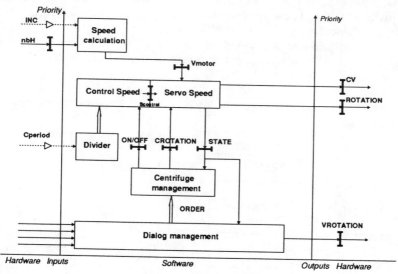

Figure 22.15   Example of the software location diagram.

- dialog management, divider, speed calculation are drivers;
- centrifuge management is a service or an agent;
- control_speed and servo_speed are services, or also agents.

Some variables - Vmotor and the set (ON/OFF, STATE, CROTATION) - are also used for coupling. Since everything must be an object, these variables must be encapsulated as data objects.

Using the object notation given in Figure 22.134 for each category, the implementation diagram is transformed directly as shown in Figure 22.16.

For each object, links in the software implementation diagram define the inputs or methods necessary. Incoming links correspond to methods that must be provided by the designated object. Outgoing links designate actions requested by other objects.

The data structure type object is a passive object. It solves conflicts and keeps internal data coherence. Actor type objects are used to generate evolution. These objects are necessarily implemented as cyclic tasks, evolving continuously or under interrupt. Agent and server type objects are generally implemented as tasks. They are invoked by an agent or actor. Centrifuge_management invoked by a single actor, can be implemented as a procedure.

Another more optimized solution can also be deduced. The point of view used consists of integrating shared data in producer objects. Consulting units then invoke the object containing the data through an entry point. This solution is more optimized since it reduces the number of application tasks thus reducing the complexity while improving performances. To show the efficiency of this process, a partial description of the ADA program, which results directly from the implementation diagram with optimization is given.

First, a description of the speed_calculation object declared as a generic package is given, thus allowing specification of the definition domain of the SPEED variable.

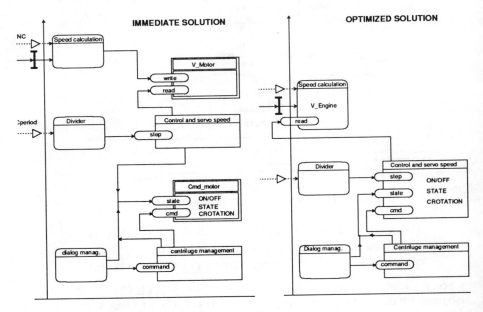

Figure 22.16   Two object-oriented organizations.

```
with ADDRESSES; use ADDRESSES;
with TYPES; use TYPES;
template
 MAX_NBH: in UNSIGNED_NATURAL;
package SPEED_CALCULATION is
 procedure READ(SPEED: out natural);
end SPEED_CALCULATION;
```

```
package body SPEED_CALCULATION is
 subtype DEF_NBH is UNSIGNED_NATURAL range 0..MAX_NBH;
task TSK_SPEED_CALCULATION is
 entry READ(SPEED: out DEF_SPEED);
 entry EVENT;
 --- for EVENT use at TIMER_SPEED;
end TSK_SPEED_CALCULATION;

task body TSK_SPEED_CALCULATION is
 SPD: DEF_SPEED:= 0;
 begin
     loop
        select
                accept READ (SPEED: out DEF_SPEED) do
                SPEED := SPD;
                end READ;
          or
                accept EVENT do
                 -- speed calculation
                 end EVENT;
        end select;
      end loop;
end TSK_SPEED_CALCULATION;
procedure READ (SPEED: out natural) is
 begin
 TSK_SPEED_CALCULATION.READ (SPEED);
 end;
end SPEED_CALCULATION;
```

The application includes DIALOG_MANAGEMENT as a background task. The CENTRIFUGE_MANAGEMENT and CONTROL_SERVO_SPEED objects are tasks. CONTROL_SERVO_SPEED generates an instance of SPEED_CALCULATION. The description of DIVIDER, which is a generic package like SPEED_CALCULATION is not given, nor are type and address declarations or the bodies of procedures and tasks.

```
with TYPES; use TYPES;
with ADDRESSES; use ADDRESSES;
with DIVIDER;
with SPEED_CALCULATION;

procedure DIALOG_MANAGEMENT is
 package SPEED_CALC is new SPEED_CALCULATION
 (MAX_NBH => 65535);

task CONTROL_SERVO_SPEED is
     entry STEP;
     entry STATE(STATE: out ON_OFF);
     entry CMD (CMD: in DEF_CMD);
end CONTROL_SERVO_SPEED;
task body CONTROL_SERVO_SPEED is
V: DEF_SPEED;
begin
     loop
        select
                accept STEP do
                SPEED_CALC.READ(V);
                -- rest of servocontrol
                end STEP;
          or
```

```
                        accept STATE (STATE: out ON_OFF) do
                        -- .....;
                        end STATE;
                or
                        accept CMD(CMD: in DEF_CMD) do
                        -- .....;
                        end CMD;
                end select;
        end loop;
end CONTROL_SERVO_SPEED;

package DIV is new DIVIDER
        (MAX_DIV => 5,
        EVENT => COMM_ASS_SPEED.STEP);

task CENTRIFUGE_MANAGEMENT is
 entry COMMAND(COMMAND: in DEF_COMMAND);
end CENTRIFUGE_MANAGEMENT;
task body CENTRIFUGE_MANAGEMENT is
STATE: ON_OFF;
CMD: DEF_CMD;
begin
        loop
          select
                        accept COMMAND(COMMAND: in DEF_COMMAND) do
                        --....
                        CONTROL_SERVO_SPEED.STATE(STATE);
                        --....
                        CONTROL_SERVO_SPEED.CMD(CMD);
                        --....
                        end COMMAND;
                end select;
        end loop;
end CENTRIFUGE_MANAGEMENT;

begin
        loop
          --scan keys
          CONTROL_SERVO_SPEED.STATE(STATE);
          --modify control value/display V_ROTATION
          --....
          CENTRIFUGE_MANAGEMENT.COMMAND(COMMAND);
        end loop;
end DIALOG_MANAGEMENT;
```

As we have just seen in the previous example, once the object-oriented implementation diagram has been defined, the method recommended by Booch is entirely applicable to define operations or methods, visibility, the interface and implementation of each object.

The graphic notation used here is specific. This is deliberate to avoid showing a preference for one of those recommended by object approach specialists. Obviously, any other notation such as Booch's diagram or Buhr's diagram, can be used. For example, it is quite conceivable that the MCSE methodology could be used to deduce Buhr's machine charts diagrams, and the CAD tools developed for this methodology could then be used.

This simple example thus shows that the process recommended in MCSE also facilitates an object-oriented design. MCSE satisfies the main question of object identification, since the software implementation diagram expresses the object specification in four categories. Second, object programming can be considered as an implementation technique.

22.10.4 Structuring with object programming

After the top-down design phase, the implementation is obtained using a bottom-up construction. It is interesting to see how object programming keeps the structure found during the design.

Let us consider a simple agent type function using the two dimensions suggested by Rosentreich. This type of function can be considered:

- for the horizontal dimension, as a data transformation function;

- for the vertical dimension, as an adaptation function between abstraction levels (client-server relation).

Some object translation rules are given for these two cases below.

-A- Horizontal structuring

The function F considered as an example is activated by an event or message reception in PORT and evaluates and updates a characteristic variable V, see Figure 22.17.

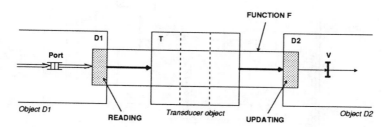

Figure 22.17   Transformation function in a data-flow.

Invoking the function will use the input data, and will then produce output data as a result of successive translations.

For the object structure, the function F can be decomposed into:

- two elementary parts for data access. These parts are procedures specific to objects D1 and D2 which encapsulate input and output data;

- a central part, located as an agent object or transducer T, itself decomposable into more elementary objects, each carrying out a transformation stage.

The structure is of the data-flow and pipeline type. Construction follows the data evolution flow induced by the design process. Each object may be a task or a procedure.

-B- Vertical structuring

To illustrate a vertical structure, we will consider the client/server type relation, for example for the transfer of information between F1 and F2 through a port with geographic distribution as shown in Figure 22.18.

The application level port is globally implemented by object O1 as an abstract object distributed on two sites.

Internally, O1 is composed of two objects O11 and O12, calling the communication service implemented by object O13. This object can also be decomposed into more elementary objects down to the physical support.

Vertical structuring is thus kept by building the implementation as a set of nested objects. Developed objects have the advantage of being directly reusable for other applications.

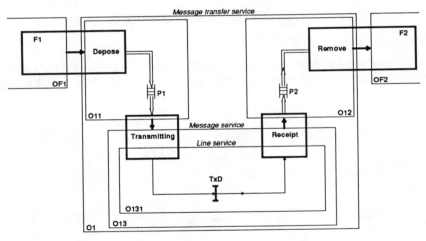

Figure 22.18   Information transfer between abstraction levels.

22.11 SUMMARY

This final chapter on implementation has described the variety of techniques and methods usable for the software implementation. The objective was to make industrial data processing designers aware of software engineering criteria, principles and techniques.

Several development processes are available to bridge the gap between application functionality and the executive support, but in the longer term it is useful to increase the functional level of the hardware support. For this purpose, one of the most promising processes is reusability based on object-oriented implementations. This chapter showed that the MCSE methodology is ahead of implementation techniques and facilitates the choice of the most appropriate technique to be used satisfying the imposed implementation constraints.

The main points in this chapter are:

- Software development must follow the process already followed for the hardware, by reuse of standard components. Not compulsory in software, this can only be the result of a deliberate attitude.

- To satisfy understandability and reusability features, the software development must respect at least two principles: abstraction and encapsulation.

- The choice among possible techniques depends on the application complexity: direct implementation for small applications, use of a real-time executive or a real-time language such as ADA for more complex applications.

- Facilitating reusability, the object-oriented implementation technique is possible with current languages such as ADA. The difficulty of the method for inducing objects concerns their identification.

- After specification of the software implementation, the MCSE methodology is a guide to find application objects. Object programming is thus shown to be a suitable tool for a bottom-up implementation technique. It maintains understandability and the design structure.

- This process facilitates reusability: in design, refinement stops when existing objects become apparent. Similarly, programming generates new abstract objects for future applications.

- More generally, for industrial data processing, object programming adds another method of developing implementations which tend to reduce development work by reuse, generating modularity and therefore system security, thus increasing understandability and consequently maintainability. This implementation technique used for real-time embedded applications avoids the need to go down to an operational detailed level in the same way as high-level languages have helped to take a step towards abstraction compared with assembler type programming.

REFERENCES PART 6

[ABBOTT-86]
> *An integrated Approach to Software Development*
> R.J. Abbott
> Wiley, Interscience Publication, John Wiley & Sons 1986

[ALSYS-83]
> *Reference Manual for the ADA Programming Language*
> ALSYS, Janvier 1983

[AMGHAR-89]
> *Méthodes de Développement d'un Système à Microprocesseurs*
> A. Amghar
> Masson, Collections Manuels Informatiques 1989

[BEN-ARI-86]
> *Processus Concurrents: Introduction à la Programmation Parallèle*
> M. Ben-Ari
> Masson, Collection Manuels Informatiques 1986

[BOOCH-83]
> *Software Engineering with ADA*
> G. Booch
> Benjamin/Cummings, Menlo Park, CA 1983

[BOOCH-86]
> *Object-oriented Development*
> G. BOOCH
> *IEEE Transactions on Software Engineering* Vol SE-12 febuary 1986,
> p 211-221

[BOOCH-87]
> *Composants logiciels réutilisables*
> G. BOOCH
> *Génie Logiciel* No 9, Novembre 1987, p 22-26

[BUHR-84]
System Design with ADA
R.J.A. Buhr
Prentice-Hall Inc, Englewood Cliffs NJ, 1984

[COX-85]
Object-Oriented-Programming: An Evolutionnary Approach
B. Cox
Addison Wesley 1985

[CARLING-88]
Parallel Processing: The Transputer and OCCAM
A. Carling
Sygma Press UK 1988

[BUHR-84]
System Design with ADA
R.J.A. Buhr
Prentice-Hall Inc, Englewood Cliffs NJ, 1984

[FLETCHER-80]
Engineering Approach to Digital Design
M.I. Fletcher
Prentice-Hall 1980

[FREEMAN-87]
Tutorial: Software Reusability
P. Freeman
Computer Society Press of IEEE NW 1987

[HOARE-78]
Communicating sequential processes
C.A.R. Hoare
Communications of ACM Vol 21 No 8 1978 p 666-676

[HOROWITZ-87]
An expensive view of reusable software
E. Horowitz, J.B. Munson
IEEE Transactions of Software Engineering September 1984 p 477-487

[INMOS-86]
An Introduction to the Transputer and OCCAM
INMOS 1986

[JACKSON-83]
System Development
M. Jackson
C.A.R Hoare Series, Prentice-Hall 1983

[JENSEN-79]
Software Engineering
R. Jensen, C.Tonies
Prentice-Hall, Englewood Cliffs, NJ 1979.

[M. JONES-88]
>   *Practical Guide to Structured Systems Design*
>   M. Page-Jones
>   Yourdon Press London 1988

[G. JONES-88]
>   *Programming in OCCAM 2*
>   G. Jones, M. Goldsmith
>   C.A.R. Hoare Series, Prentice-Hall, 1988

[D. JONES-89]
>   *To task or not to task*
>   D.W. Jones
>   *Journal of Pascal, Ada & Modula-2* September/october 1989, p 61-63

[NIELSEN-88]
>   *Designing Large Real-time Systems with ADA*
>   K. Nielsen, K. Shumate
>   Intertext Publications McGraw Hill NY 1988

[ROSEN-87]
>   *Méthode de conception orientée objets*
>   J.P. Rosen
>   *Génie Logiciel* No 9 Novembre 1987, p 16-21

[ROTENSTREICH-86]
>   *Two-dimensional program design*
>   S. Rotenstreich
>   *IEEE Transactions on Software Engineering* Vol SE 12 No 3 March 86 p 377-384

PART 7

PROJECT MANAGEMENT

Overall project control necessitates submerging the technical part of the work into a wider set of problems which must not be neglected or underestimated if satisfactory results are to be obtained. A project development does not consist exclusively of designing and implementing the product. This is even more true when the project is large.

Prior organization is necessary, taking account of the required objective and imposed constraints. Monitoring of the development is then necessary to check conformity of the implementation with predefined standards, respecting time and cost estimates. If any drift is detected, necessary corrections must be made.

Making sure that the result is conform with the customer's requirements and satisfies all constraints also involves defining a verification and validation procedure at the same time as the specification of each solution level, and then applying it at each corresponding step of the integration.

A project is never completely finished at the end of a development. Modifications, evolution and corrections are unavoidable as part of maintenance.

Moreover, a product cannot live unless it is supported by a documentation which must be produced throughout the development.

In presenting these various aspects, this part makes the reader aware of problems related to management (Chapter 23), cost estimating and scheduling problems (Chapter 24), conformity (Chapter 25), maintenance (Chapter 26), documentation (Chapter 27) and quality management (Chapter 28).

23

THE PROJECT MANAGEMENT PROCESS

"Adding manpower to a late project makes it later"

Brooks' Law

"Projects progress quickly until they are about 90 percent complete, and then remain 90 percent complete for ever".

Golub's Law

We take more interest in the individual activities of the development process rather than the work involved in the organization and monitoring of the overall life cycle. However, this must be considered as a whole, evolving like a continuous process which can and must be optimized. We will consider here that the starting point is the signature of the development contract. The feasibility study, and proposal preparation part has previously been completed.

Each project has its own nature: size, duration, technical content, work conditions, specifications to be satisfied. Management becomes a necessity for medium and large projects. Project sizes can be considered approximately:

- small < 5 man-months
- 6 < medium < 15
- large > 15 man-months

For small projects, project management information, other than product documentation can be memorized by personnel and transmitted by verbal communications. This is only true for a very small team.

With increased work complexity and team size, control and communication increases geometrically and can no longer be satisfied verbally and informally. Therefore, more companies accept project management as a tool to improve development and make efficient use of resources.

Project management means the organization and control of all technical and organizational activities necessary to obtain an acceptable solution, conform with the customer's requirements, within specified time, resource and cost constraints.

The management function can also be described using its components - planning, organization, resource management, direction, and control [FATHI-85, KOONTZ-80, RUSKIN-82]. The objective of this chapter is limited to a brief description of these various functions.

Chapter 3 introduced the global context for the technical part of any development; the project management was introduced as an encapsulating activity. We will first justify the objective by presenting the problem and will then describe management functions.

23.1 PRESENTATION OF THE PROBLEM

The development activity is a set of steps using a development process model, also called a life cycle. We will first analyze the difficulties in understanding the objective of management. This presentation is given by Jensen. It uses an analogy based on **entropy** [JENSEN-79].

23.1.1 Modeling a development step

The development process can be considered as a set of transformations which introduce state changes. The transformation in each phase is the result of the interaction of resources applied to obtain the transformation with input specifications and to produce a solution. We are now interested in the interaction part of the process. There are several specific interactions which take place:

- interaction between resources themselves;
- interaction with the development personnel;
- interaction with the management team;
- interactions with the customer, user, facilities, etc.

The transformation process as seen according to the entropy concept can be represented in Figure 23.1.

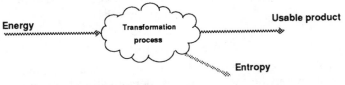

Figure 23.1   Representation of the transformation process.

Resources represent input energy. Internal interactions exist because there are many sources. Entropy is the energy dissipated during the transformation process which is not available for producing work or obtaining the product.

Inevitably, every interaction produces a certain quantity of entropy. Based on the thermodynamic analogy, the quantity of entropy for a system is proportional to random movements. Entropy expresses disorder in the system. This means that not all energy input is transformed into a usable product.

$$W = E - s \quad \text{where} \quad s > 0 \text{ (human failings)};$$

W:	is the work produced;
E:	is the input energy;
s:	is the entropy.

23.1.2 Entropy types

Entropy therefore represents negative effects. The following figure (Figure 23.2) shows inputs, outputs and forms of entropy for a transformation step such as, for example, the transition from the specifications to a design result.

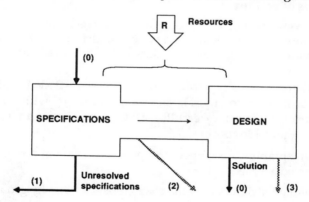

Figure 23.2   Model for the Specification --> Design transformation.

We will describe the various forms of entropy shown in this figure.

- **Line (0)** shows the direct solution with no redesign, errors, omissions, inefficiencies. It therefore represents correct and valid data. Other lines represent the entropy.

- **Line (1)** represents non-transformed input data (unresolved specifications and therefore not transformed by the design). Non-transformation may be due to:
  - inconsistencies between specifications;
  - specifications which cannot lead to a design;
  - specifications too expensive to be satisfied;
  - incomplete or incorrect specifications.

- **Line (2)** represents the disorder of the transformation activity. This is a pure energy loss. It is due to specific activities of each individual, communication defaults, use of unsuitable equipment, methods, etc.

- **Line (3)** represents the fact that the product (or solution) resulting from the phase is not perfectly complete, adequate, etc. These imperfections introduce a degree of disorder or entropy into the next phase. The state change is therefore incomplete. This line therefore transfers entropy to subsequent phases. "Entropy is about to happen".

Feedbacks to previous phases are expensive and produce high entropy. The quantity of generated entropy is a function of the phase or phases in which it appears and the length of the loopback for its correction. The later the phase, the more expensive the error is to correct.

Good management therefore consists of finding, planning and organizing (resources and methods) which minimize overall entropy. Obviously, there are local minimums to be avoided.

23.1.3 Causes of entropy

The first considerations in preparing a management strategy consist of identifying the causes of entropy in a system so that methods and tools can be found to control them. Jensen considers that causes fall into two different classes:

- **Inevitable and acceptable causes,** since related to uncontrollable situations: absence, moral, sickness, problems with hardware and software purchased externally, visits, etc. These can be limited by reducing possible abuse.

- **Non-acceptable causes**: poor cooperation, incoherence, confusion and undirected actions.

The following list describes some characteristic causes by group.

1. Underestimated project

    - scheduled time too short,
    - budget too low,
    - unaccounted inefficiencies and deficiencies.

2. Insufficient resources for the project

    - type and amount of human competence,
    - roles and responsibilities not well defined,
    - poor scheduling and resource allocation.

3. Specifications too vague

    - inadequate specifications between users, customers and main contractor,

- incomplete specification documents,
- unchecked documents,
- no understanding of the impact of modifications.

4. Design too superficial

- unidentified difficulties,
- lack of method,
- no design document,
- no development tools,
- no quality checking.

5. Unchecked implementation

- intuitive hardware development,
- no method for writing software,
- weak testing procedures,
- unchecked validation.

6. Inefficient communication

- between user and customer,
- between customer and main contractor,
- between groups working on the project,
- between designers and implementers, programmers,
- between specifiers and test groups.

7. No control over project management

- low visibility of state of progress,
- no partial reports,
- ineffective authority within the personnel organization,
- management not followed by teams.

GROUP 1 concerns resource definition and work quality.

- An inadequate level of resources as energy would lead to an incomplete and unacceptable product (first law of thermodynamics: the output energy is always less than input energy). Therefore, the resources must be reconsidered during the project.
- Poor definition and incorrect project scheduling inevitably lead to new planning and organization changes at a given stage. Roles and responsibilities are modified, moral is affected, and the entropy rate increases significantly. The addition and assimilation of new resources is the cause of a great deal of entropy. The effect may even be negative. Brook's law says: "Adding manpower to a late software project makes it later".

GROUP 6 identifies communication- related problems; in other words, bad communication and misunderstandings. Two solutions can be considered:

- reducing necessary communications by partitioning into tasks so that interfaces and exchanges are as simple as possible;
- installation of efficient and coherent communication systems wherever necessary.

GROUP 7 identifies sources of lateness compared with a schedule. There are two main types of causes:

- Expectation error:
  - inadequate analysis, implying forgotten tasks;
  - poor cost, time and equipment estimates;
  - too much optimism;
  - changed specifications;
  - resource unavailability: men and equipment;
  - late supplies;
  - interference with other projects.
- Poor monitoring of project development:
  - no will on the part of management to monitor the project;
  - no planning chart for checking progress;
  - no concrete product at the end of each step;
  - camouflaged lateness, thinking that it can be made up;
  - invisible activities: it is easy for software and design.

There may be several types of reactions when lateness is observed:
- pressure on teams to skip steps
- thoughtless reinforcement;
- arbitrary specification changes.

Without entering into management details, the following are the minimum remedies for the points raised:
- provide adequate resources;
- make tasks and resources correspond in terms of structures;
- use coherent and global methods;
- set up a project progress monitoring procedure;
- maintain coherent and efficient communication between project participants;
- make management and control effective and visible.

Management's objective is therefore to react to all previously mentioned observations and causes in order to globally reduce entropy.

23.2 MANAGEMENT ORGANIZATION

Good planning and associated control are necessary for success. Management can be decomposed into five main activities [FATHI-85, KOONTZ-80]:

- planning
- organization
- team structuring (staffing)
- directing
- control

According to Capron, these management functions can be classified into three management levels, as shown in Figure 23.3 [CAPRON-86].

The highest level corresponds to long-term planning for the company. What will customers want in five to ten years time? How to achieve this objective? At the intermediate level, managers combine human and equipment resources to satisfy the objectives of the higher level. At the lowest level, the tasks consist of managing and control activities specific to projects.

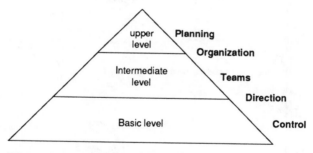

Figure 23.3   Hierarchy of management functions.

It is obvious that competence varies with the level. It will be fairly general and strategic at the top level and therefore relatively independent of products, and will become mainly technical and therefore specific at the bottom level.

Another way of describing management functions is to describe the functional organization. Figure 23.4 shows the relations between various activities.

Based on objectives to be achieved, the planning function estimates human and equipment resources, times and cost. Team organization and structuring functions suggest the resources necessary for the project.

Project management defines actions on the development. Corrections result from observing the progress of the development by a control function.

We will describe the objects and a few basic principles below for each function.

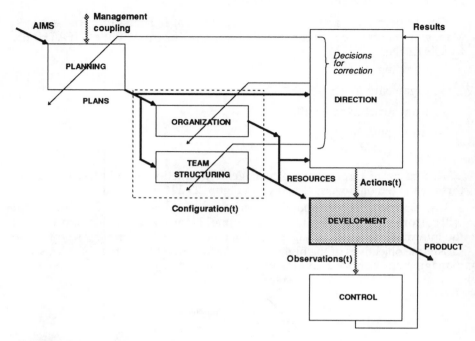

Figure 23.4   Functional management organization.

23.3 PLANNING

23.3.1 Objectives

The purpose of planning is to evaluate all tools, times and costs: who, when, where, how, how many. Every project must start by producing an action plan (project plan). It must be consistent with the company organization plan.

Planning is deciding in advance what will be done, when it will be done and by whom. Planning creates the bridge between the current situation and the desired situation. It implies the introduction of new elements.

Reifer identified three initial phases in producing any plan [FATHI-85]:

1. Definition of development and management strategies: configuration, quality assurance, documentation, which have a direct influence on company management.

2. A business plan: describing the work to be done, constraints and limitations, identification of teams by justifying the management policy.

3. A project plan: this involves describing the work as a set of manageable activities with resources and cost estimates for each. This helps to make the manager familiar with the project and to allocate and manage resources. It is obtained by a top-down type hierarchical work breakdown procedure.

The purpose of a schedule is to define when all tasks forming part of the project implementation will be performed. It is therefore a model for progress throughout the project. The manager uses this estimated model for managing the implementation. The result observed by monitoring is used to check progress.

The schedule is only one element available to the manager; it is not sufficient in itself. When it is complete, it shows the following three decisions:

- definition of an ordered time relation between tasks to be accomplished;
- assignment of equipment and human resources for executing tasks: number, abilities, duration;
- locating tasks in time.

Therefore, in order to produce a correct planning schedule, we must:

- clearly define tasks to be carried out;
- define resource methods necessary for execution;
- define the execution time with sufficient accuracy.

This latter point is very important. Many software projects are late due to incorrect program development time estimates. If uncertainty about duration is high, the estimate should be made over a very short term.

However, although a schedule is necessary for organization, organization is also essential for producing a schedule, at least to be aware of implementation methods and times.

23.3.2 Principles

Reifer describes three main principles:

1. **Precedence principle**: every project must start by planning.
2. **Effective schedule**: the schedule shall be applicable and applied. Consequently, it must be coherent with the company organization and strategy.
3. **Up-to-date planning**: schedules must be kept up to date if they are to maintain their values and be useful for control.

23.4 PLANNING TECHNIQUES

Methods normally used are [BERNARD-85]:

- Use of the GANTT diagram which describes each task and its relation with others in two dimensions. It can show the difference between planning and actual progress, as shown in Figure 23.5, but is not very suitable for showing dependence between tasks.

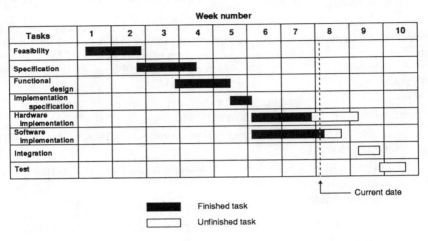

Figure 23.5   Example of GANTT diagram.

- Use of PERT diagrams. This is a chart specifying activities and events (start and end), and dependence relations. This shows the critical path as shown in Figure 23.6.

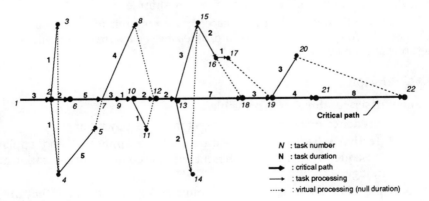

Figure 23.6   Example of PERT diagram.

The MCSE methodology is a valuable planning aid. It indicates the decomposition into tasks for completing a project. It also suggests a procedure by successive steps which facilitates time estimates (see next chapter).

23.5 ORGANIZATION

Organization concerns the structure of the company as a whole and as required for each specific project. The choice of a structure for each project must remain compatible with the company structure, and must allow sufficient flexibility for adaptations. Individuals collaborating in the implementation of an objective have a role to play and contribute to the collective effort in a very precise way. Organization defines who must do what, who is responsible for what and for what results.

Organization must be carefully thought out because it must ensure that tasks necessary for implementation of the objective are distributed, and whenever possible to the persons most capable of carrying them out.

The efficiency of an organization for a project can be defined as its ability to generate a quality product in minimum time and with minimum resources.

A few traditional organization rules:
- controlling unit (for each subordinate);
- exception (concentration on important urgency);
- limitation of the controlling range;
- structuring into departments (groups of similar activities);
- hierarchical control chain.

Reifer also quotes three common sense principles:

1. **Initial assignment of responsibilities**: a person must be named as responsible at the beginning of the project life cycle. This person must occupy a sufficiently high position in the hierarchy so that he can take on his responsibilities and make sure that decisions are applied. He must also be vigilant about the technical ability necessary to ensure that problems can be understood and solved.

2. **Interface reduction**: efficiency is inversely proportional to the number of interfaces.

3. **Parity**: in order to make progress, a balance must be maintained between the manager's authority and the responsibility of project participants.

There are three classical organization structure types:
- Functional organization. this is a grouping of common activities under the control of a single manager. The organization is of the traditional hierarchical type.

- Project-oriented organization. This involves the formation of a large number of heterogeneous groups, each responsible for its activities related to the project. This structure inevitably leads to wasted resources, inadequate communications and well-defined difficulties to evolve towards standardization.

- Matrix organization. A matrix organization is a result of associating the good characteristics of the above two organizations:

- horizontal organization for projects;
- vertical functional organization.

This last organization is not based on the only directing function: project manager or functional manager. Its advantages are that it allows long-term planning, definition of standards and procedures.

23.6 STAFFING

Groups or teams have to be formed to work on the project. Consequently, manpower requirements have to be defined previously according to the work to be carried out in order to select and evaluate participants.

Some guiding principles are:

1. **Quality**: it is better to have few experienced persons for critical tasks, rather than large unskilled teams.
2. **Perspective development for the personnel**: technical and management training are company investments which are worth while in the long term.
3. **Equality of functions**: it is realistic nowadays to consider equivalent promotion for technical and management staff (dual ladder principle).

The training strategy for existing personnel and the recruitment policy to suit project requirements are therefore very important.

23.7 PROJECT DIRECTING

Project management is an essential operational function for management. It defines instructions at all times based on results derived from control. Directing and monitoring each project allow introducing and applying necessary changes to the main plan in a controlled manner, in good time.

Monitoring takes place at regular intervals, in order to check changes and maintain integrity and visibility of the configuration throughout the life cycle. Obviously, if management is to be operational, every project must be "controllable" such that configuration modifications can be taken into account. This means that direction has checking tools and action tools to influence the development, by acting on objectives, tools and methods.

The following two objectives are essential:

- communicate objectives to subordinates;
- motivate these subordinates to achieve these objectives.

Fathi and Armstrong [FATHI-85] give three principles to satisfy these objectives:

1. **Motivation**: results-related bonus and possibilities for promotion are sources of motivation which improve productivity and quality.

2. **Leadership principle**: staff will follow whoever represents a means of satisfying personal objectives. Success is more likely if people and company objectives coincide.

3. **Communication**: productivity is related to communication efficiency. Reduction of exchanges is a method of increasing productivity.

23.8 CONTROL

The object of control is to obtain a convergence between development and planning, despite the inaccuracy of planning and disturbances during the development. This is a regular activity which must be accepted by all and which allows:

- measuring the state of progress;
- observing deviations.

Control requires the availability of measurement points, hence the implementation of a development strategy providing visibility [AMGHAR-89]. Control during specification and design is based on observing documents analyzed in reviews or audits.

Control leads to corrective actions to respect objectives, which mainly results in modifying the project configuration.

Two extreme attitudes may be observed:

- some managers are satisfied if they know the present situation;
- others try to achieve defined objectives. The schedule is a necessary tool to these managers. It is used to steer the company by defining corrections to achieve these objectives, by modifying the strategy to converge towards them.

Planning and control are two linked activities since one provides the guide or the control value for the other. The objective of control is to detect any significant deviations from the planning and to suggest methods for correcting problems.

Finally, we will mention three principles for control:

1. **Significant planning**: controls inform managers very quickly about significant drifts from the plans.

2. **Measurable work**: control is impossible without an efficient strategy for observing work progress and for checking conformity with objectives and standards.

3. **Action on exception**: the manager must concentrate his control activities on exceptions.

In summary, this chapter describes an organization model for project development. A manager is responsible for its application.

The manager's function requires experience. This experience is acquired during participation in other projects and allows the manager to structure the work and project activities in a realistic way so that resources made available can satisfy the specifications of each task at all levels. The manager must understand how all activities interact.

The next chapter gives a few indications based on MCSE about how to produce a plan and to prepare a project cost estimate.

24

PROJECT PLANNING AND COST

A project must be completed within the time allocated and assigned budget. This assumes that the time and cost were correctly estimated during the planning phase.

This chapter describes a basis for project estimating and planning. Guided by the MCSE methodology, estimates of time and resources for each step lead to a development schedule and cost.

This chapter strictly lists the necessary development constraints, and mentions possible ways of sequencing development phases in order to satisfy best external constraints imposed on the project.

Sequential chaining of steps is a linear top-down progress from the requirements definition to the operational product. Is this sequential nature really necessary, or is it possible to use a different step schedule such as concurrent steps organization, respecting the methodology principles? This question has been raised several times by industrial companies. It is a practical question since the application development context itself generates constraints which may contradict the ideal linear sequential diagram. There are various constraints to be considered, such as:

- project development incompatible with step chaining for human resource and/or equipment resource unavailability problems;
- required application running date earlier than normal realistic date;
- development dependent on other current projects or to be satisfied.

When there are incompatibilities as a result of various constraints, the procedure has to be reconsidered in more detail. The technique therefore consists of analyzing each task in each step in more detail, in order to end up with a strategy compatible with the customer's requirements.

The cost estimate requires determination of:
- all tasks to be accomplished;
- a list of resources necessary for each task in terms of manpower, equipment and facilities;
- the association of a duration with each task and assignment of dates for each resource.

The procedure proposed in the following sections consists of analyzing elementary tasks, time constraints and precedence relations for each step, and to subsequently carry out possible planning and draw a few conclusions.

24.1 EXECUTION CONSTRAINTS FOR EACH STEP

We will use the development agreement between the customer and designers as a starting point for this analysis. It is obvious that tasks involving discussions, problem analysis, cost and time estimates, and negotiations are necessary before starting the specifications.

This is a fairly theoretical macroscopic analysis, independent of special features of each project. Approximate times are given to deduce a few conclusions. It is obvious that these values have to be adjusted to give a better estimate. Secondly, disturbances have to be considered in addition for any real situation: supplying, shortages, etc. The manager is responsible for taking account of all these parameters.

For each step, the time in man-months, durations and necessary abilities are estimated. The estimate is relative using a design month as a basic unit.

24.1.1 Specification step

Starting from the requirements definition, a team of analysts produces a specification document. Meetings, discussions, site visits to observe application entities are essential for a good understanding of the problem. Objectives are then deduced and gradually refined. All information entering into specifications must be synthesized in the form of a document. This must be read, amended and then accepted by all project participants. The most important tasks during this step are therefore:
1. knowledge of the problem;
2. modeling the environment;
3. preparing specifications;
4. reading;
5. correction and validation.

Our experience with the methodology has shown that the time required to produce satisfactory specifications (Dspec), is not equal to the sum of times spent for each task, but is much higher. Second, the total time for all tasks is not inversely proportional to the number of analysts working on the specification. Only some parts of specifications can be written by a team.

Figure 24.1 shows the chronology of tasks for this step.

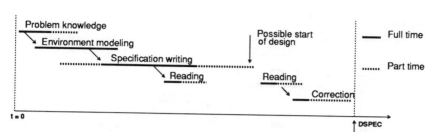

Figure 24.1   Specification tasks chronology.

As an approximate order of importance, we can consider that if a specification requires a start to end time of three months for Dspec, about Tspec = 1 man-month will have to be spent in order to obtain this result (do not confuse duration in time (D) and working time (T)).

Duration is normally fairly incompressible, since it is equal to the sum of the times necessary between each operation: meetings, discussions, visits, reading, correction, etc.

The next step, the design step, starts by an analysis phase in which inputs/ outputs have to be delimited, and may start slightly before the end of the specifications. The most realistic moment is after the functional specifications have been written, corresponding to about 2/3 of Dspec.

An engineer's competence is necessary for this step. Since the specification is the result of a transfer of expertise between customer-users and analysts or designers, a large amount of communication work is essential. The ability to synthesize will result in correct and fast specification writing.

24.1.2 Design step

If the specification document is well written, designers can work independently to produce a functional solution. Elementary tasks during the design step are as follows:

  1- delimitation of inputs/outputs;

  2- first functional decomposition;

  3- refinement of functions;

  4- global solution synthesis;

  5- design work reviews.

Each task ends with writing part of the design document. Reviews in the author/reader cycle check solution coherence and quality. Within a design team, tasks 1, 2, 4, 5 can be done jointly. Refinement of functions can only take place individually.

The chronology of design tasks is as follows in Figure 24.2:

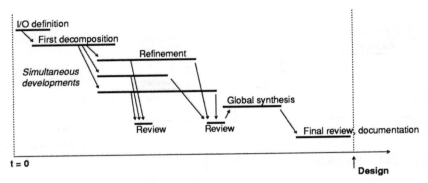

Figure 24.2   Chronology of design tasks.

To give an order of importance of the working time in man-months and the overall design time, we can consider very roughly that the design time is about three times the specification time. Obviously, this coefficient is very dependent on the nature of the problem.

$$\text{Tdesign} = 3 \times \text{Tspec (in man-months)}$$

The design work can be done full time. Since refinement tasks can be carried out in parallel by several designers, we will start from the assumption that, for the duration, half the cost of the development time can be reduced. The other half is for team activities: initial analysis, synthesis, reviews. Let N be the number of designers, then the design duration is between:

$$0.5 \times (1 + 1/N) \text{ Tdesign} < \text{Ddesign} < \text{Tdesign}$$

N depends on the size of the project. Note that efficiency reduces with the number of participants, due to the time necessary for exchanges. Therefore, a small project can be treated more efficiently by a single designer, generally the same person who wrote the specifications.

Logically, the implementation specification can only start after the functional design.

This step must be carried out by an analyst-designer. An engineer level design manager will carry out the initial and final phases, repartition of refinement tasks, monitoring developments, etc. Refinement tasks can be distributed to engineers and technicians qualified for design, depending on the complexity of problems to be solved.

24.1.3 Implementation specification step

This step leads to a result by a sequence of analyses and transformations of the functional solution. The essential tasks are as follows:

1. enhancement of the functional structure with technological constraints;
2. evaluation of timing constraints and hardware/software distribution;
3. software implementation specification;
4. hardware implementation specification.

Depending on the number of designers, some tasks can be carried out in parallel. The task chronology is as follows in Figure 24.3.

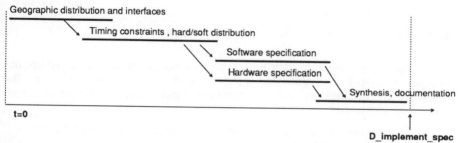

Figure 24.3   Chronology of implementation specification tasks.

In our experience with industrial projects, the time required for this step is fairly low compared with that necessary for the design. The ratio is around:

$$T\_impl\_spec = Tdesign/3$$

Designers who worked on the previous step will also be involved in this step. Depending on the number, the duration of this step is between:

$$0.5 \times (1 + 1/N)\ T\_impl\_spec < D\_impl\_spec < T\_impl\_spec$$

24.1.4 Implementation step

Implementation involves a hardware and a software part and is carried out by two categories of specialists. Without going into details of activities which may be very varied, the essential tasks are:

1. hardware implementation;
2. software implementation;
3. integration and debugging;
4. test, verification, validation, certification.

Tasks 1 and 2 can be carried out concurrently and by teams of technicians. Tasks 3 and 4 require the collaboration of two types of competence. The task chronology is as follows in Figure 24.4.

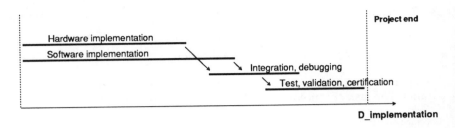

Figure 24.4   Chronology for the implementation step.

The hardware implementation may be subcontracted. This is therefore not necessarily a full time activity. Integration can then only start after the hardware is available and when a significant part of the software has been developed and tested.

The time necessary for implementation is related to the design time. We will assume a coefficient of 3 here.

$$Timplementation = 3*Tdesign$$

Since tasks can be carried out concurrently, part of the time can be reduced by increasing the number of participants. The incompressible part - coordination meetings, integration, testing, etc. - is about half. Therefore, for M implementers working simultaneously, the implementation time is between:

$$0.5 \times (1 + 1/M) \text{ Timplementation} < \text{Dimplementation} < \text{Timplementation}$$

This work can be carried out by technicians, together with one or more engineer level team leaders.

24.2 TOTAL PROJECT DURATION

The very approximate numbers given for each step give an estimate of the total project duration, and the cost in time and human resources.

We have carried out this calculation in design months. The result is given in the following table:

- N number of engineers;

- M number of technicians;

- CE cost per engineer month;

- CT cost per technician month.

Step	Duration	Time cost	Resources cost
Specification	1	0,33	0,33 CE
Design	0,5(1+1/N)	1	0,5(CE+CT)
Implement. spec	0,17 (1+1/N)	0,33	0,17(CE+CT)
Implementation	1,5(1+1/M)	3	CE+2CT
Total	3,17+0,67/N+1,5/M	4,66	2CE+2,67CT

Therefore,   if $N = 1$ and $M = 1$ then Duration = 5.34 for working time of 4.66

if $N = 2$ and $M = 3$ then Duration = 4

if $N = \infty$ and $M = \infty$ then Duration = 3.17 !!

The approximate formula given for the duration shows that adding manpower does not significantly reduce the project duration, whereas the cost in resources most probably increases.

The human resource cost calculation is also a function of the qualifications necessary for the various tasks.

24.3 SCHEDULE OPTIMIZATION

Given the result calculated, based on sequential chaining of steps, we could ask the question if it is possible to reduce the project duration while still respecting the method. To answer this, we will analyze possible modifications to the schedule within each step and between steps to introduce concurrency between steps. This is the basis of the concurrent engineering.

-A- Specification step

A different scheduling in this step does not appear to be realistic. However, design can start after the functional specifications have been written, at 2/3 of the specification period.

-B- Design step

It would appear difficult to change the scheduling during this step. It would only be possible to change the order of refinement tasks when the number of designers is less than the number of refinements to be made.

-C- Implementation specification

If the elements necessary to start the implementation specification are considered carefully, it will be noted that a start can be made on introducing interfaces as soon as the first functional structure has been obtained, regardless of any geographic distribution constraints.

Therefore, in the limiting case, some of the implementation specification tasks can start half way through the functional design, but at least half of step 3 must take place after the design.

If the problem involves fairly hard real-time constraints, task enhancement must be strictly monitored. If not, the hardware/software distribution is quickly deduced from inputs/outputs. The implementation specification can then be anticipated. There may be some risk, but sometimes anticipation is useful, or even necessary if the hardware implementation work is long and the hardware is necessary quickly for the software development and tests.

-D- Implementation

The implementation can be started a little early. This is often the case for the hardware part which is defined on constraints other than project constraints. The implementation duration is reduced by improving the technique used and the ability of software development teams. On average, the cost in time for the software is more than 70% of the total cost of the step.

-E- Minimum global duration

The above conclusions are shown on the diagram in Figure 24.5.

Thus, for N = 1 and M = 1, Duration = 4.75

for N = 2 and M = 3, Duration = 3.45

The maximum saving of time possible is therefore of the order of 10%. This shows that scheduling freedoms remain relatively low.

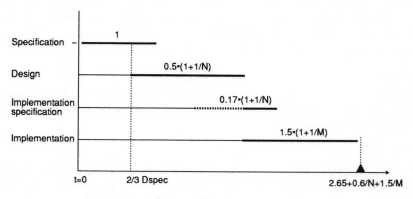

Figure 24.5 Earliest dates for a project.

24.4 METHOD OR NO METHOD

We will estimate, approximately, the comparative times with and without the method.

The lack of a method can lead to the extreme situation in which the project development starts directly with the implementation phase: development of hardware support, writing programs. Whatever the procedure, the stated problem has to be analyzed, objectives and imposed constraints have to be expressed and a solution has to be built architecturally. With no method, using a bottom-up progression, these points will gradually be clarified during the work which leads to the result.

Without being too far out, we will assume that the implementation time is at least twice the implementation time estimated when using a method (this is very probably underestimated).

Thus: time cost = 6,

duration = 3 (1 + 1/M),

human resource cost = 2 CE + 4 CT.

Therefore, the cost is greater even if the duration is not. In addition, since errors will inevitably be detected relatively late in the development cycle, the cost of correcting these errors will very significantly increase the implementation cost.

24.5 PROJECT COST ESTIMATE

Estimating development costs is a complex task which requires a detailed understanding of all the various factors which directly or indirectly influence the cost. Some factors identified by Griffin [FATHI-85] are:
- level of detail in requirements definition;
- specification stability;
- level required for documentation;
- existence and ability of support (personnel, equipment);
- necessity for training;
- ease of access to development tools;
- level required for tests (operational, qualification, certification);
- complexity of the hardware/software integration;
- level of support after delivery (maintenance, training);
- for software: size, programmers' productivity.

How can a more realistic estimate be made? Boehm mentions several estimating techniques [BOEHM-84]:
- estimating by analogy (extrapolated from previous experience);
- estimating by consulting experts;
- algorithmic estimating based on evaluation of some factors: size, difficulty, number of I/O, etc;
- estimating by analysis (top-down or bottom-up);
- price estimating accurate enough to win the contract ("Parkinson's method").

It is very difficult to make an accurate estimate when specifications are not completely defined. One possible strategy is to consider a variety of products for the need and therefore cost intervals.

The difficulty is very characteristic for a software development and variation factors of between 1 and 4 are frequently observed. First, it is impossible to estimate the number of program lines directly from the requirements definition, and secondly it is very difficult to measure productivity in this field.

Nevertheless, a large estimating effort must be made based on a method, since a good initial estimate is essential for planning and control.

Cost estimating requires determination of the following [AMGHAR-89]:

- all tasks for the project. The more detailed the decomposition is, the better the resulting estimate will be;
- the duration of each task;
- the list of necessary resources and their cost for each task. There are three types of resources: personnel, equipment, infrastructure and facilities;
- a list of supplies required for implementing the product.

The cost is then the total of the products: resource costs x duration, together with supply costs. Therefore, three factors must be well defined - tasks, resources, time. The decomposition based on MCSE is thus a good estimating basis.

In addition to the previous elements, a good manager considers the possibility of potential problems and risks such as fast technology changes, supplying delays, single manufacturing supplier, etc., and some uncertainties.

An experienced manager will add an expectation analysis of all things which could go wrong.

25

Project Verification and Validation

In order to be accepted, a system must comply with its specifications which define at least all functional and technological constraints.

Therefore, a major and essential activity consists of determining if the solution is correct. Obtaining project conformity requires a sequence of tasks called: verification, test, validation. They must be defined as procedures and must be based on the use of methods and tools. This is the purpose of this chapter.

Error is human. The more complex the problem is, the more participants are involved and therefore risks are greater. Errors are also related to the increased number of transactions between people.

Each phase in the life cycle can induce errors. Design introduces errors related to the specifications. Implementation is not completely done in accordance with designers' intentions. Errors unavoidably arise during implementation. Checks must be carried out at least between each phase to reduce error propagation.

In addition, since humans cannot implement and communicate perfectly, the development process must be accompanied by a quality management activity described in Chapter 28. Verification and validation help to obtain this quality.

25.1 TERMINOLOGY

Talking about this activity which leads to obtaining conformity, we will use the VVT notation: Verification, Validation, Test [FATHI-85]. Before we start, we will define the meaning of terms used.

1. **Reliability**. This is the probability that the system operates correctly during a period T defined by the MTBF. This is a specific quality measurement. Parameters involved are the number, frequency and complexity of errors. Verification and validation contribute to obtaining a reliable system which carries out the planned functions.

2. **Verification**. This activity helps to guarantee that each solution level correctly satisfies the specifications of the higher level. It ensures consistency, completeness and absence of errors at each stage and between development stages.

3. **Validation**. This activity ensures that the implementation developed for each subset at each level carries out its functions and satisfies the performances as described in the specifications for the corresponding level. Finally, it ensures that the final product is conforms with the customer's requirements and expectations.

4. **Certification**. This is the customer's acceptance of the product after its validation. He checks that the product interacts correctly with its environment, carries out required functions within the customer's context and satisfies required performances.

5. **Test**. This is the analysis phase for the behavior of a system, subset, function, etc, carrying out executions on data sets to find errors and thus carry out verification.

6. **Testability**. This is the suitability of a design to be efficiently tested. Quality criteria inducing testability of a design are understandability, controllability and measurability. How many modules have to be re-tested when a change is made in a module? Which modules have to be tested for a set of changes?

Figure 25.1 shows the meaning of the terms and the relation with the design steps.

25.2 OBJECTIVES

The objective of the VVT activity is to determine if a system can carry out the intended design functions and guarantee a given reliability.

The verification/validation activities can be illustrated in the V-shaped structure in Figure 25.1, which shows that each subset made must be the image of the specification document for the corresponding stage. The VVT activity therefore covers sets of procedures, activities, techniques and tools.

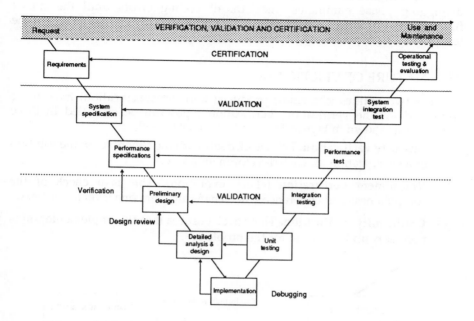

Figure 25.1   Life cycle including Verification, Validation and Certification.

We will first mention the nature of errors before considering how to detect them

25.3 ERROR TYPES

The cost of errors, including finding and correcting them, increases exponentially with the distance between the verification stage and the corresponding design stage. The main types of errors currently encountered during development are:

- bad interpretation of specifications;
- poor understanding and inappropriate use of design and development methods and tools (components, languages);
- imperfection; this is processed by quality assurance;
- syntactical, logic and semantic errors;
- critical values and side effects;
- timing, overload errors;
- performances, throughput not satisfied;
- safety (recovery).

A distinction should be made between testing and debugging. The debugging phase eliminates "mechanical" coding errors until the subset functions and produces results, which are not necessarily right. The role of the test phase is to correct them.

25.4 NATURE OF VERIFICATIONS

Since two entities (the result produced and the specification) have to be compared for the verification, verification types can be classified in three categories as shown in Figure 25.2 [FATHI-85, DUKE-89]:

- **Integrity verification.** This check deals with the coherence of the solution or a specification for each development phase.

- **Refinement verification** (check evolution). This is a check of the completeness and coherence when changing from one level to the next.

- **Conformity verification.** This check ensures that the implementation is necessary and sufficient for the problem.

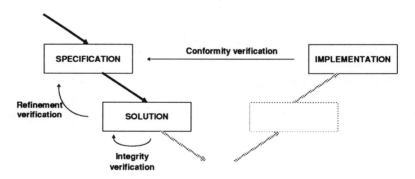

Figure 25.2   Verification categories.

Another classification is possible depending on the analysis nature - static, dynamic, formal.

-A- Static analysis

This technique detects errors by examining the product, for example by simply reading the design documents (author/reader cycle).

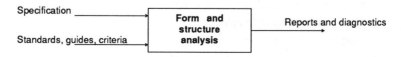

Figure 25.3   Verification by static analysis.

The analysis may be manual or automatic (for source descriptions and texts). It can inform about omission type errors and detect syntax type errors.

-B- Dynamic analysis

This can determine the validity of a subset by studying its response to a set of input data or commands. The activity of obtaining responses is called testing as shown in Figure 25.4.

This analysis is broken down into the following phases:

-   preparation of the test to be executed, including:

    -   selection of test scenarios and input sequences,
    -   formulation of results expected.

-   execution of the test;

-   results analysis to determine behavior and performances.

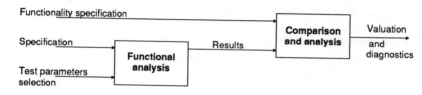

Figure 25.4   Verification by dynamic analysis.

-C- Formal analysis

This analysis is based on the use of mathematical techniques to analyze the properties of a solution. This method is normally limited to very precise subsets to prove the existence and correctness of properties. It may also consist of complexity tests. These three analysis types can be coupled to define a method as shown in the Figure 25.5.

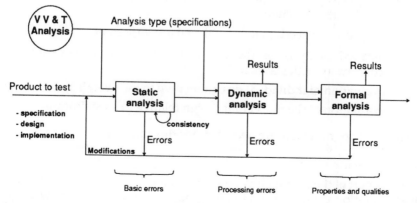

Figure 25.5   Chaining the various analyses.

The method to be used depends on the step in the development. We will review the techniques that can be used for the design and implementation phases.

25.5   DESIGN METHODS

Verifications and validations are continuous activities during design. The objective of the verification is to check the logical consistency of the design with the previous phase. Verification includes an analysis to determine if quality criteria are respected. Validation guarantees the suitability of a design to functionally satisfy the customer's requirements, in other words that it matches the specifications.

.   Usable methods are [JENSEN-79]:

- design reviews;
- models and simulations if necessary.

The result may bring out two types of defects:

- incorrect operation (or functionality);
- performance does not match the specifications.

25.5.1 Design review technique

A designer, if he is close to his design, may have introduced errors which are invisible to him, or biased solutions since they are preconceived, and which may or may not be right. On the other hand, a reader or reviewer has no initial knowledge about the design.

The principle of the method consists of using the designer's intimate knowledge about the system, but eliminating preconceived ideas, in order to bring out objectivity. This requires planning and organization carried out with precise and defined objectives.

Three aspects of objectives to be achieved are important:

1. detailed analysis of the designers work for its consistency and conformity with standards;
2. evaluation of individual design relative to the overall system;
3. evaluation of the individual design relative to specifications.

Several types of review are necessary for this purpose.

-A- Formal review

This is part of the management plan, particularly for the documentation. An initial definition is necessary, implying the association of a review with each development phase.

-B- Informal review (walk throughs)

Engineers must be prepared for participation in these meetings. This type of work is part of the daily routine and improves his knowledge and understanding of the problems. Participants make an important contribution to detecting and successfully solving problems. The solution is made based on objectives.

The reviewer is responsible for this activity, and he must acquire review materials, read, identify analysis domains and prepare the meeting. Documents for reviews are prepared and previously submitted to participants. A chronological document should be created to record decisions and eliminate redundancies.

Carrying out a review, the reviewers must firstly comment on the completeness and quality of the work. Essential problems are expressed and identified to subsequently solve them. Designers present their results. They then walk the reviewers through the design step by step, to simulate the function being analyzed in their minds. Points which require additional action are recorded and identified.

The reviewed person is responsible for carrying out all listed actions. Reviewers are informed of any actions and/or corrections; follow-up is therefore necessary to reviews. The resulting design (documentation release) is then sent for quality control.

25.5.2 Simulation/modeling as evaluation tool

This technique can be used to evaluate the various alternatives and for verification. However, the cost in time and in resources should be foreseen at the beginning.

Modeling is a representation of part of the real thing generally in a simplified abstract form. Several model levels are possible - from a conceptual model to a realistic model. A model must represent the desired characteristics of the product to be evaluated. A model is not an end in itself, but is a tool to predict properties and performances.

A simulator is a simple software tool which helps with a product development: environment simulation (test, maintenance), system simulation (design test).

Modeling must be used when verification cannot be completed by a manual analysis effort, by experimenting (costs), intuition or previous experience.

25.6 IMPLEMENTATION PHASE METHODS

The test, and therefore the dynamic analysis, is not the first solution to be used. Many errors can be found beforehand using a static analysis. These procedures are valid both for hardware and software.

25.6.1 Static analysis

Reviews and audits set at precise development stages allow static analysis and are therefore the first step in the verification and validation method.

Reviews must be held on the analysis of implementation specifications, the implementation and integration. A simple review by two people is efficient for an initial analysis. This is an inspection technique, since any one person is not very good at finding his own mistakes.

25.6.2 Dynamic analysis

This analysis is based on carrying out tests. The test can demonstrate the presence of errors, however it cannot demonstrate the absence of errors. This may justify the formal analysis stage.

The sequence of test operations is as follows: execution, observation, comparison.

Execution requires prior planning, in other words a document which specifies the following points:
- test types
- scenario
- input data
- how to observe
- how to compare.

The choice of scenarios and input data is not easy since the number of cases is very often infinite. A subset therefore has to be selected. The objective is to find the right subset.

The following rules may help the designer:
- the scenario visualizes normal and special properties, and singularities (extreme values);
- It must be able to activate all branches or components.

25.6.3 Test procedure

Divide and conquer is the general test rule. Subsets therefore have to be tested before considering integration.

-A- Basic component test (unitary test)

Delaying testing until the complete assembly stage leads to a disastrous experience. The idea is that a large percentage of errors can be discovered and corrected at the lowest level (software or hardware component). The cost is then minimized.

-B- Integration test

This involves testing the assembly of several components forming large operational sets.

The test deals with the interaction between components and interfaces. This type of test is easier if each component has been previously tested and validated. Assembly, and therefore the test sequence, follows the application structure of hierarchical organization.

25.7 INTEGRATION TECHNIQUES

We will describe techniques to be used for the final development phase, since they are essential for efficiency. These techniques can largely be extrapolated for the hardware.

Techniques can be classified into two complementary categories: assembly by phase or incremental assembly.

25.7.1 Assembly by phase

Assembly by phase consists of assembling the component at a given level with all tested components of a lower level as shown in Figure 25.6.

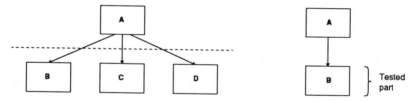

Figure 25.6   Assembly for testing by level.

The difficulty is finding the error; it may be due to the untested module A, or to the interaction with called components.

25.7.2 Incremental assembly

Incremental assembly consists of starting from one component, testing it and then adding another untested component. The error then arises either from the new component or from the interaction with the rest of the tested system. Assembly may take place in top-down or bottom-up order. For complex systems, it is better to use the bottom-up technique.

Bottom-up integration requires the use of Driver programs. A Driver activates the component under test by simulating the activity of the components in the higher level.

Top-down integration requires "stubs". These are empty components which simulate the operation of lower level components as shown in Figure 25.7.

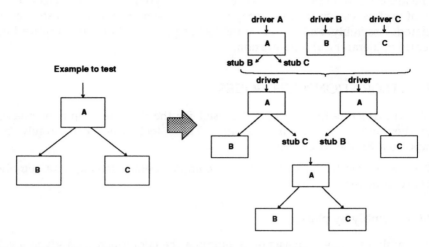

Figure 25.7   Assembly and bottom-up and top-down test.

In practice, it is recommended that a combination of these two techniques be used.

25.7.3 Objective-oriented tests

This is a different functional test from the above which can show functional possibilities very early in the test activity. This is a sequence of programs written specially for testing and which, when completed, carry out a given function.

Progress towards the final objective can be checked by plotting a curve such as that shown in Figure 25.8 indicating the variation between the planned objective and the real situation.

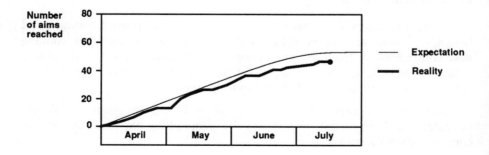

Figure 25.8   Progress recording.

The advantages of this method are as follows:
- progressive tests;
- anticipated demonstration of functionalities;
- the need to have operational parts (code, hardware);
- control of interfaces and configurations;
- fast production of a detailed documentation.

This method is based on test scenarios on path selection through the solution hierarchy.

25.7.4 Comments on these procedures

We will mention a few common sense rules to complete the above description:
- Test the most important things first. The most specific modules are at the base since they are close to the environment, particularly for real-time applications with timing constraints. Interfacing problems are thus anticipated since they are related to the environment.
- Plan a preliminary version of the system. What should preferably be finished first at the end date, the base or the skeleton? For bottom-up assembly: coding is complete but nothing actually works. Top-down assembly will demonstrate something tangible, but not completely operational with the environment. The situation is unpleasant in both cases.
- Debugging is easier using the incremental approach.
- Coding and top-down testing instead of a complete design. This should only be carried out when time is short. A top-down procedure can then only be used when the basic levels are not known.

25.8 TEST ENVIRONMENT

Every test requires a test environment. A simulated environment is generally used at the beginning instead of the real environment. Two simulation classes can be used:
- Environment simulation: this requires a parallel evolution with the system since it is necessary for input activation and output observations.
- Executive support simulation: the final support (for example, computer) is not available. The simulator may have functions facilitating debugging.

25.9 AUTOMATIC TESTS

Automatic test tools may be considered for the following reasons:
- assistance in test production and result analysis;

- reduced test times;

- test improvements and reliability.

Tools to be used depend on the phase. For the design phase, automatic analysis of the design, system simulation. For the implementation phase, static analysis for the test coverage, dynamic analysis for the performance test, etc.

25.10 TEST PLANNING

Planning for verifications, validations and tests forms an integral part of the overall development planning task. The problem is to produce a document describing VVT specifications and procedures for carrying out the verifications. The imposed requirement for the tests may depend on the application. There are three basic characteristic types:

- application size (number of instructions, for example: < 5000, between 5000 and 10 000, > 10 000);

- complexity (low, medium, high);

- critical constraints (critical, non-critical).

Since this is a control operation, it must be planned at the same time as the development. The design document must therefore include a description of test procedures and expected results. The approach for test planning is as follows:

- identification of VVT specifications, taking account of objectives;

- determination of constraints for these activities;

- selection of techniques;

- detailed plan of activities, sequencing, budgets, time, resources.

The procedure is as follows:

Problem => Mission => Approach => Plan

The objective of planning is to produce an action plan in the form of a document. An example of a plan for obtaining conformity is given in the next section, for illustration. The following is therefore necessary for testing each subset:

- define the test method(s);

- define the procedures to be followed;

- after the tests, produce a test report.

An example of a test plan is also given at the end of the chapter. Some methods for this progression may be inspection, walk throughs, reviews, tests. A temporal diagram summarizes the test sequencing based on decomposition into procedures, modules, tasks, as indicated in Figure 25.9.

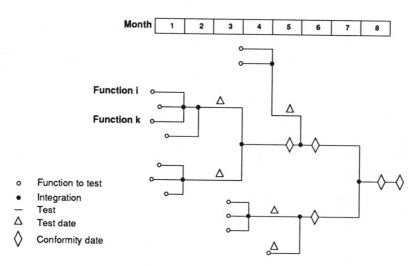

Figure 25.9   Planning representation.

25.11   TEST SPECIFICATION GUIDE

As an example [FATHI-85], the points which must be described in the synthesis document to be used as a test specification aid are given below.

-A- Objectives
- Define tangible results of the activity, measurement criteria to define if the result is satisfactory.
- Roles and responsibilities:
  • customer and suppliers, to check that the product will be accepted;
  • development/management: measurable quality and activities.

-B- Factors influencing the activity
- resources;
- the budget, scheduling constraints;
- methodologies, standards;
- personnel.

-C- Selection of tools and techniques
- produce a list of techniques and tools possible to achieve each objective;
- make an evaluation from this list and then select the solution.

-D- Development of a detailed plan
- budget, scheduling, information;
- training, development, or tool acquisition.

25.12 GUIDE FOR A TEST DOCUMENT

Test documents must be prepared during the specification and design phases. This is therefore partly the responsibility of designers. The existence of these documents and therefore prior reflection about test procedures can lead to improvements in the development to facilitate verifications.

A model of a test document which can be used as a guide is described below.

25.12.1 General information

- *Summary*
  A brief reminder about the functions of the system or subset and the tests to be carried out.

- *Environment and objectives*
  Reminder about the project origin. Identify how the system or subset fits in for the customer.

- *References*
  Previously published documents related to the project.

  Documents for similar projects.

25.12.2 Plan

- *Description of the functionality to be tested*
  Briefly describe inputs, outputs and functions carried out by the system or the entity to be tested.

- *Test location*
  Identifies participants and the test location.

- *Scheduling*
  Describes details of dates and events for the test.

- *Constraints*
  Description of necessary resources:

    • Hardware: period of use, type and quantity of essential equipment.
    • Software: list of software necessary for tests.
    • Personnel: number and ability of personnel necessary during the test phase.

- *Test documents*
    • Documentation on the tests.
    • Documentation on the function or entity to be tested.
    • Inputs for tests and observations to be made.
    • Test procedures.

- *Training for tests*

  Description of the training plan for carrying out the tests: training type specification, personnel to be trained, and team of instructors.

25.12.3 Test specification

- *Procedures*
  - Reminder about functionalities.
  - Description of functions to be tested.
  - Relation between functions and tests.
  - Test sequence: description of the test cycle.

- *Methods and constraints*
  - Methodology: description of the method and test strategy.
  - Conditions: specify the input type to be used and the data size and frequency.
  - Record results: specify the method and tools used to store test results.
  - Constraints: indicate test limitations such as interfaces and equipment.

25.12.4 Test evaluation

- Criteria: description of rules to be used to evaluate results.
- Synthesis: description of techniques to be used to deduce diagnostics from recorded data.

25.12.5 Description of tests

Description for each subset to be tested:
- type of tests: manual, automatic, semi-automatic, operation sequencing;
- inputs: describes input data and commands for the test;
- outputs: describes results expected and messages produced;
- procedures: step by step specifications of procedures to accomplish the test.

26

MAINTENANCE

"Maintenance should not be used as a training ground where junior staff are left to sink or swim"

E.T. Fathi

Judging by the number of articles on the subject, the maintenance field is a subject of increasing interest. The necessary effort can be seen from the simple observation that the cost of maintaining existing systems is at least as high as the development cost for new products. Software application managers estimate that maintenance costs can be as high as 60 to 70% of the total application cost [LELUC-86].

There are many reasons for this. First, there is a considerable increase in the number of products to be maintained. Modifications to software and specifications and the number of errors, much larger than zero at the end of the development phase, are a few reasons. Second, the lack of techniques and methods to reduce this maintenance during maintenance itself and during earlier steps amplify problems.

The following points should be considered in more detail if better results are to be obtained:

- improvements of tools, methods and techniques;
- implementation of maintenance management.

This chapter first describes the various problems and defines the terminology, and then mentions methods and techniques which can help to improve product maintenance by organizing it thus reducing operating costs. This work is complementary to the benefits of the methodology which helps to reduce maintenance problems as a result of its maintainability criterion.

26.1 MAINTENANCE TYPES

Maintenance is the execution of activities necessary to keep a system operational and to maintain its responsibility when it has been accepted as a product after the production and the guarantee period.

This therefore involves the activities which introduce modifications, changes, and corrections to the product after its development. Based on a functional definition, maintenance in its widest sense can be divided into three categories:

1. **Improvement**: change, insertion, remove, modification, extension of functions to satisfy requirements. These are improvements for functionalities, performances, maintainability, understandability. Improvement takes place after modifications to specifications due to changed requirements. This work forms part of maintenance rather than new development. This maintenance is necessary when the product is operating correctly or incorrectly: for the addition of new features when it is operating correctly, and to correct errors when it is operating incorrectly. Preventive maintenance improves understanding of the system (structure, documentation, updating, etc.). Optimization improves performance and reduces reproduction costs. The product and all its documentation have to be updated when such specification modifications are made.

2. **Adaptation**: these are the necessary modifications to satisfy a new environment, or to adapt to changes in the environment. Examples include evolution of hardware, the operating system, sensors, data, interfaces, etc.

3. **Correction**: this concerns correcting residual development errors to make the system operational. It requires an immediate reaction.

26.2 CAUSES OF MAINTENANCE

The following list gives a classification of maintenance problems according to the source:

- *System*
  - lack of quality in the maintenance system due to design, implementation, documentation.
- *System environment*
  - changing environment,
  - disturbing environment.
- *Management*
  - no maintenance policy,

- no maintenance control,
- no techniques, procedures, tools,
- no responsibilities.

- *Users*

- increased demand and features.

- *Personnel*

- no expertise,
- strategic problems,
- no attraction to maintenance.

Considering the above list, it can be seen that there are two categories of problems: technical faults and organizational faults. Rules for these two domains will be discussed below. First, we will mention some reasons which lead to problems.

26.2.1 Quality of the developed product

Lack of attention to quality during the design and implementation phases leads to high maintenance cost. Designers should be aware of this effect. This justifies the necessity for control and consequently quality rules imposed by quality assurance.

Some examples of faults are:

- poor understanding of the problem by designers;
- incorrect, incomplete or unclear specifications;
- primary and complex design, lack of discipline, individualistic design;
- poor implementation (thin coding), little structuring;
- logic errors resulting from incomplete or incorrect tests or wrong conclusions;
- use of obsolete hardware;
- bad global definition of application data, important for understanding;
- use of several programming languages: such as machine code;
- edge effects for the application;
- too many resources necessary.

Four causes should be considered for errors which require an immediate correction:

- specification errors;
- design errors;
- logic errors;
- implementation errors (hardware implementation, coding).

We should particularly notice the importance of specification quality in obtaining a correct product. Cox describes two possible designer's attitudes towards specifications [COX-85]:

- **Defensive attitude**: specifications are considered to be complete and unvarying, which is never the case, especially for large projects. Based on this assumption, the product will be made in accordance with the specifications. All modifications will be left to maintenance since they will have to be made otherwise the product will not be used.

- **Opportunist attitude**: take account of required variations as and when they arise. For this purpose, a design method which facilitates taking modifications into account has to be used. Obviously, this second attitude is preferable to reduce correction costs.

Design errors are a result of bad design or incomplete or too fast design. Implementation errors are the result of negligence or lack of responsibility. They are the easiest to correct.

26.2.2 Documentation

Documentation is necessary for communication. The maintenance man must first understand the what, how and why of each part.

There may be months or years between design and maintenance. Moreover, maintenance men are not designers. The designers may no longer be in the company. Without documentation, the information which has disappeared must be reconstituted. Good documentation is the only trace and is therefore the only method of communication. This is a long-term investment that must be prepared by designers.

26.2.3 Users

Users are very often unable to accurately define what they want. Specifications are thus incomplete and unsuitable.

The more successful a system is, the more the user will request additional features. Hence the necessity for management to filter justified requests only. Similarly, if a system does not work, there will be continuous requests to make it work.

Modification requests are often excessive, conflicting, vague and are expressed without knowledge of the impact on the maintenance work. Management is necessary to control the maintenance level by reacting to the customer informing him of the cost and consequences of his request.

26.2.4 Personnel

Maintenance work tends to be considered:

- unimportant;
- not interesting (unchallenging);
- uncreative.

It is therefore not popular with users and the rest of the company, and especially by designers. However, this work requires particularly important qualities: good will, good qualification, experience. It is therefore not to be carried out by novices or beginners since the objective is to quickly satisfy the customer by making the system operational efficiently and inexpensively.

The following qualities are required for this category of personnel:

- flexibility, self-motivation, responsibility, creativity, discipline, analytic reasoning, reasoning finesse, experience, and also intuition.

26.3 MAINTENANCE PROCEDURES

Maintenance is necessary during the product operational phase, in other words the last phase of the life cycle which corresponds to the product usage phase.

The maintenance procedure is complex and involves several persons and even several teams. This work starts when a change request is received. It is completed when the user has accepted the modification and the documentation has been updated.

The following list describes the successive steps in the maintenance procedure:

1. Determination in the need for modifications
2. Request submission
3. Request analysis
4. Request approval or rejection
5. Operation planning
6. Analysis for design
7. Review for design
8. Modification and debugging
9. Review of proposed changes
10. Test
11. Update documentation
12. Audit
13. Acceptance by users
14. Installation of modifications and impact on the product
15. End of operation

This list shows that part of the life cycle - specification, design, implementation, test - has to be repeated.

There are some difficulties. Modifications have to be made in an existing system. The older the product is (little documentation, few tools, etc.), the more difficult the problem is; the need for understanding by a regressive procedure. It is sometimes better and more cost effective to define a new product, particularly with the current hardware evolution.

Criteria are used to determine whether or not it is advantageous to continue modifications. A modification control procedure must also be imposed to reduce costs.

26.3.1 Alternative: maintenance/new design

The decision depends on the comparison between the two possible solutions - to continue with the existing product or to produce a new design.

The following list gives some reasons for a new design:
- frequent system breakdowns;
- 7 to 10 year old design for hardware or software;
- complex system structure and logic;
- obsolete technology;
- modules too large;
- use of too many resources;
- invariable parameters;
- difficulty of keeping a maintenance team;
- serious documentation deficiencies;
- specifications not satisfied or incomplete.

26.3.2 Change control method

A maintenance operation management and control policy has to be defined in order to check variations, thus implying rules.

The following list gives a few suggestions for controlling modifications:
- formal and written request for all modifications;
- review all requests and consider approved request only;
- analysis and evaluation of modification request type and frequency;
- evaluation of the degree of necessity for the change and its anticipated use;
- evaluation of modifications to check that they are not incompatible with the state of the system, no change shall be carried out without a precise idea of its complexity and repercussions;
- evaluate if the modification improves or degrades performances;
- approve a change only if its benefit exceeds its cost;
- scheduling of all maintenance;
- impose documentation and implementation in accordance with standards;
- instruct that all modifications use modern techniques;
- plan preventative maintenance.

The maintenance strategy is partly linked to the maintenance type - improvements, adaptations, corrections. According to Fathi, the work load estimate for improvements is of the order of 60% of the total maintenance effort. Requests are received from: the user, the management staff and the maintenance team.

The user is often never completely satisfied and the direction may also request developments, a normal situation in any company and which must be planned for. The maintenance team may note imperfections and potential problems.

Due to its high cost, management of maintenance is essential and must analyze requests, specify them, assign each a priority and schedule them. Reducing costs requires a global policy for coordinating requests - common points, conflicting points, etc.

Modifications represent 20% of maintenance cost. This effort is non-productive for the company. Should this work be carried out by the department which produced the system or by the maintenance team? Take care also with the difficulty of communication since designers lose interest in these problems.

Concerning corrections (the remaining 20%), the first problem is to identify errors. It is very unusual that a perfect system is produced so that this work always exists. It can be reduced by defining standards and procedures during development and maintenance. This leads to the need to respect rules and this is the role of quality assurance.

26.4 SOLUTIONS FOR IMPROVING MAINTENANCE

The technical remedy is maintainability. It is a system's facility for supporting changes to satisfy user requests and for correcting detected errors.

It is obtained by consideration throughout the life cycle. This is one of the quality criteria imposed on all developments. Hence the necessity to always bear maintenance in mind.

Some common sense rules and tools to induce this quality during design and implementation are:

- specifications guide and design guide;
- guide for writing code, hardware implementation, etc;
- use of high-level languages;
- structuring, modularity, coherence, limited coupling;
- standardization of data definitions;
- good documentation, noticable by the ease of finding information necessary for maintenance, documents up to date. This raises the problem of documentation maintenance.

Maintainability quality is not sufficient, it has to be imposed and must be observed during the early phases of development.

Quality assurance defines its observation. The review technique should be used in cooperation with a maintenance specialist:

- Review by two people: for the specification, design, programming and self-correction. This must not be taken as a method of evaluating aptitudes and performances of the reviewed person.
- Walk throughs: two heads are better than one. The person concerned makes a detailed description of the proposed solution. Reviewers ask questions to clarify points and bring out errors and potential problems.

The maintenance manager must be present:
- for good acceptance by all of the objective, refinement of good ideas and elimination of bad ideas;
- to evaluate the state of progress, understand the system, evaluate quality for maintenance.

26.5 MAINTENANCE TOOLS

Maintenance tasks require the same tools as those used for the development. In addition, procedures and tools are necessary for troubleshooting, performance evaluation and other purposes.

Since the development imposes the creation of these tools for the verification and validation phases, these tools must be usable. Consequently, the maintenance personnel must participate during the development in the specification of these tools which will subsequently be useful to them.

Also, management of corrections and modifications may be facilitated by the use of special computer tools.

26.6 MANAGEMENT OF MAINTENANCE

Managing all maintenance problems requires an organization similar to that necessary for any development project. The organization and necessary activities are mentioned here.

26.6.1 Objective and activities

The objective is simple: all systems have to be kept in working order so that they satisfy user requests satisfactorily and in good time. Maintenance managers must therefore carry out an essential task consisting of:
- keeping the maintenance activity ordered and controlled;
- keeping systems, products and applications running;
- keeping users satisfied;
- keeping maintenance personnel satisfied;
- making sure that maintenance is seen as a positive aspect which contributes to the company objectives and not as an obligation to compensate for negligence.

The manager's activities are:

- scheduling changes;
- negotiation with users;
- coordination of team activities;
- definition of tools and working rules.

The following tasks should be undertaken for each modification:
- evaluation of work for a request;
- estimate of the necessary effort;
- assigning a priority;
- scheduling;
- work monitoring;
- verification of conformity to rules during maintenance;
- deal with problems and crisis as they arise;
- improving team enthusiasm.

Management imposes techniques and methodologies. This difficult function therefore requires technical and management abilities.

26.6.2 Maintenance rules

To prevent scattering of the maintenance team's energy, we will mention a few common sense rules for reducing costs while satisfying customers:
- Review and evaluation of all requests. Each must be fully justified. The impact on other tasks must be evaluated.
- Planning and scheduling maintenance actions:
  - assigning a priority;
  - scheduling tasks;
  - execution according to priority.
- Restrict modifications to the approved and planned request.
- Update documentation and respect standards by reviews and audits.

26.6.3 Team management

This point is as important as the technical and methods aspects. Due to the gap between maintenance and development, it is interesting to gain experience in both activities during one's career to see the consequences of acts. Observing maintenance difficulties should have very positive repercussions on design.

The following advice may be used as a basis for defining a management quality policy:
- Maintenance is as important as the development: just as difficult and essential.
- Maintenance personnel must be highly qualified, competent and motivated. The team must not be isolated from the others and turnover must be low.
- Maintenance must not be considered as an essential step in which one "sinks or swims".

- Personnel rotation must allow transfer from development to maintenance and vice versa. Experience helps to increase awareness of one's acts.
- Good maintenance performances should be well remunerated, as in development.
- The team must be correctly formed. This maintains performances and minimizes problems of enthusiasm.
- Change assignments and organization to prevent some personnel having their own private empire within the organization since this leads to a loss of control and therefore a loss of efficiency.

27

PROJECT DOCUMENTATION

> *"Most programmers regard documentation as a necessary evil, written as an afterthought only because some bureaucrat requires it. They do not expect it to be useful.*
>
> *Mathematicians diligently polish their proofs, usually presenting a proof very different from the first one that they discovered..... The simplest proofs are published because the readers are interested in the truth of the theorem, not the process of discovering it.*
>
> *Analogous reasoning applies to software. Those who read the software documentation want to understand the programs, not to relive their discovery."*
>
> **D.L. Parnas**

Producing documentation for projects is an essential task which increases the product life. Essential activities cover the entire product life cycle, and documentation management and production must be planned.

The following procedure is used to justify the contents of a project documentation:

1. functional justification: why;
2. hierarchical structure for documents: what;
3. planning: when;
4. methods and procedures: how.

27.1 FUNCTIONAL JUSTIFICATION

A document represents a structured memory of a collection of information. First, a document is not useful if it is not used. It is therefore an interface element necessary between two or more activities, sometimes performed by the same person, but more frequently by different persons.

The contents of a document are defined firstly from the role that it must play in the project: who will read the document? and what knowledge of the context is necessary to these readers, see Figure 27.1?

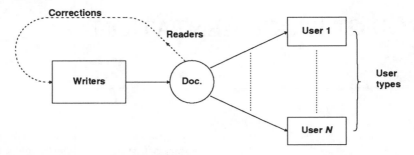

Figure 27.1   Role of the document as interface.

A document must contain only necessary and sufficient information for the assigned objective. The documentation fulfills four functions:

- communication;

- reference documentation;

- quality assurance support;

- chronological reference.

-A- Communication, interactivity

Every project involves several persons. It is thus divided into tasks or activities. To reduce the loss of efficiency due to direct exchanges between persons, the document acts as an indirect and permanent tool for the exchange. It is therefore a formalization of the exchange process. This makes it independent of persons - absence, sickness, leaving the company, etc. The role is even more important when the project is long and complex and when it requires a long maintenance period.

It must be possible to convince designers that documents represent the final product to deliver, by analogy with mechanics in which drawings are the final representations of parts. This becomes more and more true with the evolution towards completely integrated electronics, automatic component production, and automatic program generation.

-B- Reference document

This type of documentation acts as a basis for training new persons to be familiar with the product. When well done, it represents the accumulation of experience which is worthwhile passing on to others.

It is also used for product maintenance, which is generally carried out by other teams during the months and years following the development. Its use as a user manual and product reference manual must not be forgotten.

-C- Quality assurance support

To obtain quality, it must be possible to observe the product, preferably before its final implementation. Documents contribute to this observation:

- understanding the solution and therefore its structure;
- agreement with specifications, completeness, understandability.

Documents are used as a basis for analysis meetings (reviews, audits) at clearly defined steps.

-D- Chronological reference

This document stores all phases, thoughts and problem solutions. It then allows the reuse of these ideas and solutions for new projects, thus avoiding previous errors by concentrating time and energy on priority points.

27.2 DOCUMENT STRUCTURE

After having defined the objective of the documentation, we will consider its content and especially its form.

27.2.1 Document hierarchy

The problem is to describe all documents necessary for a project. Obviously, the contents of the documentation depend on the nature and complexity of the project and the methodology used for the development.

For this purpose, we consider the case of a fairly complex real-time system developed using the MCSE methodology. Figure 27.2 describes the hierarchy of the necessary documents.

The documentation is broken down into two categories:

- development documents (WHAT, HOW);
- control documents.

Development documents are technical. Control documents are used for project management.

This hierarchy is required for useful documentation when the project is signed. Other documents are necessary prior to this to obtain the contract. They may be included in the preliminaries.

The role of each document type is described in Figure 27.2.

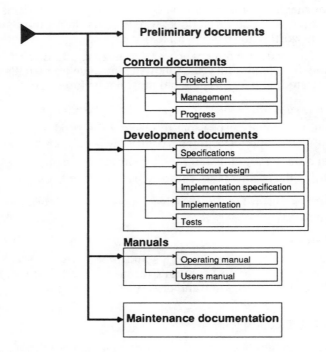

Figure 27.2 Documentation structure.

27.2.2 Preliminary documents

These documents contain:
- the request expressing the initial reason for the project;
- the feasibility study which considers the various solutions and options, and the corresponding cost. This helps to determine the best proposal;
- the initial project plan identifying essential resources, times and costs required, personnel and equipment.

27.2.3 Control documents

The purpose of these documents is to provide a method for controlling the project in accordance with the initial plan in order to observe and inform about any significant variations from the plan. These documents concern the project plan, management and progress.

-A- Project plan

The project plan is used mainly as a coordination document between the manager and all project participants. This document, or set of documents covers the complete life cycle. Note the advantage of graphic models to give a synthetic presentation (GANTT, PERT diagram, etc.). We could give the following list of constituents [JENSEN-79]:

- **Presentation of documents**: objectives of the plan and document identification.

- **Technical project description**: for understanding the document.

- **Organization plan**: organization diagram, roles and responsibilities of each element, arrangement with other companies.

- **Methodology**: common practice, standards, techniques used for quality assurance.

- **Configuration for management**: this describes how checks are carried out for each phase, dates for each document, reviews.

- **Management information plan**: all data to be transmitted to the customer and internal data: financial, laws, logistics, etc. How is data collected, formatted, transmitted.

- **Resource description**: all necessary resources and the manner in which they will be used: energy definition (manpower and equipment).

- **Documentation description**: list of all documents, supply and review dates, internal and external review procedures.

- **Test plan**: plan for all unit tests and integration tests.

- **Training plan**: users for operation and maintenance.

- **Safety plan**: case of systems with safety: procedure to be followed.

- **Scheduling**: (program plan) describes important project events - reviews, meetings, audits, etc.)

-B- *Management*

This document presents three schedules deduced from each other:
- Tasks:
    - duration,
    - number of persons and personnel qualification,
    - necessary equipment,
    - intermediate deadlines defining progress stages.

- Resources: personnel and equipment for the complete project.
- Financial:

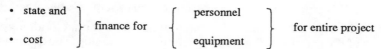

-C- *Progress and evaluation*

This document contains all information about project progress and all personnel activities.

- Progress:

    • evaluation of the method,

    • choice of alternatives,

    • analysis of errors and major problems, etc.

- Activities:

    • structure of working groups,

    • activity of each,

    • time passed for each phase, errors and correction times.

Taking the management principle into consideration, the control method used as a basis for writing the control documentation can be summarized in the following diagram (Figure 27.3).

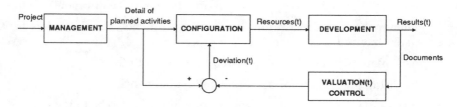

Figure 27.3   Advantage of documents for project control.

The evaluation produces a correction effect so that objectives are always satisfied as well as possible. It shows the state of progress of the project and facilitates convergence towards the objective.

The control documentation must reflect this strategy and this monitoring during the project.

27.2.4 Specification, design, implementation and test documents

These documents all describe characteristics of the products to be developed, followed by the selected solution, using a top-down presentation. The final result is a complete description of the hardware implementation and the software implementation. Test, verification and validation procedures are included in this part of the documentation, together with results obtained.

The outline for this documentation complies with the methodology used. Each part of the document is a result of completing one step. The outline for the MCSE methodology is as follows:

1. *Specification*

- environment model,
- interface with the system,
- functional specifications,
- operational specifications,
- technological specifications.

2. *Functional design*

- delimitation of the system to be designed,
- first functional decomposition,
- specification and functional refinement for each function,
- description of each elementary function,
- synthesis: final functional structure.

3. *Implementation specification*

- introduction of geographic distribution,
- introduction of interfaces with the environment,
- evaluation of time constraints,
- hardware/software repartition,
- executive structure,
- software implementation,
- hardware implementation specification.

4. *Implementation*

- hardware solution description,
- software implementation description.

5. *Tests*

- definition of rules specifying verification, validation, certification,
- test philosophy and methods,
- test procedures for each subset for each level,
- a test execution plan,
- results.

27.2.5 Manuals

A system is only usable and maintainable if manuals describe its installation, use and maintenance. Each manual type is intended for a specific category of users.

-A- Operations manual

The objective of this manual is to help understand the system behavior, especially for maintenance. For this purpose, it describes the operation of the system and the environment necessary for it to be operational. More precisely, it describes procedures for carrying out special functions on the system. It can be used as a maintenance assistance manual.

-B- User manuals

These describe system functions without describing how these functions are implemented. The objective is that every user should be capable, starting from this simple and clear description (non-technical terminology) to determine the applicability, and when and how to use the product.

There are three categories of manuals:

- "getting started" manual;
- installation manual;
- user manual.

Note the importance of quality in this category of documents. It should not be necessary to read the entire document to make use of the system. This requires classification of information into several levels of use.

27.2.6 Maintenance document

This is used to list:

- modification or evolution requests;
- corrections;
- adaptations to the environment.

Requests are then analyzed and evaluated - cost, time, priority. An evaluation is made for each change. After product modification, all previous documents concerned by changes are updated.

27.3 DOCUMENTATION PLANNING

Planning is specified by diagrams. They describe document production dates, showing the status - for example T for temporary, F for final.

Documents are produced at dates which correspond to the development schedule. They are also used for quality assurance - reviews, audits, etc. The diagram is presented in parallel with the life cycle and development steps.

The following figure shows planning for documentation using the MCSE methodology. For each step, the final document is obtained after two or three readings in the author/readers cycle, see Figure 27.4.

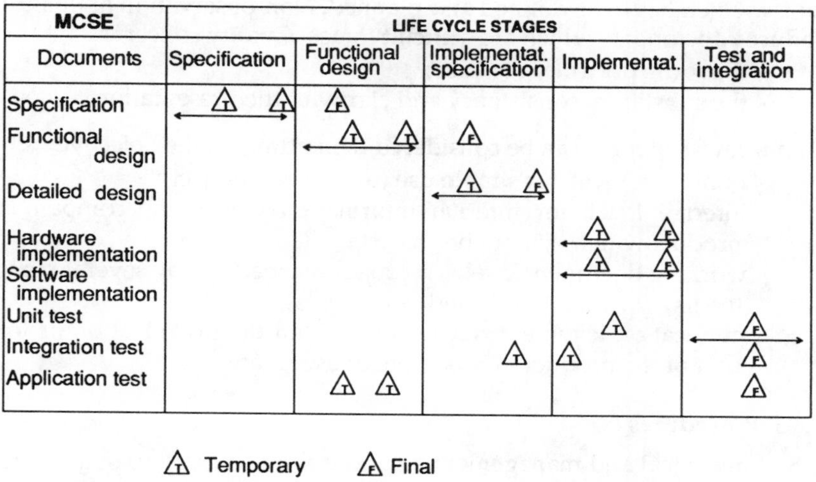

MCSE	LIFE CYCLE STAGES				
Documents	Specification	Functional design	Implementat. specification	Implementat.	Test and integration
Specification	△T ——— △T	△F			
Functional design		△T ——— △T	△F		
Detailed design			△T ——— △F		
Hardware implementation				△T ——— △F	
Software implementation				△T ——— △F	
Unit test				△T	
Integration test			△T	△T	△T ——— △F
Application test		△T △T			△F

△ Temporary   △ Final

Figure 27.4   Documentation planning for MCSE.

27.4 DOCUMENTATION PROCEDURES

27.4.1 Problems and causes

There are three types of abnormal situations for a project:
- no documentation;
- incomplete documentation;
- inadequate documentation.

There may be many causes:
- low priority for documentation;
- no resources for its implementation;
- no planning;
- no documentation specification;
- personnel attitude:
  - they don't like it,
  - unproductive and uncreative, little appreciated work,
  - invisible work.

The first four points are impersonal factors related to organization attitudes. The last point is difficult. This aptitude must be evaluated when recruiting personnel. It must then be part of a deliberate policy used by company managers.

27.4.2 Documentation quality levels

It is not sufficient to produce documents under the argument that the procedure or contract requires them. These documents must have a certain quality which has to be defined and planned. Non-observation of quality rules produces documents which are difficult to use. Quality concerns:
- the form: document outline;
- the substance: consistency and clarity of the presentation.

Four levels of form can be considered depending on the objective:
- minimum level: for simple use (one month project);
- internal level: for internal information within the company, for a product which will not be shared;
- working document level: for projects carried out by several persons or teams (typed and reviewed documents);
- publication level: for general use within the organization or forming part of the product to be supplied: user manuals.

27.4.3 Procedures

Both technical and management solutions are necessary to obtain adequate documentation. First, there must be a documentation group:
- convinced of its importance;
- supported by management;
- producing usable data and rules:
  • definition of disciplines, standards,
  • quality criteria,
  • availability of resources,
  • integration of this work into the daily work,
  • reviews to guarantee conformity with the discipline, procedures and observation of standards and guides.

For the company, the following important questions are to be asked:
- Has a decision been taken to obtain adequate documentation?
- Have rules been defined for quality?
- Has a person been made responsible for preparing the documentation and for having it developed and validated?
- Have resources been made available?
- Who is responsible for quality?
- Have relations been set up between the various development groups and between stages?
- Have time and cost for documentation been considered in project scheduling and cost?
- Do standards exist or have they been defined?
- Are tools available for writing and managing documentation?

To obtain a satisfactory result, the same principles have to be applied as those used to obtain quality for a project. Therefore, it is necessary to:
- produce a documentation plan,
- define procedures and check conformity.

Each of these points is described below.

-A- Documentation plan

First, a plan must be produced to act as a communication tool and as a work guide and control guide. This must describe the following for each necessary document:
- what document is to be produced;
- how should it be structured;
- when should it be produced;
- by whom should it be produced.

It should contain the following information describing each document:
- The document type, contents and usage.
- Its identification and format, to facilitate documentation maintenance and quality analysis. Some companies develop their own standards.
- The planning, which contains a diagram describing the necessary activities for producing the document: development stage, reviews, etc., and the documentation generation date, then author/reader cycles leading to its validation.

For large projects, all documentation is managed by a manager who maintains:
- a chronological record of significant events;
- a project document index;
- all documentation.

-B- Procedures

Formal reviews must be carried out at specific stages throughout the project life cycle. These are included in the development method since document production forms an integral part of the overall procedure.

The essential points for success of the project deal with specification analysis and design analysis at different stages.

- Specification analysis

The objective is to check that the designers have properly understood all aspects of the problem raised by the customer and that all constraints have been defined. A good specification document helps to guarantee a satisfactory result. The customer and system users must necessarily participate in meetings and approve the document. It is then used as a contractual base.

- Design analysis

Several analysis stages are necessary:

- functional design review or preliminary design review,
- detailed design review, which includes a complete analysis of the solution and test methods and procedures,
- review of the implementation solution, with the objective of analyzing the hardware solution? and the software implementation, together with the overall coherence.

- Documentation management

Documentation management is based on a description of the documentation life cycle, namely preparation, generation stages, reviews, acceptance, quality control, documentation repartition and control, archiving and subsequent updates.

27.5   DOCUMENT PRODUCTION GUIDE

Very frequently, the youngest and least experienced personnel are assigned to write the documentation and particularly the user and maintenance manuals, considering this as a very small task compared with the effort invested in the project. Consequently, manual quality is poor, incomplete and not suitable for users.

27.5.1 Faults in a document

Parnas mentions a few major points about documentation [PARNAS-86]. Documentation unused before its publication and considered as unimportant by its author will always be poor. A characteristic fault is often its lack of completeness, but this is not one of the most serious problems. If it were, the documents could be completed and corrected without difficulty. Other faults are much more difficult to correct.

-A- Bad structure

A document may be a result either of a stream of consciousness, or a stream of execution. The former expresses the fact that the author writes in the order in which he thinks, and the latter refers to the system in which events are described in the order of their appearance during the project.

The difficulty with this type of document is that readers do not know how to find the information that they want. They do not know then whether information is missing. Updating is difficult after a modification to the project.

-B- Limited description (myopic view)

A document written when the project is almost finished no longer contains information about the important decisions. It contains only small details, which make it useful only to persons who know the system well, but is impenetrable to newcomers.

27.5.2 Writing principles

The first job is to understand the situation of readers and the tasks that they must undertake with the documentation. The document outline is dependent on prior knowledge of the reader and target objectives.

The following comments can be used as guidelines [SCHNEIDERMAN-85]:

- facilitate the information search:
  - provide input points,
  - group required information.

- facilitate information understanding:
  - simple writing,
  - concrete description,
  - natural expression.

- express sufficient information for each task:
  - include all necessary information,
  - check their validity,
  - exclude what is not necessary.

After becoming aware of the difference between a good and a bad document, an effort must be made to ensure that the document is obtained when necessary and at reasonable cost.

To obtain quality documents, a complete documentation production policy must be defined.

Writing must be planned and qualified personnel must be assigned to this task.

-A- *Planning*

A document must be produced in good time if it is to be used: specification for the design step, functional design for the implementation definition, etc. All these documents are then usable for maintenance. The advantage is clear when new personnel have to be incorporated into the teams (Mythical Man-Month effect).

-B- *Structure definition*

The problem is to impose a structure on the contents of each document. It should first state the questions that it must address and then the answers have to be given.

The document should only be produced after generating the outline. Any one aspect of the system is described in one section only which facilitates updating.

The documentation is the design medium and no design decision should be taken before the solution has been incorporated into the documents. It is important that the documentation contains all alternatives considered during the project, for every problem. Every solution should be described together with the reasons for choosing it and for rejecting others.

When implemented in this way, several months or years later designers and maintenance personnel can find the answer in the documentation when they ask themselves the same questions.

27.5.3 Writing user manuals

Although we are most interested in user manuals, we should be aware of the difference between users and designers, that a good designer is not necessarily a good author, but that the success of a system may be closely related to the quality of the documentation. Writing documents is a highly creative work. Therefore, the value of this work should be recognized within the company.

Authors must bear in mind that users do not necessarily have the same knowledge as they do.

Schneiderman describes three categories of readers [SCHNEIDERMAN-85]:
- The reader familiar with the task to be carried out, but not very familiar with computers or automation. For these readers, the documentation should start from the task and associated concepts, and explain the concepts added by the product, and then the syntax for its use.
- The reader understanding the task and the benefit of the system. A brief description of concepts is sufficient, whereas the syntax has to be described in relation to operations.
- The experienced reader, who merely wants a reminder.

This decomposition into three categories shows the advantage of presenting manuals in three parts:
- an introduction to the product;
- a reference manual;
- a quick reference guide.

Another guide which can be useful in using the system is the "getting started from scratch" activity diagram. This diagram shows paths for orienting the user, showing transitions from one activity to subsequent activities.

Writing, reviewing and testing the user manual can take place before the product is completed. A good document preparation may clarify the development work since it represents the response to the need expressed by the customer. Authors then play a critical role thus participating in obtaining quality.

28

QUALITY MANAGEMENT

Zero defects will be obtained only if you detect the root cause of an error at the stage at which the error arises and then feed back information so that corrective action can be taken to prevent the error being transformed into a defect. It is not practical to detect defects in the final product, and then feed information back and take corrective action. We cannot prevent mistakes, but we can prevent them becoming defects.

Shigeo Shingo

Product development and particularly the specification and design work which concerns us, is the result of human activities. Errors are unfortunately unavoidable. However, defects resulting from errors can be eliminated, provided that error propagation is prevented.

Quality management is a preventative practice to reduce imperfections, errors and resulting defects in order to increase productivity and quality, to minimize cost, times and to maximize customer satisfaction.

Productivity gain is obtained by reducing the amount of the iterative correction procedure. Control and validation should therefore take place as early as possible to prevent the question from arising later.

Apart from a large number of implementation errors, dissatisfaction may be the result of many reasons including the following (the WHY):

- deadlines not respected;
- cost overrun;
- product not satisfying the need;
- lack of reliability;
- poor tolerance to hardware failures and human errors;
- difficulty of implementation;
- ruinous maintenance:
  - difficult corrective maintenance,
  - difficult development maintenance,
  - uneconomic solution.

Quality is now a very wide-ranging term. When talking about total quality, we consider all aspects: the product obviously, but also the service provided, the personnel in charge of its implementation, etc.

The objective of this chapter is very limited compared with this wide-ranging problem. We simply want to show quality criteria and rules, principles to be followed to obtain these qualities during the specification and design phases. Already, we need to be aware that quality criteria for these steps are not easy to express, and that measurement and quality producing methods are even harder.

The term quality does not have the same meaning in production as in design and specification writing. For production, the resulting object is completely defined. Its implementation quality is therefore quite measurable. For specification and design, the result is not known since the objective of the work is to find a solution. The measurement of quality is therefore very different.

28.1 TERMINOLOGY

We will first define the vocabulary [BUCKLEY-84]:

- **Quality**: this expresses all characteristics and features of a product which contribute to satisfying a need (user, but also producer, customer).

- **Quality assurance**: this is the set of planned and systematic actions necessary to ensure that a project is conform with the specifications and that it has the required qualities.

- **Quality control**: these actions follow on from quality assurance and are used to measure and control quality, and to detect errors in order to correct them.

Examples of types of quality are: economic, integrity, documented, understandable, modifiable, modular, error free, reliable, flexible, validated, general, testable, reusable, usable, clear, maintainable, portable, efficient, robust, progressive, optimized.

28.2 PRINCIPLE FOR OBTAINING QUALITY

The basic principle on which quality management is based consists of making sure that an intermediate product that can be observed, accepted (verifications, controls, measurements) and compared with predefined and required quality rules, is obtained after each phase in the life cycle. The organization diagram is given in Figure 28.1.

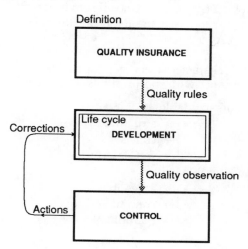

Figure 28.1   Organization of quality management.

Quality assurance defines the rules that must be respected by designers and implementers to satisfy quality objectives.

Throughout the life cycle, documents and implementations are produced during each phase expressing the solution at each intermediate level. Observation of these documents and implementations forms a basis for quality control by making a comparison between imposed rules and solutions. Corrective actions are then undertaken to satisfy rules.

28.3 QUALITY CRITERIA

Quality criteria are the expression of quality characteristics specified by quality assurance and useful for system design. The criteria are very important: see non-exhaustive list in the definition of the word quality. The main criteria are given below.

-A- Reliability

The system or product carries out functions expected by the user under normal conditions and with expected performances. For abnormal conditions, the functions are carried out, but possibly with degraded performances, but nevertheless remaining correct. The key words are:

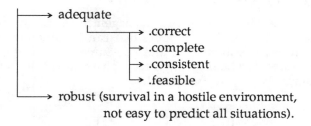

```
├──→ adequate
│        └──→ .correct
│         └─→ .complete
│         └─→ .consistent
│          └─→ .feasible
└──→ robust (survival in a hostile environment,
                 not easy to predict all situations).
```

-B- Testability

The system has characteristics facilitating testing and measuring performances in accordance with specifications. The key words are:

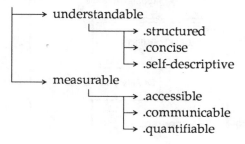

```
├──→ understandable
│         └──→ .structured
│          └─→ .concise
│           └→ .self-descriptive
└──→ measurable
          └──→ .accessible
           └─→ .communicable
            └→ .quantifiable
```

-C- Usability

The system has a user-friendly interface satisfying user's requirements.

-D- Efficiency

Performances are satisfactory without excessive resources.

-E- Adaptability (or portability)

This criterion expresses the solution independence from inputs/outputs (self-contained), and portability to other hardware. This is particularly useful for software. It minimizes costs following technological developments.

-F- Maintainability

When the simplicity and documentation is such that the system can easily be understood by personnel responsible for its maintenance, the product can easily be modified and tested when modifications are requested, or defects have to be corrected (documentation quality, testability).

-G- Other classification

The above list is obviously not exhaustive. Criteria are necessarily specifiable concepts which must be measurable for evaluation. However, they are very often fairly qualitative. They correspond to the external characteristics observed by the user during use, maintenance, transfer (validation, certification). Another classification could be made depending on the stage:

- operation (validity, reliability, efficiency, integrity, user-friendliness);
- use (transferability, configurability);
- modification (maintainability, progressiveness, testability).

28.4 QUALITY FACTORS OR ATTRIBUTES

These factors express rules to be obtained as constraints for the creative part of the work so that quality criteria stated in the previous section are satisfied. For design, Jensen mentions the following attributes [JENSEN-89, AUBRY-86]:

- **Necessity**: only performance and features requested in specifications, natural limitation to the request, are satisfied, leading to simplicity.

- **Completeness**: the specification for all modules, interfaces and the environment is complete.

- **Consistency**: all incompatibilities are identified and solved.

- **Observability**: hierarchy monitoring relating implemented functions and specified functions is possible by analysis of documents.

- **Visibility**: relations between design elements and decisions taken during the design are observable. The trace of decisions taken allows flexibility of changes to adapt to the new specifications.

- **Feasibility**: it must be possible to demonstrate (demonstration, implementation, prototyping, etc.) that critical parts can be completed within budget and on time.

28.5 QUALITY MEASUREMENT

Quality measurement is essential in order to ensure conformity with the rules stated by quality assurance. Possible measurement types are:

- complexity measurement: structural, textual, behavioral;
- performance measurement: logimetry;
- reliability measurement: defect rate.

Developments (program and system complexity measurements) are taking place particularly in the software field.

The complexity of the system must be evaluated during the design step. At least two approaches are noteworthy: that due to Yin and Winchester based on the analysis of the module structure diagram, and that due to Henry and Kafura based on analysis of the data-flow diagram [NAVLAKHA-87, ROUVE-88].

The C metric measures the intermodule coupling for each level in the hierarchy. This function is monotonic increasing. A major increase in changing from one level to the next signals that the increasing complexity is too high, suggesting a design modification.

Complexity measurements can help to detect design defects. Navlakha gives the following list for procedures, which may be extended to actions or functions of a functional structure.

- **Lack of functionality**: a large number of inputs (fan-in) and outputs (fan-out) indicates that the action or module carries out more than one function.

- **Critical point in the system**: too much complexity shows data-flow is too high. This point is critical when modifying the implementation.

- **Inappropriate refinement**: a too high fan-in or fan-out can be the result of a missing in abstraction levels.

28.6 METHOD

Two distinct and complementary methods are explained:
- checking that quality is introduced into the product from the beginning;
- verification and validation. This is a diagnostic technique which does not introduce quality. This is only a measurement of the existing quality.

The two methods are very different, and the second only becomes efficient after the first is applied.

Quality as a preventative technique is obtained as a result of coherence of three activity types: quality assurance, quality production, quality control.

-A- Quality assurance

This defines technical principles and rules, which means:
- definition and modification of rules, procedures, tools, standards tending to give quality for each project;
- prevention of causes which could harm quality;
- encouragement in the application of requirements;
- data collection, archiving and use.

-B- Quality elaboration

Quality production lies in the application of methods, rules, etc. previously defined by quality assurance. It also assumes continuous quality verification.

The use of a method such as MCSE for specification and design naturally tends to satisfy quality rules in documents and solutions. It recommends completeness and structuring for specifications and the methodology defines the procedure to be followed. In design, it facilitates selection of a simple solution by proposing template models with quality properties. Second, graphic representations - diagrams for specifications, functional structure, executive structure, implementation diagram - allow a qualitative measurement of proposed solutions.

-C- Quality control

This activity helps to obtain satisfactory results before going onto the next step by observing documents and implementations.

This activity must be carried out at the end of each step to certify that the product respects general rules and specified quality requirements.

One technique for documents is "cross-reading" by an author/reader cycle consisting of discovering errors, omissions, incompleteness, etc. Correction is the author's responsibility. Another advantage resulting from introducing readers into the development cycle, this technique introduces a good team coherence and a good knowledge of the work, allowing interchangeability.

28.7 QUALITY VERIFICATION

Two types of verifications should be considered for a project or a solution:
- Techniques for verifying that the solution complies with attributes required by quality assurance. This therefore evaluates "good design".
- Validation techniques to check that the solution complies with the customer's specifications.

Methods for this type of verifications are still very limited:
- review and inspection: these require qualified reviewers;
- internal checking at a level, coherence checking between levels;
- simulation/modeling: analysis of the dynamic aspect;
- measurement tools: complexity, testability, etc., static and dynamic.

Qualimetry tools can make more measurements on software descriptions, desirable since they are more difficult to observe than hardware implementations.

REFERENCES   PART 7

[AMGHAR-89]
   Méthodes de Développement d'un Système à Microprocesseurs
   A. Amghar
   MASSON Collection Manuels Informatiques 1989

[AUBRY-86]
   Prototypage et qualité du logiciel
   R. Aubry, Y. Martinez
   Journées "maquettage et prototypage de Logiciels" *BIGRE* No 51, 1986

[BERNARD-85]
   Les Plannings
   J. Bernard, M. Paker
   Les éditions d'Organisation 1985.

[BOEHM-84]
   Software engineering economics
   B.W. Boehm
   IEEE Transactions on Software Engineering SE-10, No 1, January 1984, p 4-21

[BUCKLEY-84]
   Software Quality Assurance and the IEEE Standards Process
   F.J. Buckley
   IEEE RCA Government Systems Division 1984

[CAPRON-86]
   Systems Analysis and Design
   H. L. Capron
   The Benjamin/Cummings Publishing Compagny, Inc 1986

[COX-85]
   Object-Oriented-Programming: An Evolutionnary Approach
   B. Cox
   Addison Wesley 1985

[DUKE-89]
   V & V of flight and mission-critical software
   E. L. Duke
   IEEE Software May 1989, p 39-45

[FATHI-85]
Microprocessor Software Project Management
E. T. Fathi, C. V. W. Armstrong
Marcel Dekker Inc 1985

[JENSEN-79]
Software Engineering
R. W. Jensen, C. C. Tonies
Prentice-Hall 1979

[LELUC-86]
Enquête sur les coûts de la maintenance
P. Leluc, Y. Salomon
Génie Logiciel No 5 Juillet 1986, p 68-71

[KOONTZ-80]
Management: Principes et Méthodes de Gestion
H. Koontz, C. O'Donnell
Collection Administration Mc Graw-Hill 1980

[NAVLAKHA-87]
A survey of system complexity metrics
J.K. Navlakha
The Computer Journal Vol 30, No 3, 1987, p 233-238

[ROUVE-88]
Logiscope: Contribution à la maîtrise de la qualité des logiciels
C. Rouve, M. Viala
Génie Logiciel et Systèmes Experts No 12, Juin 1988, p 36-44

[RUSKIN-82]
What Every Engineer Should Know about Project Management
A.M. Ruskin, W.E. Estes
Marcel Dekker Inc 1982

[PARNAS-86]
A rational design process : How and why to fake it
D.L. Parnas, P.C. Clements
IEEE Transactions on Software Engineering SE-12, No 2, Febuary 1986,
p 251-257

[SCHNEIDERMAN-85]
Designing User Interfaces
B. Schneiderman
Addison-Wesley 1985

[SHINGO-87]
Le système POKA-YOKE: Zéro Défaut=Zéro Contrôle
S. Shingo
Les Editions d'Organisation 1987

PART 8

CONCLUSION AND PERSPECTIVES

To conclude with the whole contribution of the MCSE methodology, this final part describes the contribution of each of its three aspects: a methodology as a working guide, computer tools as a working support, the designer as the main actor in developments.

Chapter 29 summarizes the essential points of the methodology.

Concerning design aid tools, rather than describing existing products in this relatively new domain, we felt it would be preferable to characterize the desired tool. The objective of Chapter 30 is to define this type of requirements definition.

Chapter 31 concerns the designer. A methodology and tools are not sufficient. The designer's competence is essential since design will remain a human activity for many years to come. Similarly, the company's commitment is an essential condition for success.

29

METHODOLOGY CONTRIBUTION

This chapter is an overview of the main points of the MCSE methodology to summarize its contribution to system and design engineering.

Although it "may" be considered superfluous for small applications, a methodology is absolutely essential for industrial projects. In and of itself, it does not form an isolated whole, but is a complementary contribution to the organization of the company, which must be integrated harmoniously.

First, we will recall the main objectives for a development which were used as a basis for formalizing this methodology. The first essential point is that the objective is to satisfy the customer. Second, deadlines and costs must be respected. Finally, the developed product must satisfy quality criteria: robustness, solution understandability which implies simplicity, and maintainability to guarantee long life.

Starting from these objectives, we will show how the proposed methodology satisfies these requirements.

29.1 THE DESIGNER'S TOOL BOX

A methodology can be compared with a tool box. This tool box contains elements useful to the designer. In this document, MCSE makes the following available:

- **Models.** Models are used partly to describe specifications and solutions, and partly for work organization: development cycle, steps sequencing, etc.

- **Methods.** Each method is a guide to obtain a result starting from input data or specifications. A methodology is a set of methods based on the use of a model or models and is made up of rules, recommendations, decision criteria and sequences, etc.

- **Project organization**. This is a scheme for the breakdown of tasks for each project, a distribution of these tasks according to the necessary ability, and a procedure for planning, estimating, organization and finally project management,

- **Solutions**. Case study examples allow the designer to work by analogy in order to enhance his experience. By the use of such examples, we can find a set of frequently encountered classical problems. This is therefore an indirect way of encouraging reuse. Some solutions are general, in that they can induce a variety of solutions. We have called them template models.

We can obviously add to these elements any other model, method and methodology which may be useful to the designer. If the necessary tool is to be found easily, the tool box has to be organized. The objective of a methodology is to provide this organizational framework. In addition, each designer is able to enhance his tool box, by expressing new models and methods and developing reusable solutions that he makes available to his collaborators.

29.2 FIELDS OF USE

In defining the fields of use of the methodology, two aspects are to be considered: the class or classes of systems concerned and the complexity of applications.

Concerning system classes, the MCSE methodology well covers the field of industrial data processing systems. The techniques to be used are well understood in the fields concerned: electronics, automation, data processing, communications, signal processing. The difficulty is more a result of the diversity of aspects to be considered than the complexity of each aspect.

Concerning application size, the methodology is fully justified for small projects and is also essential for complex projects. Using the top-down approach, a complex project is decomposed into interconnectable subsets. The subsets can then be developed separately with the certainty that integration of all components will guarantee an appropriate result.

29.3 PROJECT ORGANIZATION

MCSE is based on a hierarchical-type development cycle: system level, then subsystem level, then hardware and software. This decomposition is used as a basis for development organization.

As a guide, the development cycle facilitates tasks ahead of the technical work: estimating, planning, forecasting, resource organization and management. Scheduling several projects concurrently can also help to optimize costs and resources.

A project is not necessarily a sequential execution of steps from specification to implementation. Some projects may necessitate preliminary cycles, such as a preliminary specification phase useful for the feasibility study. For other projects, it may be decided that it is necessary to produce a prototype of a subset.

These organizations are quite possible variants from the purely linear ideal scheme.

Project monitoring necessitates observations: state of progress, document quality, solution quality, etc. A monitoring strategy has to be implemented. For the general documentation produced during the development, which is the only clearly observable result, author/reader type cycle reviews can be planned in order to validate production and if necessary to improve quality.

As a project monitoring aid, the reader will find a simplified guide model for the methodology at the end of this chapter. It demonstrates the necessity of carry out the development, verifications and tests, and document production in parallel. This guide can be used for a small project and also for the development of each subset in a more complex project.

For the organization strategy, the methodology may provide a framework for thought, but the thought itself must be intentional on the part of management in each company. This responsibility cannot fall exclusively on designers themselves. It should be the responsibility of each project manager who must then have the means to apply it. This is a technical and not administrative type of task. The organization requires that the technical content of projects be known, each of which has its special features.

29.4 DISTRIBUTION OF COMPETENCES

The MCSE methodology breaks the work down into three activity types: specification, design, implementation. The advantage of this decomposition is to clearly identify ability categories.

The first specification phase is very clearly customer and user-oriented. It requires a fast understanding of the problem raised and the need. There are three types of necessary abilities:

- **General skills**, to be able to understand and formulate a problem in a field other than electronics and industrial data processing;

- **Synthesis ability**, to clearly structure and formulate problem concepts, constraints and requirements;

- **Communication ability**, a strictly necessary condition for success. The specifier can understand the need only as a result of a dialog with the customer. This understanding is subsequently validated by clearly writing the specification document.

Obviously, success is only possible if the person responsible for this work is very interested in this type of activity.

The design phase is essentially a conceptual activity. The designer must be able to interpret specifications in order to imagine the appropriate solution. This solution is initially on a purely functional level. Expressing a solution implies a modeling activity for something which does not exist. It is therefore a creative activity.

This work is half-way between the customer request and the technical solution. Dialog with the customer, users and the specifier remains necessary to guarantee a satisfactory result. Technical ability is obviously necessary to induce practical solutions and to be able to talk with specialists responsible for the implementation.

The implementation phase is essentially technical. It requires significant competence in implementation and manufacturing techniques: mastering tools, components and technology.

Project management needs an overall ability to be able to plan, observe, understand, decide upon and guide collaborators throughout the project.

29.5 DEVELOPMENT GUIDE

A methodology is also a guide for project development. The proposed process is globally top-down. It recommends starting from the customer's problem to search for an appropriate implementation by successive approaches.

Decomposition into steps is based on the possibility of describing any system in several levels. The description by levels is based on an internal description model based on the association of three components, allowing consideration first of the interconnection between functional components and then of their evolution, and finally in resources generating this evolution. The specification which concerns an external description of the system is also based on a model with three views: the data space, the state space and the activities space.

These models are used as a basis to specify the breakdown into steps and to induce the method to be followed during each step.

A method provides a structured guide for the analysis and decisions to be taken to transform efficiently a specification into a solution.

In the same way as a seven layer OSI model was defined for communication systems, a system structure can be represented here as a five layer set as shown in Figure 29.1 which summarizes the overall recommended process.

- level 0, the highest, expresses the need;

- level 1 is an external view of the system and its environment;

- level 2 is an internal functional description independent of technology;

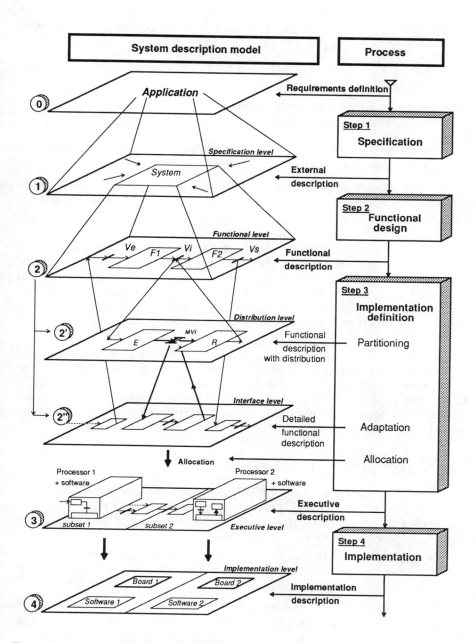

Figure 29.1   Structuring a system into five levels.

- level 3 is a solution specification for the implementation with the hardware part, and for programmable processors, the software implementation specifications;

- level 4 is the implementation description like a set of boards and software.

It is useful to add two other sub-levels at level 2:

- sub-level 2' including information transfers for distributed systems;

- sub-level 2" which introduces the technological interfaces necessary for physical coupling with the environment.

The representation by description levels is useful to show the process to be followed and to indicate the information to be added or the transformation to be carried out for each transition from one level to the next lower level.

Although the recommended process is globally top-down for design, variants are possible to allow for objectives to be achieved and constraints. In particular, it is quite possible to define the implementation and especially the hardware part at the start of the functional approach for some problems. This may then necessitate a large amount of design work which is carried out concurrently with the system level design. Secondly, some developments may result from a bottom-up approach which isolates subsets usable for other projects.

Development is also an iterative and even an evolving procedure. It may be decided after verification at the end of a step to change decisions made during the step, or possibly even during previous steps. This is a normal attitude. Correction loopbacks are inevitable since the activity is human and errors will be made; the method is only a guide. Automatic production by transformations would be the only method of eliminating the risk of errors.

29.6 PROJECT DOCUMENTATION

An essential function of the MCSE methodology is to act as a guide in producing documentation. This is obviously necessary for long product life. Developed particularly for maintenance, it is also imposed for the methodology itself to allow verifications on completion of each step.

The documentation is thus produced and verified incrementally, step by step. It then contains the relevant decisions and reasons for these decisions which led to the selected solution.

Documentation fulfils several objectives:

- **Communication**. Readable by all participants, the documentation defines an information exchange standard for the project. It also informs all other persons thus preventing project completion from being particularly dependent on one designer.

- **Maintenance**. Carried out by other persons, maintenance depends on knowledge of the solution and decisions which resulted in certain choices. Documentation is absolutely necessary for these reasons.

- **Historical references**. This is a chronological record of past developments. This forms a guarantee since personnel mobility exists in all companies.

The documentation presents the solution in a top-down form, even if the development was carried out using a different procedure. The content matters, rather than the manner of obtaining them.

29.7 DIFFICULT ASPECTS OF DESIGN

We will mention here a few of the main principles of the MCSE methodology recommended to obtain the best results. These principles solve problems often encountered by designers.

Beforehand, it is useful to remember that development is a human activity involving a methodology and a social system. Both parts are important for success. Therefore, a positive attitude by designers is a strictly necessary initial condition for success of the procedure.

-A- Specification step

The specification step is the first and most difficult step. There are at least two problems in this work. First, the most appropriate model has to be selected to model the environment considering its nature and level of detail. If it is to be good, the analysis must be functional and not hardware related. This is a frequent mistake. The nature of the model is deduced from the analysis - in order of complexity, data/event static model, global dynamic model, activities model. Modeling is carried out at the necessary, but just sufficient, level of detail to solve the problem. It must not involve the system to be designed.

Finally, the functional specifications to be produced must be limited to an external description of the system. System functions must be only application functions and must not be confused with internal system functions.

-B- The design step

In this step, the first important point is that the design should be technology-independent. Consequently, all geographic distribution and interface problems must be avoided, to consider the functional aspect alone.

Second, the solution should be found based on the necessary internal variables rather than based on internal functions. The recommended approach leads to an easier to understand and easier to implement solution. Solution concepts can also be deduced from template solution models. The advantage is having a guide to help the search for variables.

In general, the designer should forget all preconceived ideas, otherwise he will carry out his development based on his own idea without trying to evaluate other solutions which may be better.

-C- Implementation specification step

In this step, interfaces are introduced to adapt to the characteristics of the environment. The most appropriate solution has to be found, particularly for the man-machine interface.

Timing constraints must be correctly evaluated in order to prove beforehand that the application will work correctly.

Second, in determining the hardware/software distribution, the objective is to minimize the development. This involves minimizing the hardware first, then the software. The software is composed of two parts: the operational part; strictly necessary for it to work and therefore relatively incompressible if the behavioral specification was well written and the organizational part concerning relations between functions. This second part is compressible and the objective of transformations to create the software implementation diagram(s) is to minimize this part. The MCSE methodology facilitates this reduction.

This approach is fully justified for dedicated real-time applications in which the development is made once and for all.

29.8 LONG LIFE OF THE METHODOLOGY

Although the MCSE efficiency and limits are difficult to define precisely, we have significant experience of its use which has demonstrated its real efficiency. The overall efficiency is clearly related to the quality of designers: aptitude for rigorous working, systematically considering all problems in detail, aptitude to acquire technical skills and to inform oneself about available solutions, aptitude for working in groups. Also, the management's will in each company is a determining factor since the application of a methodology is a technical problem but it is also an organizational problem in which human factors are essential.

Developed especially for real-time systems, this does not automatically restrict its field of application to this problem class alone. Interesting experiments in the field of VLSI components (design of specific components with silicon compilers), parallel architectures, interactive systems, communication systems, show how useful this type of methodology can be. Its open nature makes it complementary to other methodologies.

Long life is another feature difficult to evaluate. Note that concepts used and description natures are technology independent. Second, the essential contribution of the methodology concerns phases prior to implementation techniques. This type of methodology will therefore remain essential as long as these phases are not carried out by automatic production tools, and will not happen tomorrow.

30

REQUIREMENTS FOR A COMPUTER-AIDED SYSTEM ENGINEERING TOOL

A methodology is not enough. A computer tool is essential as a development aid. This is obvious, but what should its role be?

There are two ways of analyzing this problem: doing a survey of existing tools, or defining the need based on a methodology.

A variety of tools as methods support are already available to satisfy this new market with fairly different characteristics [SCHINDLER-87, FALK-89, HAREL-88]. These software-oriented tools are referred to as CASE (Computer-Aided Software Engineering). For the hardware part, tools are called CAD or CAE (Computer-Aided Design or Computer-Aided Engineering).

The objective of each is to satisfy the need. The question therefore becomes what is the need? Obviously, every designer would like to have a "magic" tool which starts from specifications and produces hardware solutions and executable code. This tool could be used to develop any type of system and would design, develop and finally implement the solution. Man's intervention would be simply an interface between expressing the need and the tool. However, this tool is decades away.

This CAE tool market is separate from "front-end" products used for the initial specification and design phases and "back-end" tools for producing solutions. The first category includes data-flow diagram and schematic editors. The second category includes cross-compilers, application generators, and silicon compilers for components.

Attempts are being made to link the two categories in order to cover the whole development life cycle.

The possibilities of each tool have to be analyzed, looking at two aspects:
- the part of the development cycle covered by the tool;
- the method(s) and model(s) supported.

Instead of analyzing the features of existing tools which is difficult for a field in full evolution, it seemed preferable to define the need. This can then be used as a basis for specifying tool characteristics and facilitating the analysis of existing products.

30.1 OBJECTIVES

Since we are interested in systems with hardware and software aspects, the functionalities described below are mostly those of "CASE" products, with "S = System". They must simultaneously cover electronics and computers fields, even though at the present time the market includes two categories of products.

The phases covered by a required tool can be described by considering the development life cycle. Figure 30.1 uses the V cycle to show the advantage of covering all phases from specification to maintenance and product monitoring.

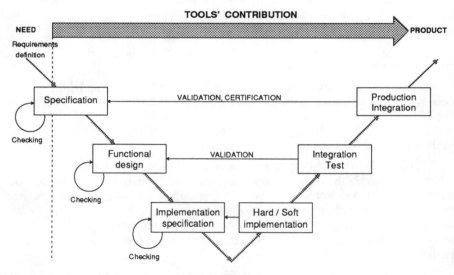

Figure 30.1   Project phases and contribution of a tool.

The impact of using a computer-aided tool for the early development phases, as shown in Figure 30.2, is particularly essential for the maintenance phase [SCHINDLER-87, DECLERFAYT-88].

But this observation applies to the current time. The important long-term objective is to increase productivity. In Martin's and McClure's book [MARTIN-88], it states that productivity resulting from the use of databases and Search Query Languages (SQL), database generators and application generators, is of the order of 1 000 compared with those using structured programming which remains between 0.25 and 0.75.

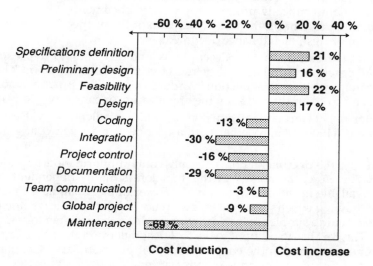

Figure 30.2   Cost gain using a tool.

Evolution thus inevitably requires the creation of automatic production tools in order to reduce development time and therefore cost.

The next section describes the functions necessary to satisfy these objectives.

30.2 NEEDED FUNCTIONALITIES

Functions are described in the order of priority, starting from the results produced by the designer up to project management.

30.2.1 Description

An initially necessary function is to be able to describe the solution selected and developed by the designer. This function is equally applicable for a specification as for a design or an implementation solution.

However, the description method will depend on the nature of the model: text for syntactical descriptions, graphics for graphical models.

What is the advantage of this function by itself? Simply that the description can be modified and then reprinted. This tool therefore acts more as a word processor or a CAD tool.

30.2.2 Documentation

Description capabilities lead to the availability of a set of documents concerning the project within the tool. The objective of the documentation function is to automatically produce appropriate documents with a structure and content dependent on the use to be made of them: specification, design, implementation, test, maintenance document, etc.

A document associates text descriptions and graphics to a predefined outline. All description updates will be reflected in the documentation. The tool must be configurable for this function in order to modify the structure and form of documents to be produced to suit the organization or company's constraints.

The document formatting function is the equivalent of a Desk Top Publishing (DTP) system, together with a document manager: configuration, update.

Obviously, the documentation will only contain information provided by the user. Therefore, the quality of this function is highly dependent on the features available in the description tools. For example, imagine a functional structure drawing which was input by a graphical editor. The design document must also contain a simple analysis drawing made by the designer to justify this solution. This text has to be input to the tool. Another example for the format of the document required is the equivalent of that given in Part I Chapter 6 to describe the solution for the cruise control system.

30.2.3 Verification, validation

Describing an object with a specification, a functional structure, an algorithm, etc. does not guarantee that the object is correct. The term "correct" concerns the contents of the described element and its integration into the overall solution. Therefore, the tool also needs a description verification and validation function.

Verification deals more with the form: static verification and checking against the description model. Validation is more concerned with the proof of a correct solution; this brings in the dynamic aspect.

This functionality requires specific verification tools based on description models and simulation tools for the validation. These types of tools are only possible for descriptions based on formal models.

To illustrate the role of this function, consider the current capabilities of CAE tools in electronics. The designer describes his schematics based on symbols available in the library. A check is then made on the coherence of the schematics to obtain the netlist of connections. The designer works by simulation to validate his solution. He defines the test pattern vectors to be applied to the inputs of the system or function. The system is simulated based on the behavior of all symbols. Models of these components form part of the tool library. The designer observes the results and deduces whether or not his solution works properly. Obviously, this type of tool alone does not perform validation since this is the designer's responsibility, but it shows what is meant by verification and validation. This functionality would be desirable for other levels and other implementation techniques: specification, functional design, software implementation. It requires the availability of a "universal" top-down type simulator, applicable either to a system or to hardware and software subsets! In the absence of this tool, much of this work is carried out by making prototypes.

30.2.4 Production

The above functionalities do not increase designer's productivity. On the contrary, it is possible that they spend more time with tools for inputting descriptions. However, productivity increase is an essential condition for the future.

Tools must therefore be available for the automatic production of solutions starting from descriptions. The resulting advantages are at least:
- Reduced solution search time. This alone fully justifies the description function.
- Reduced verification work, since automatic tools produce working solutions only if the tools are correct.

Again, to illustrate the benefit of this type of tool, we will consider two examples, cross-compilation for software and silicon compilation for components.

When an application has to be developed on a target microprocessor board, the process is to describe the solution in a high-level language on a development system tool. This has a processor which may be different from that on the target board. The program designer checks and validates his program for a test set. After debugging the program, he then uses a cross-compiler which starts from the validated description and produces an executable code on the target board. The solution is normally operational, except for adaptations to suit the board hardware characteristics. There is therefore a development saving of time, partly because it is no longer necessary to develop his application in assembly language, and second because the translation is automatic if the processor is changed.

For integrated circuits, the designer describes and validates his schematics by simulation as indicated in the previous section. He then inputs the manufacturer technology and the packaging type, uses a silicon compiler and automatically obtains a drawing of all layers of the integrated circuit (the layout). This description is then sent to the founder for manufacture. In this case, the productivity gain is considerable, since there is no longer any need to draw each transistor and a circuit with 20 000 transistors can be produced in less than a week.

The above two examples show the advantage of this production function. Obviously, we must not be satisfied with what already exists. Every designer would like more sophisticated tools which avoid the need for him to go down to a level too close to the technology so that he can invest his time in the initial phases.

Progress is already being made towards these tools. The objective is to start from a description, and to automatically produce a quality solution satisfying the description specifications.

The description level will gradually increase to approach the requirements. As the description level becomes higher, the constraints increase, but there is also more latitude for finding a solution. Therefore, these tools must more integrate designers' expertise, technical characteristics and implementation technologies more often.

The current level of these tools is very variable depending on the field. For example, application packages can be used for the automatic production of an application starting from a configuration. In the digital signal processing filters field, tool prototypes can be used to directly obtain a component satisfying filter specifications.

As shown in Figure 30.3, this functionality is the most essential in the future for increasing productivity. In each field, it requires that description models of the objects to be produced, solution models and processes for progressing from the specification to an implementation best satisfying the problem, are perfectly formalized. The development of methodologies is an essential, intermediate stage.

The curve should be asymptotic at the specifications level since we will always have to formulate the customer's requirements ourselves.

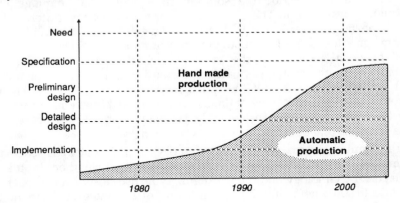

Figure 30.3   Contribution of automatic production tools.

In the real-time systems field, there is even more work to be done. Imagine automatically obtaining a solution starting from a functional description. For example, a functional structure input by a graphics editor including functions written in ADA. For this purpose, the application would already have to be validated, the timing constraints would have to be expressed and the hardware solution necessary would have to be described or found so that the tool could automatically produce the software part. Finally, a guarantee that the application would work correctly and satisfy timing constraints would be necessary since this is an essential condition in the real-time field.

30.2.5 Project and version management

Firstly, projects become more complex which requires breaking down the work for many teams. Second, each application or system has a life unfortunately which is considerably longer than its development. Product maintenance is therefore necessary.

To satisfy these essential requirements, a project and version management function is absolutely necessary. It concerns two parts:

- **Development**. Each developer contributes to one or several projects. The tool is used to integrate the various parts of the development. Any modification made to a subset becomes available to the entire project. The reusability concept therefore has to be managed to take advantage of developments made in other projects.

- **Maintenance**. It is obvious that products which have to last 10 or 15 years will be subject to modifications and improvements. Hardware and software may no longer be compatible. It must be possible to manage the various application versions in order to carry out maintenance correctly.

For this function, the tool then has to be a development integration platform, a version and installed system monitoring manager, and must manage participant rights.

30.2.6 Project management

Managing projects necessitates preliminary activities including project planning, evaluation and distribution of human and equipment resources, cost estimating, controlling the activities throughout the development of each project, namely estimating the state of progress, observing deviations from the schedule, measuring development quality, etc.

A computer-aided design tool therefore must provide these functionalities. For preliminary activities, it is useful to decompose a project into its various elements in accordance with a development life cycle and the methodology used. Based on previous estimates, it helps to estimate a new project and to define a load distribution strategy taking account of resources already used in other projects.

Management activities will be based on observations of the state of all descriptions used in the project: not started, start date, end date, test, certification, etc. Quality may be deduced starting from descriptions and quality criteria using qualimetry tools.

Global project monitoring helps to react in good time to correct drifts from the schedule or even estimating errors.

This type of tool already exists but they have to be fully integrated into other functions to avoid the need to input checking information useful for monitoring and difficult to obtain from designers.

30.3 SYNTHESIS OF FUNCTIONALITIES

In this section, we will reconsider each function to show its role in project developments. Figure 30.4 shows that each function must be based on models. Methods are used for production, verification and project management.

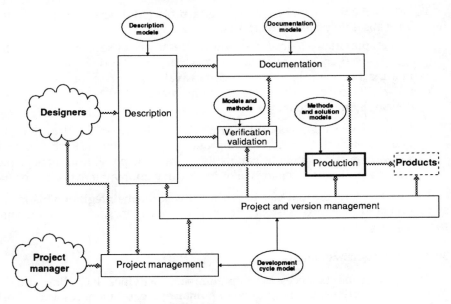

Figure 30.4   Tool functionalities for the development.

Figure 30.4 above shows the importance of the description inputs when they can be used to produce output results. The essential function in which the factor of 10 to 100 can be obtained in production.

This figure also helps to understand the nature of the two types of existing tools - "front-end" for specification and design descriptions, and "back-end" tools dealing with the product itself. Current developments towards coupling the two types of tools will therefore lead to a more complete integration of desired functionalities.

30.4 TOOL STRUCTURE AND CHARACTERISTICS

Starting from the required functionalities, it is fairly simple to outline the structure and characteristics of this kind of tool.

We will start with its coupling with the environment. To facilitate description input, a tool must have easy-to-use interfaces. Since most of descriptions are graphical, it is best to use a workstation with a multiwindow manager and an icon driven interface to help follow the methodology.

The output documentation requires the use of high resolution devices such as laser printers.

Production provides output documents satisfying interfaces suitable for implementation tools: ASIC manufacturer, printed-circuit board manufacturer, EPLD and EPROM programmers, emulators, etc.

Then, the tool must internally manage a large quantity of information in very different formats. The core of the system is therefore a database, preferably object-oriented, to facilitate management of the diversity. The various tools, each associated with a specific function and possibly a specific field, will be installed around this database.

The tool structure will be as shown below.

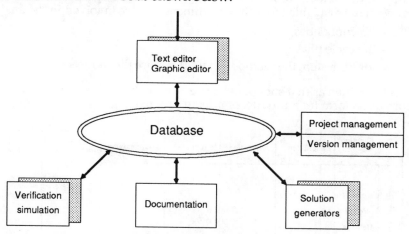

Figure 30.5   Structure of a tool for project development.

Tools features can be deduced from this functional organization.

First, the tool must be used simultaneously by all participants in one or several projects. Each user must have his own local workstation with a powerful graphic display to use the description tools. The workstation is a suitable tool.

But since all project information must be accessible at all times and from all workstations, the database must be functionally centralized (its implementation may be distributed).

All complementary tools must also be accessible to participants. The hardware structure is thus a computer network including a set of workstations and servers for information management and for making specific tools available.

The operating system for this structure must be a framework for the database and tools.

Due to the complexity of tools to be developed and their development costs, it will be impossible to find all useful tools from the same company. For any one organization or company, an appropriate tool will probably be the result of combining tools from different sources. This type of solution will only be satisfactory if all component tools interface correctly. A standard for database access will be essential. A uniform, and previously defined, platform is therefore a necessity. This effort is recognized today by tool developers searching for openness and complementary rather than specific features.

30.5 TOOL ANALYSIS GUIDE

To complete this chapter in which we defined the role and structure of a computer-aided tool, we suggest a simple guide for analyzing characteristics of commercially available tools. Several dimensions are involved in the analysis:

- functionalities;
- life cycle phases;
- for each step, the method(s) and therefore the models.

A table such as that shown in Figure 30.6 can be used to produce an information form for a product or a set of products.

Function \ Steps		Description	Verification	Production	Documentation	Version management	Project management
S P E C I F I C A T I O N	Models Methods						
⋮							
P R O D U C T I O N	Models Methods						

Figure 30.6   Information form for a tool.

The following integration constraints should be added to this form:
- the database used and its interfaces and access;
- each tool interface.

Another approach based on need consists of making a list of the specific needs of the user organization to produce an analysis basis for studying existing solutions. This is then the tool specification and design problem. Obviously a methodological approach will facilitate this work.

31

REALITIES AND PERSPECTIVES

In a sense, the programmer's job is inhuman because we require him to write a large amount of complex code without errors. Error-free coding is not natural for our animal-like brain. We cannot handle the meticulous detail and the vast number of combinatorial paths. Furthermore, if we want 1000 lines of code produced per day, the job is even more inhuman. It is a job for machines not people. Only recently have we understood how to make machines do it.

It is likely that historians in the future, looking back on the extraordinary evolution of computing, will say that the true computer revolution was the one that automated the processes of design and programming. Manual structured techniques were a necessary preliminary to the automation but were not by themselves the true revolution.

J. Martin and C. McClure

In conclusion, it is important to consider the designer himself and his context. Since he plays an essential role in the development process, it is useful to consider the manner in which he acquires the necessary skill to accomplish his goals. Second, the organization in which the designer works has an important responsibility since it either encourages or does not encourage the use of a methodology. Finally, we will look a few years into the future to attempt to get a glimpse of what we should be looking for now in order to gain this objective.

31.1   THE DESIGNER'S ABILITY

It is now recognized that designer's competence is essential. But how is it acquired? Two complementary methods may be considered:

- **Training**. This involves following a methodology course in order to acquire the basis, concepts, models and methods. In other words, to be able to use its tool box and to be familiar with and know how to use all its tools. As an analogy, the handyman may buy his own tool box, but that does not make him a competent craftsman.

- **System development**. This second point is essential since the only way of widening his experience is to solve problems. Experience is the result of using the process, analysis work and decision making. The designer can evaluate the appropriateness of his own decisions only after having made choices during a development. This result gives him additional experience.

Therefore, ability is acquired by solving problems. Training requires processing case studies which can be solved by analogy with other problems and solutions. Experience is thus also acquired by reusing this ability in developments.

But experience takes a long time to acquire. If this problem is not understood at the beginning, results will be poor. This type of ability can only be acquired in individual steps and requires time spent thinking about real problems in individual or team work. We think that six or twelve months is a minimum investment.

Ability is based on two types of knowledge:

- methodological knowledge, which is the objective of this book;

- scientific, technical and technological knowledge necessary to define and make products.

This second category requires a minimum level of knowledge at the beginning, but also subsequently requires a regular investment in time to follow advances in the technical field. This suggests a deliberate effort, for example conscientiously and regularly reading specialized technical journals. This work effort gives the designer a certain hardware and software culture allowing him to know what exists, what to do and by using what tools.

Faced with the problems to be solved, the designer must adopt attitudes favorable to success. First, he must eliminate all preconceived ideas from his mind, this is very difficult since he has learnt these solutions with experience. Second, his reflex should be to attack the most difficult points first, whereas the reverse is more natural. Finally, since error is human, the designer must be able to reconsider his own solution to correct errors inherent in any development.

31.2 THE ORGANIZATION RESPONSIBILITIES

The designer alone has a very limited impact on developments within a company, despite all his good intentions. Since the use of a methodology requires an increased investment during the early phases of a development in order to significantly reduce the cost of the final phases, it cannot be done without the agreement and commitment of management.

A project organization using a methodological approach is a long-term capital-intensive investment. The initial investment is partly in training, assimilation and experimentation, and also involves an increase in human resources during the initial specification and design phases.

The return on investment can take on several forms: reduction in the cost of project manufacturing phases, and also and especially by team reuse of experience gained by each participant. This gain is also obtained by a reduction of communication costs due to the documentation and the single uniform way of processing problems and describing solutions. All these gains are difficult to measure: ideally, it would be necessary to make a comparison but this would be unrealistic.

Success using a methodology requires a commitment within the organization and by the person(s) responsible for obtaining the expected results. This problem is comparable to the quality approach in companies.

31.3 LONG-TERM PERSPECTIVES

In evaluating long term perspectives, we will make use of Martin's and McClure's analysis for software and particularly for structured programming [MARTIN-88].

First observation, according to Jones [JONES-88], structured programming improves productivity by only 25 to 75%. Therefore, software productivity remains very much lower than that necessary to satisfy demand. Remember also that progress for hardware is exponential due to reuse of components, whereas it remains linear for software.

According to Martin and McClure, there are three phases of evolution towards using a technique before it reaches the maturity stage:

- crisis and recognition of a need;

- development of means and start training;

- assimilation and practice.

Figure 31.1 shows this evolution, particularly concerning the use of structured software techniques.

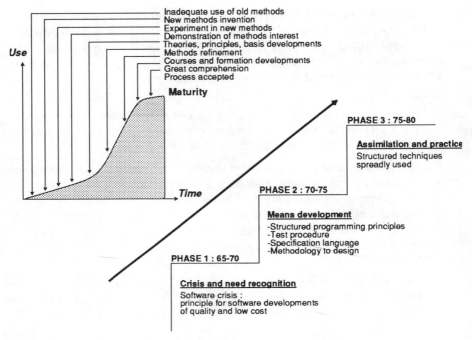

Figure 31.1 The three phases for the use of structured techniques.

Martin and McClure conclude that the use of structured techniques is quite insufficient to absorb the "software crisis". The solution is automatic code production starting from the design.

As an example, consider what is happening in the system design field. We will use this point of view to place the three phases for the use of methodologies:

- the crisis phase: 75-80;
- the development phase: 80-87;
- the maturity phase: 88-90.

Methodologies are therefore entering into a maturity phase. This is a period in which design processes are available to satisfy developer's needs. Training gradually results in a wider spread thus increasing the quality of developments. CASE tools are at the initial stage and we can hope to see some uniformity and wider use in the period 92 to 95.

The contribution of methodologies will be observed during the maturity phase. Although essential for quality, as was the case for structured programming, productivity will not be greatly increased. As indicated by Martin and McClure, the solution for a significant productivity increase for real-time systems is also automatic solution production. The process is then specification description, verification and validation, and automatic solution production satisfying constraints. Figure 31.2 shows a vision of this long-term progression. The horizontal axis of the diagram represents the description nature which varies from idea to formal, and the vertical axis represents the phases of a development.

Automatic production is only possible if the "object" to be obtained is fully specified in a formal manner. The same must apply for the production method.

Although the current situation using methods is on an intermediate trajectory, a medium-term objective is to consider that the description of the functional level is the interface between the human activity of the designer and automatic production. This description must be validated, requiring automatic tools, and production tools are then necessary, for example for the design of VLSI components. The silicon compiler for architectural synthesis clearly demonstrates the evolution towards this objective.

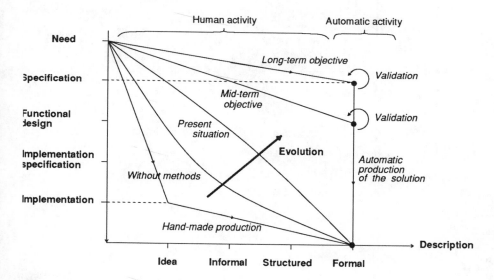

Figure 31.2   Evolution for solution production.

The same reasoning can be used for the longer term, but using the specifications as interface.

The future perspective in the real-time systems field is therefore to start from current methodologies based on solution description and possibly specification models, to find formal description verification methods since a solution developed by man always contains errors, and solution production methods forming part of design tools.

Imagine for a moment a specification given to a tool. After checking the coherence of the specifications, the tool would produce documents and the implementation as output. In this futurist scenario, the MCSE methodology will have made a contribution during the intermediate stage between the human design phase and the automatic design phase.

References Part 8

[DECLERFAYT-88]
  "Software Through Pictures" de IDE: Outils et Méthodes
  O. Declerfayt
  Bigre No 58, Janvier 1988, Spécification de Logiciel, p 57-67

[FALK-89]
  Software vendors serve up varied palette for CASE users
  H. Falk
  Computer Design January 1989, p 70-80

[HAREL-88]
  STATEMATE: a working environment for the development of complex reactive systems.
  D. Harel, H. Lachover et al.
  Proceedings of 10th International Conference on Software Engineering Singapore, 11-15 april 1988, p 396-406

[JONES-88]
  Practical Guide to Structured Systems Design
  M. Page-Jones
  Yourdon Press London 1988

[MARTIN-88]
  Structured Techniques: the Basis for CASE
  J. Martin, C. Mc Clure
  Prentice-Hall, Englewood Cliffs, NY 1988

[SCHINDLER-87]
  Advanced tools finally start to automate software design
  M. Schindler
  Electronic Design November 27, 1987, p 61-68

INDEX